Two major issues have troubled economists in recent work on saving: First, what was the cause of the substantial decline in the saving rate of most industrialized countries over the past two decades, and second, why has the traditional life cycle theory of saving, which seemed to offer an acceptable explanation for aggregate saving patterns, produced unsatisfactory results when faced with macro data? Drawing heavily on Italian data, this book provides new explanations for both questions.

For many years Italy had one of the highest saving rates of leading industrial countries, but the rate's decline in recent years has been more pronounced than in other countries. At the same time, Italy has combined an extremely generous social security and government transfer system with relatively less-developed capital markets. The simultaneous presence of these two features makes it possible to assess the impact on saving decisions of the growth in government and private transfers of capital market imperfections, both individually and in combination.

This book offers original contributions on most of the significant aspects of saving and consumption behavior. It reveals new evidence on the relative importance of precautionary saving and the bequest motive; it provides further explanations for the increased tendency to save of younger consumers and the slow rate of wealth decumulation of the elderly. The controversial role of liquidity constraints is a recurrent theme; these are seen to shape many aspects of households' behavior, from the durable/non-durable tradeoff to the timing of inter-vivos transfers.

The articles that make up this volume should be of interest to economists working to advance our knowledge of the determinants of personal consumption and saving patterns, the consequences of capital market imperfections and the relationships between fiscal policy and saving.

T0312106

Saving and the Accumulation of Wealth

Saving and the Accumulation of Wealth

Essays on Italian Household and Government Saving Behavior

Edited by
ALBERT ANDO, *University of Pennsylvania*
LUIGI GUISO, *Bank of Italy*
IGNAZIO VISCO, *Bank of Italy*

CAMBRIDGE UNIVERSITY PRESS

CAMBRIDGE UNIVERSITY PRESS
Cambridge, New York, Melbourne, Madrid, Cape Town, Singapore, São Paulo

Cambridge University Press
The Edinburgh Building, Cambridge CB2 2RU, UK

Published in the United States of America by Cambridge University Press, New York

www.cambridge.org
Information on this title: www.cambridge.org/9780521452083

A catalogue record for this publication is available from the British Library

Library of Congress Cataloguing in Publication data
Ando, Albert.
Saving and the accumulation of wealth : essays on Italian
household and government saving behavior / Albert Ando, Luigi Guiso,
Ignazio Visco.
p.   cm.
Includes index.
ISBN 0-521-45208-2
    1. Saving and investment – Italy.   2. Consumption (Economics) –
    Italy.   3. Households – Italy.   I. Guiso, Luigi.   II. Visco,
    Ignazio.   III. Title.
HC310.S3A7   1994
339.4′3′0945–dc20   93-34758
                                                              CIP

ISBN-13 978-0-521-45208-3 hardback
ISBN-10 0-521-45208-2 hardback

ISBN-13 978-0-521-03223-0 paperback
ISBN-10 0-521-03223-7 paperback

Contents

Foreword

The supply of saving and the accumulation of capital are at the core of economic life and of economic analysis. In an awareness of the crucial role of saving and investment activity in the wealth and welfare of nations and their deep relationship with money, credit markets and financial intermediation, central banks closely monitor the evolution of saving, pay great attention to the analysis of saving decisions and act in order to preserve the purchasing power of accumulated assets.

This book, *Saving and the Accumulation of Wealth. Essays on Italian Household and Government Saving Behavior*, presents the results of a research project on saving promoted by the Bank of Italy and carried out by members of its Research Department in cooperation with economists from other institutions. The project was launched at the end of 1989, when policy-makers and international organizations were beginning to acknowledge the possibility that the decline in saving rates experienced by most OECD countries over the previous decade might represent a serious obstacle to the financing of investment, the more so at a time when the pressing need for economic reform in East European countries was anticipated to raise strong demands on available funds.

The Italian experience is of particular interest and concern in light of the financing requirements induced by the country's high public debt and the need to guarantee sufficient funds for private investment in light of the tendency to a decline in private saving, which nevertheless remains high by international standards. An understanding of the reasons for this decline is a necessary preliminary to designing policy measures to reverse the trend. The Bank of Italy project was accordingly intended to initiate a wide-ranging enquiry into the numerous and complex factors underlying decisions on saving, using Italy as its country of reference. It is hoped that the methodology developed during the project and the conclusions reached may both offer insight into the causes of the decline in saving and be of use to other countries.

Antonio Fazio
Governor of the Bank of Italy

Contributors

Albert Ando
Department of Economics, University of Pennsylvania, Philadelphia
Fabrizio Barca
Servizio Studi, Banca d'Italia, Roma
Andrea Brandolini
Servizio Studi, Banca d'Italia, Roma
Agar Brugiavini
Dipartimento di Scienze Economiche, Università di Venezia
Luigi Cannari
Servizio Studi, Banca d'Italia, Roma
Daniele Franco
Servizio Studi, Banca d'Italia, Roma
Jagadeesh Gokhale
Research Department, Federal Reserve Bank of Cleveland
Luigi Guiso
Servizio Studi, Banca d'Italia, Roma
Tullio Jappelli
Istituto di Studi Economici, Istituto Universitario Navale, Napoli
Laurence J. Kotlikoff
Department of Economics, Boston University
Livio Maccan
GRETA, Venezia
Nicola Rossi
Dipartimento di Scienze Economiche, Università di Modena
Nicola Sartor
Servizio Studi, Banca d'Italia, Roma
Daniele Terlizzese
Servizio Studi, Banca d'Italia, Roma
Ignazio Visco
Servizio Studi, Banca d'Italia, Roma
Guglielmo Weber
Dipartimento di Scienze Economiche, Università di Venezia

Figures

Tables

Acknowledgments

This book brings together the findings of a research project on saving conducted at the Bank of Italy. We are grateful to the former governor of the Bank of Italy, Carlo Azeglio Ciampi, and to the current governor, Antonio Fazio, for their encouragement to pursue this research. Pierluigi Ciocca provided useful suggestions in the course of the project. Some of the results were presented at the conference: *Saving in Italy. Past and future trends, household and government behavior*, held in Rome on January 10-11, 1992. The essays that make up this volume have benefited greatly from the comments and suggestions received from the participants in the conference. We are particularly grateful to Chris Carroll and Angus Deaton for their help in assuring the success of the conference with invited papers and comments; to Franco Modigliani, who made illuminating comments on all of the issues raised; to Carlo Andrea Bollino, Onorato Castellino, Sean Craig, Elsa Fornero, Giampaolo Galli, Giuseppe Marotta, Marco Pagano, Alessandro Petretto, Luigi Spaventa and Guido Tabellini for their discussion of the papers presented at the conference. The full responsibility for the contents of this book rests, however, with the editors and with the authors of the individual essays.

Liliana Pulcini patiently and competently participated in every stage of the organization and realization of this volume; Raimondo Urbanetti skillfully helped with the drawings; Silia Migliarucci scrupulously verified the bibliographical references; Carla Lucidi, Roger Meservey, John Smith and Margaret Wayne greatly helped revise and polish the English; Gianfranco Nucci and Giuseppe Rodomontini conscientiously prepared the manuscript and assembled the various papers; Luisa Dell'Armi carefully checked the formal consistency of the text and helped us bring it to completion. Their efforts have greatly improved the quality of the book.

Albert Ando
Luigi Guiso
Ignazio Visco

Introduction

ALBERT ANDO, LUIGI GUISO
and IGNAZIO VISCO

Starting in the period between 1970 and 1975, most OECD member countries saw a more or less marked decline in national and personal saving rates. In Italy, the net private saving rate adjusted for inflation and including net investment in consumer durables hovered around 19 percent during the sixties, declined in the seventies and early eighties and has fluctuated around 14 percent since then. This makes the level of the Italian saving rate generally higher than the average for OECD countries throughout this period, but the size of the decline is also greater for Italy than for other countries.

These patterns have given rise to concern about the ability of the economies to accommodate a sufficiently rapid capital accumulation. An increase in the rate of capital accumulation on a global level has been viewed as necessary in order to meet the financial needs of many developing regions, including Eastern Europe, which are to be set on a stable path of economic recovery and development. A reversal of the declining trend of investment in the developed economies has also been called for in order to meet the capital requirements needed to enhance the economic and social welfare and to sustain the rates of growth necessary to reduce the high levels of unemployment, which have prevailed, especially in the European Community, in the last fifteen years (for a most recent contribution on some of these issues, see the collection of papers in Heertje, 1993).

In order to assess whether or not these concerns are justified, and if they are, to search for a set of policy measures to alleviate the problem, we must first answer a number of analytical and empirical questions. Above all, we need to have a better understanding of the factors and mechanisms which cause the fluctuations of the saving rate. We should also try to clarify the nature of the interactions between the level of saving in a society and its economic progress. The essays in this volume are primarily devoted to the first of these two issues. We seek to clarify and to expand important aspects of the theory of saving, and to relate them to critical evidence from the Italian economy. We hope and expect that the results in the volume will also be useful in understanding saving behavior and its implications in other developed countries.

Before we summarize the main findings, however, we wish to report on some guidelines that we have found useful in both formulating our theoretical framework and organizing the results. There are two propositions that have recurred persistently throughout the project that has led to this volume.

First, the motives for saving are complex, and none of the elegant, unified theories which seek to explain the saving behavior of all the members of a society is especially helpful, at their current stage of development, in dealing with actual data. One can start with a unified theory such as a generalized life-cycle model (which allows for bequest motives and for the presence of liquidity constraints), but it has to be recognized that a number of variations are needed to deal with, for instance, newly formed young households, middle-aged families with children, and retired families concerned with potential illness. Different models can thus be utilized, each designed to deal with a particular problem or to highlight a specific feature of behavior. As emphasized in the recent review by Deaton (1992), the above recognition raises doubts about the general usefulness of aggregate models based on the assumption of the representative agent and leads naturally to consider models in which the heterogeneity of consumers is acknowledged, especially when they are faced with the limited working of financial and insurance markets.

These issues are considered in this volume, with particular emphasis being given to the specific behavior of somewhat specialized groups such as the old and the young, to the effects of borrowing constraints and intergenerational transfers, to the role of uncertainty and of social security. Even if not dealt with explicitly in the various chapters of the book, it is therefore acknowledged that the aggregation process leading to a theory of aggregate saving behavior is by no means trivial, making a number of approximations inevitable. We can improve our understanding of the determinants of saving by looking at the phenomenon from many different perspectives, such as those which have been adopted in this volume.

Second, it is helpful to remember that virtually all variations of theories of saving lead to a decision rule both at the household and at the aggregate level which can be stated in terms of adjustment to a target wealth-income ratio. Let us illustrate the usefulness of this proposition in terms of the stylized consumption function implicit in most of the essays collected in this volume:

$$C_t = a_Y YL_t + a_A A_{t-1} \tag{1}$$

where C is private consumption, YL is labor income and A is total end-of-period private assets.

Equation (1) is usually associated with the life-cycle hypothesis, but it can be consistent with any theory which explicitly or implicitly implies a target wealth-income ratio. When it is used to describe the behavior of individual families, it requires the assumption that the underlying utility function be homothetic, so that the parameters α_Y and α_A do not vary with the levels of YL and A, even if they may be functions of age, family composition, the structure of preferences, the rate of return on assets, the relative position of the family in the income distribution, the strength of the bequest motive and so on. The presence of social security wealth and liquidity constraints can also be handled within the framework of equation (1), while the effect of uncertainty can be accommodated with some approximation, given that no exact closed-form solution exists in general. When equation (1) is used with aggregate time series data, to allow clear interpretation of parameter estimates, the usual set of additional assumptions on the lack of correlation between values of independent variables and parameter values over the micro units to be aggregated is needed (see Theil, 1954).

Equation (1) may be thought of as implying an error correction behavior on the accumulation of wealth. Let Y_t be total private disposable income, s_t and a_{t-1} the aggregate saving and asset-income ratios, a^* the target wealth-income ratio, g and ϱ the real rates of income growth and return on assets. After simple manipulation, the saving rate can be espressed as

$$s_t = ga_{t-1} + \beta(a^* - a_{t-1}) \tag{2}$$

where

$$s_t = S_t/Y_t, \; a_{t-1} = A_{t-1}/Y_t, \; Y_t = YL_t + \varrho A_{t-1}$$
$$\beta = \alpha_A + g - \alpha_Y\varrho, \; a^* = (1 - \alpha_Y)/\beta.$$

Equation (2) says that the saving rate is equal to the rate of growth of income times the actual wealth-income ratio (the proposition made famous by Harrod and Domar), adjusted by a fraction of the difference between the target wealth-income ratio and the actual initial value. On the equilibrium growth path, the saving rate equals the growth rate times the wealth-income ratio. The latter, in turn, is a function of the rate of growth but, subject to this qualification, we can also expect the saving rate to vary more or less proportionately with the growth rate.

When the behavioral theory underlying equation (2) is founded on the standard life-cycle model, it is easy to see how the aggregation process can bring about a positive correlation between the rate of growth of aggregate income and the saving rate envisaged in equation (2). In a "stripped-down" version of the model, since households before retirement have positive saving while those after retirement should dissave, an increase in the population growth rate would shift the weight in the measured aggregate saving rate from the old to the younger households, and the aggregate saving rate would hence become higher. An increase in the rate of growth of productivity would raise the income of the young relative to that of the old, again leading to an increase in the saving rate. In terms of equation (1), if it were derived from the "stripped-down" version of the life-cycle model, the coefficient of A_{t-1}, a_A, would increase asymptotically to unity as the household age rises, starting at a very small number (say less than 0.02 at the age of 25). The aggregate coefficient is the weighted average over this range, and hence, the higher the weight of younger families in the population, the smaller the value of a_A would be in the aggregate equation. From equation (2) we can see that, as a_A decreases, the target wealth-income ratio increases, and hence, for a given growth rate, the saving rate also increases.

The "stripped-down" version of the life-cycle model is not, however, the only one able to produce these results. Models where wealth accumulation is driven by bequest or precautionary motives may have similar implications. In what follows, we will attempt to summarize the findings reported in each of the three parts of this volume within the framework developed above.

1   Saving trends, government deficit and demographic changes

On several accounts Italy is an ideal laboratory for a study on saving. It has been, and still is, a high-saving country; during the last two decades, its saving rate has declined markedly while the rate of growth of income has slowed down significantly; population increase has come to a halt while life expectancy has lengthened substantially; unlike bank credit to firms, the markets for private insurance and credit to households are still rather thin, potentially exposing a large share of households to uncertainty and borrowing constraints; the public sector (as well as the public debt) is very large and the social security system has become one of the most generous among the OECD countries. These features, which have been hotly debated in the literature on wealth accumulation, make a study of the Italian saving experience both interesting and potentially fruitful.

The two aspects which characterize Italy's postwar wealth accumulation process are thus the high saving rate and the marked decline recorded since the early seventies, which has exceeded that observed in most other countries. As shown by equation (2), the high saving rate may in part be explained, for a given wealth-income ratio, in terms of the high rate of growth that has characterized the Italian economy (as well as those of other high-saving nations, such as Germany and Japan). The positive effect of growth on aggregate saving may also have been strengthened in Italy by particularly high target wealth-income ratios. As we shall see, this possibility is investigated under various perspectives, and at different levels of aggregation, in basically all the chapters of the book.

Furthermore, the relatively high wealth-income ratio may have made the decline in the saving rate associated with the reduction in growth of the last two decades particularly large. As equation (2) suggests, part of the decline of the saving rate may also have been due to a widening of the disequilibrium component, either through a rise of the actual wealth-income ratio or through a reduction of the related target. Among the factors that may have produced such effects, those related to the fiscal policies that have been followed and the demographic changes that have occurred in the period may have been especially important.

A positive correlation between income growth and the aggregate saving rate is not specific to Italy: it has been found repeatedly in cross-country studies and observed in many countries. In Italy, however, it appears to be more pronounced than in most other OECD nations.

Ceteris paribus differences in the rates of growth of income (as well as those of its basic components, population and productivity growth) are not sufficient to explain the difference in the level of saving between Italy and other countries. A major role must thus be played by differences in the elasticity between saving and growth. A positive elasticity is not necessarily implied by standard life-cycle models, nor is it implied, as observed by Campbell (1987), by permanent income models with an infinite horizon. In the latter case, in fact, saving should fall when the household anticipates a permanent increase in future income. In the former, for the life-cycle aggregation mechanism to insure a positive correlation between saving and productivity growth, it needs to be cohort-specific and the earnings profile to be relatively flat up to retirement. If earnings are upward sloping, and capital markets are perfect, the young would like to dissave; in such a case, provided that borrowing is not constrained, an increase in growth may even lead to a reduction in aggregate saving.

Several factors could in principle have strengthened the effect of growth on aggregate saving. They include the accumulation of precautionary assets or of buffer stock savings, the presence of incentives to postpone consumption to provide for larger needs later in the life cycle, the desire to leave a bequest, the thinness of consumer credit and insurance markets which may lead either to borrowing constraints or to insufficient protection against uncertainty. All these factors are considered in the various chapters of the book, and all are shown to matter to some extent, thus justifying the relatively high asset-to-income ratios necessary to account for saving rates being higher in Italy than elsewhere.

In Chapter 1, however, Guiso, Jappelli and Terlizzese argue that the limited size of the Italian markets for insurance and credit to households is likely to play the major role in fostering, via a high wealth-income ratio, the link between saving and growth. Consumer credit and mortgages are extremely limited as a percentage of consumption expenditure when compared with the other major OECD countries. Insurance premiums also represent a particularly small proportion of total domestic product. It can be argued that Italian households may have a low propensity to borrow or to insure, or that the pattern of earnings over life, the structure of uncertainty and the demographic characteristics of Italian households result in their expressing a low demand for loans and insurance. The evidence provided in the paper nonetheless suggests that the thinness of the credit and insurance markets is more likely to reflect the terms at which credit and insurance are offered, barriers to entry and regulation specific to the markets, as well as the restrictions on the type of contracts available to individuals.

The presence of borrowing constraints may thus provide a possible explanation for a relatively higher asset-income ratio in Italy than in other countries. It may also account for the stronger impact on the Italian saving rate of a decline in the rate of growth of the economy such as that recorded in the last two decades. In Chapter 2, Rossi and Visco estimate that the growth slowdown explains about two thirds of the reduction in the aggregate private saving rate. Obvious candidates to account for the residual one third are therefore changes in fiscal policy and demographic characteristics.

Besides the direct effect of government deficits on national saving, there are a variety of channels through which changes in taxation, government consumption, intergenerational redistribution policies and net social security benefits can affect private saving behavior. Rossi and Visco concentrate on the latter. The impact of fiscal policies on saving has in fact been thoroughly scrutinized in Italy, but most of the research has aimed at assessing the validity of the Ricardian neutrality proposition in the country with the highest public debt among the major industrial nations. The proposition has been generally rejected, and this result is confirmed by the Rossi and Visco estimates. Less attention has been devoted to the role of the intergenerational redistribution of resources operated through the social security system. In principle, however, as the simulations performed by Kotlikoff (1979) within a life-cycle context clearly confirm, the existence of an unfunded social security system can have strong effects on the equilibrium capital stock. Casual evidence indicates that Italy has an extremely generous social security system: in fact it has the highest pensions-to-GDP ratio of all the western countries.

Net government transfers have increased in Italy from a level of about 2 percent of national income in the years before the mid-seventies to about 6 percent in most of the eighties. The rise can be attributed almost entirely to the growing imbalances of the national social security system and it may have differentially affected the consumption decisions of various age-cohorts of Italian consumers. The main result emerging from the Rossi and Visco time series and cross-section analysis is that more than a quarter of the overall decline in the saving rate in the last two decades can be attributed to the startling increase in social security wealth. In particular, during the postwar period and until 1962, the introduction of the new pay-as-you-go system had the effect of slowing down the increase in the saving rate prompted by the rapid growth associated with postwar reconstruction and development. Between the seventies and the eighties, major variations in the traditional life-cycle pattern of income were exogenously introduced through the overhaul of the pension system, thus significantly reducing private capital accumulation. The saving rate decline of little more than 2 percentage points between these two decades can be almost entirely explained by increases in social security wealth.

In Chapter 3, Cannari examines the effects of demographic changes, and in particular the very rapid decline in the fertility rate that occurred in Italy in the eighties. He concludes that the effects of such changes on the propensity to save, operating through the life-cycle aggregation process, have been negligible. The fall in the personal saving rate which took place in the last decade appears rather to be due to the increase in the propensity to consume of all age-groups in the population. Not all groups, however, contributed equally. Using Bank of Italy survey data covering the 1980-89 period, Cannari shows that, although the average propensity to consume increased for all age-groups, it increased more for retired households. This finding is consistent with the results of Rossi and Visco discussed earlier: *ceteris paribus*, an increase in the size of social security transfers should have affected the consumption of the elderly proportionally more than that of the younger. A further finding is that the increase in the average propensity to consume is mainly due to homeowners and to households in the upper tail of the income distribution, perhaps as a consequence of the large capital gains on housing and stocks that occurred in the eighties.

The results in this paper are analogous to those found for the United States by Bosworth, Burtless and Sabelhaus (1991) and by Attanasio (1992) and suggest that the decline in the saving rate observed in Italy as in many other countries during the eighties may have little to do with the rapid changes in the age structure of the population. This conclusion is basically due to the lack of substantial dissaving by the elderly: if retired households continue to save or if they dissave very little, changes in the age distribution of the population will have very modest effects; movements in the aggregate propensity to consume will be due mainly to changes in the propensities of specific groups. On this issue two observations are in order. The first is that changes in the fertility rate may have more direct effects on consumption decisions, besides affecting the weight of groups in the population with different propensities to save. On the one hand, a decline in fertility reduces family consumption as there are fewer dependent children; on the other, a lower planned fertility tends to tip consumption towards young age as incentives to accumulate for larger future family needs are lower. A decline in fertility could also weaken the saving for bequests as less or no heirs are expected to be around. Second, the effects of other demographic changes, such as those in life expectancy and in the retirement age, have been neglected, and this is likely to be an important omission. In fact, part of the increase in social security transfers that took place in the last decade may have been due to such demographic changes. Above all, these changes may have a considerable impact on future socio-economic conditions in Italy.

As shown in Chapter 4 by Franco, Gokhale, Guiso, Kotlikoff and Sartor, the combination of Italian demographic changes and fiscal imbalances poses a very serious threat. Building on previous work by Auerbach, Gokhale and Kotlikoff (1991), a consistent system of generational accounts is set up to evaluate the likely burden imposed on future generations of Italians by the current course of fiscal policy. The paper, written before the December 1992 reform of the Italian social security system, blends some of the crucial facts of the recent course of Italian fiscal policy and demographics. It shows how the very high stock of public debt, the mentioned generosity of the pay-as-you-go pension system and the projected rapid decline of the Italian population may interact and create a very significant gap in the tax burden of current and future generations. Given these trends and in compliance with the government's intertemporal budget constraint, the paper concludes that net payments to the government by future generations of Italians, in present value terms and *ceteris paribus*, may be almost three times more than those of current newborn Italians over the entire course of their life.

Although the results of exercises such as the one presented in this chapter are based on strong assumptions about the very distant future patterns of fertility, interest rates and productivity growth, to mention only a few factors, they have value in suggesting that when fiscal policy becomes visibly unsustainable, as seems to be the case in the present situation, measures need to be taken to safeguard the welfare of future generations. And such measures would best be taken soon after the policy is found to be on an unsustainable track. From this perspective, the recent reform of the Italian social security system certainly goes in the right direction, even if it may still be insufficient to fill the generational gap in the tax burden. Finally, as Franco *et al*. point out, fiscal policy measures aimed at filling the gap may have important consequences for the national saving rate. They estimate that a complete restoration of the generational balance might bring the saving rate back to the levels prevailing in the sixties.

2 Life-cycle saving and precautionary motives

A distinctive feature of the life-cycle theory of saving is its implications for the behavior of consumers at various stages of the life cycle. In particular, in a growing economy individuals are expected to dissave when young and when old and to finance this dissaving with the accumulation of assets in their middle years. However, these implications are often contradicted by the evidence: consumption appears to trail income too closely over the life cycle, leading to less consumption smoothing at low frequencies than implied by the standard life-cycle model. Consequently, there is little dissaving at the two extremes of the life cycle, so that the aggregation mechanism is insufficient to account for the strong positive effect of the rate of growth on the aggregate saving rate. Since the life-cycle hypothesis is a much more flexible framework than the standard version of the model, we are led to ask what modifications are needed to account for the observed facts. In particular, a reasonable theory of saving behavior should probably account for individual families increasing their saving rate when faced with a rise in their disposable income.

In Chapters 5 and 6, Ando, Guiso and Terlizzese explore a number of possibilities that may explain observed deviations from the predictions of the standard life-cycle model while retaining the spirit of the life-cycle hypothesis, that is, a rational allocation of total available resources to consumption in all remaining periods of the life cycle, plus a bequest.

In the first paper they concentrate on young households and individuals. Contrary to the standard life-cycle model, which would require them to borrow, it appears that both in Italy and Japan young households save a significant fraction of their income and accumulate substantial assets. This is surprising in consideration of the fact that both countries are characterized by high income growth and thus by strong incentives to smooth consumption. Ando *et al*. argue that explanations based on simple forms of borrowing constraints, or on imperfections in the consumer loan market when earnings are uncertain, are not likely to be able to account for the behavior of the young. An alternative explanation appeals to the existence of strong incentives to postpone consumption over the life cycle besides those provided by market interest rates in excess of subjective rates of time preference.

There are at least two reasons why this type of situation is plausible. The first is simply that future needs may be greater, for instance to allow for anticipated additions to family membership. This particularly includes cases in which, in the absence of extra saving now, the household may find itself liquidity-constrained in the future. The second possibility is that a consumer may find himself wholly uncertain concerning future preferences. He may be quite aware of the possibility that the acquisition of additional experience, learning and association with different social groups lead him to develop a new pattern of tastes that will enable him to derive greater satisfaction from a given expenditure at a later date than he would obtain from the same expenditure now. The authors provide some evidence from Italian and Japanese data that is consistent with these hypotheses. These theories are supplementary, rather than alternative, to the basic thesis of the life-cycle theory, namely that in their major decisions consumers attempt to plan for a fairly long horizon extending over the remainder of their life and beyond.

In the second paper, Ando *et al.* study the saving (or dissaving) behavior of older families in Italy. This topic has been the subject of a number of studies covering several countries in recent years. As in other countries, older families in Italy decumulate their net worth on average, but by a far smaller amount than is consistent with the "stripped-down" version of the life-cycle model, in which they would plan to reach a zero wealth level at the time of death.

The critical question is to identify the reasons why these families attempt to maintain their wealth, and end up leaving substantial bequests at the time of their death. For most families, an explicit bequest motive does not seem to be the central consideration. In fact, when they are directly asked to choose among alternative motives for saving, only a few cite the bequest motive as being even subsidiary. Furthermore, it should be recalled that even at a moderate productivity growth the earnings of the younger generation would, on average, be much larger than those of an older generation. For instance, if the generational gap is 35 years and the average annual productivity increase is 1.5 percent (a figure considerably below the Italian rate), the younger generation's earnings would be some 70 percent higher than those of the older generation. Thus, if transfer decisions are affected by the relative wealth of donors and recipients, as the results in Ando *et al.* suggest, and if there is mutual concern among different generations, the transfers should flow from the younger to the older generation and not *vice versa*. The exception would be the relatively few families at the top of the income distribution; since wealth is highly concentrated in these families, the aggregate transfer of wealth at the time of death must depend heavily on their behavior.

On the other hand, the decumulation of wealth appears to be somewhat more pronounced for families with independently living children than for families without, suggesting that significant *inter vivos* transfers do take place, perhaps to alleviate the consequences of liquidity constraints faced by younger families. As we shall see, however, these transfers do not appear to be large enough to overcome completely the effects of liquidity constraints. It also appears that households with children are more likely to hold life insurance than those without.

On the whole, then, we must conclude at this point that the factors considered so far are not sufficient to explain why older families decumulate their wealth as little as they apparently do. There are three additional considerations that may contribute to the explanation of this behavior. The first is the nature of residential arrangements. Most families live in their own houses by the time they retire, and they appear to have a strong preference for staying there until their death. If annuities markets were not available, homes would tend to be left as unintended bequests. Secondly, older persons do not, obviously, know exactly when they will die, and any prudent family must act as though it will continue to live longer than the life expectancy charts indicate, leading again to unintended bequests. Thirdly, older persons may fear the possibility of major disasters (serious illness or other events involving large expenses) and they may feel the need to maintain reserve funds to meet such contingencies. The second and third types of uncertainty may overlap, and a unified reserve can cover both.

The effects of these uncertainties on the saving behavior of older families in Italy have not yet been formally investigated. A different type of uncertainty has been studied instead, namely that regarding future earnings. This type of uncertainty is clearly not very relevant for older, retired persons, but may be important for very young families and may help explain why their saving rate is so high.

In theory, earnings uncertainty should lead to lower consumption and higher saving for prudent consumers. The empirical relevance of this motivation for saving remains a matter of controversy. Simulations performed for example by Skinner (1988) and by Caballero (1991) seem to indicate that income risk might explain a substantial fraction of accumulated assets. This contrasts, however, with the difficulty usually found in empirical literature to identify a precautionary motive, let alone to measure its contribution to the accumulation of wealth. The two papers by Guiso and Jappelli (Chapter 7) and by Guiso, Jappelli and Terlizzese (Chapter 8) provide new evidence on both the existence and the relevance of a precautionary motive. The main conclusion is that a precautionary motive exists, but appears to contribute very little to savings, at least in Italy. It should be noted, however, that the analysis was confined to a specific source of uncertainty, namely that related to future labor earnings, and that direct information is available only for one-year-ahead expectations. Further studies on other types of uncertainty are therefore needed before a conclusion on its effects on the saving rate can be reached.

The paper by Guiso and Jappelli tests for the presence of precautionary saving that relies on the insurance role of the family. The simple, yet unexplored intuition is used, that households with multiple earners can pool their earnings and thus share risks. Accordingly, households with multiple earners should, *ceteris paribus*, have a higher propensity to consume than households with a single earner. This implication is not rejected by the data; households where both husband and wife work consume a higher fraction of lifetime resources than households where only the husband works.

Though the classification of households into *a priori* reasonable income risk groups can shed some light on the existence of a precautionary motive, it has a number of shortcomings, including the fact that classification criteria may be correlated with other characteristics that affect consumption decisions. Furthermore, while such tests make it possible to measure the difference in the saving propensities of the groups, they do not allow to measure the extent of the precautionary motive, as this would require knowing the level of risk faced by the specific household. The second essay follows a more direct approach and allows some of these deficiencies to be overcome. Guiso *et al.* exploit a unique source of information on the subjective probability distribution of earnings growth contained in the 1989 Bank of Italy Survey of Households Income and Wealth. In this survey households were asked to attach probabilities to specified classes of one-year-ahead changes in nominal income and prices. From this rather unusual information a measure of the subjective variance of real earnings was constructed, which was then used to test for the existence of precautionary saving. Perhaps surprisingly, the result obtained is that, while uncertainty lowers consumption, as implied by the theory, the effect is on average rather small. Consistently with decreasing prudence, the effect of earnings uncertainty increases as wealth decreases but is of significant importance only for the poorest consumers. These results are confirmed if the measure of uncertainty is used in a wealth accumulation regression: the theory would imply that consumers facing more uncertainty should end up accumulating more assets. Guiso *et al.* show that this is indeed the case, but earnings uncertainty can only account for about 2 percent of the stock of accumulated assets.

3   Borrowing constraints, intergenerational transfers and bequests

As repeatedly argued, a distinctive feature of the Italian economy is the imperfect working of insurance and credit markets for households. Virtually every aspect of households' behavior is affected by the thinness and limitations of the mortgage, consumer loan and insurance markets. Several of the papers already mentioned have directly or indirectly dealt with this feature of the Italian economy. We now turn to specific issues concerning the presence of borrowing constraints, starting with their diffusion across Italian households.

In Chapter 9, Maccan, Rossi and Visco directly address the problem of measuring the diffusion of borrowing constraints; using Mariger's (1987) methodology and adopting a definition of borrowing constraints extended to allow also for difficulties in access to the mortgage market (in addition to the more traditional constraints in the consumer loan market), they arrive at the conclusion that in Italy restricted borrowing affects between one sixth and one fourth of the population.

Such a widespread presence of liquidity constraints is likely to cause severe loss of welfare to consumers who, in turn, are provided with an incentive to take action to circumvent the constraints or, at least, to limit their effects. For example, if the constraint is currently binding, or is expected to bind, they might increase their current labor supply: the higher income obtained would in fact ease the constraint, if currently binding, or allow the accumulation of more assets in order to prevent the constraint from binding in the future. Some evidence of this effect, based on the Bank of Italy survey data, is provided by Nicoletti-Altimari and Thomson (1993). The main message is that borrowing constraints may alter the leisure-consumption choice. But they might also alter the trade-off between durable and non-durable consumption. If durables can affect the amount consumers can lend, perhaps because they can be used as collateral, then the presence of borrowing constraints might affect the relation between durables and non-durables. In Chapter 10, Brugiavini and Weber show that the effect on the stock of durables depends on the value of the durable as collateral; if it has low collateral value, consumers will tend to purchase more non-durables, while they will hold a comparatively larger stock of durables if this effectively signals credit worthiness. They find empirical support for these propositions from the Italian experience and are able to confirm that for credit-constrained households the relation between durables and non-durables is shifted towards the latter.

Besides adapting their choice of actions, consumers might react to the absence or imperfect working of finacial markets by developing alternative ways of effecting transactions: when markets are poor or inefficient, there is a strong incentive for individuals to develop parallel, informal institutions to overcome the impediments to trading in official markets. In Chapter 11, Guiso and Jappelli ask whether the observed inefficiencies in the consumer loan market might be overcome by private transfers and loans taking place through the family network. They indeed find that transfers are mainly targeted towards liquidity-constrained households. This result implies that to ignore the existence of informal markets might lead to significant overstatement of the welfare cost of the inefficiency of the official market for loans. Empirically, Guiso and Jappelli notice that for those who receive the transfer, its amount (which averages almost 40 percent of net transfer income) appears sufficient to release completely the constraint and to allow these consumers to reach their optimal consumption path. However, it also appears that transfers are not widespread enough to allow all consumers to overcome the constraint: only 17 percent of liquidity-constrained households receive a money transfer. Thus, a large fraction of households remains liquidity-constrained even after transfers have taken place.

These results are consistent with those of Ando, Guiso and Terlizzese (Chapter 6) already discussed; according to these findings, the presence of borrowing constraints induces households to anticipate the timing of bequests to when they are most needed. Since, however, the pattern of wealth accumulation is only marginally altered by the anticipation of bequests, we may infer that *inter vivos* transfers are not as widespread as would be necessary for them to be an effective substitute for official borrowing. This conclusion is also supported by the evidence provided by Barca, Cannari and Guiso in Chapter 12. Computing the share of intergenerational transfers in the form of both bequests and *inter vivos* transfers, they find that the latter account for only 12 percent of overall transfers. Thus, while informal markets and consumers' reactions may limit the welfare cost of borrowing constraints, they are by no means a substitute for a well-functioning credit market.

4   Conclusions

The project underlying this book focused on several factors contributing to the level and changes of the Italian saving rate between the mid-fifties and 1990. For this reason, virtually all the essays in this volume are set within a generalized life-cycle framework, allowing for liquidity constraints, intergenerational transfers, the effects of the social security program and some forms of uncertainty.

It is useful to summarize our discussion in terms of equations (1) and (2). While these equations are often associated with the standard life-cycle model, they are almost definitional relations and are applicable to a much broader class of hypotheses. We can then see that, for a given target wealth-income ratio, the saving rate is proportional to the growth rate of income. The wealth-income ratio is indeed a declining function of the growth rate of income, but less than proportional for a plausible set of values of the basic parameters. Thus, it is not surprising that the saving rate in Italy is closely related to the growth rate of income. Both the wealth-income ratio and the growth rate are higher than the OECD averages throughout the period.

The growth rate, however, does not by itself explain the level and changes of the saving rate completely. It accounts, jointly with the relatively high level of the wealth-income ratio, for some two thirds of the reduction in the saving rate during the period considered. The results of the papers collected in this volume suggest that:

1) As the present value of social security benefits (social security wealth) rises, it is perceived by the private sector as partially accumulated wealth, thus reducing the target wealth-income ratio and the actual saving rate.

2) The credit and insurance markets for households are significantly less developed in Italy than in other major OECD countries, and this directly or indirectly leads many households to consume less early in the life cycle, increasing Italy's saving rate. *Inter vivos* transfers from older families alleviate this problem, but not completely.

3) Older families are fairly reluctant to decumulate wealth, though they seem to do so to a small extent. The motivation for this behavior is not yet fully understood, but an explicit bequest motive does not appear to be the dominant one. This behavior makes the aggregate Italian saving rate less sensitive to changes in the demographic structure of the country than is implied by a naive life-cycle model. It also increases the aggregate target wealth-income ratio.

4) Although uncertainty regarding future earnings seems to increase the saving rate, its quantitative effect appears small. However, it should be recognized that the consequences of many types of uncertainties involving major expenditures, such as those associated with illness, the need to assist family members, and still others, have not been explored.

Looking ahead, it is probable that the private saving rate in Italy will continue to rise or fall with the rate of growth of income in association with medium-term movements in productivity and population. Such fluctuations in the saving rate should, however, be considered as contributing to the efficient functioning of the economy, since they help to keep the wealth-income ratio of households more stable and tend to accommodate investment needs. Thus, any adjustment of government policy aimed at moderating or reversing the decline in the saving rate should take into consideration only that part of the decline that is not prompted by an exogenous slowdown in the growth rate of the economy.

This naturally raises the problem of the adequacy of the current capital-output ratio. Although optimal growth theory warns us that the maintenance of a very high capital-output ratio is not necessarily welfare-enhancing, it would appear that in the leading OECD economies, including Italy, this ratio is below the critical level established by the "Golden Rule" (see Abel *et al*, 1989). There seems thus to be a case for policies aimed at increasing national savings, even if their importance is probably limited by the fact that, on average, the actual capital-output ratio is not likely to fall short of the Golden Rule level by more than a small margin.

The above would not apply if the rate of growth of productivity were dependent on investment (and thus on savings), as in recently developed endogenous growth models. In such circumstances even small variations in the saving rate could have a substantial impact on the level of output and on welfare, through their effect on the rate of growth of productivity. Although the empirical status of endogenous growth models is not yet clarified, we may note that even in traditional growth models with exogenous technical progress, if the nature of capital is putty-clay (that is, if existing capital cannot be modified to take advantage of new technologies developed after it is put in place), then the improvement of productivity will depend on new investment, and hence on saving, except in the very long run.

Apart from its possible effects on long-term growth, the decline in the saving rate could cause concern for other reasons. Some types of investment, particularly those that carry the characteristics of public goods, such as environmental improvements or cultural and educational facilities, may have social rates of return that are higher than the market rate, and in order to undertake them the society may need a high rate of saving. On a global level, and for some time, we cannot ignore the need for an unusually high level of investment in order that some regions, such as Eastern Europe and the less developed countries, may be set on the path to economic recovery and development. If these countries are to receive the assistance they require, the OECD economies will have to generate high levels of saving: the indirect benefits for the latter countries should amply justify the outlay. It should be pointed out, then, that in Italy a higher saving rate may be needed in order to eliminate dependence on net foreign savings and be in a position to participate with other developed nations in efforts to bring about a permanent improvement in the economic conditions of other regions.

If we accept even some of these lines of approach we must conclude that the maintenance of a relatively high level of national saving (aside from the fluctuations associated with medium-term variations in the growth rate) is an important policy objective. So what are the prospects of achieving this if current financial market conditions and demographic trends continue under the policies foreseen to prevail in the immediate future? And if the saving rate is considered too low, what are the alternative policy options?

We have noted that financial market imperfections, precautionary saving and bequest motives have together contributed to a higher level of saving in Italy. Consumer credit and insurance markets may be expected to become more efficient in the near future and, if our analysis is correct, this should lower the saving rate somewhat. We have also concluded that the effects of demographic changes on the saving rate were fairly mild in the past. If, however, the current low birth rate in Italy continues for a significant period of time, it will bring more radical changes in the age structure of population than anything we have experienced so far. It will also alter family structure and this in turn may affect the aggregate saving rate. Since we find that young families save on average more than the rest of the population, and retired families save less (though they do not dissave significantly), we must expect the saving rate to decline to some extent when the effects of the current dramatic reduction in the birth rate become visible.

On the other hand the effects on saving of the projected rationalization of the social security system and its interaction with demographic developments are complex. As the social security system is rationalized and made sustainable, the social security wealth of the private sector should decline, leading to a higher private saving rate in the younger, working population. On the other side, since support for the retired, older population will be necessarily less generous than it is now, compared with the average earnings of workers in the economy, dissavings by retired families should increase if the retirement age remains the same. However, the retirement age will rise both because the statutory age of entitlement to social security benefits will be raised and because families will perceive the need to accumulate more assets before retirement. Finally, if the current low birth rate continues and the aging of the population progresses more than is currently projected, further rationalization of the social security system may become necessary. It may be thus quite important that older individuals – perhaps those between the ages of 60 and 75 – who are able to do so, continue in employment. If even relatively small numbers of this older population switch from the ranks of the retired to those of the actively employed it could make a major difference to output capacity and the saving rate. The elimination of the disincentive feature for older individuals to work currently incorporated into the social security program, under which older individuals lose pension benefits if they work and earn income, should be helpful in this regard. For example, the benefit schedule can be adjusted so that the present value of the benefits measured at a given age remains the same regardless of how much the individual chooses to work. Such a provision may end up reducing the social security deficit in addition to increasing the labor force participation of older individuals.

It seems fair to conclude that it is unlikely that private saving will recover spontaneously in the near future, even taking into account the effects of the recent reform of the social security system. Further, from all we know about the value of the intertemporal elasticity of substitution in consumption, it is equally unlikely that tax-based incentives to save can reverse or even slow down current declining trends in private saving rates. Thus a recovery in Italian national saving must come mainly from higher government saving. However large the private sector saving rate, the economy will not be able to improve the welfare of its citizens if private saving is offset by public sector dissaving (net of public investment in productive resources). The fundamental issue here is the availability of resources for investment not only in productive resources but also in the domestic social overhead capital. Consideration should also be given to the fact that the developed countries as a whole should make funds available to guarantee the improvement of economic conditions in distressed parts of the world. For these purposes, what matters is the level of saving, rather than the saving-income ratio: this calls for the full utilization of resources accompanied by the production of as large an output as is consistent with other objectives such as the maintenance of stable prices. Closer coordination of policies among the leading OECD countries aimed at the fuller utilization of capacity should help to achieve this.

REFERENCES

Abel, A.B., N.G. Mankiw, L.H. Summers and R.J. Zeckhauser (1989). 'Assessing Dynamic Efficiency', *The Review of Economic Studies* **56**: 1-19.

Attanasio, D. (1992). 'A Cohort Analysis of Saving Behavior by U.S. Households', Stanford University, mimeo.

Auerbach, A.J., J. Gokhale and L.J. Kotlikoff (1991). 'Generational Accounts: A Meaningful Alternative to Deficit Accounting', in D. Bradford (ed.), *Tax Policy and the Economy*, Cambridge, MA: National Bureau of Economic Research, Vol. V.

Bosworth, B., G. Burtless and J. Sabelhaus (1991). 'The Decline in Saving: Evidence from Household Surveys', *Brookings Papers on Economic Activity* **1**: 183-256.

Caballero, R. (1991). 'Earnings Uncertainty and Aggregate Wealth Accumulation', *American Economic Review* **81**: 859-71.

Campbell, J.Y. (1987). 'Does Saving Anticipate Declining Labor Income? An Alternative Test of the Permanent Income Hypothesis', *Econometrica* **55**: 1249-73.

Deaton, A. (1992). *Understanding Consumption*, Oxford: Clarendon Press.

Heertje, A. ed. (1993). *World Savings. An International Survey*, Oxford: Blackwell.

Kotlikoff, L.J. (1979). 'Social Security and Equilibrium Capital Intensity', *Quarterly Journal of Economics* **43**: 233-54.

Mariger, R. (1987). 'A Life-Cycle Consumption Model with Liquidity Constraints', *Econometrica* **55**: 533-57.

Nicoletti-Altimari, S. and M. Thomson (1993). 'The Effects of Liquidity Constraints on Consumption and Labor Supply: Evidence from Italian Households', University of Pennsylvania, mimeo.

Skinner, J. (1988). 'Risky Income, Life Cycle Consumption and Precautionary Saving', *Journal of Monetary Economics* **22**: 237-55.

Theil, H. (1954). *Linear Aggregation of Economic Relations*, Amsterdam: North-Holland.

I

SAVING TRENDS, GOVERNMENT DEFICIT AND DEMOGRAPHIC CHANGES

1   Why is Italy's saving rate so high?*

LUIGI GUISO, TULLIO JAPPELLI
and DANIELE TERLIZZESE

1   Introduction

Two features characterize the Italian saving rate. By international standards, Italy is a "high-saving" country; the Italian saving rate has declined markedly in the last three decades. We provide a consistent framework to interpret these facts. According to the life-cycle hypothesis, they should be explained mainly by differences in demographics and productivity growth between countries and over time (Modigliani, 1990). However, as we argue in Section 2, the differences in the growth rates between Italy and the other major OECD countries are rather small when compared with the large differences in their saving rates: growth appears to generate more saving in Italy than elsewhere. Thus, growth alone cannot account for the high Italian saving rate and for its sharp decline.

We argue that capital market imperfections provide a plausible explanation of the evidence. An economy in which households are liquidity-constrained exhibits a higher saving rate than an economy with perfect markets, even if the two economies grow at the same rate. This implies that an identical reduction in growth leads to a greater reduction in saving in the economy with imperfect markets (Jappelli and Pagano, 1994). Thus, the interaction between growth and capital market imperfections may explain not only why Italy's saving rate is high; it may also explain why the reduction in the rate of productivity and population growth of the eighties was accompanied by a sharp reduction in saving.

In Sections 3.1 and 3.2 we present evidence to show that the level of development of Italian consumer credit and insurance markets is by far the lowest of the major industrial countries. Regulations, high downpayments for the purchase of durables and housing, wide interest rate spreads and limited competition make it considerably more difficult to obtain access to credit and insurance in Italy than in almost all other industrialized countries of comparable level of development.

One important objection to stressing the role of capital market imperfections as a determinant of households' saving behavior is that the public sector and informal financial arrangements may overcome private market imperfections. Italians may borrow less and buy less insurance because the family or the government provide insurance efficiently and help them to circumvent liquidity constraints. In Section 3.3 we address and reject both explanations on the grounds that: (i) private transfers are not disproportionately targeted towards households that face higher income uncertainty or credit constraints, and (ii) the public provision of insurance is no greater in Italy than in other OECD countries.

Having shown that supply factors, rather than other factors, are the likely explanation for the low level of consumer debt and insurance provisions in Italy, we evaluate the impact of capital market imperfections on households' saving decisions. Given the complex interaction between insurance and credit markets, we provide a number of empirical tests to assess the effect of credit market imperfections and earnings uncertainty on households' saving.

Where capital markets are imperfect, consumption growth can be expected to correlate with income growth. We provide standard tests of excess sensitivity for the purpose of comparing the degree of excess sensitivity in Italian data with that of other countries (for the latter case we rely on existing studies). Using aggregate time series and panel data, we find a comparatively high level of excess sensitivity in Italy (Section 4.1), a result which is consistent with the hypothesis that credit market imperfections are the source of the empirical failure of the permanent income hypothesis. However, these tests have little power to discriminate between liquidity constraints and other competing explanations of Euler equations failures (e.g. myopia and durability of goods). So we turn to more direct evidence of the influence that market imperfections may have on saving, using the 1989 Bank of Italy Survey of Household Income and Wealth (SHIW).

In Section 4.2 we investigate whether downpayment restrictions, transaction costs and other mortgage market imperfections force households to save more than they would in a properly functioning mortgage market. We find that the desire to purchase a house, in conjunction with the inability to borrow, increases the aggregate saving ratio by 2 to 3 percentage points (depending on the specification and sample used).

In Section 4.3 on the basis of the findings of two studies on precautionary saving included in this volume we conclude that risk affects saving and wealth accumulation in a direction predicted by the theory, but the amount of precautionary saving in response to earnings uncertainty is small.

In Section 5 we evaluate alternative explanations for the high Italian saving rate and for its sharp decline, and reject the role of bequests and the slope of the earnings profiles as possible causes. In Section 6 we summarize the evidence and suggest that the approach used in this study is useful to analyze the inter-country differences in saving rates and the response of the Italian saving rate to the on-going liberalization of European financial markets.

2   The Italian saving rate in an international perspective

From its peak in the early sixties, the Italian gross national saving rate declined by almost 7 percentage points by the end of the eighties (Table 1.1, column (1)). It would appear that the reduction in the national saving rate was due entirely to a dramatic reduction in public saving, while the private saving rate remained roughly constant, or even increased slightly. However, this measure of saving is not adjusted for the erosion in purchasing power of the stock of nominally denominated debt due to inflation or for the depreciation of the capital stock.[1]

Owing to the depreciation's increased share of gross national income, net saving declined by 10 percentage points between 1960 and 1988 (Table 1.1, column (4)).[2] After the maximum reached in the early sixties, corresponding to the peak of the long cycle of the so-called economic "miracle", the national saving rate diminished in the late sixties. In the early seventies saving recovered, but fell sharply after the second oil shock. In the eighties the saving rate continued its long-term decline.

The inflation adjustment is extremely important in Italy, on account of its high rate of inflation, especially in the seventies and early eighties, and the high level of the stock of public debt in the eighties. In contrast to the unadjusted figures, the inflation-adjusted saving rates indicate that both private and government saving contributed in roughly equal measure to the reduction in the national saving rate (Table 1.1, columns (8) and (9)). This brings us to the first fact: the Italian saving rate – whether national or private – has declined substantially over time.

Table 1.2 reports the net national saving rates and the net private saving rates adjusted for inflation of the seven major industrialized countries (from here on, G7) and of three North-European countries.[3] As we will see, Finland, Norway and Sweden feature relatively low saving rates and relatively developed household credit markets, and represent an interesting comparative set. For each country we also report averages of the rate of growth of gross domestic product over ten-year periods.

Table 1.1 Saving and growth in Italy, 1954-1990 (a)

Period	Gross saving rates (b)			Net saving rates (c)			Net saving rates adjusted for inflation (d)			Growth
	NS (1)	PS (2)	GS (3)	NS (4)	PS (5)	GS (6)	NS (7)	PS (8)	GS (9)	ϱ (10)
1954-60	26.8	25.1	1.8	16.0	14.3	1.7	16.0	12.4	2.7	5.8
1961-65	28.0	26.2	1.8	19.8	18.3	1.5	19.8	15.8	4.0	4.6
1966-70	27.0	26.8	0.2	19.8	19.9	-0.1	19.8	17.9	1.9	5.9
1971-75	25.4	28.7	-3.3	17.0	21.9	-4.1	17.0	15.4	1.6	2.7
1976-80	25.8	30.1	-4.3	16.1	21.2	-5.1	16.1	13.1	3.1	4.7
1981-85	22.2	28.6	-6.4	11.2	18.8	-7.6	11.2	10.0	1.2	1.6
1986-90	20.6	26.2	-5.6	9.9	16.6	-6.7	9.9	11.6	-1.7	3.1

NS = national saving; PS = private saving; GS = government saving; ϱ = average percentage rate of growth of gross domestic product.
(a) In 1985 the national accounts were subject to major revisions. Official statistics exist for a few main aggregates only after 1970. The data for earlier years have been estimated on the basis of the old national accounts. *Source*: Pagliano and Rossi (1992).
(b) Gross saving as a percentage of gross domestic product.
(c) Net saving as a percentage of net domestic product.
(d) The adjustment for inflation has been made with reference to holdings of government debt, currency and net external financial assets, using the year-to-year percentage change of the CPI as well as survey measures of inflation expectations (see Pagliano and Rossi, 1992).

Table 1.2 Net saving rates and growth in the OECD countries (a)

	Average 1960-1970			Average 1971-1980			Average 1981-1987			Differences 1980s - 1960s			Ratio of private saving to the growth rate of GDP		
	NS (1)	PS (2)	ϱ (3)	NS (4)	PS (5)	ϱ (6)	NS (7)	PS (8)	ϱ (9)	ΔNS (10)	ΔPS (11)	$\Delta\varrho$ (12)	1960s (13)	1970s (14)	1980s (15)
Canada	11.3	8.0	4.7	13.3	11.5	3.8	9.4	12.1	3.1	-1.9	4.1	-1.6	1.7	3.0	3.9
U.S.A.	10.6	8.3	3.5	8.9	8.2	2.9	3.9	6.8	3.1	-6.7	-1.5	-0.4	2.4	2.8	2.2
Japan	25.6	18.1	9.5	24.6	20.0	4.9	20.2	15.4	3.7	-5.4	-2.7	-5.8	1.9	4.1	4.2
France	19.3	14.5	5.0	16.3	11.5	3.4	8.0	5.4	1.8	-11.3	-9.1	-3.2	2.9	3.4	3.0
Germany	19.9	13.8	4.1	14.3	11.0	2.8	10.7	8.8	1.6	-9.2	-5.0	-2.5	3.4	3.9	5.5
Italy	19.8	16.8	5.2	16.6	14.2	3.7	11.0	10.8	1.9	-8.8	-6.0	-3.3	3.2	3.8	5.7
U.K.	11.2	6.1	2.6	8.2	0.8	1.8	6.2	4.7	3.2	-5.0	-1.4	0.6	2.3	0.4	1.5
G7 average	16.9	12.2	4.9	14.6	11.1	3.3	9.9	9.1	2.6	-7.0	-3.2	-2.3	2.5	3.4	3.5
Finland	15.7	7.4	4.8	14.2	7.8	3.8	10.7	7.7	3.3	-5.0	0.3	-1.6	1.5	2.0	2.4
Norway	16.1	8.5	3.8	14.0	5.5	4.8	15.8	2.4	3.9	-0.3	-6.1	0.1	2.2	1.1	0.6
Sweden	16.6	7.6	4.2	11.8	8.0	2.1	6.0	5.5	2.4	-10.6	-2.1	-1.8	1.8	3.8	2.3
OECD average	16.6	11.4	4.9	15.3	11.9	3.4	10.3	9.0	2.4	-6.3	-2.4	-2.5	2.3	3.5	3.8

(a) Net national saving (NS) and net private saving adjusted for inflation (PS) are expressed as a percentage of net domestic product. For Italy the inflation adjustment is defined in note (d) to Table 1.1. For all other countries the inflation adjustment is the product of the rate of change of the private consumption deflator and the stock of outstanding government debt at the beginning of each year. Growth (ϱ) is the average percentage rate of growth of GDP. Source: Modigliani (1990) and Pagliano and Rossi (1992).

Table 1.2 indicates that, by all standards, Italy is a high-saving country, with private and national saving rates consistently above both the OECD and the G7 averages. In terms of national saving rates, Italy ranks second in the three decades (after Japan); in terms of private saving, it ranks second in the sixties and seventies (after Japan) and third in the eighties (after Japan and Canada). This is the second fact: the Italian saving rate is high by international standards.

Columns (10) and (11) of Table 1.2 indicate that saving rates declined in most OECD countries. But the decline in the Italian rate was more evident: between the 1960s and the 1980s the private saving rate declined by 6 points, against a G7 reduction of 3.2 points and an OECD decline of 2.4 points.

The life-cycle hypothesis points mainly to differences in population and productivity growth rates to explain why saving changes over time and why it differs between countries. However, the differences in the rate of growth of Italy and the G7 are not sufficient, *ceteris paribus*, to explain the large differences in the respective saving rates. In the sixties the Italian private saving rate, adjusted for inflation, was almost 5 percentage points above the G7 average, but its growth rate was only 0.3 percentage points above average. In the seventies the differences were 3.4 and 0.4 points respectively, while in the eighties private saving in Italy was 2 percent above average, but growth was actually below average (−0.7 points).

Not even the stripped-down version of the Modigliani-Brumberg (1980) life-cycle model, which emphasizes the effect of growth on saving by assuming a flat earnings profile through the entire life of the individual, can explain these large differences in saving only by relying on differences in growth. According to this model, the predicted difference between the Italian and the G7 saving rates is only 0.6 percent in the sixties, 1.1 percent in the seventies and negative in the eighties.[4]

One way of checking that growth alone cannot explain the difference in saving between Italy and the G7 is to compare the ratios between saving and growth among countries (Table 1.2, columns (12), (13) and (14)). By this measure, Italy ranked first in the sixties and eighties, and second in the seventies.[5] This ranking already shows that the Italian saving rate was high not only in absolute terms, but also in relation to its growth rate.[6]

Another possibility is that Italy has a higher-than-average private saving rate because it has a higher-than-average government deficit. This would be the prediction of the much discussed Ricardian Equivalence Proposition (Barro, 1974), which asserts that one should refer to the national rather than to the private saving rate, because people incorporate the budget constraint of the government in their own budget constraint. However, as implied by the figures in Table 1.2, in the last three decades the Italian current deficit (adjusted for inflation) has not been on average higher than in the OECD area. Further, contrary to the proposition, private saving has not risen to offset the increase in government deficit in the eighties (if anything, the opposite is true).[7]

A more formal way of checking that growth alone cannot explain Italy's high saving rate is to run a pooled regression over countries and (ten-year) periods that excludes Italy to predict its saving rate. In all cases, and even when we add other OECD countries or other regressors – such as the dependency ratio – the coefficients tend to underpredict substantially the Italian private saving rate in all the three periods considered (the 1960s, the 1970s and the 1980s). Two typical regressions for the three decades, both excluding Italy from the sample, are as follows:

$$S_p = \underset{(0.048)}{0.092} + \underset{(0.591)}{2.361}\,\varrho - \underset{(0.319)}{0.178}\,S_g - \underset{(0.139)}{0.191}\,Dep \qquad \text{SE=0.038; Sample: 18 observations of 6 G7 countries}$$

$$S_p = \underset{(0.027)}{0.094} + \underset{(0.420)}{1.429}\,\varrho - \underset{(0.175)}{0.486}\,S_g - \underset{(0.080)}{0.064}\,Dep \qquad \text{SE=0.042; Sample: 60 observations of 20 OECD countries}$$

where S_p and S_g are, respectively, net private and public saving adjusted for inflation, ϱ is the rate of growth of gross domestic product, Dep is the ratio of the population under 15 to the total population, and standard errors are reported in parentheses.

In the first regression the differences between the predicted and the actual Italian saving rates are –3.3 in the sixties, –3.3 in the seventies and –2.5 in the eighties. In the second regression the differences are: –4.8 in the sixties, –3.4 in the seventies and –1.1 in the eighties.[8] Regressions with the national saving rate as the dependent variable yield similar results. The data tell us that, by international comparison, the Italian saving rate tends to be high even when differences in growth and other variables are taken into account.[9]

Since differences in growth cannot explain the evidence, we turn to other factors that can account for the high Italian saving rate as well as for its sharp decline. The issue which we think deserves the closest scrutiny is the possibility that the main difference between Italy and the other OECD countries is the level of development of its credit and insurance markets. When credit markets are imperfect, households are prevented from borrowing to finance flow consumption, and must save to acquire durable goods and homes in anticipation of future borrowing constraints (Zeldes, 1989; Mariger, 1986). And if risks are uninsurable, households accumulate assets to be run down in hard times. In both cases young individuals accumulate more assets than required by the standard life-cycle model with perfect capital and insurance markets.

In the absence of population or productivity growth, capital market imperfections do not, of course, generate positive aggregate saving. But once one allows for growth, an economy with capital markets imperfections exhibits a higher saving rate than an economy with perfect markets. Jappelli and Pagano (1994) illustrate this point in the context of a three-period overlapping generations model where the young are liquidity-constrained and productivity growth is exogenous. In a closed economy the saving rate is the product of the growth rate and the capital-output ratio: they show that for any given level of the growth rate, liquidity constraints raise the capital-output ratio and therefore saving. In other words, the effect of growth on saving is greater in an economy with liquidity constraints: an identical change in growth – for instance, from zero to positive growth – generates a greater change in saving in an economy with liquidity constraints.[10]

This interaction between saving, growth and liquidity constraints may also explain why Italy's saving rate declined so sharply in the eighties. In the G7 the decline in growth was of the same order of magnitude as in Italy, but the decline in private saving was only 3.2 percent (against 6 percent in Italy). Thus, in Italy the reduction in growth has been associated with a greater reduction in saving than in other countries. This pattern is consistent with the idea that in Italy liquidity constraints are more severe than elsewhere.

Besides liquidity constraints, however, there are other factors that may explain the two features of the Italian saving rate: the Italian earnings profile may be flatter than elsewhere, or the bequest motive in Italy may be stronger. As with capital market imperfections, in the absence of growth there is no saving, independently of the bequest motive and the shape of the earnings profile. But allowing for growth, a strong bequest motive or a flat earnings profile may induce a high saving rate.[11] These issues will be addressed in Section 5.

3   The Italian capital markets in an international perspective

In the real world there is substantial interaction between credit markets and insurance markets. For instance, most mortgage contracts are signed in conjunction with a life insurance policy, with the insurance company repaying the loan if the borrower dies prematurely. Mortgages and instalment-sales of durables are generally linked with fire insurance. The combination of credit and insurance allows maturities to be lengthened and moral hazard reduced. Credit lines and credit cards also serve an insurance purpose, since they protect the consumer against a sudden drop in income. Moreover, credit cards help the consumer face unexpected changes in credit rating and the possibility of being denied loans in the future (Jaffee and Stiglitz, 1990).

The interaction between credit and insurance market imperfections has received considerable attention in the theoretical literature. When insurance is not available, credit provides *ex-post* insurance: if current income turns out to be lower than expected, the individual can borrow against future earnings. Since future borrowing constraints prevent the individual from buying insurance *ex-post*, the individual accumulates assets to use in the event of hard times (Deaton, 1991).[12] In this case credit market imperfections reinforce the effect of uncertainty on saving.

Even when insurance is available, it has to be bought in advance. If the individual can only buy a future contingent claim by paying a premium today, he might want to borrow to finance the premium. This feature implies that credit markets must be unrestricted if the individual is to be able to use insurance markets efficiently. The interaction between saving and the structure of capital markets is considered more closely in Appendix 1.

Although it is hard to devise a framework to account for all possible interactions between saving and capital markets, theory suggests that countries such as Italy with less "perfect" capital markets should be expected to save more than countries where capital markets are more developed and closer to the perfect market paradigm.[13] In this section we try to establish whether the proposition that Italy has less developed capital markets is also backed by an international comparison of the credit and insurance markets.

Ideally, it would be best to compare direct indicators of rationing in capital markets (such as interest rates differentials or quantity constraints, if any). However, in many cases it is difficult to find reliable and comparable evidence, and in some important areas we lack sufficient information. In these cases, our approach – like that of Jappelli and Pagano (1989) – is to show that Italian credit and insurance markets are small and to establish that it is "supply" factors rather than "demand" factors that affect market performance.

3.1 Credit markets

In Figure 1.1 we plot the ratio of total household liabilities to net national income from 1964 to 1989. The ratio overestimates the sum of personal consumer credit and mortgage loans granted to households because unincorporated businesses are included in the household sector. But even this overestimation indicates that borrowing has always financed a trivial portion of households' expenditure and investment. Table 1.3 reports figures for consumer credit and mortgages in the main OECD countries and in three North-European countries (columns (1) and (4)). Both markets are between five and ten times smaller in Italy than in most other countries listed in the table.

Table 1.3 Households' liabilities in the OECD countries

	Consumer credit in 1988 (a)	Number of credit cards (b)	Durables share of total consumption in 1988 (c)	Mortgages in 1982 (d)	Average downpayment as a percentage of the sale price (e)	Ownership (percent) (f)
	(1)	(2)	(3)	(4)	(5)	(6)
Canada	22	–	16	60	20	62
U.S.A.	23	200	11	61	11-33	65
Japan	18	–	7	25	35-40	60
France	8	20	9	44	20	47
Germany	15	26	–	65	30	37
Italy	4	4	11	6	40-50	59
U.K.	10	30	11	45	15	59
G7 average (g)	14	–	–	44	–	56
Finland	39	–	13	42	20	61
Norway	48	–	10	60	–	67
Sweden	39	–	12	61	20	57

(a) As a percentage of private consumption expenditure in 1988 (for Japan and France in 1987, for Sweden in 1986). *Sources*: OECD, *Financial Accounts*, Paris, 1989. Data for Italy are from Banca d'Italia, *Relazione annuale*, Roma, 1990. Data for Finland, Norway, Sweden and Japan have been provided by the Finland Central Bank, the Norge Bank, the Sverige Riksbank and the Japan Information Centre Corporation. – (b) In millions, at the end of 1988. *Source*: Banca d'Italia, *Relazione annuale*, Roma, 1989, p. 290. – (c) *Source*: OECD, *National Accounts*, Paris, 1992. – (d) As a percentage of private consumption expenditures in 1982. *Sources*: Boleat (1987), Table 21.8, p. 218. For Italy, Banca d'Italia, *Relazione annuale*, 1983, Appendix, Table aD29. Data for Finland, Norway and Sweden have been kindly provided by the Finland Central Bank, the Norge Bank and the Sverige Riksbank. – (e) The average downpayment is the amount of personal funds required to buy a house even when individuals borrow from different institutions. For the U.S., the figure refers to 1985. The two numbers refer to the downpayments of first-time buyers and repeat buyers, respectively (Summers and Carroll, 1987, Table 7). For Canada, Finland, France, Germany, the figures refer to 1982-3 (Boleat, 1987, pp. 102-3). For Japan, Hayashi, Ito and Slemrod (1988, pp. 223-4) report 35-40 percent for the downpayment of first-time and repeat buyers in the eighties. For Italy, the numbers are our own estimates based on conversations with market specialists. The figure for the U.K. is the average ratio of mortgage advances to house prices for first-time home buyers in 1988 (Muellbauer and Murphy, 1990, p. 366). – (f) For Canada, Japan, France and Germany the figures refer to 1978; for the U.S., Italy, the U.K. and Sweden to 1981; for Finland and Norway to 1980. *Source*: Boleat (1987), Table 29.1. – (g) Average figures are unweighted averages for all countries.

Consumer credit

In 1989 consumer credit was equal to only 4 percent of consumption expenditures (Table 1.3, column (1)).[14] This figure includes outstanding debt on credit cards, which in Italy is far below the G7 average (Table 1.3, column (2)). The number of credit cards is an important indicator of credit market imperfections because it is a gauge of the amount that consumers can borrow if their income falls unexpectedly.

Figure 1.1

**Total households' liabilities and medium- and long-term liabilities
as a percentage of net national income, 1964-1989**

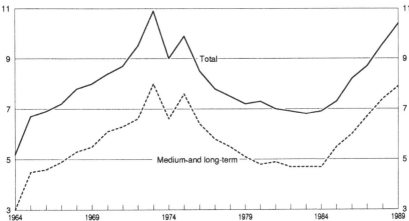

The terms of consumer credit to households are a likely explanation for the small size of this market. In 1987-89 the average downpayment on cars was 25 percent (Table 1.4, column (5)) and that on other consumer durables exceeded 50 percent. In 1989 the average interest rate charged by consumer credit companies was 24.1 percent (Table 1.4, column (2)).[15] The average maturity of these loans was slightly longer than one year. In 1989 the after-tax return on a one-year government bond was 10.9 percent, so the spread between the borrowing and the lending rate was 13.2 points (see Table 1.4, column (4)).[16] In contrast, in 1986 the spread was 6.5 points in the U.S. and in 1987 it was 3.5 points in the U.K.

An alternative explanation for the small size of consumer credit is that Italian households have a low propensity to borrow, either because their demographic characteristics and earnings differ from those of other OECD households or simply because they are thrifty. However, simulations by Jappelli and Pagano (1989) suggest that the earnings profiles and the age structure of the population do not exhibit a pattern that should induce Italian households to borrow less than their OECD counterparts.

In countries with large consumer credit markets, most household loans finance the purchase of durable goods. An indirect indicator of the potential impact of borrowing constraints on consumption expenditures is provided in Table 1.3 (column (3)), where we report the ratio of outlays on durables to total consumption expenditures. The figures show that the "preference" for durable consumption is not lower in Italy than in most OECD countries. This implies that if borrowing constraints exist in Italy, they do not prevent households from acquiring durable goods. The share of durables in total consumption expenditure is comparable with that of the other OECD countries. But clearly, if credit finances a very small share of consumption, most durables will be purchased by drawing on accumulated saving rather than by borrowing.

Table 1.4 Consumer credit in Italy, 1986-1989

	Ratio of consumer credit to consumption expenditures (percent) (a)	Borrowing rate (b)	Lending rate (c)	Spread	Downpayment on cars
	(1)	(2)	(3)	(4)	(5)
1986	3	25.3	11.2	14.1	–
1987	3	23.8	9.7	14.1	24.9
1988	4	23.1	9.6	13.5	26.1
1989	4	24.1	10.9	13.2	23.4

(a) Figures on consumer credit refer to both banks and finance companies. The loans made by the finance companies are imputed from a sample of 25 institutions estimated to cover 80 percent of such loans. *Source:* Bollino and Casini (1989) and D'Alessio (1990).

(b) Average annual interest rate, inclusive of all transaction costs. The figures refer to finance companies only.

(c) After-tax rate of return on one-year government bonds. *Source:* Banca d'Italia, *Relazione annuale,* Roma, 1990, Appendix, Table aD30.

Mortgage markets

Regulation plays an important role in mortgage markets. For all mortgage loans, the minimum downpayment is set at 50 percent. This proportion can be reduced somewhat for new home-buyers, according to their income and other factors. By law, in no case can it be lower than 25 percent for first-time buyers. However, downpayments for new home-buyers are rarely less than 40 percent, so that by a conservative estimate the average downpayment is between 40 and 50 percent, as opposed to 20 percent in the United States and Canada, 15 percent in the U.K., 20 percent in Finland and Sweden and 35-40 percent in Japan (Table 1.3, column (4)).[17]

The effect of inflation on mortgage markets has been very damaging, also in light of the fact that indexed mortgages were introduced only at the beginning of the eighties. The average maturity of mortgage loans declined substantially, from 20 years in the sixties to 10 years in the seventies. It was only after 1984 that mortgage indexing became widespread. Today, the maximum mortgage maturity is set at 25 years, but an estimate of the average mortgage maturity ranges from 10 to 15 years. This contrasts with other housing finance systems. Boleat (1987) reports that in the early eighties the "typical" mortgage had a maturity of 25 years in Canada, 25 to 30 years in the U.S., 20 to 25 years in Germany, and 15 to 20 years in France.

Between 1980 and 1985 the spread between the interest rate wedge on home loans was 3 percentage points.[18] This wedge does not include other transaction costs; in the absence of official statistics, these costs are difficult to measure, but we suspect they are not trivial.[19]

In countries like the U.S., Canada and the U.K., loan applications are processed rapidly because specialized credit reference agencies provide information on the credit histories of all potential borrowers, and creditors share information about insolvent consumers (Pagano and Jappelli, 1993). Such agencies do not exist in Italy, so the extent of asymmetric information between lenders and borrowers is more severe than in other countries.

In almost all European countries there is direct government involvement in the provision of mortgage loans, either directly or through the tax system (Boleat, 1987). In Italy, by contrast, government intervention in housing finance is very limited, while government incentives are hard to obtain and have been reduced over time.[20]

Because of high downpayments, high interest rate spreads and low maturities, it is not surprising that the Italian mortgage market is one of the smallest in the OECD (see Figure 1.1 and Table 1.3, column (4)).[21] However, mortgage market imperfections have not prevented Italian households from becoming home owners. The home ownership rate increased from 46 percent in 1961 to 59 percent in 1981.[22] The small size of the mortgage market cannot be attributed to a relatively low percentage of owner-occupation; in Italy the latter is actually higher than in several OECD countries (Table 1.3, column (6)). The fact that the mortgage market is so small implies that many households buy houses borrowing very little or not at all.

3.2   Insurance markets

The most direct indicator of the relative importance of the insurance market in the OECD is the ratio of premiums to national income. Column (1) of Table 1.5 indicates that the average Italian buys less private insurance than citizens of all the other OECD, except Greece. The Italian ratio of 2.4 percent is between 2 and 3 times smaller than that of any other major OECD country.[23] Among OECD countries, Italy ranks 23rd in the market for life insurance (Table 1.5, column (2)), and this market is between 5 and 10 times smaller than those of all the other G7 countries. Figure 1.2 indicates that Italians have always bought little insurance, at least since we have reliable data.[24]

Figure 1.2

**Life insurance and other insurance premiums
as a percentage of national income, 1964-1988**

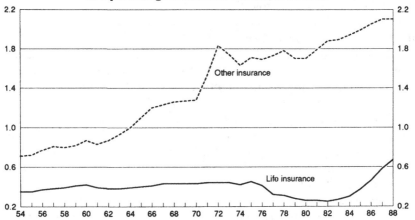

It is very unlikely that differences in preferences and risks across countries explain the pattern of Table 1.5, for, under suitable assumptions, the amount of insurance that individuals buy may even be independent of their preferences, even when insurance is not fair.[25] And there is no absolute evidence that Italy is a less risky environment than other OECD countries. On the other hand, a close examination of the Italian insurance market suggests that regulation is a more likely candidate to explain the small size of this market.

In Appendix 2 we report evidence that regulations put severe barriers to entry for firms and strong restrictions on the types of contracts that individuals may wish to buy. Premiums are set by a regulatory agency and strictly enforced. Though some progress towards liberalization has been made in recent years, regulation is substantially more pervasive than in any other major European country.

There is one other possible explanation for the small size of the Italian insurance market, i.e. that in Italy there is much more public insurance and/or that Italian families provide more insurance than those of any other OECD country. We shall concentrate on this explanation below.

Table 1.5 Insurance premiums as a percentage of gross national product *(a)*

	Total premiums	Life insurance premiums	Other premiums
	(1)	(2)	(3)
Canada	5.41	2.62	2.79
U.S.A.	9.07	3.69	5.38
Japan	8.69	6.43	2.26
France	5.06	2.15	2.91
Germany	6.40	2.86	3.54
Italy	2.36	0.51	1.85
U. K.	8.35	5.25	3.10
G7 average (b)	6.47	3.36	3.12
Finland	5.31	3.33	1.98
Norway	5.08	2.03	3.05
Sweden	4.49	2.50	1.99
Australia	5.31	1.79	3.52
Austria	4.75	1.44	3.31
Belgium	4.17	1.23	2.94
Denmark	4.30	1.67	2.63
Greece	1.24	0.40	0.84
Ireland	12.24	7.60	4.64
Luxembourg	3.35	0.84	2.51
Netherlands	6.29	2.92	3.37
New Zealand	5.64	3.30	2.34
Portugal	2.69	0.35	2.34
Spain	3.31	1.27	2.04
Switzerland	8.02	4.45	3.57
OECD average (b)	5.52	2.67	2.85

(a) Sources: Sigma, Zurich, March 1990 and Istat, *Annuario statistico italiano*, Roma, 1989, Table 16.18. All data refer to 1987.

(b) Average figures are unweighted averages for all countries.

3.3   Public insurance and informal financial arrangements

Efficient social insurance programmes may substitute for private health and life insurance. In principle, the government may provide the most efficient form of insurance because it has the largest pool of applicants. Thus the fact that Italians buy so little insurance may merely indicate that public insurance covers all types of risk efficiently and at a low social cost. There are three reasons why we think the role of the government cannot explain the failure of the private market: (i) for most programmes, social expenditure in Italy is no greater than in other industrialized countries; (ii) the increase in public insurance in Italy has not been greater than that of other countries and, if anything, the public coverage of most risks is lower; (iii) private insurance markets were small even before the growth of the public provision of insurance actually took place, i.e. in the fifties and sixties (see Figure 1.2).

Table 1.6 reports the ratios of the main expenditures on social programmes to GNP for the same set of countries that we have analyzed so far. In most types of social expenditure Italy is not among the OECD leaders, and for unemployment and housing its outlays are actually among the lowest.[26] The share of public health expenditure is in line with that of most other European countries.[27]

On the other hand, the ratio of pension benefits to GNP is one of the highest in the OECD. In the last three decades the social security system has been extended to the totality of the working population; the ratio of the average pension to the average pre-tax earnings of employed workers rose from 26 percent in 1960 to 43.7 percent in 1987.[28]

As far as pensions are concerned, two considerations are important. First, and more importantly, social security is generally advocated to explain a reduction in asset accumulation, not a high saving rate.[29] Second, theoretically and empirically, it is not clear to what extent social security substitutes for annuities, life insurance and disability insurance (Kotlikoff, 1989).

A generous social security system may however be unsustainable.[30] And the fear for the future solvency of the social security system is greatest in countries where people rely exclusively on social security, unsupplemented by fully funded pension plans, to provide for old age. In Italy private pension plans cover only 2 percent of all workers, by far the smallest proportion among the countries listed in Table 1.6.

Even if the public provision of insurance in Italy is not particularly high by international standards, it is still possible that private transfers may serve as a form of insurance against risk. If risks are not perfectly correlated across generations and individuals, then there is scope for implicit contracts based on private transfers (Kotlikoff and Spivak, 1981). A similar argument applies in the case of credit markets, i.e. affluent parents may relieve the borrowing constraints of their children. In other words, a network of informal financial arrangements may overcome credit and insurance market imperfections (Mace, 1991).

Table 1.6 Public expenditure on the main social programmes and number of workers in pension funds in 1985 *(a)*

	Health	Unemploy- ment	Housing *(b)*	Pensions	Workers in private pensions funds *(c)*
	(1)	(2)	(3)	(4)	(5)
Canada	6.4	3.3	–	5.4	–
U.S.A.	4.4	0.4	–	7.2	52
Japan	4.8	0.4	–	5.3	55
France	6.8	2.8	0.7	12.7	86
Germany	6.4	1.5	0.2	11.8	87
Italy	5.4	0.7	0.1	12.8	3
U. K.	5.2	1.8	0.9	6.7	51
G7 average (d)	5.6	1.6	–	8.8	–
Finland	5.6	0.5	–	7.1	–
Norway	6.2	0.7	–	8.0 *(b)*	–
Sweden	8.5	0.7	–	11.2	–
OECD average (d)	5.6	1.8	–	8.9	

(a) All data are percentages of gross domestic product. *Sources:* Duskin (1987) and OECD Social Data Bank. The data are not strictly comparable because they are provided by the OECD on the basis of national accounts and OECD's own estimates. For Italy the data have been updated with the figures available from the new national accounts.
(b) 1984 figures.
(c) 1980 figures as a percentage of the working population.
(d) The G7 and OECD figures are unweighted averages; the OECD figures exclude Portugal and Greece.

To be effective, transfers have to be timed correctly. They have to occur when they are most needed, i.e. in case of emergencies or when credit constraints are binding. Bequests are very unlikely to serve these purposes. Gifts or loans have to occur *inter vivos*. But all surveys of Italian households indicate that private transfers are not widespread. In a typical survey no more than 2 or 3 percent of households receive either monetary gifts or loans from relatives and friends. This contrasts with the U.S. (the only country where private transfers have received wide attention), where more than 10 percent of households report receiving transfers during a one-year period (Cox, 1990). Guiso and Jappelli (1994) report that some of these transfers in Italy are directed towards liquidity-constrained households, a finding that is consistent with the hypothesis that informal markets help remove borrowing constraints.[31] However, since such transfers are not widespread, most households remain liquidity-constrained even after private transfers have been made. Some transfers are large and are likely to come on "special" occasions, such as marriage and the purchase of a home. Since the role of gifts and bequests in the provision of housing is potentially important, it will be further taken up in Section 4.2.

3.4   Assessment

Italian capital markets are significantly at variance with the paradigm of perfect capital markets that is required by rational consumers to smooth income fluctuations and acquire durable goods and homes without distorting the consumption profile. But more importantly, Italian capital markets are much less developed than those of other OECD countries that are at a comparable level of economic development in several other respects. Our evidence suggests that regulation, transaction costs and adverse selection are the likely reasons for these market failures.[32] Evidence on private transfers suggests that the family has a role in overcoming credit market imperfections, but that this role is limited. Overall, the role of the government in providing insurance against risks does not appear any more important than in other OECD countries. Government intervention to circumvent borrowing constraints in the mortgage market is actually much less significant than in the rest of Europe.

To summarize, we list the factors that are likely to inhibit the proper functioning of Italian credit and insurance markets:

(i)   the terms of the contracts, in part imposed by regulation, limit credit and insurance availability. In credit markets the most important impediments are high downpayment requirements, large interest rate spreads and the short maturities of loans; in insurance markets severe barriers to entry limit competition (see Appendix 2).

(ii) The pace of financial innovation has been slow. Indexed mortgages and variable rate life insurance contracts were not marketed until the second half of the eighties.

(iii) The extent of asymmetric information between borrowers and lenders is more severe in Italy than in other countries.[33]

4 Measuring the effect of capital market imperfections

In this section we test for the effect of borrowing constraints and uncertainty on consumption. We first estimate Euler equations for the consumption of non-durables on aggregate time series and panel data. In this case we are able to relate our evidence to that available in other OECD countries. We then turn to structural estimation of the consumption function on data drawn from the 1989 SHIW in order to assess the potential impact of mortgage market imperfections and earnings uncertainty on households' behavior. We then summarize our recent work on the effect of earnings uncertainty on consumption.

4.1 Excess sensitivity

According to the life-cycle-permanent income hypothesis *cum* rational expectations, in the absence of borrowing constraints consumption growth should not be correlated with either lagged disposable income or anticipated growth in current income. Following Hall (1978) and Hayashi (1982), we estimate Euler equations for non-durable consumption and test whether the time series data and the panel data are consistent with the pure version of the permanent income hypothesis. In both cases we choose specifications that allow an international comparison.

Using aggregate annual data, we regress the growth rate of consumption, C, on the expected growth rate of disposable income, Y, choosing a specification and estimation method similar to those adopted by Campbell and Mankiw (1991) for six OECD countries. We improve with respect to previous studies with Italian data because we use the series from the revised national accounts. The top panel of Table 1.7 reports that, contrary to the theoretical predictions, consumption growth – either of non-durables or of non-durables and the imputed flow of services – is very sensitive to expected income fluctuations.[34] This result confirms those of other time series studies reporting high values of the excess sensitivity parameters in Italy (of the order of magnitude reported in Table 1.7).

The size of the estimated coefficient is consistent with the hypothesis that it is liquidity constraints in the market for personal consumer credit that induce the failure of Euler equations. In fact, there is by now considerable evidence that the excess sensitivity parameter is negatively correlated with

Table 1.7 Excess sensitivity tests: aggregate time series and panel data
(t-statistics in parentheses)

Aggregate data: annual data, 1954-1988 (a)			Dependent variable: ΔlnC_t		
Dependent variable	Constant	ΔlnY_t	$R^2(Y)$	$R^2(C)$	R^2 (INST)
	(1)	(2)	(3)	(4)	(5)
1. ND (b)	0.016 (2.99)	0.566 (4.03)	0.16	0.21	−0.09
2. ND + IFD (b)	0.013 (2.72)	0.608 (5.23)	0.41	0.37	0.10
3. ND (c)	0.013 (1.71)	0.650 (3.22)	0.04	0.13	0.02
4. ND + IFD (c)	0.011 (2.30)	0.652 (5.41)	0.38	0.37	0.30

$R^2(Y)$: adjusted R^2 of the regression of ΔlnY_t on the instruments;
$R^2(C)$: adjusted R^2 of the regression of ΔlnC_t on the instruments;
$R^2(INST)$: adjusted R^2 of the residuals of 2SLS regression on the instruments;
ND   : consumption of non-durables and services;
IFD   : imputed flow of the consumption of durables.

(a) Data sources: see notes to Table 1.1.
(b) In regressions 1 and 2 the instruments are the first and second lags of the growth rate of disposable income and consumption, and the first lag of the consumption-income ratio.
(c) In regressions 3 and 4 the instruments are the second and third lags of the growth rate in disposable income and consumption, and the second lag of the consumption-income ratio.

Panel data: 820 observations (d)	Dependent variable: ΔlnC_t (e)	
Constant	Y_{87}	R^2
0.019 (7.92)	−0.17 (8.50)	0.07

(d) In 1987 the Bank of Italy interviewed 8,026 households. Of these, 1,268 were interviewed again in 1989. After excluding households with missing observations for the relevant variables and those that experienced a major change in family status between 1987 and 1989, a sample of 820 observations remains.
(e) The dependent variable is the growth rate of the consumption of non-durables and services between 1987 and 1989. Besides disposable income in 1987 (Y_{87}), the regression also includes a set of demographic variables (age, occupational dummies, gender and regional location).

the size of the market for consumer credit. Combining the results of three recent studies, it appears that excess sensitivity is highest in Italy and France; reaches intermediate values in the U.K., Ireland and Japan; is lower in Canada and the U.S., and lowest in Sweden and Denmark.[35] The degree of development of the market for consumer credit (Table 1.3, column (1)) is indeed negatively correlated with this ranking of excess sensitivity. On the other hand, there is no evidence that other factors that may induce excess sensitivity, such as myopia, are more important in Italy than in other countries.

To check that the international pattern of results is not affected by aggregation problems, in the lower panel of Table 1.7 we regress the rate of change of consumption of non-durables on the lagged value of disposable income using panel data. If households wish to borrow but have no access to credit markets, an increase in income increases current consumption relative to future consumption, thus reducing consumption growth. In fact, the income coefficient is negative (-0.17) and significantly different from zero. More importantly, the coefficient is larger, in absolute value, than the values found in other countries. Zeldes (1989), using the U.S. Panel Survey of Income Dynamics (PSID), estimates a coefficient that varies from -0.021 to -0.081, depending on the sample split; Hayashi (1986) finds values ranging from -0.041 to -0.130 using Japanese (pseudo) panel data; Runkle (1988) – also using the PSID – finds an insignificant coefficient.[36]

These patterns are consistent with the hypothesis that Italians react more strongly to current disposable income because they are more likely to be subject to borrowing constraints. However, Euler equations have no power to detect the behavior of households that do not conform strictly to the permanent income hypothesis. In fact, while acceptance of the Euler equations is consistent with the permanent income hypothesis, its failure can be induced by several factors, liquidity constraints being only one possibility. This is why in the next section we turn to structural estimation of the consumption function, which allows us to isolate the specific role played by liquidity constraints.

4.2 Saving and mortgage markets imperfections

In Section 3.1 we argued that high downpayment requirements, short maturities and high interest rates have been an obstacle to households from borrowing to purchase houses. The stock of mortgage loans to consumption expenditures is estimated to be on the order of 6-7 percent, a strikingly low value when compared to the size of the mortgage market in all the other major developed economies. There is thus a strong presumption that mortgage market imperfections distort households' optimal consumption profile and force them to save when young to finance the purchase of houses.[37] With perfect markets, by contrast, households would borrow early in life, and repay the loan over a long horizon which is, in principle, their entire life.

Mortgage market imperfections distort the consumption profile if households desire to own a house, rather than rent it; this requires assuming that a house owned yields a higher utility than the identical house if rented. This can be justified in three ways: (i) owning eliminates the principal-agent relationship if one rents from oneself, i.e. he can alter the house as desired and is not subject to a risk of rent termination or rent increase in the future (Hayashi, Ito and Slemrod, 1988); (ii) often there are tax incentives to owning; (iii) in Italy there is often no alternative as to owning because of imperfections and regulations in the rental market for housing.

Figure 1.3

Home ownership ratio by age-group in Italy, the U.K. and the U.S.
(age-groups identified by average age)

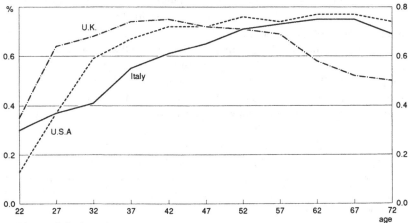

Figure 1.3 plots the incidence of owner-occupied dwellings by age groups in Italy, the U.S. and the U.K.[38] In Italy the proportion of owner-occupation increases slowly with age, and reaches a peak before retirement.[39] This pattern contrasts sharply with the experience of the other two countries, where the profiles reach an early peak. In 1985 the average age of U.S. and U.K. first-time buyers was only 28 and 29 years, respectively, while in Italy it was 41 years in 1988.

The patterns of Figure 1.3 are consistent with the hypothesis that mortgage market imperfections force Italian households to accumulate more funds when young than they would if the markets were perfect. Italians may desire a profile similar to that of the U.S. or the U.K., but mortgage market imperfections prevent them from doing so.

A second possibility is that intergenerational transfers in the form of housing eliminate the need for an organized mortgage market. If young households expect to receive a house as a bequest, they may choose to rent, rather than buy, while waiting to receive the bequest. This strategy will avoid the need to save large amounts to meet high downpayments and distort the consumption profile: the Italian pattern of owner-occupation by age displayed in Figure 1.3 is also consistent with the choices of a large group of households who expect to receive a bequest around the age of forty.[40]

In Figure 1.4 we plot the proportion of owner-occupation including and excluding households who received their house as a gift or bequest. We note that: (i) only 13 percent of the sample (22 percent of home owners) received the house as a bequest;[41] (ii) the two profiles are very similar, i.e the timing of bequests does not affect the overall pattern of housing tenure. We infer that expected bequests are likely to affect the behavior of only a minority of the population.[42]

Figure 1.4

Home ownership ratio by age-group in Italy *(a)*
(age-groups identified by average age)

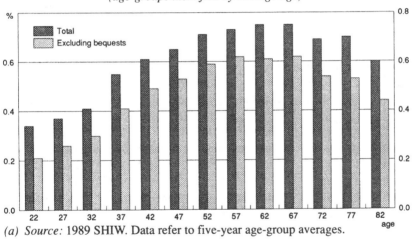

(a) Source: 1989 SHIW. Data refer to five-year age-group averages.

To assess the impact of mortgage market imperfections on consumption, we evaluate how much renters would consume if they were not subject to mortgage market constraints. We follow a strategy similar to that adopted by Hayashi (1985) and Zeldes (1989). We assume that homeowners are not constrained in the mortgage market, estimate their desired consumption and use the estimated coefficients to predict the desired consumption of renters. With either formal or informal perfect markets, the gap between desired and actual consumption of renters should be zero. If the gap is positive, we infer that renters are accumulating assets in excess of those that they would accumulate under perfect mortgage markets.

This estimation strategy does not require the sample of renters to be constrained, only that the sample of owners is unconstrained (otherwise the estimates would not be consistent). This assumption is reasonable, because homeowners have accumulated substantial collateral, so they are unlikely to face constraints in the mortgage market, even if they wish to purchase another house. One objection is that owners are repaying relatively short-term loans and are saving in excess of what they would along the unconstrained accumulation path. But the number of these households in the sample is trivial.[43]

Since the choice of becoming a homeowner is endogenous to the consumer optimization problem, the coefficients are potentially affected by selection bias. Accordingly, we estimate a probit equation for the choice of owning, and desired consumption by Heckman's Generalized tobit on the sample of owners.

The SHIW contains detailed information on labor income, consumption of durables and non-durables, wealth and several demographic characteristics drawn from a sample of 8,027 households. It also contains a section on housing, with questions about properties, mortgages and house characteristics. The survey defines the household head to be always the male, if present in the household. Only for widows, singles or singles with children is it possible for the head to be a female. All variables refer to the year 1989 (see the Methodological Appendix in the volume for details).

Theory suggests that tenure choice and consumption are a function of permanent rather than current earnings. Thus, we construct an income variable that purges current earnings from transitory earnings and age effects. This variable is similar to the King and Dicks-Mireaux (1982) concept of permanent income, i.e. normal earnings adjusted for cohort effects; the details of the estimation of permanent earnings are given in the paper by Guiso, Jappelli and Terlizzese (1994).

We exclude from the sample households that are not in the labor force and households that report zero labor income. For these households, in fact, permanent earnings are difficult to impute. We also exclude households whose head is over 55 – the peak age of housing tenure – because older households might run down assets accumulated when young and may therefore be over-consuming with respect to their optimal consumption profile.[44]

Table 1.8 reports sample means of selected variables for the sub-samples of renters, buyers, and those who have received the house as a bequest, as well as for the whole sample. The group of renters exhibits a lower propensity to consume than the group of buyers (0.78 against 0.91). The propensity to consume of those who received the house as a bequest is similar to that of buyers (0.89 versus 0.91). But the three groups have different characteristics. For instance, renters are younger, poorer and have permanent earnings that exceed current earnings. Thus, a proper test of the proposition that renters save more than homeowners requires that all characteristics – income, wealth and demographics – be held constant.

Table 1.8 Sample means for owners and renters

Variables (a)	Renters	Buyers	Received the house as a bequest	Total sample
	(1)	(2)	(3)	(4)
Consumption of non-durables	22.39	29.73	27.15	26.26
Total consumption	24.83	32.88	29.98	29.06
Current earnings	27.98	34.20	29.93	31.00
Permanent earnings	28.74	32.58	31.18	30.76
Net worth	70.95	261.61	244.89	177.72
Age	37.99	42.58	40.58	40.35
Family size	3.22	3.63	3.47	3.43
Gender	0.87	0.93	0.91	0.90
Education	10.08	10.06	10.22	10.09
Ratio of non-durable consumption to current earnings	0.80	0.87	0.91	0.84
Ratio of non-durable consumption to permanent earnings	0.78	0.91	0.89	0.85
Sample size	1,958	2,033	573	4,564

(a) Consumption, income and wealth are in millions of 1989 lire. Observations excluded from the sample refer to: (i) households where the head is not in the labor force; (ii) households with zero disposable income; (iii) households with head older than 55. The dummy for gender takes the value of 1 if the head is male, 0 if female.

Table 1.9 Probit estimates: probability of ownership *(a)*

Variables *(b)*	Coefficients	*t*-statistics	Coefficients	*t*-statistics
	(1)	(2)	(3)	(4)
Permanent earnings	0.14E–04	4.66	0.15E–04	4.73
Education	–0.0021	–0.09	–0.008	–0.33
Resident in the North	–0.257	–4.81	–0.225	–3.96
Resident in the South	–0.049	–0.86	–0.064	–1.06
Price index of housing	–0.45E–03	–7.14	–0.35E–03	–5.31
Demographics				
Age < 25	–0.824	–10.53	–0.898	–10.69
25 ≤ Age < 35	–0.591	–9.57	–0.633	–9.70
35 ≤ Age < 45	–0.191	–3.24	–0.189	–3.08
Number of children	–0.246	–4.45	–0.219	–3.68
Married	–0.053	–0.68	0.019	0.09
Family size	0.229	4.32	0.211	3.69
Gender	–0.039	–0.48	–0.018	–0.21
Occupation				
Operative	–0.121	–0.82	–0.029	–0.18
Clerical	0.059	0.41	0.118	0.75
Precision craft	0.152	1.00	0.196	1.19
Professional	0.046	0.25	0.089	0.51
Manager	0.039	0.25	0.118	0.60
Self-employed	0.192	1.32	0.267	1.70
Sector				
Agriculture	0.394	3.36	0.304	2.37
Industry	0.047	0.81	–0.001	–0.01
Services	–0.012	–0.24	–0.025	–0.45
Constant	0.375	1.40	0.005	0.02
Observations	4,564		3,991	
Number of owners	2,606		2,033	
Likelihood at binomial	–3,117		–2,909	
Final likelihood	–2,861		–2,523	

(a) In column (3) the sample excludes households who received the house as a bequest.

(b) Excluded attributes are: Resident in Central Italy, Age > 45, Non-married, Females, Working in the Public Administration. Dependent variable = 1 if owner, 0 otherwise.

Table 1.10 Generalized tobit estimates

Variables (a)	All owners		Buyers only	
	Coefficients	t-statistics	Coefficients	t-statistics
	(1)	(2)	(3)	(4)
Permanent earnings	0.566	21.58	0.602	19.21
Transitory earnings	0.341	27.60	0.349	25.50
Net worth	0.008	14.18	0.007	11.59
Age	0.73E–04	2.62	0.72E–04	1.99
Family size	0.99E–03	6.74	0.86E–03	4.82
Gender	–0.57E–03	–0.99	–0.68E–03	–0.98
Education	0.23E–03	4.81	0.25E–03	4.49
Constant	–0.14E–03	0.08	0.99E–03	0.44
Mill's ratio	–0.010	0.29	–0.059	1.26
Adjusted R^2	0.358		0.352	
Sample size	2,606		2,033	

Gap between desired and actual consumption
(as a percentage of non-durable consumption)

Sample of renters	Observations	Gap for renters	Total sample gap
	(1)	(2)	(3)
No exclusions (b)	1,958	11.7	2.4
No exclusions (c)	1,958	18.1	3.7
Excluding $W<20$ and $W>200$ (c)	1,269	19.5	2.6
Excluding $W<30$ and $W>300$ (c)	1,048	17.9	2.2
Excluding $W<50$ and $W>500$ (c)	606	14.7	1.3

(a) All variables are divided by permanent earnings.

(b) The gap is computed using the coefficients estimated on the sample of all owners (column (1)).

(c) The gap is computed using the coefficients estimated on the sample of buyers only (column (3)). Net worth (W) is in millions of 1989 lire.

The first stage probit regression includes permanent earnings, demographic variables and variables associated with the price and quality of housing (regional location, occupation and a constructed price index of housing in different regions and urban areas). The results, reported in Table 1.9, indicate that the conditional probability of owning is an increasing function of age, number of children, family size and permanent income and a decreasing function of the index of house prices. Residents in Central Italy and in rural areas are more likely to own their homes.

In the second stage we regress the ratio of consumption of non-durables and services to permanent earnings on beginning-of-period net worth, permanent and transitory earnings and a set of households' characteristics (age, gender, education and family size).[45] Transitory earnings are defined as the difference between actual and permanent earnings. The estimated coefficients of the consumption equation for the entire sample of owners are displayed in column (1) of Table 1.10.

Since the probability of buying a house and that of receiving a bequest might be functions of different sets of variables, we further exclude the 573 beneficiaries of housing bequest from the sample. The results of the probit and generalized tobit regressions are reported in column (3) of Table 1.9 and in column (3) of Table 1.10, respectively.[46] In both regressions of Table 1.10 permanent earnings are found to have a greater effect on the consumption to income ratio than transitory earnings. Schooling, age and family size also influence the ratio of non-durables to permanent earnings.

We then evaluate the gap between the desired and actual consumption of renters using the coefficients of Table 1.10. An upper estimate of the gap can be computed by assuming that all renters are subject to mortgage market imperfections. This is shown in the first two rows of the lower panel of Table 1.10. Borrowing constraints lower the consumption of the constrained households by 18 percent of permanent earnings (12 percent if the whole sample of owners is used in the estimation). The total sample gap is 2.4 percent (3.7 percent using the sample of buyers).

These gaps do not take into account the fact that some renters do not have plans to purchase a house. Only those who have such plans face borrowing constraints in the mortgage market. There are two reasons why renters may not plan to buy a house: (i) they are lifetime poor and cannot afford it; (ii) they have the resources to buy a house, but have chosen not to buy one. We therefore exclude "extreme" observations from the sample of renters, according to different levels of households' net worth.[47] The last three rows in the lower panel of Table 1.10 correspond to different (and somewhat arbitrary) assumptions about the price of the "typical" house that renters desire to buy. We find that even excluding households with net worth of less than 50 million lire and very rich households (with assets greater than 500 million lire), the estimated gap for renters remains sizable (14.7 percent). Since the number and characteristics of renters changes in each case, the overall shortfall in consumption also changes. In the aggregate, these gaps range from 1.3 to 2.6 percent of non-durables consumption.[48]

4.3 Earnings uncertainty and precautionary saving

Since in Italy insurance markets are far less developed than in the other OECD countries (see Section 3.2), Italian households might be expected to engage in substantial precautionary saving. Most studies that have confronted this question have limited the focus to earnings uncertainty which is only one risk that households face, and perhaps not even the most important one. The 1989 Survey of Household Income and Wealth included questions about the subjective probability distribution of earnings in 1990, and allows one to derive a measure of subjective uncertainty and estimate the amount of precautionary saving. We estimate a consumption function using this self-reported measure of uncertainty and find that earnings uncertainty raises saving and wealth accumulation (Guiso et al., 1994). However, evaluated at the sample means, the increase in saving in response to uncertainty is a modest 0.14 percent of current labor earnings. The share of wealth accumulated in response to earnings uncertainty is only 1.8 percent.

As an alternative approach, we compare the consumption choices of households with different numbers of income earners (Guiso and Jappelli, 1994). Households with multiple incomes are more easily protected against income shocks than those with sole breadwinner. Since the formers' need for precautionary saving is lower, the saving rate of households with one income recipient should be higher than that of households with multiple earners. We find that households with two income earners have an average propensity to consume out of lifetime wealth that is about 0.1 percentage points higher than that of single-income households; this implies that risk pooling leads to an increase in consumption of roughly 2.5 percent of current earnings.

These results suggest that earnings uncertainty alone does not explain a large fraction of saving. One possibility is that households that have accumulated substantial amount of assets early in the life cycle – perhaps, as in the previous section, because they want to buy a house – can largely dispense with precautionary saving. But one should not rule out the possibility that other important types of risk, such as health risk, are important determinants of saving.

5   Bequests and earnings profiles

So far we have neglected the potential role of the slope of the earnings profile and of the bequest motive in the explanation of the high correlation between saving and growth documented in Section 2. In fact, one objection to our analysis is that the age-earnings profile is flatter in Italy than in other countries. The life-cycle model suggests that in an economy with a flat earnings profile the young save relatively more (or borrow less) than in economies in which resources are more concentrated later in life. As mentioned in Section 2, for any given growth rate, the resulting saving rate is higher than in an economy with a steep earnings profile.

Data on earnings profiles in Italy, the United States and Japan do not support this hypothesis (Table 1.11). The Italian cross-sectional profile is similar to the American, but flatter than the Japanese. Once we correct the cross-sectional profiles for the effect of productivity growth, it appears that the U.S. profile is the flattest, i.e. closest to that implied by the stylized version of the life-cycle model. In Italy, households have been confronted with a steep earnings profile, a consequence of the relatively high economic growth rate.

Table 1.11 Earnings profiles in Italy, the United States and Japan
(age-group 40-49 = 100)

Age	Cross-sectional profiles (a)			Profiles adjusted for productivity growth (b)		
	Italy	U.S.A.	Japan	Italy	U.S.A.	Japan
	(1)	(2)	(3)	(4)	(5)	(6)
20-29	65	65	32	30	50	11
30-39	87	92	79	59	81	47
40-49	100	100	100	100	100	100
50-59	83	85	104	97	97	174
60-69	25	42	45	54	54	126

(a) *Sources:* Italy: 1989 Bank of Italy Survey of Household Income and Wealth. United States and Japan: Hayashi (1986, Table 3, p. 170). Data for Japan refer to 1980; data for the United States to 1972-1973.

(b) The adjustment for the cohort effect is the average annual rate of growth of GNP per employed worker between 1960 and 1988, i.e. 3.9 percent in Italy, 1.3 percent in the United States and 5.3 percent in Japan.

A second possible objection is that the reason Italians save more is that they have a strong bequest motive. In a growing economy in which households pass a fraction of their lifetime resources on to future generations, the saving rate will be higher than in an economy without bequests. An increase in the growth rate leads then to an increase in aggregate saving: this effect will be stronger the stronger the bequest motive (whether voluntary or involuntary).[49]

Table 1.12 Wealth profiles in Italy, the United States and Japan
(age-group 56-65 = 100)

Age	Cross-sectional profiles *(a)*			Profiles adjusted for productivity growth *(b)*		
	Italy	U.S.A.	Japan	Italy	U.S.A.	Japan
	(1)	(2)	(3)	(4)	(5)	(6)
< 25	26	20	11	6	12	2
26-35	41	52	41	13	35	9
36-45	75	87	81	35	67	29
46-55	99	89	94	68	78	56
56-65	100	100	100	100	100	100
66-69	63	74	99	82	81	122
70-74	62	73	98	102	86	136
75-79	45	86	65	86	107	104
> 80	31	40	74	67	52	134
Amount *(c)*	154	86	17	599	136	106

(a) Sources: Italy: 1989 Bank of Italy Survey of Household Income and Wealth. United States: 1979 Household Pension Survey, Ando and Kennickell (1987), Table 7.1, p. 163, line NW79. Japan: 1979 National Survey of Family Expenditure, Ando and Kennickell (1987), Table 7.9B, p. 195, line ARM.

(b) The adjustment for the cohort effect is the average annual rate of growth of GNP per employed worker between 1960 and 1988, i.e. 3.9 percent in Italy, 1.3 percent in the United States and 5.3 percent in Japan. We assume that the average age of individuals in the first age-group is 20.

(c) Wealth is the sum of real and financial wealth, net of liabilities. The last row of the table indicates the values of net worth in the age-group 56-64. For Italy this number is in millions of 1987 lire, for the United States in thousands of 1979 dollars, for Japan in millions of 1979 yen.

There is little direct evidence on the role of bequests in Italy. The specific importance of intergenerational transfers in the form of housing has been studied by Barca, Cannari and Guiso (1994), with the finding that in 1987 the bequeathed wealth accounted for 35 to 50 percent of aggregate wealth,[50] a value that is not high if compared with available estimates of the share of inherited wealth in the United States (see, for instance, Kotlikoff and Summers, 1988). As mentioned in Section 3.3, Guiso and Jappelli's (1994) evidence also suggests that few households receive *inter vivos* monetary transfers in any given year; in the previous section it was noted that only 13 percent of the households received the house as a gift or bequest.

Indirect evidence on the potential role of intergenerational transfers can be inferred from the age-wealth profiles in Italy, the United States and Japan. The pattern of wealth decumulation, as shown in Table 1.12, does not indicate that Italians have a particularly strong bequest motive. If anything, the Italian profile indicates the presence of more wealth decumulation by the elderly than in the other two countries and is much more hump-shaped than in Japan, where bequests are thought to be very important.[51]

More formal analyses have been made of the pattern of wealth decumulation. King and Dicks-Mireaux (1982) find that in Canada the rate of wealth decumulation between age 65 and age 85 ranges from 0.7 to 1.5 percent per year. In the United States, Hurd (1987) finds a rate of decumulation of 1.5 percent, and Hubbard (1986) finds even lower values. On the other hand, Brugiavini (1987) replicates these studies and finds a rate of wealth decumulation ranging from 1.5 to 8 percent, according to the model specification. Both the (limited) direct evidence on bequests, and the indirect evidence from the patterns of wealth decumulation by the elderly suggest that a strong bequest motive is not a valid explanation of the high Italian saving rate.

6   Conclusions

In this paper we argue that capital markets imperfections are one of the likely explanations for the high Italian saving rate. Further, their interaction with growth can account for its recent decline. Italian credit and insurance markets are considerably smaller than those of other comparably developed countries. Credit finances a trivial share of household consumption and investment, and Italians buy very little insurance. Public and private insurance do not appear more important than elsewhere in insuring risks or circumventing borrowing constraints. Wealth decumulation by the elderly is actually greater in Italy than in Japan or the United States, implying that Italians do not have any special bequest motive. The evidence suggests that

Italians are not "different" in any major respect from other OECD citizens; rather, it is Italian capital markets that are different.

Empirical evidence on the effect of capital market imperfections suggests that the degree of excess sensitivity in Italy is high by international standards. Given the international evidence, it is likely that the under-development of the Italian market for consumer credit is responsible for the high correlation between income and consumption growth. Mortgage market imperfections appear to distort the consumption profile, forcing people to save when young to purchase houses and postponing consumption until later in life. The saving behavior arising from income uncertainty is consistent with the theory of precautionary saving, but the overall effect of risk on saving is small. We suggest two possible explanations: first, that income risk is only one of several risks that households face, and perhaps not the most important one; and second, that with decreasing prudence households obliged to accumulate substantial amounts of wealth can largely dispense with precautionary saving. Accordingly, credit market imperfections may outweigh imperfect insurance markets in explaining the behavior of Italian households.

The approach taken in this study is useful in analysing inter-country differences in saving rates. Previous literature has focussed mainly on the role of productivity growth, demographic variables and fiscal policy to explain the cross-country differences in saving rates (e.g., Modigliani, 1990), but rarely explored the role of capital market imperfections. The international evidence presented in Table 1.2 suggests that the high degree of development of credit and mortgage markets in Finland, Norway and Sweden may be responsible for their relatively low saving rates. Similarly, as shown also by Hayashi *et al.* (1988), mortgage market imperfections may partly explain the high Japanese saving rate. Our results are therefore consistent with those of Jappelli and Pagano (1994), who use the same approach and find that indicators of capital market imperfections, such as minimum downpayment ratios and the volume of consumer credit, account significantly for the inter-country differences in the OECD saving rates.

This study also carries implications for the evolution of the saving rate in Italy. Financial deregulation and European integration will bring more competition to Italian financial markets. Some changes have already taken place; regulation has eased somewhat, particularly in the insurance industry, several financial instruments are now indexed and competition is intensifying. Compliance with the EEC Directive on Consumer Credit and application of the Third Directive on Fair Insurance will lower downpayments to 25 percent for all mortgages, restrictions on maturities will be abolished, legal costs reduced and second mortgages introduced. A credit reference agency already operates on a very small scale, but is expanding rapidly. These changes will undoubtedly sharpen banking competition and insurance and credit terms for consumers will improve accordingly. If financial deregulation will relieve consumers from binding borrowing contraints it might also stimulate the convergence of the Italian saving rate towards those of the other major industrial countries.

APPENDIX 1

The interaction between uncertainty and borrowing constraints

At the theoretical level, credit markets are a constrained version of insurance markets. A complete set of Arrow-Debreu (AD) securities allows individuals to use resources in the desired amount at each point in time and in each of the events that might occur at any point, resulting in perfect insurance and perfect credit markets. Perfect capital markets are available when all securities have the same yield in each state.

A combination of borrowing and insurance replicates the optimal allocation that could be achieved by a full set of AD securities. To show this, let us consider the problem of a consumer who maximizes a separable utility function over a two-period horizon. Income in the second period is uncertain; it can take only two values, y_1 and y_2 $(y_1 < y_2)$ with probabilities p and $(1-p)$ respectively. The consumer can buy fair insurance and borrow against future income. Assuming that the real interest rate r is equal to the rate of time preferences δ, the consumer faces the following problem:

$$\max \quad u(c_1) + pu(c_{21}) + (1-p)u(c_{22})$$
$$\text{st.} \quad c_1 + s + \pi q = y$$
$$c_{21} \qquad\qquad = y_1 + s + Rq$$
$$c_{22} \qquad\qquad = y_2 + s$$
$$q \geq 0$$

where s is saving, q is the (non-negative) amount of insurance that can be purchased paying the premium π, and R is the compensation that the consumer receives if income happens to be low. Fair insurance implies that $\pi = pR$. Using this condition, the optimal levels of saving and insurance are:

$$s^* = \frac{y - y_2 + p(y_1 - y_2)}{2}, \qquad q^* = \frac{y_2 - y_1}{2} > 0.$$

Substituting s^* and q^* in the budget constraint and using the condition $\pi = pR$, consumption is seen to be equal across states and periods:

$$c_1^* = c_{21}^* = c_{22}^* = \frac{y + py_1 + (1-p)y_2}{2}.$$

These are the same values of consumption that could be achieved with a full set of AD securities. Note that if expected future income is equal to current income, $s^* = p(y_1 - y_2) < 0$ and $\pi q^* = p(y_2 - y_1)$. Total saving, defined as income minus consumption (i.e. $s^* + \pi q^*$), is zero, and the premium is entirely financed by borrowing. In this example, access to credit markets also allows access to insurance markets.

Now suppose that borrowing is not allowed, so that $s \geq 0$.

If $y_1 \leq y \leq y_2 + p(y_2 - y_1)$, the borrowing constraint will bind, so that:

$$s^{**} = 0 \qquad \text{and} \qquad q^{**} = \frac{y - y_1}{R(1 - p)}.$$

The consumer will want to buy insurance if the worst outcome of future income is lower than current income. But since he cannot borrow against the good realization of income, the demand for insurance will be lower, so that $q^{**} < q^*$. In this case total saving ($s + \pi q$) rises. In fact, when the consumer can borrow:

$$s^* + \pi q^* = \frac{y - [py_1 + (1 - p)y_2]}{2}, \quad \text{while if he cannot borrow:}$$

$$s^{**} + \pi q^{**} = \frac{p(y - y_1)}{1 + p}.$$

Since $s^* + \pi q^* \leq 0$ if, on average, income is not expected to decline, while $s^{**} + \pi q^{**} > 0$ provided that $y > y_1$, it follows that $s^* + \pi q^* < s^{**} + \pi q^{**}$.

Suppose now that the individual has no access to insurance or credit. In this case there is the possibility that total saving declines with respect to the previous case. Accumulating assets to smooth future income fluctuations is an inefficient way of dealing with uncertainty, for if future income happens to be high, the future resources will have a smaller marginal utility than the current ones. On the other hand, access to fair insurance allows an intertemporal reallocation of resources when they are most needed. Thus if borrowing is not allowed it might be optimal to save more when insurance is available than when there is no insurance (depending on the form of the utility function and on the stochastic process generating income).

The table below summarizes this discussion. In the table saving is defined as the difference between current income and current consumption (and therefore includes insurance premiums).

Insurance market	Credit market	
	perfect	*borrowing is not allowed*
perfect	s_{11}	-
only non-negative quantities can be traded	s_{21}	s_{22}
no insurance is possible	s_{31}	s_{32}

The cell in the upper-right corner is logically impossible, since a perfect insurance market (unrestricted trade of AD securities) can always replicate a perfect capital market. Since the non-negative restriction on insurance can be overcome by borrowing, $s_{11} = s_{21}$. In each of the other cases saving is at least as great as s_{21}. The case s_{31} is the standard case of precautionary saving. The case s_{32} has been analyzed in this appendix: the anticipation of future borrowing constraints increases current saving, so that $s_{32} \geq s_{31}$. If the consumer cannot borrow to finance the purchase of insurance, there will be less purchase of insurance, but total saving rises, i.e. $s_{22} \geq s_{21}$. Finally, the comparison between s_{22} and s_{32} is ambiguous *a priori*, i.e. it is impossible to establish if in the absence of borrowing and insurance saving is greater than the sum of the savings obtained by eliminating one market at a time.

However, it is clear that the value of saving in the second column of the table is always higher than that of the first column: borrowing constraints will always increase saving. And with respect to the perfect market case (s_{11}), each cell in the table indicates that saving rises.

APPENDIX 2

Regulation in the Italian insurance market[52]

The Italian insurance market is heavily regulated. Although some rules were changed in 1986, three main factors still severely limit competition. First, there is a rigid distinction between life insurance and other types of insurance. Companies may specify premiums and coverage only for life insurance. For other types of insurance, the premiums are set by law for at least one year, and may be revised each year. In both branches, new entrants must obtain a license from the Ministry of Industry. The license authorizes the company to sell specific contracts (for instance, auto insurance). Until 1986 this license was granted on a totally discretionary basis, so that in practice only a few insurance companies were authorized to enter the market after World War II. From the mid-sixties to 1985 the number of insurance companies ranged from 215 to 220. No new life insurance company was licensed. In 1986 licensing was made non-discretionary. Now it is sufficient for applicants to satisfy a number of requisites, such as specified financial ratios. The fact that 36 companies obtained the license to sell insurance between 1986 and 1989 is indirect evidence that the authorization process previously limited entry.

Second, firms are required to turn over to I.N.A., a public insurance company, 30 percent of their life insurance premium income for the first 5 years, 20 percent for the following 5 years and 10 percent forever.[53] This regulation, the only one of its kind in Europe, is extremely damaging to competition, especially since it is a powerful deterrent for potential entrants.[54]

Third, minimum premiums for auto insurance are set each year by law, whereas life insurance premiums are subject to approval by the Ministry of Industry. The actual premiums are the sum of three components: a fair premium, a spread to compensate the insurance company and a commission to agents. The first two are either set directly or subject to approval by the central authority and the third by the insurance agents themselves, who are a strong lobby. In principle, if a company sold insurance at a price below that set by the regulating agency, its licence could be revoked. Thus in practice the premiums for any given risk category are virtually identical.[55]

Almost all insurance policies are intermediated by agents. In countries such as the U.K., Germany and the U.S., brokers have an important role, since they search for the best contracts and bid for the client. But in Italy insurance brokers were not allowed to operate until 1985. Today they intermediate 13 percent of total premiums, but operate exclusively on behalf of firms, not households. In other countries, brokers are very active: in Europe, the share of premiums covered by brokers is more than 40 percent, in the U.S. it is 80 percent (*Sigma*, Zurich, April 1989).

Life insurance. The great majority of life insurance contracts terminate with the option of collecting the capital. There are tax incentives to collect the capital, which is taxed at 12 percent; on the other hand, 60 percent of the flow of income from the same capital is subject to income tax. Premiums are taxed at the rate of 2.5 percent. Deductibles discourage annuities: since 1986, premiums up to 2.5 million lire a year have been tax deductible, but if one buys a pure annuity there are no further deductions. The deductibility of premiums applies only if the individual does not borrow for the first 5 years of the contract.

The returns on life insurance contracts have been consistently negative. Until 1973 contracts provided no protection at all against inflation. Starting in 1974 the yield on life insurance was adjusted at a fixed rate of between 3.5 and 4 percent. With inflation at 20 percent, the returns were substantially negative throughout the seventies and early eighties. From 1974 to 1983 very few individuals signed new contracts, and those bound by old contracts continued to suffer tremendous losses: in the early eighties the life insurance market was near collapse. After 1985 life insurance companies started to sell equity linked contracts. The yields are only partially indexed to the rate of return on mathematical reserves, with a degree of indexation equal to 80 percent, but receive a fixed return of 4 percent. It is therefore not surprising that even during the early eighties the return on life insurance was considerably lower than that provided by other financial investment, such as government bonds.

Regulations and negative real returns explain why the market for life insurance has always been minuscule (see Figure 1.2 in the text). In addition, tax disincentives limit the demand for pure annuities. The number of these contracts has fluctuated between 6,000 and 10,000 in the eighties (0.1 percent of the population over 65), one twentieth of the figure in the U.S., where 2 percent of the elderly hold annuities (Friedman and Warshawsky, 1990).

Health insurance. The market for private health insurance is negligible: the ratio of premiums to GNP has been 0.05 percent throughout the last 30 years. By law, health insurance premiums can be changed every year. In some cases, insurance companies offer an option to buy health insurance for 10 years in conjunction with life insurance, but it is not clear whether this practice is legal. Even in these cases, the insurance company has the right to cancel the contract if there has been a serious illness in the previous year, i.e. when the need for insurance is greatest. These constraints have the following consequences:

(i) with the exception of a few companies that provide health insurance for their employees, only a very few elderly buy health insurance; and even then they are not covered when they need it most, i.e. in case of serious illness;

(ii) since only the very old buy health insurance, its cost is very high; this in turn exacerbates the well-known problem of moral hazard, raising costs still further.

NOTES

* We are greatly indebted to Onorato Castellino, Giampaolo Galli, Franco Modigliani and Marco Pagano for their comments and many useful suggestions. An earlier version of this paper was presented at the International Conference on "Saving Behavior: Theory, International Evidence and Policy Implications", Helsinki, May 26-28, 1991, and a shortened version was published in the *Scandinavian Journal of Economics*, 94, 1992. We thank seminar participants for helpful discussions and comments. We retain responsibility for all mistakes.

1 In 1985 the Italian national accounts were substantially revised, and no official estimate of depreciation consistent with the new accounts exists before 1980. The data for the depreciation of private capital stock are unofficial estimates based, in part, on the old national accounts. In measuring current government saving, the depreciation of the stock of public capital is included among outlays. Given the nature of public capital, this depreciation, as a percentage of the capital stock of the public sector, is considerably smaller than the depreciation of private capital. However, this item is likely to be underestimated in the national accounts reflecting, in part, the difficulty of estimating depreciation of infrastructure and public buildings. If public depreciation is underestimated, government and national saving are actually smaller than those reported in columns (4), (6), (7) and (9) of Table 1.1.

2 Any theory of saving refers to net, rather than gross, saving. Note, however, that the depreciation adjustment is appropriate if the introduction of new capital equipment does not bring new technology into the production process. If the old technology is replaced by new technology, growth could be fast even if net capital formation is zero. For this and other issues regarding the correction of national saving for depreciation, see Lipsey and Kravis (1987).

3 The unadjusted private saving rates are misleading because Italy has a higher-than-average inflation and stock of public debt. Thus, they are not reported. Since income, consumption and depreciation are not strictly comparable across countries, some of the differences emerging from Table 1.2 may merely reflect different accounting practices (Hayashi, 1986).

4 In this version of the model individuals live L years, work in the first M years and earn a constant income through their working life. The labor income of each generation grows at a rate γ. If the rate of interest and the rate of time preferences are equal to zero, the aggregate saving rate s can be written as:

$$s = 1 - \frac{M}{L} \frac{(1 + \gamma)^L - 1}{L (1 + \gamma)^{L-M} [(1 + \gamma)^M - 1]}.$$

The calculation in the text assumes a value of 53 for L and 40 for M. The values of γ are given in Table 1.1. For Italy, the simulated saving rates in the three decades are 19.0, 15.9 and 9.9 percent. The corresponding values for the G7 are 18.4, 14.8 and 12.6 percent. The model also consistently underpredicts the differences between the Japanese and G7 saving rates. On the other hand, the model consistently overpredicts the saving rates of Finland, Norway and Sweden and cannot account for the their low saving rates.

5 We have also run pooled time series and cross-country regressions of saving on growth in the G7 countries, excluding one country at a time. The largest reduction in the coefficient is obtained when Italy is excluded from the sample. For brevity, the results are not reported.

6 Also in Japan in the seventies and in the eighties the ratio between saving and growth is high by international standards; in these periods Japan's extraordinary performance is not enough to account for its high saving rate. On the other hand, the Scandinavian countries' private saving rate is low not only in absolute terms, but also with respect to their rate of growth, which was roughly in line with that of the other OECD countries.

7 In the context of the Italian economy the issue of Ricardian equivalence is analyzed by Modigliani and Jappelli (1987) in a historical study and by Nicoletti (1988) in an international comparative study.

8 The data source is Modigliani (1990). The OECD countries not included in the estimation are Italy, New Zealand, Yugoslavia and Turkey.

9 A similar Italian saving "puzzle" was discovered by Koskela and Viren (1989). In a cross-country analysis of the determinants of saving, they use a dummy for Italy on the ground that "the household saving rate behaves in a way that cannot be simply accounted for by the explanatory variables specified in the equation."

10 In a small open economy saving is no longer the product of growth and the capital-output ratio, but the proposition that the saving rate is higher in the economy with liquidity constraints still holds. Liquidity constraints generate higher saving also in a version of the model with endogenous growth *à la* Romer (1986).

11 In a general version of the life-cycle model, the sign of the effect of growth on saving is *a priori* ambiguous. For instance, if earnings are upward sloping, and capital markets are perfect, the young would like to dissave: an increase in the growth rate may then even result in a decline in aggregate saving. Similarly, the permanent income hypothesis with infinite horizon predicts that saving should fall if people anticipate an increase in future income. We do not claim that there is always a positive relation between saving and growth, only that in an economy with capital market imperfections the link between saving and growth is stronger. In such an economy households' behavior is closer to that predicted by the stripped-down version of the life-cycle hypothesis even when the earnings profile slopes upwards.

12 Deaton (1991) assumes that consumers are impatient, i.e that the subjective discount rate δ is greater than the rate of interest r. If, instead, $\delta < r$, liquidity constraints would almost never be binding because people would quickly accumulate enough assets to avoid having to borrow altogether. However, if individuals have finite horizons, future liquidity constraints may be binding even if $\delta = r$, provided that there is a low degree of absolute prudence as defined by Kimball (1990).

13 Two recent surveys report that when Italian households are asked about their reasons for saving, one third indicates that the main reason is "emergencies" and more than 15 percent indicate "to acquire a house or to buy a durable good." Only 25 percent indicate that the main reason for saving is to provide for old age or to provide an estate for the family (Censis, 1988).

14 While Italy has some 20 percent of the EEC population, its share of credit cards is less than 4 percent. There are more credit cards in Boston or London than Italy!

15 As there is no standardized way of quoting interest rates on personal loans, the terms of the contracts are very often obscure and households are commonly induced to sign expensive agreements. In 1989 an EEC Directive called on member countries to standardize the way interest rates are quoted on consumer credit. The Directive has been applied in Italy only in 1992.

16 The comparison is based on government bonds because interest payments on consumer credit are not deductible in Italy.

17 There is no official estimate for actual downpayments in Italy. The figures in Table 1.3 are based on Boleat (1987) and on our conversations with market operators.

18 See Jappelli and Pagano (1989, Table 2, p. 1095). They also report that the spread in Italy is larger than in Sweden, the U.S.A., the U.K. and Japan.

19 There is almost invariably a 6-month waiting period to obtain the loan. In the meantime, a "bridging loan" is offered, but this credit is much more expensive than the regular mortgage because it is a short-term loan without collateral (Beltratti and Fornero, 1989). Banks require up to nine documents to approve a mortgage, including court certificates, references from the applicant's employer and tax forms. Obtaining some of these documents is costly and time-consuming. Mortgages must be registered in courts, an expensive and lengthy operation. Fire insurance is also charged to the borrower.

20 Until 1976 all interest payments were tax-deductible. From 1976, 3 million lire was deductible (4 million after 1980) for all mortgages. Except for first-time buyers, deductibility was abolished in 1990. The other incentives to housing were those provided by the so-called Goria Law, enacted in 1984 and abrogated in January of 1991. That law set stringent eligibility requirements for incentives: the head of the household had to be less than 45-years-old, employed continuously for at least 2 years and not already a home owner. The maturity of the loan was 20 years, the downpayment 25 percent and the mortgage could not exceed 60 million lire, twice the average household income. The interest on the loan was subsidized in proportion to household income and ranged from 5.5 to

13 percent. A strong disincentive to these loans was the fact that the home could not be sold before the entire mortgage was repaid, i.e. before 20 years.

21 An upper estimate of the size of mortgage markets is simply the difference between total household liabilities and short-term liabilities (less than 18 months maturity). This is the series that we have plotted in Figure 1.1.

22 Source: Census data.

23 Half of these premiums are represented by compulsory auto insurance, which is strictly enforced.

24 In 1933-1937 an estimate of the ratio of all insurance premiums to net national income was 2.1 percent. Life insurance premiums accounted for about half of the market. Source: Istat, *Annuario statistico italiano*, Roma, 1935 to 1939 editions.

25 The assumption that is required to obtain this result is that the utility function is state-independent (Arrow, 1974). While restrictive, it is not unreasonable and is widely adopted in the literature.

26 In Italy unemployment benefits are negligible. Substantial benefits are provided only for temporary lay-offs (a subsidy equal to 50 percent of the wage rate for three months and sometimes up to a year), but these benefits only cover people employed in manufacturing firms with more than 15 workers.

27 However, the coverage is far from complete, particularly for the elderly. For example, very few social programmes finance nursing homes. More generally, the quality of the national health service is poor and people often have to turn to private institutions.

28 Source: Istat, *I conti della protezione sociale*, various issues.

29 Rossi and Visco (1994) find that the increase in retirement benefits accounts for a substantial fraction of the decline in the Italian private saving rate over the past 15 years.

30 According to Censis (1988), the main reasons why people are worried about the future are illness (58 percent) and the deficit of the social security system (20 percent). This may explain Brugiavini's (1987) finding that pension wealth is only a very imperfect substitute for private net worth.

31 In the 1989 SHIW 1.7 percent of the households surveyed received gifts or loans from relatives or friends. In 1987 the proportion was 2.6 percent. About 20 percent of these transfers were loans, the other 80 percent gifts.

32 A possible complementary explanation for the failure of credit markets is that in Italy there are substantial costs of enforcing contracts and of disposing of collateral. Due to the slowness of the judicial process, debt collection and repossession is extremely time consuming. It takes an average of 4 years to repossess a house in case of mortgage foreclosure (EC Mortgage Federation, 1990). So credit grantors have to require high downpayments and high interest rates to compensate for these costs. Credit rationing results when no interest rate that official financial institutions can possibly charge will make expected profits positive.

33 Even if the quality and quantity of the information shared varies from country to country, a rough indicator of the amount of information sharing is the number of

credit reports issued, which in 1990 ranged from 400 million in the U.S., 60 million in the U.K. and 18 million in Germany to none in Italy (Pagano and Jappelli, 1993).

34 We also introduce a measure of the expected real interest rate in the regression, using as instruments one or two lags of the real rate itself. The resulting coefficient is negative (–0.08) and not significantly different from zero. We also find that the excess sensitivity parameter does not show any tendency to change over time. We add a multiplicative dummy on expected income growth. Even when the dummy is chosen as to maximize the likelihood function, it is not significantly different from zero.

35 See Campbell and Mankiw (1991), Jappelli and Pagano (1989) and Giavazzi and Pagano (1990). The latter study reports that in 1988 the ratio of consumer credit to consumption expenditures was 37 percent in Denmark and 11 percent in Ireland. The sample periods of the estimates are 1954-1988 for Italy, 1972-1988 for France, 1957-1988 for the U.K., 1962-1987 for Ireland, 1972-1988 for Canada, 1953-1985 for the U.S.A., 1972-1988 for Sweden and 1966-1987 for Denmark.

36 Mork and Smith (1989), using a Norwegian panel data and a different specification from the studies mentioned in the text, do not reject the permanent income hypothesis.

37 The same reasoning also applies to durable goods, the great majority of which are acquired with cash. In this paragraph we concentrate on housing because it is the single major durable good that households buy and because the 1989 SHIW does not contain enough detailed information on other durable goods.

38 We compute the profiles in Figure 1.3 using the 1980 Consumer Expenditure Survey for the U.S., the 1986 Family Expenditure Survey for the U.K. and the 1989 SHIW for Italy.

39 Japan exhibits a pattern of housing tenure that is similar to the Italian one. Hayashi et al. (1988) suggest that the main explanation for the difference between the U.S. and the Japanese housing systems is the downpayment required by creditors. They show, by means of simulations, that a reduction of 20 percent in the downpayment ratio could lead to a reduction in private saving of 2 percent of national income in Japan, not a trivial figure if one considers that the difference between the inflation adjusted Italian private saving rate and the G7 average was 2 percent in the 1981-1987 period (Table 1.2, column (8)). The effect of mortgage market imperfections on saving in Italy might be even more pronounced than in Japan. In fact, the downpayment in Italy is higher than in Japan, and the size of the mortgage market is much smaller (Table 1.3, column (4)).

40 Similarly, if it is more common for affluent relatives to subsidize first-time buyers in Italy, renters would not save more than homeowners, and differences in downpayments and other terms of the loans would not be able to account for the different pattern of owner-occupation (and saving) across countries.

41 This figure does not include non-occupied dwellings. Including them would raise the proportion of households who inherited a house or received it as a gift to 23 percent.

42 Even those who received a house as a bequest may have accumulated to purchase a house. The bequest may not have been anticipated, or may have been expected to occur too late in life.

43 At the end of 1989, 57 percent of the households whose head was under 55 years of age owned their homes, and 7.8 percent of them owed mortgage debt. Many of these mortgages were small loans to finance housing repairs and additions. Out of 4,564 households, only 60 had mortgages outstanding in excess of 50 million lire. And only 25 households faced annual mortgage payments that exceeded 10 percent of their yearly permanent income. The comparison with the United States mortgage market is striking: in 1983, 64 percent of households were homeowners; for these home owning families, 57 percent owed mortgage debt, and 26 percent of them had mortgages outstanding in excess of $25,000. Source: our computations on the 1983-1986 Survey of Consumer Finances.

44 A similar issue arises in the analysis of precautionary saving (Skinner, 1988).

45 The results excluding households with earnings less than 6 million lire in 1989 are similar to those reported in Table 1.10.

46 For instance, parental wealth and permanent income are likely to be important determinants of the probability of receiving a house as a bequest. These variables are not observed in the cross-section.

47 We have also partitioned the sample of renters according to different levels of permanent income and age. For each subsample, the implied gaps for renters are similar to those displayed in Table 1.10.

48 One objection to our analysis is that the consumption rule of buyers should not be used to evaluate what renters would consume in the absence of borrowing constraints. Owners faced the same constraints in the past, and may now be consuming relatively more than implied by the unconstrained consumption optimization. Households who received a bequest may be a more appropriate sample to evaluate desired consumption of renters, because they are less likely to have faced mortgage market constraints in the past. There are three responses to this objection: (i) we exclude households whose head is over 55 precisely to control for this effect; (ii) those who received a bequest may live in more "connected" families, and their consumption rule may differ from that of more "isolated" consumers, possibly because the former have a stronger bequest motive; (iii) the sample of young households who received a bequest is too small to obtain precise estimates of their consumption rule.

49 This is in fact the main explanation that Hayashi (1986) offers for the high Japanese saving rate.

50 This estimate is based on direct information on the years in which real estate was received as bequests, and does not include financial wealth.

51 The Japanese age-wealth profile is strongly affected by the presence of extended families, i.e. by the tendency of the elderly to merge with younger households. Wealth decumulation is more evident if one isolates nuclear families, which

represent 50 percent of Japanese households (Hayashi, 1986). The Italian profile would look more similar to the U.S. one if extended families were more widespread in the U.S. But the proportion of individuals older than 60 living with younger households is 5 percent in Italy but only 3 percent in the U.S. Sources: Our estimate on the 1989 SHIW for Italy and Yoshikawa and Othake (1989, Table 2, p. 1004) for the U.S.

52 We would like to thank Gianpaolo Crenca of ISVAP, the Italian National Supervision Institute for Private Insurance, and Dario Focarelli of the Research Department of the Bank of Italy for providing us some of the information contained in this Appendix.

53 I.N.A. may even refuse contracts that it does not like. There are two major consequences of this option: (i) I.N.A. indirectly controls all contracts that are signed; (ii) in practice, I.N.A. supervises the operations of all other companies, especially those recently established. Before 1985 the rule was even more severe. Insurers were required to turn to I.N.A. 40 percent of their premiums for the first 10 years of operation, 30 percent and 20 percent for the following 10 and 20 years respectively, and 10 percent forever.

54 Since this violates EEC rules on fair competition, the Italian government has been repeatedly reprimanded by the EEC court in Brussels.

55 In 1990, for example, the excess of actual premiums over the fair premiums for life insurance only ranged from 18 percent to 20 percent.

REFERENCES

Ando, A. and A.B. Kennickell (1987). 'How Much (or Little) Life Cycle Is There in Micro Data? The Cases of the United States and Japan', in R. Dornbusch, S. Fischer and J. Bossons (eds.), *Macroeconomics and Finance. Essays in Honor of Franco Modigliani*, Cambridge, MA: MIT Press.

Arrow, K.J. (1974). 'Optimal Insurance and Generalized Deductibles', *Scandinavian Actuarial Journal* 1: 1-42.

Barca, F., L. Cannari and L. Guiso (1994). 'Bequests and Saving for Retirement. What Impels the Accumulation of Wealth?', *this volume*.

Barro, R.J. (1974). 'Are Government Bonds Net Wealth?', *Journal of Political Economy* 82: 1095-118.

Beltratti, A. and E. Fornero (1989). 'Risparmio e acquisto dell'abitazione: un'analisi del comportamento delle famiglie', Torino, mimeo.

Boleat, M. (1987). *National Housing Systems: A Comparative Study*, London: Croom Helm.

Bollino, C.A. and M.C. Casini (1987). 'Il credito al consumo in Italia, principali risultati dell'indagine della Banca d'Italia', *Bollettino Statistico* 42: 435-47, Banca d'Italia.

Brugiavini, A. (1987). 'Empirical Evidence on Wealth Accumulation and the Effects of Pension Wealth: An Application to Italian Cross-Section Data', Discussion Paper 20, London School of Economics, Financial Markets Group.

Campbell, J.Y. and G.N. Mankiw (1991). 'The Response of Consumption to Income: A Cross-Country Investigation', *European Economic Review* **35**: 723-56.

Censis (1988). *La nuova domanda di sicurezza e l'offerta previdenziale*, Milano: Angeli.

Cox, D. (1990). 'Intergenerational Transfers and Liquidity Constraints', *Quarterly Journal of Economics* **105**: 187-217.

D'Alessio, G. (1991). 'Le indagini campionarie sulle società di leasing, di factoring e di credito al consumo', *Supplemento al Bollettino Statistico* **44**, 1, Banca d'Italia.

Deaton, A. (1991). 'Saving and Liquidity Constraints', *Econometrica* **59**: 1221-48.

Duskin, E. (1987). 'Social Security in the EEC Countries', Paris: OECD, mimeo.

EC Mortgage Federation (1990). *Mortgage Credit in the European Community*, Brussels: Artigraph.

Friedman, B.M. and M.J. Warshawsky (1990). 'The Costs of Annuities: Implications for Saving Behavior and Bequests', *Quarterly Journal of Economics* **105**: 135-54.

Giavazzi, F. and M. Pagano (1990). 'Can Severe Fiscal Contractions Be Expansionary? Tales of Two Small European Countries', *NBER Macroeconomics Annual 1990*, Cambridge, MA: MIT Press.

Guiso, L. and T. Jappelli (1994). 'Intergenerational Transfers and Capital Market Imperfections. Evidence from a Cross-Section of Italian Households', *this volume*.

Guiso, L., T. Jappelli and D. Terlizzese (1994). 'Earnings Uncertainty and Precautionary Saving', *this volume*.

Hall, R.E. (1978). 'Stochastic Implications of the Life-Cycle-Permanent Income Hypothesis: Theory and Evidence', *Journal of Political Economy* **86**: 971-87.

Hayashi, F. (1982). 'The Permanent Income Hypothesis: Estimation and Testing by Instrumental Variables', *Journal of Political Economy* **90**: 895-916.

Hayashi, F. (1985). 'The Effect of Liquidity Constraints on Consumption: A Cross-Sectional Analysis', *Quarterly Journal of Economics* **100**: 183-206.

Hayashi, F. (1986). 'Why Is Japan's Saving Rate so Apparently High?', *NBER Macroeconomics Annual 1986*, Cambridge, MA: MIT Press.

Hayashi, F., T. Ito and J. Slemrod (1988). 'Housing Finance Imperfections, Taxation and Private Saving: A Comparative Simulation Analysis of the United States and Japan', *Journal of the Japanese and International Economies* **2**: 215-38.

Hubbard, G.R. (1986). 'Pension Wealth and Individual Saving: Some New Evidence', *Journal of Money, Credit and Banking* **22**: 167-78.

Hurd, M.D. (1987). 'Savings of the Elderly and Desired Bequests', *American Economic Review* **77**: 298-312.

Jaffee, D. and J. Stiglitz (1990). 'Credit Rationing', in B. M. Friedman and F. Hahn (eds.), *Handbook of Monetary Economics*, Amsterdam, North-Holland, Vol. II.

Jappelli, T. and M. Pagano (1989). 'Consumption and Capital Market Imperfections: An International Comparison', *American Economic Review* **79**: 1088-105.

Jappelli, T. and M. Pagano (1994). 'Saving, Growth and Liquidity Constraints', *Quarterly Journal of Economics*, forthcoming.

Kimball, M.S. (1990). 'Precautionary Saving in the Small and in the Large', *Econometrica* **58**: 53-73.

King, M. and L-D.L. Dicks-Mireaux (1982). 'Asset Holdings and the Life Cycle', *Economic Journal* **92**: 247-67.

Koskela, E. and M. Viren (1989). 'Taxes, Credit Market Imperfections and Inter-Country Differences in the Household Saving Ratio', Bank of Finland Discussion Paper 21.

Kotlikoff, L.J. (1989). *What Determines Savings?*, Cambridge, MA: MIT Press.

Kotlikoff, L.J. and A. Spivak (1981). 'The Family as an Incomplete Annuities Market', *Journal of Political Economy* **89**: 372-91.

Kotlikoff, L.J. and L.H. Summers (1988). 'The Contribution of Intergenerational Transfers to Total Wealth', in D. Kessler and A. Masson (eds.), *Modelling the Accumulation and Distribution of Wealth*, New York: Oxford University Press.

Lipsey, R.E. and I.B. Kravis (1987). 'Is the U.S. a Spendthrift Nation?', NBER Working Paper 2274.

Mace, B.J. (1991). 'Full Insurance in the Presence of Aggregate Uncertainty', *Journal of Political Economy* **99**: 928-56.

Mariger, R. (1986). *Consumption Behavior and the Effects of Government Fiscal Policies*, Cambridge, MA: Harvard University Press.

Modigliani, F. (1990). 'Recent Declines in the Saving Rate: A Life Cycle Perspective', *Rivista di politica economica* **80** (English version): 5-42. (Also in M. Baldassari, L. Paganetto and E.S. Phelps, *World Saving, Prosperity and Growth*, New York: St. Martin's Press, 1993.)

Modigliani, F. and R. Brumberg (1980). 'Utility Analysis and Aggregate Consumption Function: An Attempt at Integration', in A. Abel (ed.), *The Collected Papers of Franco Modigliani*, Cambridge, MA: MIT Press, Vol. II.

Modigliani, F. and T. Jappelli (1987). 'Fiscal Policy and Saving in Italy since 1860', in M. Boskin, J. Flemming and S. Gorini (eds.), *Private Saving and Public Debt*, Oxford: Basil Blackwell.

Mork, K.A. and V.K. Smith (1989). 'Testing the Life-Cycle Hypothesis with a Norwegian Household Panel', *Journal of Business and Economic Statistics* **7**: 287-96.

Muellbauer, J. and A. Murphy (1990). 'Is the UK Balance of Payments Sustainable?', *Economic Policy* **11**: 347-95.

Nicoletti, G. (1988). 'A Cross-Country Analysis of Private Consumption, Inflation and the 'Debt Neutrality Hypothesis'', *OECD Economic Studies* **11**: 43-87.

Pagano, M. and T. Jappelli (1993), "Information Sharing in Credit Markets', *Journal of Finance*, forthcoming.

Pagliano, P. and N. Rossi (1992). 'The Italian Saving Rate: 1951 to 1990 Estimates', in *Income and Saving in Italy: A Reconstruction*, Temi di discussione 169, Banca d'Italia.

Romer, P. (1986). 'Increasing Returns and Long-Run Growth', *Journal of Political Economy* **94**: 1002-37.

Rossi, N. and I. Visco (1994). 'Private Saving and the Government Deficit in Italy', *this volume*.

Runkle, D.E. (1988). 'Liquidity Constraints and the Permanent Income Hypothesis', *Journal of Monetary Economics* **27**: 73-98.

Skinner, J. (1988). 'Risky Income, Life-Cycle Consumption and Precautionary Saving', *Journal of Monetary Economics* **22**: 237-55.

Summers, L.H. and C. Carroll (1987). 'Why Is U.S. National Saving so Low?', *Brookings Papers on Economic Activity* **2**: 607-42.

Yoshikawa, H. and F. Othake (1989). 'An Analysis of Female Labor Supply, Housing Demand and the Saving Rate in Japan', *European Economic Review* **33**: 997-1022.

Zeldes, S.P. (1989). 'Consumption and Liquidity Constraints: An Empirical Investigation', *Journal of Political Economy* **97**: 305-46.

2 Private saving and the government deficit in Italy*

NICOLA ROSSI and IGNAZIO VISCO

1 Introduction

According to official sources, aggregate Italian saving rates have declined substantially in recent years. The precise timing and extent of this change largely depend on the definition of saving adopted and on the researcher's attitude toward the host of measurement issues involved. However, major trends are undisputably under way with regard to gross and net rates, national and private measures and "adjusted" and "unadjusted" values, and provide a rather surprising description of the behavior of Italian consumers.

In the second half of the eighties private saving rates (net of depreciation, adjusted for durables and inflation and computed as ratios to net national disposable income) fluctuated around 14 percent, 5 percentage points lower than the average in the sixties.[1] In the same years government saving (adjusted for inflation) plunged to an unprecedented minus 1 percent, after more than thirty years of current account surpluses averaging 3 percent. As a result, the overall Italian saving rate is 9 percentage points lower today than during the so-called "Italian economic miracle".

Several alternative explanations for the fall in the saving rate have been put forward in recent research.[2] In particular, the impact of fiscal policy on private sector behavior has been repeatedly scrutinized, although no definite conclusion has been drawn.[3] Nevertheless, this paper proposes that a thorough assessment of the interplay of private and public decisions can shed light on the evolution of the saving rate in recent decades. In particular, it appears that the dynamics and composition of government saving figures, together with changes in productivity growth, are important factors for explaining private saving rates.

Section 2 reviews aggregate saving figures in postwar Italy and highlights the role of accounting conventions in the measurement of national and sectoral saving rates. A detailed analysis of major items of the government current account balances suggests that attention should be paid to the composition of government saving and particularly to the role played by social transfers. Section 3 takes an empirical approach and examines the time series aggregate consumption function over the period 1951-1990. On the basis of the aggregate evidence, a hypothesis concerning the role of public transfers in the seventies and the eighties is put forward. In Section 4, an econometric model of consumer behavior allowing for borrowing constraints estimated on microeconomic data provides fresh and independent evidence concerning the effect of selected social transfers on saving. Specifically, Section 4.2 evaluates the impact of structural changes in the social security system in the late sixties and early seventies on the private saving rate, while Section 4.3 treats the same issue with a view to the future, assessing the impact on the household saving rate of the recent Government measures to reform the Italian pension system. Section 5 concludes.

2 Saving rates in the postwar period (1951-1990)

Before examining the trends of Italian saving rates in the last forty years, a number of issues relating to data and definitions need to be considered. Concerning definitions, it should be stressed that the standard national accounts (NA) definition is inadequate in various respects. First of all, consumption is usually defined as total expenditure on consumer goods and services. The former include expenditure on consumer durables, which it would be more correct to treat as a component of household investment. A proper (economic) definition of consumption should, by contrast, only include the services provided to households by the stock of durables.

Second, the NA definition of income includes interest payments and receipts at their nominal value. It has long been recognized, however, that income should be adjusted for the loss of purchasing power of the stock of nominal debt due to inflation.[4] This is especially relevant when national saving is divided into its private and government components. Disregarding the loss of principal due to inflation implies overestimating private savings and thus neglecting a possibly important source of government revenue, the so-called "inflation tax".

Finally, saving should probably be considered net of the depreciation of the capital stock. In principle, the replacement of old capital equipment may spur the growth of income when the new equipment incorporates technological innovations; in practice, however, much investment spending is simply intended to replace worn-out equipment and machinery.

In this section the movements of national, private and government saving rates will be examined, comparing the standard NA definition with the one that allows for a proper treatment of consumer durables (which we will call the "economic" definition). The latter will then be adjusted to take account of the "inflation tax" and both the household and the corporate components of private saving will be considered. All figures will be presented net of the capital stock depreciation and all saving ratios computed in relation to the (net) national disposable income.

As for the issue relating to data, in 1985 the Italian NA statistics were substantially revised, and official estimates released since then only cover the years since 1970 for most of the variables of interest here. It has thus been necessary to undertake a major reconstruction of the data. Analytical income accounts from 1970 onwards have been constructed by Marotta and Pagliano (1992); at a more aggregate level, the time series since 1951 considered in this work (inclusive of those estimates and of the official ones when available) are presented in Pagliano and Rossi (1992). While we refer readers to those papers for the details of the reconstruction, we point out here that in adjusting the saving rates for inflation the inflation tax has been computed as the "expected" inflation loss on government debt, on the grounds that consumers may only base their decisions on anticipated real interest revenues (expected inflation being derived from survey measures of consumer price expectations).

2.1   The various definitions of saving

Net national saving rates are shown in Figure 2.1. The difference between the economic and the NA definitions is mainly one of levels, even if it widened from only about 1 percentage point in the fifties to above 3 points

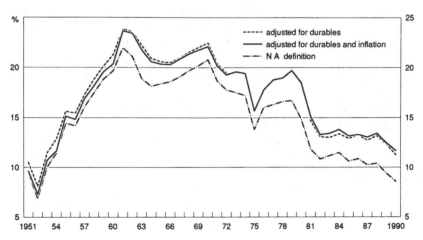

Figure 2.1

Net national saving rate

in the eighties. At the national level the adjustment for inflation is plainly negligible, reflecting the smallness of Italy's net foreign financial position over the period. From a peak of about 24 percent at the beginning of the sixties, the national saving rate turns out to have declined to an average level of below 15 percent in the past decade.

By contrast, the adjustment for inflation is extremely important when private and government saving rates are considered. As reflected in Figure 2.2, under the economic definition of saving (as well as the NA definition), on an unadjusted basis the private saving rate rose dramatically by 10 points in the fifties and continued to rise in the next two decades, albeit at a much slower pace; it only began to fall progressively in the late seventies, dropping by 1990 to a level more than 7 points lower than its 1979 peak.

Figure 2.2

Net private saving rate

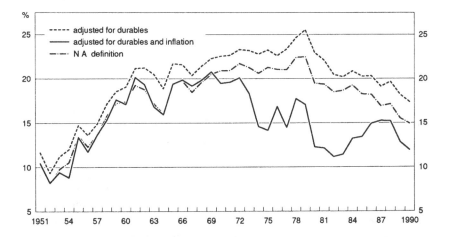

Correcting for inflation, after rising markedly in the fifties the private saving rate appears instead to have stabilized from the beginning of the sixties to almost the mid-seventies. Subsequently, even if with non-negligible fluctuations, it progressively declined until the end of the eighties, accounting for much of the 7-to 8-point reduction observed in the same period for the national saving rate.

Accordingly, the large reduction in the public sector saving rate beginning in the early seventies (Figure 2.3), when sizable current account deficits began to be recorded, was completely offset by the "inflation tax" until 1983-84. Only then, with the substantial fall in the inflation tax together with the slowdown in inflation, and notwithstanding the rise of the public debt, we begin to observe a reduction in government saving and the formation of deficits on the current account even adjusting for inflation.[5]

Figure 2.3

Net government saving rate

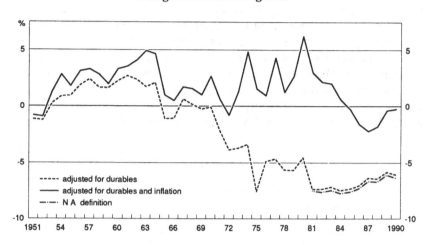

2.2   National, private and government saving rates compared

Figure 2.4 presents national, private and government saving rates (corrected for durables and inflation) and clearly shows that the Italian saving rate began to decline just before the middle of the seventies, in conjunction with the first oil shock, when the growth rate of the Italian economy started to fall. It was not until the eighties, however, that the reduction in the national saving rate became considerable, fully reflecting the progressive decline of government saving that combined with the negative trend of private saving.

Adjusted for inflation, government saving was substantially lower in the years from 1965 to 1975 than in both the preceding low-inflation and the following high-inflation years (until 1984). In the latter period, the "inflation tax" was a substantial source of revenue for the government. Its reduction after that was not accompanied by a corresponding curbing of government expenditure and transfers, with the end result of a remarkable decline in government saving. The components of government saving are examined in some detail in Section 2.3 below, in order to single out the main determinants of the decline. The subsequent sections are mainly devoted to investigating the effects that major changes in these components may have had on private sector behavior. As a preliminary, however, it might be useful to consider how the evolution of private saving has been determined by its households and "corporate"[6] components.

Figure 2.4
National, private and government adjusted net saving rates

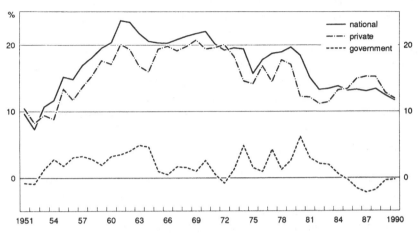

These components are presented in Figure 2.5. It is clear that the pattern of the private saving rate is dominated by households' saving. The decline in the latter from 1973 onwards was even more pronounced than that in the former. While the corporate saving rate, after a modest rise in the second half of the sixties, basically fluctuated around a constant level until the end of the eighties, the rather large recovery in the private saving rate between 1983 and 1987 was for the most part an artifact due to the cyclical reduction in firms' profits between 1981 and 1983.

Figure 2.5
Private, household and corporate adjusted net saving rates

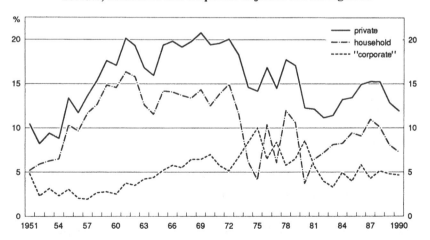

2.3   The components of government saving

As we have observed, the government saving rate fell substantially in the course of the eighties. Even when adjusted for inflation, the public sector budget actually showed a current account deficit from 1985 on. This combined with the appreciable deficit on the capital account (which over the whole period increased slightly from nearly 4 to about 5 percent of GDP), producing an overall deficit that is a matter of serious concern.

To identify all the determinants of the decline in government saving with some precision would require an extensive discussion of institutional and policy details. In this section we will therefore limit ourselves to highlighting and providing insight on the trends of the major components of government saving with the help of a number of graphs.

Tax receipts are presented in Figure 2.6.[7] After having remained basically constant until the mid-seventies, the tax-to-income ratio rose strikingly by more than 10 percentage points between 1976 and 1990. As can be seen from the figure, the rise was mainly due to the increase in direct taxation. This was chiefly a result not so much of increases in the tax rate, but of rising nominal incomes (in the presence of high inflation rates) in combination with a given progressive tax structure (so-called "fiscal drag").[8]

Figure 2.6

Tax receipts

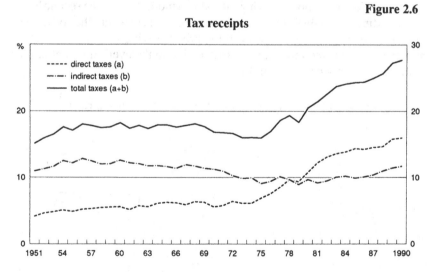

The relative growth in government consumption, that is to say expenditure on consumer goods and services plus wages and salaries of public employees, was much less pronounced than that of tax receipts (Figure 2.7). In particular, the average ratio of government consumption to net national income increased to a level around 19 percent in the eighties, about 3 points higher than in the seventies. As a consequence, the amount by which total taxes exceeded government consumption grew progressively from 1975 onwards and is now equal to more than 8 percent of total income.

Figure 2.7

Taxes and government consumption

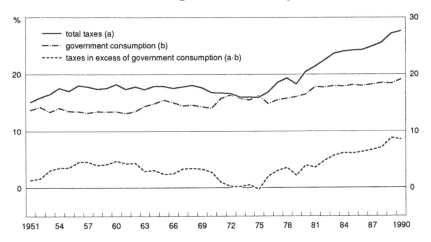

Interest payments are shown in Figure 2.8. The key thing to note is that, once the inflation tax is properly evaluated, net interest payments were negative throughout the seventies and became positive and large only in the second half of the eighties. On the one hand, this change reflected the substantial reduction in the inflation tax, which, though still non-negligible, ceased being a conspicuous source of revenue for the government. On the other, in the most recent years high real interest rates combined with an extremely large and growing public debt (the consequence of the sizable overall deficits accumulated over the years) to produce what is by now a major component of the current account deficit (equal to around 4 percent of net national income in 1990).

Subtracting inflation-adjusted net interest payments from the variable that results from the difference shown in Figure 2.7, in Figure 2.9 we obtain a value that may be labelled "non-transfer government saving", the excess of total tax receipts (including the inflation tax) with respect to current government outlays for consumption and interest payments. This variable remained positive and high over the whole period under review. After having risen considerably in the years of high inflation, non-transfer government saving fell back during the eighties to around 5 percent of net income, a level not much higher than that recorded until the beginning of the seventies.

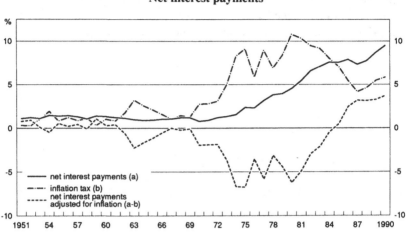

Figure 2.8
Net interest payments

net interest payments (a)
inflation tax (b)
net interest payments
adjusted for inflation (a-b)

The other component of government saving that remains to be considered is net transfers. Figure 2.10 shows that total transfers rose dramatically over the whole period, from 8 to more than 22 percent of net national income. Since transfers to firms only show a permanent increase of about 1 percentage point from 1975 onwards, social transfers to households were clearly the main determinant of the trend of total transfers. Among these, most of the rise (about 9 points) was due to pensions. The rest is attributable to the increase in spending on public health services.

Figure 2.9
Non-transfer government saving

taxes in excess of government consumption (a)
interest payments adjusted for inflation (b)
non-transfer government saving (a-b)

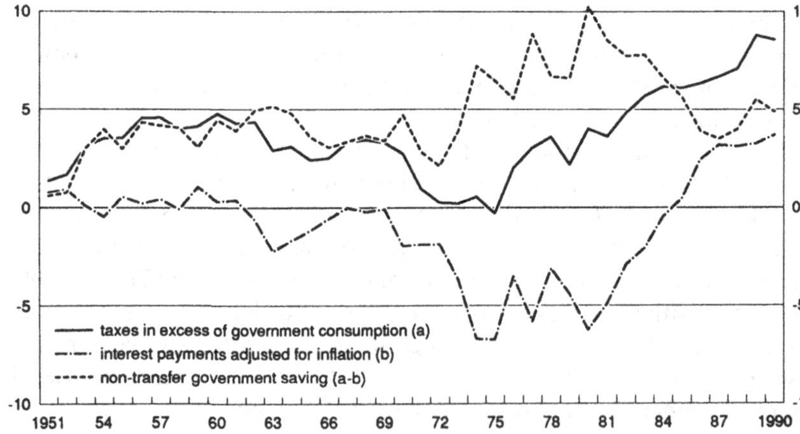

Figure 2.10

Government transfers

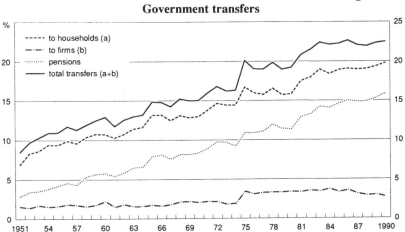

It has been observed that "Italy is the western country in which public expenditure on pensions is highest in relation to GDP".[9] An analysis of the rapid growth in pension expenditure suggests that, in addition to demographic trends, substantial increases in the number of pensions (throughout the period) and in average benefits (from 1976 onward) should be identified as the leading factors of this trend.[10]

Figure 2.11

Net government transfers

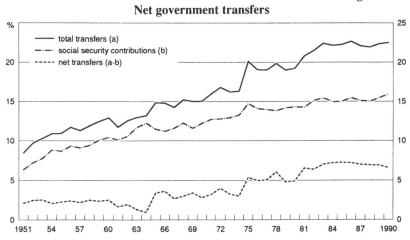

A very relevant fact is that the spectacular increase in social transfers (and particularly in pensions) was not matched by the growth in social contributions from whatever source (both employers and employees).

Between 1951 and 1990 total transfers in relation to the net national income almost tripled (with three eye-catching "jumps" in 1965, 1975 and 1980, when major institutional changes took place, with further consequences for the following years). The corresponding increase in social contributions was by no means modest, having amounted to 2.5 times that in the national income, but was insufficient to prevent net transfers from rising from about 2 percent of income until the mid-seventies to about 6 percent in most of the eighties (Figure 2.11), reflecting almost entirely the growing imbalance of the national social security system.

The increase in net transfers was offset until the beginning of the eighties by the growth of explicit and implicit taxation in excess of government expenditure and interest payments. Figure 2.12 shows, however, that as the inflation tax started declining[11] and interest payments adjusted for inflation began to become significant, net transfers continued to grow both in absolute and in relative terms. They thus ended up by more than offsetting the non-transfer saving component, which, despite the above-mentioned increase in interest outlays, was still highly positive and above the levels recorded before the first oil shock. All this caused the overall government saving rate to fall by an average of around 4 percentage points between 1974-1983 and 1984-1990.[12]

Figure 2.12

Government saving

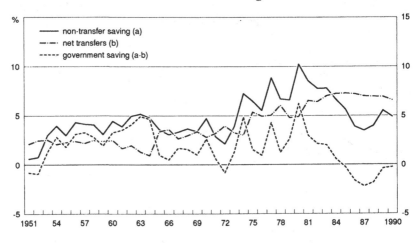

2.4   Government transfers and private saving

It has been shown above that the Italian economy witnessed far-reaching changes in the structure of government outlays and receipts in both the seventies and the eighties. As a result, the relationship between the private and public sectors underwent important changes that are not necessarily reflected by aggregate figures such as government current balances.

In this context, focusing on the interplay of aggregate measures of private and public savings is likely not to be particularly revealing. For one thing, the evolution of variables such as government deficits cannot easily be interpreted as representing, in a certain sense, the result of an experiment *à la* Barro (1974) – that is, of changes in (lump-sum) taxation matched, for a given path of government expenditure, by opposite changes in government debt. On the contrary, over and above tax rates changes, government current balances in Italy appear to have been affected by changes in expenditure policy particularly as regards transfer payments.

To clarify this point, assume that any decrease (increase) in government expenditure is associated with a corresponding decrease (increase) in borrowing. The impact of such a decrease in borrowing on consumption and saving will depend on how the path of future tax payments is expected to change.[13] Leaving aside distributional issues for the time being, the analysis would apparently parallel the standard treatment of changes in lump-sum taxation. However, this would be only part of the story. Taxes and transfers affect economic activity primarily by altering individual budget constraints. In contrast, changes in the level of government expenditure on goods and services (i.e., in the provision of public goods) tend to influence individual behavior through their direct effect on consumers' utility. Furthermore, transfer programmes, as opposed to taxes, often have notable intertemporal implications whose impact should be explicitly taken into account.

Consider the case of transfer payments, with particular reference to social security programmes. As long as some fraction of the population is liquidity-constrained at a given point in time, transfer programmes tilted toward the lower income segments of the population might be expected, everything else being equal, to have a relatively significant positive effect on consumption (Romer 1988, Wilcox 1989).

Moreover, an increase in pension benefits by way of, say, changes in the rules on social security (such as those repeatedly enacted in Italy in the seventies and eighties) could affect the saving behavior of all individuals through their impact on expectations, since, in a life-cycle framework and for a given retirement age, it would, *ceteris paribus*, create an incentive for the current generation to increase its consumption.[14] Under such circumstances, an increase in transfer payments signalling a permanent increase in pension benefits[15] (the bill eventually being footed by later generations) could be expected to have an appreciable negative impact on private savings and hence, for a given level of current income, on the private saving rate. The shrinking private saving rate would be added to the larger government deficit, thereby causing an even larger drop in the national saving rate.[16]

Changes in government current outlays affect economic activity through a number of additional channels. In particular, the impact of the provision of public goods and services, of which health care is a prominent example in the Italian setting,[17] will depend on the degree of substitutability or complementarity between those goods and services and aggregate private expenditure. In turn, this will depend on the nature of individual preferences. If public expenditure programmes are perfect substitutes for the corresponding items in private budgets, attention should be focused (as in the Barro experiment) on the implied change in public borrowing and the perceived time path of future tax payments.[18] If, however, publicly provided goods and services turn out to be complements to private consumption, additional effects will work through, although their precise magnitude would of course be rather difficult to quantify.

In short, if both government current outlays and receipts vary, evaluation of the interplay of private and public saving on the basis of the evolution of their aggregate current balances is likely to obscure the main issues, preventing a satisfactory assessment of the effects of fiscal policy on private consumption.

In this paper we suggest that the channels outlined above are of paramount importance for understanding the evolution of the Italian saving rate. Accordingly, the empirical sections of the paper will focus on the growth of pension expenditure that occurred "from the turn of the sixties onwards, reflecting the impact of the introduction of special plans for self-employed workers and increased use of disability pensions for welfare purposes. This rapid growth carried over into the seventies in connection with the switch in 1968 from a contributions-based system to an earnings-based system and the far-reaching reform of INPS pensions in 1969, in particular the introduction, and subsequent improvement, of methods of indexing pension benefits to prices and real earnings" (Franco and Morcaldo 1990, p. 107). This overhaul of the postwar social security system appears to have introduced large and exogenous variations in the traditional life-cycle pattern of income, reducing private capital accumulation.

Needless to say, the impact of social security on saving is far from a novel issue and has been widely debated at both the theoretical and empirical levels.[19] The controversy over the validity of the life-cycle model extended à la Feldstein (1976) is still very much an open issue and we certainly do not expect to settle it here. Indeed, Auerbach and Kotlikoff (1983), thoroughly examining recent cross-section and time series tests of the social security savings question, argue that on the basis of current data neither type of test has much potential for settling the controversy. Along with Williamson and Jones (1983), they point out that specification problems can lead to highly unstable coefficients and to rejection of the null (given by the extended life-cycle setting) when it is in fact true. Nevertheless, we feel that the numbers at stake in the social security debate are so large that a careful and cautious application of standard methods still deserves a chance, especially when, as in the Italian case, the evidence is, at best, scattered.[20]

We shall, however, take Auerbach and Kotlikoff's concern seriously and focus in Section 3 on a period centred on the enactment of social security reform, exploiting the information contained in the behavior of the economy around the time of enactment and thereby avoiding what they correctly regard as a major source of misspecification. Moreover, to strengthen our results, microeconomic simulation will be used in Section 4 to "replicate" the aggregate experiment independently. While we are quite willing to recognize that aggregation and other sources of bias may affect the standard "reduced-form" consumption function, we believe that there is still a lot to be learned from the parallel use of macro and micro data.

3   Macroeconomic evidence

Section 4 will propose that the behavior of about three quarters of Italian consumers can be adequately represented by the simple model of rational, utility-maximizing agents who at a given date optimally allocate resources to consumption over their future life span. We therefore begin the empirical investigation by making explicit reference to the "stripped-down" version of the life-cycle hypothesis of saving as reviewed, for example, by Modigliani (1986).[21]

As is well known, under a set of somewhat restrictive assumptions[22] the aggregate equilibrium behavior of consumers can be described by a very simple aggregate consumption function, linear in aggregate labor income (y^l) and beginning-of-period wealth (w):

$$c = \alpha y^l + \delta w \tag{1}$$

where α and δ are (approximately) constant aggregate coefficients determined by the structure of preferences, the length of life, the length of retirement, the rate of growth of population and productivity (g) and the real interest rate (r). Letting $y = y^l + rw$, where y stands for disposable income, and $s = y - c$, equation (1) implies

$$\frac{s}{y} = (1 - \alpha) - (\delta - \alpha r)\frac{w}{y} \tag{2}$$

which (since, in steady state, $s = gw$) leads to the celebrated steady-state relationships for the wealth-to-income and saving-to-income ratios: $w/y = (1 - a)/(g + \delta - ar)$ and $s/y = g(1 - a)/(g + \delta - ar)$.

As Feldstein (1974) first suggested, if labor-leisure choices are unaffected, the social security system should influence a family's consumption through the effect of social security taxes and benefits on the family's lifetime budget constraint. If there are no constraints on net worth prior to the time of death, then the social security impact is summarized by the family's lifetime social security wealth, which is simply the discounted value of lifetime social security benefits minus the discounted value of lifetime social security taxes. In such a case total net worth (w) is simply the sum of two components: net non-human (real and financial) wealth (w^r) and net social security wealth (w^s). Equation (2) would then read:

$$\frac{s}{y} = (1 - a) - (\delta - ar)\left[\frac{(w^r + \theta w^s)}{y}\right] \tag{3}$$

with the parameter θ allowing for a difference between the aggregate coefficients on net private assets and social security wealth.

Moreover, following Modigliani and Brumberg (1980) and Ando and Modigliani (1963), a more flexible specification would allow δ to vary with the real interest rate and the rate of growth of the economy, so that $\delta = \bar{\delta} + \mu r + \lambda g$. Hence:

$$\frac{s}{y} = (1 - a) - \bar{\delta}\frac{w}{y} - \lambda g \frac{w}{y} + (a - \mu)r\frac{w}{y} \tag{4}$$

where $w = (w^r + \theta w^s)$ denotes total net wealth.

Expanding around given steady-state values of the total wealth-to-income ratio, of the growth rate and of the real interest rate ($\bar{w}$, $\bar{g}$ and $\bar{r}$), we would obtain:

$$\frac{s}{y} = \phi_0 + \phi_1 g + \phi_2 r + \phi_3 \frac{w^r}{y} + \phi_4 \frac{w^s}{y} \tag{5}$$

where

$$\phi_0 = 1 - a + \lambda \bar{g}\bar{w} - (a - \mu)\bar{w}\bar{r}, \quad \phi_1 = -\lambda\bar{w},$$

$$\phi_2 = (a - \mu)\bar{w}, \quad \phi_3 = -(\bar{\delta} + \lambda\bar{g} - (a - \mu)\bar{r}), \quad \phi_4 = \theta\phi_3.$$

Equation (5), which is an equilibrium linear relationship between the saving rate, the income growth rate, the real interest rate, the net non-human wealth to income ratio and the net social security wealth-to-income ratio, provides the benchmark for the empirical analysis conducted in this section.

3.1   Time series analysis

Recent developments in the theory of cointegration permit economic equilibrium relationships between a set of variables such as the one depicted by equation (5) to be linked explicitly with statistical models of those variables (Engle and Granger 1987). To pursue the example given by equation (5), the realized values of the saving rate should not necessarily be expected to move in parallel with the wealth-to-income ratio, but agents' intertemporally optimizing behavior brings them back into line if they are not so. With shocks in every period, equation (5) never needs to hold, yet agents act to absorb those shocks and, if the theory is correct, the two ratios never drift too far from their equilibrium values. If the saving rate is non-stationary (e.g. integrated of order one, I(1)) the wealth-to-income ratio will be so too, but some linear combination of both ratios may be stationary because agents' behavior makes this set of variables cointegrated.

Table 2.1 Univariate statistics for testing unit roots

	Period	Without trend	With trend
$\ln(c/y)$			
DF	1952-90	−1.858 (−2.938)	−1.816 (−3.528)
ADF (1)	1953-90	−2.212 (−2.940)	−2.248 (−3.531)
g			
DF	1953-90	−7.055 (−2.940)	−8.148 (−3.531)
ADF (1)	1954-90	−3.567 (−2.942)	−4.460 (−3.535)
r			
DF	1952-90	−2.620 (−2.938)	−2.582 (−3.528)
ADF (1)	1953-90	−1.938 (−2.940)	−1.881 (−3.531)
w^r/y			
DF	1953-90	−3.304 (−2.940)	−3.141 (−3.531)
ADF (1)	1954-90	−2.463 (−2.942)	−3.164 (−3.535)
w^s/y			
DF	1952-90	−1.057 (−2.938)	−3.467 (−3.528)
ADF (1)	1953-90	−0.600 (−2.940)	−2.963 (−3.531)

Note: 95 percent critical values in parentheses.

In testing for the existence of cointegration, it is necessary to establish first that the individual series are I(1) and then that there exists some non-trivial function of them which is I(0). The most common approach is to start testing for a unit root in the univariate representations of the individual series and then in the least squares linear combination. The upper panel of Table 2.1 lists the values of the Dickey-Fuller (DF) and augmented Dickey-Fuller (ADF) statistics for the following variables:[23]

(i)   the log of the expenditure-to-income ratio $\ln(c/y)$, where c stands for real "economic" consumption and y denotes consumers' net real disposable income, defined as net real disposable income of the private sector adjusted for inflation and inclusive of net government transfers.[24] Clearly, $\ln(c/y) \simeq -s/y$, where s stands for net private savings.[25] Note that these private saving rate figures do not match the corresponding figures reported in Figures 2.2, 2.4 and 2.5, since the latter are computed as ratios to net national disposable income whereas the former refer to net private disposable income (adjusted for inflation). As a result, the overall pattern of the private saving rate remains hump-shaped, but the decline observed in the seventies and eighties turns out to be somewhat larger (Figure 2.13);

Figure 2.13

Net private saving rates

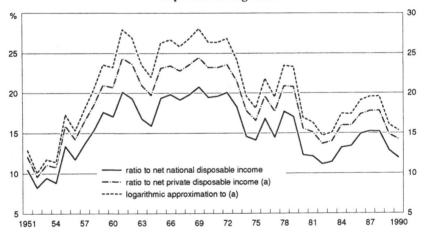

(ii)   the growth rate of real disposable income of the private sector (g);
(iii)   the real interest rate (r) defined as $\ln[(1+R)/(1+\pi)]$, where R is the nominal interest rate on long-term government bonds and π is the expected annual rate of change in consumer prices;[26]
(iv)   the ratio of private wealth to net disposable income $(w^r/y,$ Figure 2.14), where w^r denotes net non-human (real and financial) private sector wealth;

(v) the ratio of net social security wealth to net disposable income (w^s/y, Figure 2.14). This is, needless to say, a rather elusive quantity whose measurement involves formidable assumptions at both the individual and the aggregate levels.[27] Briefly, net social security wealth should measure the actuarial value of the social security benefits individuals expect to receive net of the actuarial value of the social security taxes they expect to pay. As such, this quantity should reflect changes over time in such factors as the composition of the population by age and sex, life expectancy, social security coverage and benefit and tax rules. In what follows we shall make use of a careful reconstruction of this variable.[28]

Figure 2.14

Wealth-income ratios

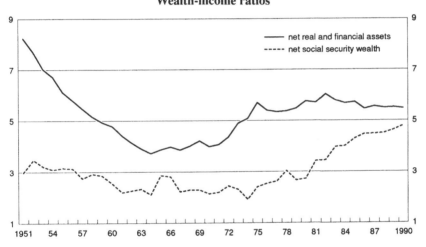

On the basis of the statistics reported in Table 2.1, the hypothesis of a unit root is clearly rejected, at the 5 percent level, only for income growth (g). In a multivariate context, however, there is a number of cointegrating regressions linking the saving rate, the real interest rate and the wealth-to-income ratios. We therefore revert to the recent work of Johansen (1988), testing for the maximum number of cointegration vectors (v) and providing a maximum likelihood estimate of such vector(s) (Table 2.2). As it turns out, the hypothesis of a single cointegration vector cannot be rejected at customary confidence levels.[29]

3.2   A basic consumption function

In a relatively small sample like the present one, an attractive alternative to the multivariate time series methods used above is to estimate a conditional error correction model and formally test the significance of the adjustment coefficient.[30] Assuming, therefore, on the basis of the results reported in Table 2.2, that $\ln(c/y)$, r, w^r/y and w^s/y are cointegrated, Table 2.3 presents the estimated error correction model. It has the general form of the theoretical model (5) but contains additional lags and variables designed to shed light on the short-run impact of income and government expenditure, as well as to take account of a possible oversensitivity of consumption to current income due to some agents being constrained from their optimal consumption plan in any period. In deriving the implied long-run (steady state) solution of the model, these constraints will be disregarded.

Table 2.2 Maximum likelihood cointegration analysis
(sample: 1954-1990)

Lag length in VAR (in years): 4, non-trended variables	
Non-zero eigenvalues of the stochastic matrix: .897, .436, .342, .074	
W test (H$_0$: $v \leq 3$; H$_1$: $v = 4$)	2.695 (9.243)
W test (H$_0$: $v \leq 2$; H$_1$: $v = 3$)	14.665 (15.672)
W test (H$_0$: $v \leq 1$; H$_1$: $v = 2$)	20.024 (22.002)
W test (H$_0$: $v = 0$; H$_1$: $v = 1$)	79.665 (28.138)

Note: 95 percent critical values in parentheses.

Cointegration vector associated with the largest eigenvalue:

$\ln(c/y)$	intercept	r	w^r/y	w^s/y
−1.000	−.359*	−.463*	.029**	.013*

Note: * (**), significant at the 95 (90) percent level.

To estimate the vector of short-run responses of consumption to changes in different components of income (y), we separately investigated the role of taxes, social contributions, public transfers and (real and nominal) interest payments, thereby allowing for the possibility of separate marginal propensities to consume from different kinds of income. However, none of these variables turned out to play a significant role, with the exception of transfers to firms, which showed a zero short-run impact on private consumption and were therefore eliminated from the definition of income applicable in the short run.

Table 2.3 Error correction representation
(sample: 1954-1990)

Least squares estimates:

$$\Delta \ln c_t = \underset{(.045)}{.439} \ \Delta \ln(y{-}x)_t \ \underset{(.115)}{-.324} \ \Delta \ln z_t + \underset{(.142)}{.291} \ \Delta \ln c_{t-1}$$

$$- \underset{(.090)}{.503} \ \{\ln(c/y)_{t-1} + \underset{(.036)}{.380} + \underset{(.125)}{.468} \ r_{t-1} - \underset{(.004)}{.036} \ [(w^r/y)_{t-1} + \underset{(.091)}{.209} \ (w^s/y)_{t-1}]\}$$

$\overline{R}^2 = .797$ $DW = 1.905$ $\sigma = .0094$

Serial correlation	$F(1,28)$	$= .190$	Functional form	$F(1,28) = .099$
Normality	$\chi^2(2)$	$= .672$	Heteroscedasticity	$F(1,36) = .457$
Arch	$F(1,28)$	$= .153$	Predictive failure	$F(10,19) = .327$

Instrumental variables estimates:

$$\Delta \ln c_t = \underset{(.139)}{.671} \ \Delta \ln(y{-}x)_t \ \underset{(.193)}{-.404} \ \Delta \ln z_t + \underset{(.151)}{.554} \ \Delta \ln c_{t-1}$$

$$- \underset{(.141)}{.500} \ \{\ln(c/y)_{t-1} + \underset{(.062)}{.464} + \underset{(.167)}{.594} \ r_{t-1} - \underset{(.007)}{.041} \ [(w^r/y)_{t-1} + \underset{(.136)}{.325} \ (w^s/y)_{t-1}]\}$$

$\overline{R}^2 = .623$ $DW = 2.073$ $\sigma = .0129$

Validity of instruments	$\chi^2(2) = 2.122$		Serial correlation	$\chi^2(1) = .199$
Functional form	$\chi^2(1) = .893$		Normality	$\chi^2(2) = .862$
Heteroscedasticity	$\chi^2(1) = 2.178$			

Note: In parentheses, White's standard errors.

Table 2.3 also reports coefficient estimates, associated standard errors and diagnostic statistics, where available, for the LS and IV estimates.[31] In the table, x stands for government transfers to firms and z for real government consumption. The following points appear to be noteworthy.

In the LS estimates, the short-run (impact) marginal propensity to consume out of behavior income is around 0.35. This figure is revised upwards by the IV estimates: the short-run marginal propensity to consume out of income averages out to 0.54. Interestingly, government expenditure turns out to be a mild substitute for private consumption in the short run (as in Rossi 1991).

Reverting to the long-run solution (corresponding to equation (5)), all long-run coefficients reported in Table 2.4 appear to be rather precisely determined.[32] θ is calculated to be 0.21 in the LS and 0.32 in the IV estimates, thereby implying in equilibrium a sizable replacement of private savings by social security.[33] Assuming that the combined effect of public transfer flows and social security contributions does not reduce saving, so that the latter falls only because of the wealth effect of the social security programme, partial equilibrium computations would lead to the conclusion that social security reduced aggregate private savings in 1990 by about one third, lowering the capital stock by the same amount.[34]

Table 2.4 Long-run coefficients of the saving rate equation
(eq. (5); dependent variable: s/y; sample: 1954-1990)

Parameter estimates	LS	IV
ϕ_0	.380 (.045)	.464 (.082)
ϕ_1	1.180 (.444)	.356 (.786)
ϕ_2	.468 (.039)	.594 (.216)
ϕ_3	−.036 (.005)	−.041 (.007)
ϕ_4	−.007 (.003)	−.013 (.005)
α	.563 (.036)	.503 (.063)
δ	.056 (.004)	.059 (.005)
$\bar{\delta}$	.045 (.004)	.047 (.006)
λ	−.197 (.074)	−.059 (.131)
μ	.485 (.053)	.404 (.092)

Note: In parentheses, asymptotic standard errors; the values reported in the lower panel of the table refer to the parameters of equation (4) and are computed from the set of relations given with equation (5), under the assumption of steady-state values $\bar{w} = 6$, $\bar{g} = \bar{r} = .035$.

In assessing the impact of the social security system on private saving, it should be observed that θ is expected to diverge from one for a number of reasons (see also Williamson and Jones, 1983), among which are: (i) the presence of a bequest motive, (ii) the estimate of the social security wealth variable, w^s, which is gross of income taxes, (iii) the double counting between y and w^s implied by the standard definition of disposable income, and (iv) the possible perception of a risk of unsustainability of the social security system. In the light of the available evidence the first two effects are likely to cancel out. Moreover, the extent of the double counting (due to the fact that disposable income and social security wealth both include the pensions of current retirees and are net of social security contributions of individuals currently at work) can be roughly estimated to be on average less than 10 percent of social security wealth in the sample period. As a result, the estimated θ is likely to reflect mostly the household perception of future developments of the social security system, apart from unavoidable measurement errors. To evaluate the robustness of the results, the error correction model was re-estimated with social security wealth simply defined as the discounted sum of future gross benefits to the currently working population (thus ignoring the difference between the discounted sums of future benefits to current retirees and contributions by current workers). Results very close to those reported in Table 2.3 were obtained with, if anything, a slightly stronger effect of social security wealth on private consumption.

In the light of equation (5) and for $\bar{w} \simeq 6$ and , $\bar{g} = \bar{r} \simeq 0.035$,[35] the long-run coefficients reported in the upper panel of Table 2.4, along with the assumption $\theta \simeq 0.3$, imply a set of values for the underlying structural coefficients in line with the outcome of the simulations referred to in Modigliani and Brumberg (1980) and Ando and Modigliani (1963). These are reported in the lower panel of Table 2.4 and imply a response of the steady state saving rate to income growth of about 3.[36] Interestingly, they seem to suggest that the standard assumption by Modigliani and Ando ($\mu \simeq \alpha$; Ando 1974, fn. 4; Modigliani 1975, pp. 15-16) is not greatly at variance with the data.

In short, the error correction estimates have a plausible economic interpretation and appear to possess acceptable statistical properties. Comparison of LS and IV estimates further suggests that conditioning upon income does not lead to substantially different results (although at least one coefficient is not negligibly altered by the IV estimation).

Finally, to assess the relevance of Auerbach and Kotlikoff's (1983) assertion about the likely instability of aggregate time series relationships, we have carefully investigated the stability of the estimated model and inspected the sequence of one-step ahead residuals. The equation standard errors corresponding to the latter show little variation, in spite of the substantial changes in the series under observation. Inspection of similar evidence for the LS estimated coefficients based on the recursive estimator has provided further evidence of parameter constancy, with the partial and notable exception of the estimate of θ, which fluctuated around zero until the early seventies reflecting a negligible sample information, reached 0.2 by the early eighties and remained remarkably stable thereafter. Finally, the accuracy of the empirical model has also been evaluated by re-estimating it over the period 1954-1980 and computing *ex-post* forecasts for the remaining 10 years. Actual values turn out to lie well within the relevant confidence interval for predictions, as the predictive failure statistics show.

In the light of the above remarks, we now turn to the interpretation of recent trends in the Italian private saving rates on the basis of the equilibrium parameters derived from the IV estimates presented in Table 2.4. The upper panel of Table 2.4 makes it clear that looking at LS estimates would not change the results appreciably.

As can be seen from Table 2.5, the large increase of the private saving rate between the fifties and the sixties was mostly attributable to the declining non-human wealth-to-income ratio and hence to the unprecedented growth of the postwar Italian economy until 1962. At the same time, the contribution of social security wealth arising from the appearance of new pay-as-you-go pension schemes was far from negligible, exceeding one percentage point on average. In the subsequent period (between the sixties and the years following the first oil shock) rising housing prices, coupled with the productivity slowdown, produced an upward trend in the non-human wealth-to-income ratio, accounting for more than one half of the total fall in the steady-state saving rate. Almost two percentage points of the fall were due to the decline in the real interest rate. In the same period further structural changes in the social security system began to feed into consumption decisions, accounting for less than one percentage point of the overall reduction in the saving rate.

Table 2.5 Changes in the aggregate private saving rate and their determinants (changes between period averages; 1954-1990)

	1962-72	1973-79	1980-90	1980-90
	1954-61	1962-72	1972-79	1962-72
$\Delta (s/y)$	.059	−.036	−.036	−.072
$\Delta [-\ln (c/y)]$	.063	−.045	−.044	−.089
$\Delta [-\ln (\hat{c}/y)]$	.047	−.070	−.022	−.092
Contributions of:				
Δg	−.003	−.009	−.001	−.010
Δr	−.014	−.018	.035	.016
$\Delta (w^r/y)$	.079	−.035	−.036	−.072
— of which: financial assets	.006	.001	−.009	−.008
real assets	.073	−036	−.027	−.064
$\Delta (w^s/y)$	−.011	−.007	−.019	−.026

Note: Changes in the aggregate private saving rate are computed from period averages of ratios of actual saving figures to the net disposable income of the private sector adjusted for inflation; the logarithmic approximation used in the estimation involves a slight overestimation of the actual saving rate figures.

In the last decade (1980-1990) the rapid growth in private financial assets (mainly public debt) combined with the rise in housing prices, but the negative effect on private saving of the rise of the non-human wealth to income ratio was almost entirely offset by the positive contribution of higher real interest rates. The "pension effect" coming from the growing imbalance of the national pension system, reflected in a further rise in the social security wealth to income ratio, accounted then for almost the entire estimated further fall in the steady state private saving rate. Finally, comparing the eighties with the sixties, more than a quarter (2.6 percentage points) of the total reduction in the saving rate appears to have been due to the rise in the social security wealth to income ratio.

4   Microeconomic evidence

The foregoing aggregate analysis has proposed that the rise in the pension expenditure to income ratio could have been responsible for a substantial part of the decrease in the private saving rate observed over the last twenty years. In this section we supplement the aggregate evidence with the insights provided by the simulation of a microeconometric model of consumers' behavior that allows for borrowing constraints.

In fact, a thorough assessment of the role of borrowing constraints is a key element in the evaluation of the impact of the social security system. If there are no constraints on net worth prior to the time of death this impact is fully summarised by the social security wealth variable (as in the aggregate equation estimated in Table 2.3, apart from the short-term elements of the error correction model). However, the presence of a social security system could make binding borrowing constraints other than the terminal one either more likely or, if already present, more severe. As a result, with fixed retirement age, the reduction in the capital stock induced by social security could be lower.

4.1   A model of consumers' behavior with varying planning horizons

The econometric model underlying the simulation exercise is described in the Maccan, Rossi and Visco's contribution to this volume, which offers a full account of the specification and estimation and of the underlying data set. The model is based on the theoretical results of Yaari (1965) and Blanchard (1985) and draws heavily on the recent work of Mariger (1986, 1987). In short, it is a structural life-cycle consumption model incorporating (endogenously determined) borrowing constraints in the form of a minimal level of net worth. In the model, rational agents attempt to maximize the expected utility derived from their household consumption over planning horizons that do not necessarily extend over the agent's (and his spouse's) lifetime. In fact, as long as borrowing constraints are binding, the household's lifetime ends up being subdivided into two or more distinct intervals, with the constraints only being binding in the final period of each interval.

The most notable implication of the model, estimated on the sample of households surveyed in the Bank of Italy Survey of Household Income and Wealth for the year 1987[37] and on which the baseline case for the simulation exercise rests, is that about one fourth of Italian consumers turn out to have planning horizons that do not extend over their entire future life span. In particular, 27.6 percent of the sampled households appear to be liquidity-constrained (that is, their planning horizon is unlikely to extend for more than a single period). Moreover, liquidity constraints appear mainly to affect households whose heads are 30- to 40-years-old and that are located in Southern Italy and the Islands (Sicily and Sardinia).

The microeconometric model then lends itself quite naturally to the study of the phenomena described in Section 2 and analyzed, at the aggregate level, in Section 3. The presence of widespread borrowing constraints leaves room for substantial distributional effects of government policy. At the same time, the large proportion of "life-cycle planners" suggests that the influence of structural changes in the social security system, by affecting the time path of life-cycle non-interest income, could be far from negligible.

4.2   Simulating the social security reforms of the seventies

The features of the estimated structural consumption model can therefore be used to assess to what extent the structural change in the social security system in the late sixties and early seventies contributed to the subsequent fall in the private saving rate. In designing the simulation experiment we cannot hope to incorporate all the numerous changes in laws and regulations that were introduced at that time and which are reviewed, *inter alia*, in Franco and Morcaldo (1990) and Franco (1992). The simulation experiment therefore focuses on three main changes to retirement provisions that were adopted in the period in question: (i) the introduction in the late sixties of special schemes for self-employed farmers and other self-employed businessmen (mainly shopkeepers and the like), (ii) the indexation from 1975 onwards of pensions to minimum contractual wages in industry and hence to productivity growth, as well as to inflation, and (iii) the rise in above-minimum pensions due to the increase in their reference base from 65 percent of pensionable earnings in 1968 to 80 percent in 1976. Given the estimated 1987 preference parameter vector, the micro-econometric model is asked to generate a consumption time path for all the households in the sample, restoring the pension system prevailing in the sixties and still allowing for a net worth constraint.[38]

In assessing the design of the simulation experiment, note that, as in the aggregate equation estimated in Section 3, the micro model is estimated under the assumption that social security wealth is to an extent indistinguishable from other forms of wealth in its effect on consumption. However, in contrast with the aggregate exercise, in the present case θ is not affected by the double counting implied by the standard definition of disposable income. Therefore, fixing θ equal to 0.3 might imply an underestimation of the replacement rate. Furthermore, in the estimated micro model the possibility of future disability pensions and old-age pensions for persons over 65 lacking adequate means of support is neglected. As a conservative choice, θ was therefore set equal to 0.5 to account for all the differences in the specification of the model and in the definition of the relevant variables. Finally, it should be borne in mind that the design of the experiment is such that it does not reallocate resources over the life cycle, but simply re-establishes the original non-interest income profile for the final phase of the life cycle.

Simulating the microeconometric model, households' aggregate average propensity to consume net disposable income would have been 2.7 percentage points lower under the laws and regulations in force in the sixties (the equivalent of 2.4 percent of the private sector's net disposable income):[39] a result remarkably similar to the outcome of the aggregate time series exercise. This lower propensity is rather uniformly distributed by region of residence, head's age and length of the planning horizon. Interestingly, the evidence indicates that by tilting the non-interest income profile upward the social security reforms actually exacerbated borrowing constraints, thereby partly counteracting the depressive effect on the saving rate of a steeper income profile over the remaining life span.

To sum up, the microeconomic simulation exercise lends further support to the hypothesis proposed earlier and suggests that changes in retirement provisions could well have been responsible for a substantial part of the fall in the private saving rate since the mid-seventies.

4.3 Looking ahead: reforming the social security system

Sections 3 and 4 have provided independent evidence of the substantial impact of the Italian pension system on the aggregate saving rate and, in particular, of the importance of changes in retirement provisions. As Franco and Morcaldo (1990) have stressed, those changes have made Italy the western country with the highest pensions expenditure to GDP ratio. It is widely recognized that, in the absence of corrective measures, this expenditure will continue to grow in the coming decades as a result of demographic factors and the maturation of pension plans. It comes as no surprise, therefore, that in recent years Italy's pension system has been the subject of lively discussion centring on the future pattern of expenditure and appropriate legislative changes. It thus appears fruitful to exploit the analytical device used in Section 4.1 to assess the likely impact of one such reform on the aggregate saving rate.

The objectives of a structural reform of the Italian social security system have been clearly stated in Franco and Morcaldo (1990, pp. 154-156) and Morcaldo (1992) and are explicitly incorporated in the recent Government measures aimed at halting the rapid growth in outlays on pensions. These measures modify some of the main eligibility requirements by raising the retirement age by five years (to 65 years for male and 60 for female workers) and extending the period for calculating pensionable earnings. Furthermore, the indexation to minimum contractual wages is to be replaced by indexation to prices only. In short, two offsetting effects are at work: on the one hand, the higher retirement age tends to reduce the need for saving, while, on the other, the extension of the computation period and, more generally, all cuts in average retirement benefits imply an increased need for saving.

It is thus worth reporting the outcome of a simulation experiment designed to evaluate the impact of these changes on the aggregate saving rate and on the behavioral distribution of consumers.[40] The main results suggest that the households' aggregate propensity to save could decline by as much as two percentage points after the reform owing mainly to the higher retirement age (whose impact on the aggregate propensity to save is sizable and negative) and the return to a simple price-based indexation mechanism (working in the opposite direction). However, since the simulation exercise neglects the impact on younger workers of the extension of the computation period to cover their entire working life, the above result is likely to overestimate the effect of the reform plan on the aggregate propensity to consume of households, which may therefore be expected to remain basically unchanged. The national saving rate, however, would be obviously raised by a significant reduction of current social security imbalances.

5 Conclusion

The central proposition of this paper is that the changes in Italy's social security provisions in the late sixties and early seventies weakened the link between contributions and benefits, allowing a time path of aggregate consumption in excess of what would have occurred in the absence of such changes. The measures adopted entailed both a replacement effect, due to the introduction of an unfunded social security system for specific segments of the population, and a lifetime wealth increment.

The combined evidence emerging from aggregate time series and survey data provide a rather clear-cut picture, indicating that net government transfers substantially contributed to the decline in private saving in the course of the seventies and the eighties. One third (or about 2.5 percentage points) of the decline in private saving in relation to net private disposable income since the sixties may be attributed to the rise in the ratio of net social security wealth to income. Even if the pension system were restored to a flow equilibrium and the negative effect on the private saving rate completely offset, the new steady state of the economy would be characterized by appreciably lower capital intensity (although, partial equilibrium results, such as those reported above, may tend to overestimate the extent of the steady state changes). As shown by the aggregate estimates, it should be finally observed that the major role in the evolution of the private saving rate was played by the changes in the net non-human real and financial wealth to income ratio, substantially affected, in turn, by the growth path experienced by the Italian economy.

APPENDIX

Do households pierce any veil?

The empirical exercise conducted in Section 3 assumes that (i) households' behavior is not affected by the division of corporate earnings between cash distributions and retentions, and (ii) consumption is not determined as a function of dynastic resources. Hence, while households pierce the corporate veil, they do not pierce the government veil. A formal test of both propositions involving the long-run solution of the equation estimated in Table 2.3 requires, in the present setting, the use of non-nested testing procedures, since the models corresponding to the different competing hypotheses cannot be obtained one from the other by means of parametric restrictions. In particular, (i) all variables appearing as ratios to net private disposable income in the estimated equation have to be redefined in terms of net household disposable income and net national disposable income (net of government consumption), and (ii) the wealth variables have to be redefined accordingly (respectively as household or national wealth). Moreover, it should be kept in mind that in a Ricardian world the net social security wealth variable would be expected to carry a zero coefficient: the main response to more social security would be a shifting of private transfers by an amount sufficient to restore the previously chosen balance of income across generations.

Table 2.A1 Non-nested testing procedures
(sample: 1954-1990)

Test procedure	Temporarily null hypothesis	
	"private"	"household"
Variance encompassing tests:		
N–test [N(0,1)]	−1.908	−3.210
NT–test [N(0,1)]	−1.588	−2.696
W–test [N(0,1)]	−1.396	−2.188
J–test [N(0,1)]	−1.508	2.409
JA–test [N(0,1)]	−1.459	2.261
Parameter encompassing test:		
F(6,23)	2.331	3.355
Akaike Information Criterion: 2.086 (in favor of the "private" concept)		
	"private"	"national"
Variance encompassing tests:		
N–test [N(0,1)]	−1.307	−3.809
NT–test [N(0,1)]	−1.001	−2.826
W–test [N(0,1)]	−.935	−2.271
J–test [N(0,1)]	1.108	3.075
JA–test [N(0,1)]	.985	2.210
Parameter encompassing test:		
F(6,23)	.826	3.560
Akaike Information Criterion: 3.458 (in favor of the "private" concept)		

Table 2.A1 reports a model discrimination criterion (known as the Akaike Information Criterion) and a number of non-nested testing procedures designed to evaluate (i) the model incorporating the "private" as opposed to the "household" concept of income and wealth, and (ii) the former against the "national" concept of income and wealth.

If the emphasis were on goodness of fit (allowing for parsimony), the model embedding a "private" notion of income and wealth would definitely be the preferred one. In the present case, however, the interest lies in model specification – that is, in the ability of a model (temporarily declared to be the maintained hypothesis) to predict the performance of the alternative. As such, non-nested testing procedures are often interpreted as model specification tests, as the (temporarily) alternative model is used as a guide in testing the specification of the (temporarily) "true" model. Notice that the nature of non-nested testing procedures, which are mainly directed toward detecting misspecification, does not prevent their use in a model discrimination setting: in this case, however, one of the two models can be accepted or both can be accepted or rejected.

Mizon and Richard (1986) have characterized the whole set of non-nested tests as "variance encompassing" (such as the test procedures labelled N, NT, W, J and JA) or "parameter encompassing" (such as the F-test). The first set of procedures can be shown to be asymptotically equivalent. They differ, however, in their small sample behavior: in a dynamic setting (characterized by a similar number of regressors in the competing models) the W and JA tests show an acceptable performance. In the present case, for customary significance levels, all test procedures suggest that the model incorporating a "private" concept of income and wealth variance encompasses both the "household" version and the "national" one.

Finally, encompassing with respect to the structural parameters provides additional insights on the nature of the model misspecification. In this respect, Table 2.A1 suggests that the model allowing households to pierce the corporate but not the government veil is again the preferred one.

NOTES

* We would like to thank Albert Ando, Onorato Castellino, Daniele Franco, Luigi Guiso, Marco Pagano, Luigi Spaventa and Daniele Terlizzese for their most helpful comments and criticisms, Luca Beltrametti for his contribution in the estimation of social security wealth, and Giampaolo Lopez, Livio Maccan and Renato Serafini for their help in handling the data. Nicola Rossi gratefully acknowledges partial financial support from the Italian National Research Council (CNR). The usual disclaimer applies.

1 In relation to net private disposable income, the average private saving rate was around 16 percent in the second half of the eighties, some 8 percentage points lower than in the sixties.

2 In addition to the papers in Fornero and Castellino (1990) and Jappelli (1991), the interested reader is referred to Modigliani (1990) and Guiso, Jappelli and Terlizzese (1994).

3 The debate has focused chiefly on the so-called Ricardian equivalence proposition. On one side, Modigliani and Jappelli (1987, 1993) and Modigliani, Jappelli and Pagano (1985, 1989) have forcefully argued against the relevance of that proposition for the Italian economy. On the other, Onofri (1987) and Nicoletti (1988) have suggested that substantial tax discounting could actually

have been effective in the seventies and eighties. Nicoletti (1990) has attempted to discriminate between short-run and long-run tax discounting. Finally, Rossi (1989) and Gambetta and Orsi (1991) have warned against the straightforward use of aggregate data to discriminate among competing hypotheses such as those referred to above. The Appendix to the present paper provides fresh evidence relating to the issue.

4   The classic reference is Hicks (1939). For evidence on the Italian case, see Banca d'Italia (1986) and references therein.

5   In assessing the evolution of government current account balances, note that the line between current and capital government expenditure is far from clear-cut. In Italy part of the latter might actually be disguised subsidies to publicly owned enterprises.

6   The national accounts currently employ a definition of "private sector" that comprises households (both "pure", i.e. consumer households, and producer households) and financial and non-financial enterprises. For simplicity, we define the "corporate" sector as including all the above except consumer households.

7   In this and the other figures, all variables are expressed as ratios to the net national disposable income.

8   Tax rates were periodically revised to account for price increases, but this only prevented a more pronounced growth in the *ex-post* average rate of personal income taxation. From 1989 to 1991 tax rates have been indexed to the general price level.

9   Franco and Morcaldo (1990), p. 105.

10   Franco (1992) reviews the postwar evolution of government transfers in Italy and provides a detailed account of their determinants.

11   This was the consequence of the gradual disinflation that followed the second oil shock of 1979 and, in contributing to the inflation tax, more than offset the large simultaneous growth of the Italian public debt. On the disinflation, see Gressani, Guiso and Visco (1988). See, also, Giavazzi and Spaventa (1989), where the role of the inflation tax in financing part of the rise in net government transfers is properly identified.

12   The government saving figures shown in Figure 2.12 do not exactly match those in Figure 2.3 owing to minor sundry items.

13   In what follows endogenous government behavior (as, for example, in Bohn 1992) is disregarded, as in practically all the literature on Ricardian equivalence.

14   If the retirement age is not fixed, the effect in question may be partly offset by induced early retirements.

15   It is implicitly assumed here that the increase in transfer payments is perceived as sustainable by the agents. This cautionary note strongly applies to the Italian case, where the inherent risk of unsustainability of the social security system is now widely recognized.

16   This would not necessarily be the end of the story. If returns on pension wealth (a non-marketable asset) and on the public debt positively covariate, an increase in

pension wealth might push up the rate of return on the public debt and hence on interest payments, adding to government current account imbalances (see Giraldi, Hamaui and Rossi 1992).

17 The national accounts include public health care expenditure in government transfers.

18 This would naturally be the case of health care programmes if we could assume (rather unrealistically, in the Italian case) that the efficiency of publicly provided health services paralleled that of private health institutions.

19 See the pioneering work of Feldstein (1974) and Barro (1974).

20 Aggregate but inconclusive time series evidence is reported in Modigliani and Sterling (1983). Brugiavini (1991) exploits cross-section evidence on private net worth accumulation to conclude that unfunded social security reduces household wealth accumulation by a much smaller amount than predicted by the life-cycle model. Notice, however, that cross-section tests are not without pitfalls (see Auerbach and Kotlikoff, 1983).

21 For earlier applications of the life-cycle saving hypothesis to the Italian experience, see Modigliani and Tarantelli (1975) and Frasca et al. (1979).

22 Among these, possibly the least restrictive concerns the income time path, which could be allowed to grow around a trend line as long as departures are not very long lasting.

23 All estimates reported in this section and in the Appendix were obtained using Microfit 3.0 (Version 386, see Pesaran and Pesaran 1991, where specific references for test statistics are also reported).

24 The empirical exercise conducted in this section therefore assumes that households pierce the corporate veil but not the government veil. Evidence regarding this set of assumptions is presented in the Appendix.

25 Notice, incidentally, that while the saving ratio is a bounded variable (at least from above), $(\ln c/y)$ is not.

26 Unweighted average of semi-annual observations; see Visco (1984).

27 Aggregate estimates of social security wealth in Italy have been computed by Castellino (1985) for the year 1983, Brugiavini (1991) for the year 1984 and Beltrametti (1988), for a specific social security programme, for the period 1959-1983.

28 The reconstruction was performed by Luca Beltrametti (see Appendix B to Rossi and Visco, 1992; see also the Statistical Appendix to this volume).

29 Although quite similar, the maximum likelihood estimates of the cointegration vector do not match the estimated coefficients of the corresponding static Engle-Granger regression, thereby signaling the small sample bias of the latter estimates.

30 As Banerjee et al. (1986) suggest, this test can be more powerful than the unit root test on the cointegration regression since the estimation of the error correction model allows a much richer short-term dynamics. They also show that in finite samples the static estimator of the cointegrating vector can be badly biased towards zero relative to the corresponding estimator in the error correction model.

31 Besides the predetermined variables present in the equation, and $\Delta \ln z_t$, the list of instruments includes $\ln x_{t-1}$, $\ln(c/y)_{t-2}$, $(w^r/y)_{t-2}$ and $(w^s/y)_{t-2}$.

32 It should be recalled that the approximation $s/y \simeq -\ln(c/y)$ and the steady-state assumption $\Delta \ln c = \Delta \ln y = \Delta \ln x = \Delta \ln z = g$ have been used here.

33 The replacement rate turns out to be three times the one suggested in Brugiavini (1991).

34 The latter is implied by the figures for social security wealth and non-human wealth for 1990: 5,500 and 6,000 trillion lire respectively. Notice, however, that partial equilibrium computations are known to overstate the impact of a pay-as-you-go scheme substantially. See Kotlikoff (1979).

35 That is, for steady-state values inherently consistent with the linearization given in equation (5) and the corresponding coefficient estimates.

36 Or 3.124 for the LS and 3.529 for the IV estimates, with asymptotic standard errors of 0.250 and 0.401, respectively.

37 A detailed description of the structure of the survey is presented in the Methodological Appendix to this volume.

38 We therefore assume that preference parameters (including household equivalence scales) are invariant with respect to the policy changes mentioned.

39 It is worth recalling that the latter variable is used in the macroeconometric exercise, whereas the microeconometric exercise is based on households' income.

40 The simulation also accounts for the increases in employees' social security contributions since 1987, including those envisaged by the most recent legislation.

REFERENCES

Ando, A. (1974). 'Some Aspects of Stabilization Policies, the Monetarist Controversy, and the MPS Model', *International Economic Review* **15**: 541-71.

Ando, A. and F. Modigliani (1963). 'The 'Life Cycle' Hypothesis of Saving: Aggregate Implications and Tests', *American Economic Review* **53**: 55-84.

Auerbach, A.J. and L.J. Kotlikoff (1983). 'An Examination of Empirical Tests of Social Security and Saving', in E. Helpman, A. Razin and E. Sadka (eds.), *Social Policy Evaluation: An Economic Perspective*, New York: Academic Press.

Banca d'Italia (1986). 'Modello trimestrale dell'economia italiana', Temi di discussione 80.

Banerjee, A., J.J. Dolado, D.F. Hendry and G.W. Smith (1986). 'Exploring Relationships in Economics through Static Models: Some Monte Carlo Evidence', *Oxford Bulletin of Economics and Statistics* **48**: 253-77.

Barro, R.J. (1974). 'Are Government Bonds Net Wealth?', *Journal of Political Economy* **82**: 1095-118.

Beltrametti, L. (1988). 'Stima della ricchezza da sicurezza sociale per il fondo pensioni lavoratori dipendenti', *Rivista internazionale di scienze sociali* **96**: 23-44.

Blanchard, O.J. (1985). 'Debts, Deficits and Finite Horizons', *Journal of Political Economy* **93**: 1045-76.

Bohn, H. (1992). 'Endogenous Government Spending and Ricardian Equivalence', *Economic Journal* **102**: 588-97.

Brugiavini, A. (1991). 'Effetti delle pensioni sul risparmio nella teoria del ciclo vitale', in Jappelli (1991).

Castellino, O. (1985). 'C'è un secondo debito pubblico (più grande del primo)?', *Moneta e credito* **38**: 21-30.

Engle, R.F. and C.W. Granger (1987). 'Co-Integration and Error Correction Representation, Estimation and Testing', *Econometrica* **55**: 255-76.

Feldstein, M. (1974). 'Social Security, Induced Retirement, and Aggregate Accumulation', *Journal of Political Economy* **82**: 905-26.

Feldstein, M. (1976). 'Social Security and Saving: The Extended Life Cycle Theory', *American Economic Review* **66**: 77-87.

Fornero, E. and O. Castellino (eds.) (1990). *Formazione e impiego della ricchezza delle famiglie*, Torino: Fondazione Giorgio Rota.

Franco, D. (1992). 'L'espansione della spesa pubblica in Italia (1960-90)', in Ente Einaudi, *Il disavanzo pubblico in Italia: natura strutturale e politiche di rientro*, Bologna: Il Mulino, Vol. I.

Franco, D. and G. Morcaldo (1990). 'The Italian Pension System: Development and Effects on Income Distribution and Poverty', *Labour* **4**: 105-24 and 133-59.

Frasca, F., E. Tarantelli, C. Tresoldi and I. Visco (1979). 'La funzione del consumo: analisi su serie trimestrali e su dati cross-section', in F. Frasca, N. Rossi, E. Tarantelli, C. Tresoldi and I. Visco, *La funzione del consumo in Italia*, Banca d'Italia, Modello econometrico dell'economia italiana (M2BI), Roma.

Gambetta, G. and R. Orsi (1991). 'Formulazione empirica di ipotesi teoriche e loro valutazione econometrica', in M. Faliva (ed.), *Il ruolo dell'econometria nell'ambito delle scienze economiche*, Bologna: Il Mulino.

Giavazzi, F. and L. Spaventa (1989). 'Italy: The Real Effects of Inflation and Disinflation', *Economic Policy* **8**: 133-71.

Giraldi, C., R. Hamaui and N. Rossi (1992). 'Vincoli istituzionali e differenziali di rendimento delle attività finanziarie', in *Ricerche applicate e modelli per la politica economica*, Roma: Banca d'Italia, Vol. I.

Gressani, D., L. Guiso and I. Visco (1988). 'Disinflation in Italy: An Analysis with the Econometric Model of the Bank of Italy', *Journal of Policy Modeling* **10**: 163-203.

Guiso, L., T. Jappelli and D. Terlizzese (1994). 'Why Is Italy's Saving Rate so High?', *this volume*.

Hicks, J. (1939). *Value and Capital*, London: Clarendon Press.

Jappelli, T. (ed.) (1991). *Bilancio pubblico e risparmio privato*, Milano: Angeli.

Johansen, S. (1988). 'Statistical Analysis of Cointegrating Vectors', *Journal of Economic Dynamics and Control* **12**: 231-54.

Kotlikoff, L.J. (1979). 'Social Security and Equilibrium Capital Intensity', *Quarterly Journal of Economics* **43**: 233-54.

Maccan, L., N. Rossi and I. Visco (1994). 'Saving and Borrowing Constraints', *this volume*.

Mariger, R. (1986). *Consumption Behavior and the Effects of Government Fiscal Policies*, Cambridge, MA: Harvard University Press.

Mariger, R. (1987). 'A Life-Cycle Consumption Model with Liquidity Constraints: Theory and Empirical Results', *Econometrica* **55**: 533-57.

Marotta, G. and P. Pagliano (1992). 'Income Accounts by Institutional Sectors: 1970 to 1979 Estimates', in *Income and Saving in Italy: A Reconstruction*, Temi di discussione 169, Banca d'Italia.

Mizon, G.E. and J.-F. Richard (1986). 'The Encompassing Principle and Its Application to Testing Non-nested Hypotheses', *Econometrica* **54**: 657-78.

Modigliani, F. (1975). 'The Life Cycle Hypothesis of Saving Twenty Years Later', in M. Parkin (ed.), *Contemporary Issues in Economics*, Manchester: Manchester University Press.

Modigliani, F. (1986). 'Life Cycle, Individual Thrift and the Wealth of Nations', *American Economic Review* **76**: 297-313.

Modigliani, F. (1990). 'Recent Declines in the Saving Rate: A Life Cycle Perspective', *Rivista di politica economica* **80** (English version): 5-42. (Also in M. Baldassari, L. Paganetto and E.S. Phelps, *World Saving, Prosperity and Growth*, New York: St. Martin's Press, 1993.)

Modigliani, F. and R. Brumberg (1980). 'Utility Analysis and Aggregate Consumption Functions: An Attempt at Integration', in A. Abel (ed.), *The Collected Papers of Franco Modigliani*, Cambridge, MA: MIT Press, Vol. II.

Modigliani, F. and T. Jappelli (1987). 'Fiscal Policy and Saving in Italy since 1860', in M. Boskin, J. Flemming and S. Gorini (eds.), *Private Saving and Public Debt*, Oxford: Basil Blackwell.

Modigliani, F. and T. Jappelli (1993). 'Why Has the Italian National Saving Rate Declined?', in S. Biasco, A. Roncaglia and M. Salvati (eds.), *Market and Institutions in Economic Development*, London: Macmillan.

Modigliani, F., T. Jappelli and M. Pagano (1985). 'The Impact of Fiscal Policy and Inflation on National Saving: The Italian Case', *Banca Nazionale del Lavoro Quarterly Review* **38**: 91-126.

Modigliani, F., T. Jappelli and M. Pagano (1989). 'The Impact of Fiscal Policy and Inflation on National Saving: A Reply', *Banca Nazionale del Lavoro Quarterly Review* **42**: 239-44.

Modigliani, F. and A. Sterling (1983). 'Determinants of Private Saving with Special Reference to the Role of Social Security. Cross-Country Tests', in F. Modigliani and R. Hemming (eds.), *The Determinants of National Saving and Wealth*, London: Macmillan.

Modigliani, F. and E. Tarantelli (1975). 'The Consumption Function in a Developing Economy and the Italian Experience', *American Economic Review* **65**: 825-42.

Morcaldo, G. (1992). La riforma del settore previdenziale', *Oggi Domani Anziani* **5**: 15-32.

Nicoletti, G. (1988). 'A Cross-Country Analysis of Private Consumption, Inflation and the 'Debt Neutrality Hypothesis'', *OECD Economic Studies* **11**: 43-87.

Nicoletti, G. (1990). 'Consumption and Government Debt in High Deficit Countries: Is Tax Discounting Stable Over Time?', Document de Travail 90-09, OFCE.

Onofri, P. (1987). 'Analisi empirica delle relazioni fra consumo e debito pubblico in Italia (1970-1984)', in *Ricerche quantitative e basi statistiche per la politica economica*, Roma: Banca d'Italia, Vol. II.

Pagliano, P. and N. Rossi (1992). 'The Italian Saving Rate: 1951 to 1990 Estimates', in *Income and Saving in Italy: A Reconstruction*, Temi di discussione 169, Banca d'Italia.

Pesaran, M.H. and B. Pesaran (1991). *MICROFIT 3.0. An Interactive Econometric Software Package*, Oxford: Oxford University Press.

Romer, D. (1988). 'What Are the Costs of Excessive Deficits?', in S. Fischer (ed.), *NBER Macroeconomics Annual 1988*, Cambridge, MA: MIT Press.

Rossi, N. (1989). 'The Impact of Fiscal Policy and Inflation on National Saving: A Comment', *Banca Nazionale del Lavoro Quarterly Review* **42**: 224-38.

Rossi, N. (1991). 'Spesa pubblica, tasso di interesse reale e risparmio delle famiglie', in Jappelli (1991).

Rossi, N. and I. Visco (1992). 'Private Saving and Government Deficit in Italy (1951-1990)', Temi di discussione 178, Banca d'Italia.

Visco, I. (1984). *Price Expectations in Rising Inflation*, Amsterdam: North-Holland.

Wilcox, D.W. (1989). 'Social Security Benefits, Consumption Expenditure, and the Life Cycle Hypothesis', *Journal of Political Economy* **97**: 288-304.

Williamson, S.H. and W.J. Jones (1983). 'Computing the Impact of Social Security Using the Life Cycle Consumption Function', *American Economic Review* **73**: 1036-52.

Yaari, M.E. (1965). 'Uncertain Lifetime, Life Insurance, and the Theory of the Consumer', *Review of Economic Studies* **32**: 137-50.

3 Do demographic changes explain the decline in the saving rate of Italian households?

LUIGI CANNARI

1 Introduction

The 1980s witnessed a worrying decline in the propensity to save of Italian households; official estimates report[1] a decrease in the personal saving rate of more than 4 percentage points in the last decade (from 20.6 in 1979-1981 to 16.3 per cent in 1989-1990). Several causal factors might, theoretically, have been at work. Some of them have been thoroughly investigated; Rossi and Visco (1994), for instance, emphasize the role of social security, while Guiso, Jappelli and Terlizzese (1994) examine the interaction between growth and capital market imperfections in order to understand the pattern of Italian saving. In this paper I focus on the effects of demographic changes.

Saving rates may differ across households because of differences in family composition. For example, the cost of providing for children may have a significant impact on consumption needs; household size may affect the propensity to save, as larger households may benefit from economies of scale in consumption. Moreover, according to the life-cycle theory, the propensity to consume should vary over the lifetime, being low before retirement and increasing thereafter. Therefore, changes in the structure of the population might be expected to help explain the decline in the saving rate.

Several studies examine the effects on saving of demographic changes. Davies (1988) explores the consequences of incorporating family size in life-cycle models. His analysis leads to the conclusion that increasing family size reduces aggregate saving. Cutler et al. (1990) argue that the decline in the U.S. private saving rate from an average above 7 percent during the 1970s to about 3 percent during 1986-89 is greater than their analysis suggests can be justified by demographic factors. Avery and Kennickell (1991) use data from the Survey of Consumer Finances for 1983 and 1986 to examine the saving behavior of U.S. households. Using several models, they are able to explain only about 7 percent of the variation in the level of saving. Demographic factors do not appear to be very significant explanatory variables.

Auerbach and Kotlikoff (1991) start from the assumption that relative consumption and income profiles remain constant over time and measure the variations in saving due to changes in the age structure of the population. Their research suggests that the drop in U.S. national saving in the 1980s reflects a change in consumer behavior rather than demographic changes. This conclusion is also reached by Bosworth, Burtless and Sabelhaus (1991); they decompose changes in the overall saving rate of U.S. households into changes in saving rates within age groups, in the age distribution of households, and in relative incomes, and show the trivial contribution of demographic factors to saving trends.

Jappelli and Rossi (1989) apply a similar method to Italian data. Using the 1986 Bank of Italy Survey of Household Income and Wealth, they estimate the average propensity to save for different age groups. They then estimate the overall average propensity, using the age distribution of the population drawn from census data over several decades while maintaining constant (at 1986 values) the intra-group propensities to save. They find a small but not negligible effect on saving of the change in the age structure of the population.

In Italy the past decade has witnessed significant demographic changes, involving not only the distribution of the population by age, but also the average size of households and their distribution by number of children. The decline in the population share of young individuals and the corresponding increase in that of the elderly, prompted by a dramatic drop in the birth-rate, was accompanied by a sharp reduction in the share of large households (five or more members) and an increase in the share of unattached individuals and households without children.

The effects of these changes are taken into account in this paper. Following Bosworth *et al.* (1991), I assess the importance of demographic factors using two different cross-sections. Three demographic variables are considered: the age of the household head, the household size and the number of children.

The main conclusion is that demographic change has not been the main determinant of the decline in the Italian saving rate. Demographic variables can at best account for only a small part of the decline in the saving rate. Rather, the decline is common to most population groups and is not sensitive to the demographic criteria used to classify the sample. Saving rates fell across the board, whether households were classified by age-group, family size, number and age of children or number of women working. When they are classified by permanent income, however, significant differences do emerge: those in the top two quintiles (40 percent of the population, with about 60 percent of income) substantially reduced their saving rate, while those in the bottom two quintiles showed only a minor change in average propensity to save. These data thus suggest that the overall decline in the saving rate is mainly attributable to the most affluent part of the population; household behavior seems to have changed only for higher income classes.

The paper is organized as follows. Section 2 describes the survey data; Section 3 details the main demographic changes that took place in the 1980s; Section 4 shows the effect of demographic changes on the decline in the saving rate; Section 5 compares the average propensity to consume in different periods (1980-1982 and 1987-1989); and Section 6 offers some concluding observations.

2   Household Survey Data

The data used in this paper are drawn from the Survey of Italian Household Income and Wealth (SHIW) conducted by the Bank of Italy. The survey is based on a two-stage stratified sample of about 8,000 households randomly selected from the General Registry Office's lists.[2] Data on social and demographic characteristics of household members, wages and salaries, self-employment income, pensions and other transfers and rents are collected on an individual basis. Interest and dividends refer to the household as a whole.

Over the years the survey has undergone several changes, and some adjustments have been necessary to ensure comparability. Specifically, sampling weights have been modified in order to remove the bias produced by the 1980-1983 sample design, which implied an oversampling of larger households. Appendix A gives the details of these adjustments.

3   Demographic changes in the eighties

Life expectancy has been rising for many years, reaching the remarkable figure of 79.2 years for women and of 72.6 for men in 1987. In the period 1981-1987 it increased by 1.6 and 1.5 years respectively for men and women.

The lengthening of life expectancy contributed to the increase in the population share of elderly individuals. The share of persons aged 65 or over rose by 1.3 percentage points, from 13.2 percent in 1980 to 14.5 percent in 1989. In the eighties, Italy was one of the "oldest" countries in the world: few countries showed a higher share of the elderly.[3]

The overall fertility rate declined from 1.58 in 1981 to 1.31 in 1987, a level that only a few years ago would have been thought outlandish. The birth-rate dropped by 0.16 percentage points in the last decade. In 1987 it was less than the corresponding figures for France, Germany and the United Kingdom (Golini, 1988).

The fall in the fertility rate seems to be related to the decline in the marriage rate and to an increase in the mean age at marriage and at child-bearing. It is not only social and economic factors (unemployment, a tax system lacking incentives for procreation, the legalization of abortion) that may explain the drop in the fertility rate. It is probable that the change is mainly due to cultural factors, such as the new role of women in Italian society, as shown by the remarkable 10-point increase in the female labor force participation rate in the last decade.

On account of these factors the incidence of children under 15 declined sharply (from 22.0 percent in 1980 to 16.7 in 1989). In just a decade the ratio of the elderly to the young population rose from 60 to 87 percent (Table 3.1).

Table 3.1 Age structure of the Italian population, 1980-89
(percentages)

	Age			Birth rate (per 1,000)	Marriage rate (per 1,000)
	0 – 14	15 – 64	65 and over		
1980	22.0	64.8	13.2	11.3	5.7
1982	20.7	65.8	13.5	10.9	5.5
1984	19.6	67.3	13.1	10.3	5.2
1986	18.4	68.2	13.4	9.7	5.2
1987	17.8	68.5	13.7	9.6	5.3
1988	17.2	68.7	14.1	9.9	5.5
1989	16.7	68.8	14.5	9.7	5.4

Sources: Relazione generale sulla situazione economica del paese, volume III, Istituto Poligrafico dello Stato, Roma, 1990, and Istat, Annuario statistico italiano, various years.

The dramatic reduction of fertility and the increase in life expectancy brought about a striking change in family structure, as shown in Table 3.2. There was a pronounced decline in the share of larger households (5 or more members) from 16.2 to 11.3 per cent and a simultaneous rise in the share of single-person households. The average household size shrank from 3.2 to 3.0; the share of households with elderly heads (aged 65 or over) rose from 19.4 to 21.4. Households with one, two, and three or more children declined by 3.9, 2.4 and 0.7 percentage points respectively.

Table 3.2 Distribution of households by selected demographic characteristics (percentages)

Characteristics	Years	
	1980	1989
Age of head		
30 or under	7.4	7.6
31 – 40	18.4	17.5
41 – 50	22.6	23.1
51 – 64	32.2	30.4
65 or over	19.4	21.4
Number of children (a)		
none	65.2	72.2
1	19.9	16.0
2	11.9	9.5
3 or more	3.0	2.3
Household size		
1 member	10.5	15.4
2 members	24.3	23.9
3 members	26.1	24.6
4 members	22.9	24.8
5 members or more	16.2	11.3
All households	100.0	100.0

Source: Bank of Italy Survey of Household Income and Wealth.
(a) Aged 13 or under.

These demographic changes have aroused considerable anxiety in Italy. Economic concerns have focused on the burden that an aging population will place on the economy. The social security system provides very substantial coverage, and the growing elderly population implies that the burden of dependency will increase: fewer workers will bear the cost of providing for a larger number of individuals no longer able to support themselves. Moreover, according to the life-cycle theory, the propensity to consume should increase following retirement. Thus, a growing elderly population might be expected to bring about a drop in the average saving rate.

The concern is compounded when one considers the fairly strong inertia characterizing demographic changes. On the basis of long-term population projections, the share of persons aged 65 and over is expected to increase from 14.5 per cent in 1989 to 20.1 in 2008, and to 25.7 percent in 2028 (CNR and IRP, 1988).

Although long-term projections may not be perfectly accurate, rising life expectancies and an increase in the population share of the elderly appear to be certain. If changes in the age structure of the population and/or other demographic changes can explain a significant part of the past drop in the average propensity to save, a considerable reduction in the saving rate should be expected in the future as well.

4   How much have demographic changes contributed to the decline in the saving rate of Italian households?

Changes in the age structure of the population can affect the aggregate saving rate through the life-cycle aggregation effect: for example, a decline in the rate of population growth should contribute to a decline in the overall saving rate even if there has been no change in the individuals' propensities to save, because a slowdown in population growth determines an increase in the share of pensioners, whose propensity to consume is greater than that of the working population.

More generally, changes in the distribution of the population by different characteristics, such as household size or number of children, can modify the overall average propensity to consume. This aggregation effect can occur because of the variation in the relative incidence of the population subgroups, each with its specific propensity to save.

Following Bosworth *et al.* (1991), the importance of demographic changes in explaining the decline in the saving rate can be assessed using two different cross-sections. In a given year t the sample is divided into G_h groups according to a classificatory variable h (the age of the household head, the household size or the number of children). The economy-wide propensity to consume is expressed as:

$$C_t = \sum_{i=1}^{G_h} w_{it}^h \, y_{it}^h \, c_{it}^h \tag{1}$$

where (omitting the h index for simplicity):
C_t = aggregate propensity to consume at time t
w_{it} = proportion of households in the i-th group at time t
y_{it} = ratio of average income in the i-th group to the overall average at time t
c_{it} = average propensity to consume of the i-th group at time t
G = number of groups.

Equation (1) shows that the aggregate propensity to consume depends on the relative weights of the population groups, on their income shares and on their specific propensities to consume.

The aggregate average propensity to consume is obviously independent of the classificatory variable used to split the sample; on the contrary, the weights of the cells and the average propensity to consume within each cell depend on the classificatory variable.

Other things being equal (the share of income, y_{it}, and the average propensity to consume, c_{it}), an increase in the relative weight of households with a high propensity to consume increases the aggregate propensity. By the same token, if the income share going to households with a high average propensity to consume increases, the aggregate saving rate declines.

Changes in income shares (induced, for example, by productivity growth), or in the relative weights of different age cohorts of consumers are the main mechanism posited by the life-cycle theory to explain the pattern of aggregate saving over time. Following the same logic, but without restricting the classification of consumers to year of birth alone, the significance of demographic changes as an explanation for the observed changes in the saving rate can be assessed by replacing w_{it}^h ($t = 1989$) with $w_{it_0}^h$ ($t_0 = 1980$) in equation (1). This gives us the propensity to consume that would have been recorded in 1989 if the distribution of the population with respect to variable h had remained the same as in 1980.[4]

If the change in the distribution of the population did contribute to the decline in the aggregate saving rate, then the hypothetical economy-wide average propensity to consume computed by aggregating the average propensities to consume in 1989 according to the 1980 weight of each cell should be lower than the actual 1989 figure.

Clearly this is true only on the assumption that changes in the demographic structure do not affect the propensity to consume of any population group, an assumption that is not necessarily valid. For example, a decline in fertility might weaken the bequest motive and lead to a lower propensity to save for childless individuals and for the economy as a whole. Thus, this methodology might underestimate the real contribution of observed demographic changes to the decline in households saving rates.

The computation is based on the 1989 survey data. Income and consumption are those reported in the survey without any adjustment. The income variable includes wages and salaries, self-employment earnings, pensions and other transfers, rents, interest and dividends. All the income components are net of taxes and social security contributions.

Column (a) of Table 3.3 shows the hypothetical average propensity to consume that would have been obtained in 1989 holding the demographic structure constant at its 1980 value for several possible classifications of the sample. Column (b) displays the difference between the actual average propensity to consume in 1989 and the estimated value.

Table 3.3 Effects of demographic characteristics on the change in the average propensity to consume between 1980 and 1989

Classificatory variable used to define the 1980 weights	Estimated average propensity to consume (a) and change in the propensity to consume (b)	
	(a)	(b)
Age of household head	73.5	0.1
Number of children in the household	74.1	–0.5
Household size	73.7	–0.1

Source: Bank of Italy Survey of Household Income and Wealth.

The role played by demographic change in the decline of the saving rate turns out to be negligible. While the overall average propensity to save decreased by about 4 percentage points over the decade, the change in the age distribution of the household heads can account for only 0.1 points.

The other two demographic factors considered appear to have worked in the opposite direction, moderating rather than amplifying the fall in the saving rate. The changes in household size increased the saving rate by 0.1 and changes in the number of children by 0.5 percentage points.

The limited significance of demographic change can be explained, by making reference to Table 3.4, as follows:

(i) The propensity to consume of small households does not differ markedly from that of larger households, so the shift in weight from the latter group to the former has little effect on the saving rate.

(ii) The propensity to consume does increase sharply from 71.7 percent for households without children to 77.6 percent for households with one child;

a further increase, though less pronounced, accompanies the shift to households with two and with three or more children. The reduced incidence of children in the population thus noticeably affects the saving rate, but raising rather than lowering it.

(iii) The propensity to consume of the elderly (households with head aged 65 or over) increases slowly with age and is only marginally higher than the average for households headed by persons aged 51-64. Therefore the increased incidence of elderly household heads can explain only a small part of the decline in the saving rate.

Table 3.4 Average propensity to consume of households with various demographic characteristics (percentages)

	Average propensity to consume
Age of household head	
30 or under	82.3
31 – 40	75.6
41 – 50	74.1
51 – 64	71.3
65 or over	71.5
Number of children *(a)*	
none	71.7
1	77.6
2	79.1
3 or more	81.4
Household size	
1 member	75.7
2 members	74.0
3 members	71.5
4 members	73.7
5 members or more	75.9
All households	73.6

Source: Bank of Italy Survey of Household Income and Wealth, 1989.
(a) Individuals aged 14 or under.

The relatively flat age profile of the propensity to consume is not confirmed by the dissaving implied by the decumulation of wealth. Several factors might theoretically be at work. First the observed pattern of the propensity to consume by age of household head may be subject to sampling bias, mainly due to older people merging into younger households (Ando, 1985). Preliminary estimates indicate that such effects are not substantial in Italy, since extended families are only a small share of total households (see Ando, Guiso and Terlizzese, 1994). Second, the flat profile may be determined by a higher increase in the propensity to consume of the younger age-cohorts. If the age profile of the propensity to consume shifted upward for the young in the last decade the cross-sectional profile would be flatter than the longitudinal one. On the other hand, the decumulation of wealth itself could be consistent with saving by the elderly if intergenerational transfers take place from the elderly to the young (see Ando *et al.*, 1994). To examine this issue I used the 1987 and 1989 waves of the SHIW panel. After selecting the households participating in both surveys, total saving was computed as the average annual change in household wealth (at 1989 prices), estimated as one half of the difference between the value of total wealth reported in 1989 and that reported in 1987. Estimates were carried out for different age-groups and were compared with saving estimated as the difference between income and consumption for the same groups.

The propensity to save based on wealth figures exceeded that based on income and consumption data for households in the age classes "up to 30 years" and "40-50 years" and was lower for those in the class "60-65 years" and, to a lesser extent, in the class "65 or more". In the remaining age classes the two measures of the propensity to save showed minor differences. The pattern seems to be consistent with *inter vivos* transfers and the bequest motive. The young could receive a "dowry" from their parents (aged 60-65 years) when they get married and begin their independent life (at about age 30). After, on average, 15 years (at the age of 40-50 years) they will receive bequests and will continue accumulating until they in turn become the donors.

An alternative explanation of the relatively flat age profile of the propensity to consume is based on the bias that the presence of inflation induces on the propensity to consume measured as a ratio of consumption to income. After adjusting income for the inflation-induced losses on financial net wealth, the age profile of the propensity to consume becomes steeper; the income adjustment, in fact, affects the elderly (households with head aged 65 or over) proportionately more as their ratio of financial net wealth to income is higher than that observed for the remaining age-classes.

Though the propensity to consume of the elderly increases after adjusting for inflation, the previous results are not significantly changed.

The decline in the aggregate saving rate might be explained by changes over time in income shares going to different groups of households. To examine this issue SHIW data are not fully adequate. The Bank of Italy surveys do not allow intertemporal comparisons of a comprehensive measure of family income throughout the 1980s without adjustments for changes in survey design and the definitions of the variables (see Brandolini and Cannari, 1994). However, using the income components collected over the period 1980-1989 and adjusting with respect to the national accounts as described in the next section, I found that the changes in income shares (classifying households by age of head, size and number of children) had a negligible effect on the saving rate.

A similar exercise based on data from the Istat Survey of Italian Household Balance Sheets (SIHBS) (Istat, 1983 and 1990) confirms that the effect of the change in relative incomes between 1980 and 1988 is negligible (less than 0.05 percentage points). This result, however, has to be taken cautiously, due to the limited intertemporal comparability of SHIW data and to quality problems involving the SIHBS income data (Brandolini, 1993).

5   Who is responsible for the saving decline?

The findings of the previous section imply that the decline in Italian households' aggregate propensity to save has stemmed mainly from a decrease in the propensity to save within each group, not from an increase in the incidence of groups with a lower propensity to save.

To gain some insight into possible causes for such a change in behavioral patterns, the evolution of the propensity to consume has been investigated for various groups generated using different classification criteria. The idea is to find the "culprit" or "culprits" in the hope that doing so will shed light on the causes of the decline.

The analysis is based on the Bank of Italy survey data over the last decade, with the necessary adjustments to take account of changes in survey design and the definitions of the variables and thus permit intertemporal comparisons. In particular, the 1980-1983 sampling weights have been modified as described in the Appendix to remove the bias produced by the sample design until 1983. To further improve comparability, the 1987 oversample and the 1989 panel have been excluded from the analysis.

Households' disposable income has been redefined to comprise only the components that are observed over the entire period; thus, interest and dividends, data on which were not collected over the period 1980-1981, have been excluded (see Table 3.5, income definition 1). For the period 1982-1989, however, a more comprehensive measure of disposable income can be computed (see Table 3.5, income definition 2), and this has been used to check the robustness of the results. Moreover, experiments using the SHIW income components adjusted with respect to the national accounts have been conducted using three correction procedures: 1) the SHIW income components (wages and salaries, self-employment earnings, rents, pensions, interest and dividends) have been proportionally increased until their totals were equal to the corresponding national accounts figures (for details on the ratios between SHIW estimates and national accounts figures see Brandolini and Cannari, 1994); 2) wages and salaries and self-employment earnings have been proportionally increased until their ratios to the number of full-time equivalent workers in the survey were equal to the corresponding national accounts ratios. The total amount of pension income was proportionally increased until its ratio to the number of pensions in the survey was equal to the same figure from the national accounts. The remaining income components were increased following method (1).

Table 3.5 Income definitions

(a) Wages and salaries	Net of taxes and contributions to social security and similar schemes
(b) Self-employment income	Net of taxes and contributions to social security and similar schemes; net of consumption of fixed capital
(c) Pensions and social security benefits	After tax; net of in-kind benefits
(d) Rents	After tax; including imputed rents of owner-occupied dwellings
(e) Interest and dividends	After tax

(a)+(b)+(c)+(d)   = definition 1 (available over the period 1980-89)

(a)+(b)+(c)+(d)+(e) = definition 2 (available over the period 1982-89)

This procedure allows for the discrepancy between the survey estimates of the number of full-time equivalent workers and the national accounts figures, the latter including an estimate of hidden employment positions (second jobs). Moreover, it accounts for the fact that the survey does not include persons living in institutions, which is presumably relevant to the underestimation of pensions; 3) after implementing the second method of adjustment, labor income (wages and salaries plus self-employment earnings) was increased until the survey total was equal to the total labor income given in the national accounts. By this method labor income from hidden activities is attributed in the same proportion to employees and the self-employed, whereas by method (1) wages and salaries from hidden activities are imputed to employees and self-employment earnings to the self-employed.

Finally the series of surveys has been divided into three periods to reduce the sampling variance of estimates. For income definition 1, the intervals are: 1980-1982, 1983-1986, 1987-1989. For the more comprehensive measure of income (income definition 2), since interest income and dividends data were not collected in 1980-1981, the intervals are 1982-1983, 1984-1986, 1987-1989.

The pattern of the average propensity to consume in the past decade, according to the different definitions and adjustments of income, is displayed in Tables 3.6 and 3.7. Obviously, these results must be treated cautiously. For one thing, trends in the propensity to consume according to household characteristics may be affected by selection bias. For instance, decisions by the elderly to merge into younger households upon reaching retirement age or of young people to marry and to leave their parental households could have effects on the observed patterns of the propensity to consume.

Second, some income components (mainly interest and dividends but also self-employment earnings) are underestimated. The methods for data adjustment assume proportional underreporting, but in reality the phenomenon could be concentrated on specific subsets, whose propensity to consume would thus be somewhat distorted.

Finally, for the adjusted data, the national accounts and survey definitions do not coincide exactly, and figures from the two sources have to be put on a comparable basis. The main difficulty is that direct taxes are not broken down by type of income and an arbitrary criterion of imputation must be adopted. In this paper, after-tax incomes are derived from the national accounts by assigning each type of income a proportional share of direct taxes. Since the tax system changed over time, the observed pattern of the adjusted propensities could be biased, the bias depending on the tax rates and on the distribution of each type of income.

Notwithstanding these limitations, the statistical breakdowns show convincingly that demographic factors have been relatively unimportant, simply because the saving rate has declined within almost all the subgroups considered.

Disaggregating the sample according to a series of different characteristics, the propensity to consume increased uniformly during the decade with few exceptions (Tables 3.6 and 3.7).

First among the exceptions is that the increase for elderly households was greater than average. Rossi and Visco (1994) argue that this might be due at least partly to the generous increases in pension benefits and public programmes for the elderly in the eighties.

Second, homeowners' propensity to consume rose more sharply than that of tenants, which is consistent with the hypothesis that capital gains on housing may have helped increase the former's propensity to consume, while the latter may have been saving in order to accumulate the downpayment on a house (as suggested in Maccan, Rossi and Visco, 1994).

Third, there is some evidence that the propensity to consume increased more for households without children. If the current absence of children were also an indication that the household plans to remain without children, then the higher propensity to consume would be consistent with a weakening of the bequest motive for saving. On this hypothesis the decline in the birth-rate would directly affect the propensity to consume of specific households and thus the aggregate propensity to consume. If this were the case, demographic factors might have had a greater role in the decline in the propensity to save.

Finally, dividing the sample into permanent income quintiles,[5] the decline in savings is mainly accounted for by the most affluent groups. The average propensity to consume of the top quintile increased by 12.7 percentage points, that of the fourth quintile by 7.5 percentage points (income definition 1, unadjusted data). For the two bottom quintiles, the increase was below average (unadjusted data, income definitions 1 and 2).[6]

The many changes in the Italian tax code, involving direct and indirect taxes, might contribute to explain differential changes in behavior depending on relative income. The degree of progressivity of income tax diminished in the last two decades. The number of brackets dropped from 32 in 1974 to 7 in 1989, while the top marginal tax rate was lowered from 72 to 50 percent. The tax burden on capital income increased and the deductibility of interest payments on mortgage loans was considerably restricted (Jappelli and Pagano, 1993). The incidence of indirect taxes on total revenue dropped from 51.1 percent in 1980 to 46.5 in 1991. In the same period the overall tax burden (measured as the ratio of total taxes to GDP) increased from 18.8 percent to 25.7 percent. The assessment of the net impact of these changes on household saving would, however, require further analysis.

Table 3.6 Average propensity to consume - Income definition 1 (a)
(indices, 1980-82=100)

Household characteristics		1983-86 unadjusted data	1987-89	1983-86 adjustment 1	1987-89	1983-86 adjustment 2	1987-89	1983-86 adjustment 3	1987-89
Age of household's head:	Under 30	99.0	105.3	97.0	98.4	104.2	105.2	98.7	101.1
	31-40	100.2	105.7	101.1	101.5	105.9	106.0	100.4	101.8
	41-50	99.9	105.7	100.5	102.2	105.1	105.9	100.0	102.0
	51-65	102.5	109.3	102.7	107.6	107.4	109.8	103.2	106.3
	Over 65	104.9	108.3	110.4	110.8	108.6	105.7	107.0	104.4
Job status of household's head:	Employee	100.5	105.9	102.4	110.5	106.7	111.1	101.5	106.7
	Self-employed	103.2	113.3	105.6	111.2	107.9	108.2	102.8	104.4
	Other	101.3	104.3	103.6	104.2	102.9	100.4	101.2	99.3
Quintiles of permanent income (b):	First	99.7	98.5	98.1	100.1	102.1	97.2	101.2	96.6
	Second	97.7	99.4	100.5	98.1	105.0	103.5	101.4	100.6
	Third	104.7	109.7	106.4	110.1	111.3	113.7	106.0	110.4
	Fourth	99.7	107.5	99.9	109.5	103.8	107.8	99.2	103.5
	Fifth	102.7	112.7	102.8	104.2	107.8	110.5	102.7	106.5
Tenure of dwelling:	Homeowner	101.1	107.9	102.9	107.9	106.1	108.5	101.8	105.1
	Tenant	102.0	106.1	101.7	99.1	107.4	105.5	102.3	101.6
	Other	103.0	108.0	102.1	101.5	109.6	108.7	105.2	105.5
Family size:	1 member	99.6	100.9	102.2	99.0	105.4	99.2	103.1	97.6
	2 members	102.4	104.7	105.4	104.7	107.9	104.3	104.5	101.9
	3 members	99.8	106.5	100.1	101.7	105.1	106.2	100.4	102.5
	4 members	99.8	105.9	99.3	102.9	104.5	106.6	99.3	102.5
	> 4 members	103.3	112.0	103.8	110.6	108.2	112.6	103.4	108.5
Number of elderly:	None	100.2	106.2	100.4	102.8	105.3	106.3	100.3	102.4
	1	106.7	112.8	109.3	112.3	112.2	112.9	109.1	110.5
	> 1	102.9	107.7	107.6	110.4	107.1	106.4	105.4	105.1

Table 3.6 (cont.)

Number of children:	None	102.5	108.4	104.0	106.6	107.6	108.2	103.4	104.9
	1	99.4	106.0	98.7	101.1	104.6	106.2	99.5	102.2
	>1	99.8	105.7	99.7	104.3	105.0	107.1	99.8	103.1
Number of employees:	None	100.2	103.0	105.8	103.8	104.1	96.7	101.1	94.6
	1	99.2	102.8	101.0	106.0	104.7	105.8	99.8	102.0
	2	100.0	109.8	102.2	112.6	105.9	114.7	100.8	110.3
	>2	104.6	117.6	109.9	122.5	110.8	122.9	105.8	117.9
Number of self-employed workers:	None	101.0	105.2	102.2	107.3	107.0	110.1	102.7	106.7
	1	101.4	112.4	105.4	111.2	107.1	108.2	102.2	104.4
	>1	118.3	128.2	121.8	124.9	122.2	119.9	115.3	115.6
Number of workers in agriculture:	None	101.5	106.9	102.5	103.8	107.0	107.4	102.5	103.9
	>0	96.5	107.2	94.7	108.1	98.9	106.0	94.6	102.3
Type:	Husband-wife	102.0	108.0	106.4	107.8	108.6	108.6	105.2	106.2
	Other	101.0	106.7	101.2	103.7	106.0	106.9	101.3	103.2
Wife's job status:	Occupied	100.9	105.6	102.9	103.8	106.5	105.7	102.5	102.5
	Other	101.4	109.5	99.7	105.3	106.0	110.4	100.6	106.3

Source: Bank of Italy Survey of Household Income and Wealth.

(a) For the definition of income see Table 3.5. Income and consumption have been deflated by the consumer price index.

(b) Permanent income computed as the predicted value of the regression of household labor income and pensions on: age, education, professional status and sector of activity of household head, number of employees in the household, number of self-employed in the household, number of retired individuals in the household, number of employed in agriculture, working-wife dummy, geographical regions and population of townships.

Table 3.7 Average propensity to consume - Income definition 2 (a)
(indices, 1982-83=100)

Household characteristics		1984-86 unadjusted data	1987-89 unadjusted data	1984-86 adjustment 1	1987-89 adjustment 1	1984-86 adjustment 2	1987-89 adjustment 2	1984-86 adjustment 3	1987-89 adjustment 3
Age of household's head:	Under 30	98.8	103.7	100.2	101.2	107.1	106.3	101.0	102.5
	31-40	98.8	103.4	102.6	102.5	106.6	105.7	100.9	102.1
	41-50	99.5	103.6	100.1	101.5	105.4	104.8	100.1	101.6
	51-65	102.1	106.1	103.7	107.6	107.7	108.4	103.3	105.6
	Over 65	101.8	103.2	114.0	111.7	110.1	105.5	108.5	104.4
Job status of household's head:	Employee	100.2	103.9	103.0	109.5	108.5	110.5	103.0	106.8
	Self-employed	99.0	107.0	102.5	108.4	101.6	103.3	96.6	100.1
	Other	102.1	102.9	112.9	110.6	109.4	104.8	107.6	103.8
Quintiles of permanent income (b):	First	101.1	99.7	103.0	105.0	106.0	102.2	104.7	101.3
	Second	98.2	98.1	106.8	101.2	111.9	104.7	107.6	102.4
	Third	102.5	103.9	107.1	107.8	112.1	112.0	106.7	109.2
	Fourth	98.7	105.5	101.3	109.3	106.9	109.1	102.1	105.6
	Fifth	101.5	109.2	102.3	104.5	104.0	106.6	98.8	103.4
Tenure of dwelling:	Homeowner	99.5	104.5	103.1	107.6	105.7	107.4	101.4	104.6
	Tenant	101.2	103.2	103.4	98.9	109.2	104.2	103.5	100.8
	Other	108.6	110.6	112.2	110.6	118.6	116.0	113.9	113.2
Family size:	1 member	99.8	96.6	107.4	100.6	109.5	99.6	107.2	98.3
	2 members	100.0	100.9	109.1	107.1	109.6	105.2	106.1	103.1
	3 members	99.0	104.0	101.9	103.1	105.4	105.8	100.6	102.7
	4 members	100.6	105.1	100.2	103.6	105.3	106.4	100.1	103.0
	>4 members	101.0	108.0	102.6	108.5	107.7	110.2	102.3	106.7
Number of elderly:	None	99.8	104.1	101.7	103.6	106.2	106.0	101.0	102.8
	1	104.5	106.7	110.4	110.2	111.6	108.9	108.5	107.0
	>1	99.9	103.4	111.4	112.9	108.8	107.7	107.0	106.5

Table 3.7 (cont.)

Number of children:	None	101.7	105.1	105.4	106.7	108.7	107.4	104.5	104.8
	1	98.2	103.9	100.1	102.7	104.9	106.3	99.5	102.8
	>1	97.5	103.1	97.7	102.5	103.3	105.0	97.7	101.4
Number of employees:	None	98.8	99.8	109.9	107.0	104.8	98.4	101.8	96.6
	1	98.3	100.9	102.0	106.6	105.6	106.0	100.5	102.7
	2	99.0	107.6	103.1	112.2	107.0	114.1	101.6	110.4
	>2	104.4	112.5	102.5	106.5	110.7	112.3	104.8	108.5
Number of self-employed workers:	None	100.8	103.2	104.5	107.9	109.5	110.0	105.0	107.2
	1	97.5	106.6	103.4	108.8	102.3	104.0	97.3	100.9
	>1	118.5	124.7	121.7	123.3	117.2	115.1	110.8	111.7
Number of workers in agriculture:	None	100.7	104.1	104.0	104.3	107.9	106.6	103.2	103.7
	>0	95.5	105.1	94.3	107.9	98.0	105.2	93.4	102.0
Type:	Husband-wife	101.5	104.4	107.4	107.0	111.0	108.2	107.4	106.1
	Other	100.1	104.1	102.5	104.3	106.4	106.1	101.5	103.0
Wife's job status:	Occupied	100.0	102.8	104.6	104.4	107.6	105.3	103.4	102.7
	Other	101.3	107.2	100.3	105.0	106.7	109.2	101.0	105.7

Source: Bank of Italy Survey of Household Income and Wealth.

(*a*) For the definition of income see Table 3.5. Income and consumption have been deflated by the consumer price index.

(*b*) Permanent income computed as the predicted value of the regression of household labor income and pensions on: age, education, professional status and sector of activity of household head, number of employees in the household, number of self-employed in the household, number of retired individuals in the household, number of employed in agriculture, working-wife dummy, geographical regions and population of townships.

6   Concluding remarks

Theoretically the decline in the overall average propensity to save could be explained by changes in the distribution of Italian households according to such demographic factors as age, number of children or household size. However, this study finds no evidence of this. Rather, the effects ascribable to demographic factors prove to be negligible. The change in the distribution by age of household head explains only 0.1 percentage point of the overall drop, while the other demographic factors considered actually appear to have worked to brake the decline: changes in the distribution of households by size and by number of children are estimated to have produced increases in the overall saving rate of 0.1 and 0.5 percentage points respectively.[7] Nor can changes in the distribution of household income with respect to demographic characteristics account for the decline in saving.

In conclusion, the decline in the Italian households' aggregate propensity to save observed during the eighties reflected a decline within each of the household categories considered, not changes in their relative incidence on the aggregate.

APPENDIX

1   Sample adjustment

The sample for the Bank of Italy Survey of Household Income and Wealth was originally taken from the electoral rolls, and the probability of a household to be included was thus proportional to the number of members aged 18 or over. Because of the correlation between household size and survey variables, income and consumption expenditure were overestimated. The total number of employed individuals also was likely to be overestimated (for further details see the Methodological Appendix to this volume).

This shortcoming was remedied following the 1983 survey. Thus, to make possible intertemporal comparison over the entire decade of the eighties, the data from 1980 to 1983 must be adjusted.

Theoretically the adjustment procedure is simple: sampling weights should be divided by the number of members aged 18 and over living in each household. The method was applied for the period 1980-1983. With this correction, the number of small households increased and that of the largest households (5 or more members) decreased sharply. These results compared rather closely to the corresponding figures estimated by Istat, even though the latter's definition of household differs from the Bank of Italy's "economic household".[8]

Given this definitional disparity,[9] the simple adjustment procedure described above was not fully satisfactory for estimating the size distribution of economic households.[10] Accordingly, a different method was adopted. First, the distribution of economic households by size was estimated by using a probability model with time and a "sample design" dummy as exogenous variables, thus obtaining estimated distributions net of the bias caused by the sample design used until 1983. Second, for the period 1980-1983, sample weights were adjusted so as to obtain a distribution of households by size equal to the estimated figures net of the bias.

The probability model was defined as follows:

$$P_{iT} = \frac{e^{a_i + \beta_i T - \lambda_i D_T}}{1 + \sum_{k=1}^{(r-1)} e^{a_k + \beta_k T - \lambda_k D_T}} \qquad \begin{aligned} i &= 1, ..., (r - 1) \\ T &= 0, ..., 9 \end{aligned} \qquad (1a)$$

$$P_{iT} = \frac{1}{1 + \sum_{k=1}^{(r-1)} e^{a_k + \beta_k T - \lambda_k D_T}} \qquad \begin{aligned} i &= r \\ T &= 0, ..., 9 \end{aligned} \qquad (1b)$$

where P_{iT} is the percentage of households of size i ($i=1,..., r$; $r=6$) at time T, D_T is the 1980-1983 sample design dummy,[11] and a_i, β_i and λ_i are parameters to be estimated.

In this model the bias due to the 1980-1983 sampling scheme is related to the coefficients λ_i of the variable D_T.

Thus, after estimating the parameters of model (1), it was possible to obtain an unbiased estimate of the distribution by setting D_T equal to zero in the period 1980-1983.

Adjustment coefficients were computed as the ratio of unbiased estimated percentages to estimated percentages; this yielded a set of adjustment coefficients (c_{iT}; $i=1,...,r$; $T=0,...,3$):

$$c_{iT} = e^{\lambda_i} W_T \qquad i = 1, ..., (r - 1) \qquad (2a)$$

$$c_{iT} = W_T \qquad i = r \qquad (2b)$$

where W_T values, computed according to model (1), are:

$$W_T = \frac{1 + \sum_{k=1}^{(r-1)} e^{a_k + \beta_k T - \lambda_k}}{1 + \sum_{k=1}^{(r-1)} e^{a_k + \beta_k T}}. \qquad (2c)$$

Finally, 1980-1983 sample weights were multiplied by the adjustment coefficients.

NOTES

* I wish to thank Albert Ando, Luigi Guiso and Ignazio Visco for their very useful comments. I retain full responsibility of all remaining errors.

1 For a detailed description of the decline see Pagliano and Rossi (1992); see also Rossi and Visco (1994).

2 See the Methodological Appendix to this volume for a detailed description of the sampling methodology and the information content and comparability of the survey data over the last decade.

3 Among them, Sweden (16.9 percent of individuals aged 65 or over), the United Kingdom (15.1 percent) and Germany (14.5 percent). These figures are taken from Cantalini, Lori and Righi (1988) and refer to the year 1985.

4 Replacing $w_{it}^h y_{it}^h$ with $w_{it_0}^h y_{it_0}^h$ in equation (1) the joint effect of demographic factors and relative income shares can be assessed.

5 Permanent income was computed as the predicted value of the regression of household labor income and pensions on: age, education, professional status and sector of activity of household head, number of employees in the household, number of self-employed in the household, number of retired individuals in the household, number of employed in agriculture, working-wife dummy, geographical regions and population of municipality of residence.

6 Data adjusted with respect to the national accounts show a slightly different pattern, but in any case the propensity to consume of the more affluent part of the population (third to fifth quintile) increased more rapidly than that of the poorest (first and second quintiles).

7 In the past decade the occupational structure of the population also changed. Self-employed workers increased by 3.5 per cent from 1981 to 1989; employees by 1.8 percent. But this trend cannot explain the drop in the saving rate. On the contrary, the increase in the share of self-employed workers should have stimulated saving, because the self-employed have a higher propensity to save than wage and salary earners.

8 Istat uses administrative data from the General Registry Office; the SHIW adopts an economic definition independent of the address where an individual is registered.

9 See Istat (1985).

10 One shortcoming is that until 1983 households in the Istat survey were selected with probability proportionate to the number of members aged 18 or over and *registered* at the same address; the Bank of Italy survey collected data on the individuals *living* at the same address, and the adjustment procedure was based on the number of individuals aged 18 or over living at the same address. These two numbers do not necessarily correspond.

11 The variable T is zero in 1980; the dummy variable D is equal to one over the period 1980-1983.

REFERENCES

Ando, A. (1985). 'The Saving of Japanese Households: A Micro Study Based on Data from the National Survey of Family Income and Expenditure 1974 and 1979', Department of Economics, University of Pennsylvania, mimeo.

Ando, A., L. Guiso and D. Terlizzese (1994). 'Dissaving by the Elderly, Transfer Motives and Liquidity Constraints', *this volume*.

Auerbach, A.J. and L.J. Kotlikoff (1992). 'The Impact of the Demographic Transition on Capital Formation', *Scandinavian Journal of Economics* **94**: 281-95.

Avery, R.B. and A.B. Kennickell (1991). 'Household Saving in the U.S." *Review of Income and Wealth* **37**: 409-32.

Bosworth, B., G. Burtless and J. Sabelhaus (1991). 'The Decline in Saving: Evidence from Household Surveys', *Brookings Papers on Economic Activity* **1**: 183-256.

Brandolini, A. (1993). 'A Description and an Assessment of the Sample Surveys on the Personal Distribution of Incomes in Italy', Discussion Paper 3, University of Cambridge, Department of Applied Economics, Microsimulation Unit.

Brandolini, A. and L. Cannari (1994). 'Methodological Appendix: The Bank of Italy's Survey of Household Income and Wealth', *this volume*.

Cantalini, B., A. Lori and A. Righi (1988). 'Invecchiamento della popolazione', in CNR and IRP (1988).

CNR and IRP (1988). *Rapporto sulla situazione demografica in Italia*, Roma.

Cutler, D.M., J.M. Poterba, L.M. Sheiner and L.H. Summers (1990). 'An Aging Society: Opportunity or Challenge?', *Brookings Papers on Economic Activity* **1**: 1-73.

Davies, J.B. (1988). 'Family Size, Household Production and Life Cycle Saving', *Annales d'Economie et de Statistique* **9**: 141-65.

Golini, A. (1988). 'La popolazione italiana: una visione d'insieme', in CNR and IRP (1988).

Guiso, L., T. Jappelli and D. Terlizzese (1994). 'Why Is Italy's Saving Rate so High?" *this volume*.

Istat (1983). 'La distribuzione quantitativa del reddito in Italia nelle indagini sui bilanci di famiglia – Anni 1980-1981-1982', *Supplemento al Bollettino mensile di statistica* **25**.

Istat (1985). *Indagine sulle strutture ed i comportamenti familiari*, Roma.

Istat (1990). 'La distribuzione quantitativa del reddito in Italia nelle indagini sui bilanci di famiglia – Anno 1988', *Collana d'informazione* **7**.

Jappelli, T. and M. Pagano (1993). 'Government Incentives and Household Saving in Italy', in J. Poterba (ed.), *Public Policies and Household Saving*, Chicago: University of Chicago Press.

Jappelli, T. and N. Rossi (1989). 'Dinamica della popolazione e risparmio privato', in *Ricerche e metodi per la politica economica*, Roma: Banca d'Italia, Vol. II.

Maccan, L., N. Rossi and I. Visco (1994). 'Saving and Borrowing Constraints', *this volume*.

Pagliano, P. and N. Rossi (1992). 'The Italian Saving Rate: 1951 to 1990 Estimates', in *Income and Saving in Italy: A Reconstruction*, Temi di discussione 169, Banca d'Italia.

Rossi, N. and I. Visco (1994). 'Private Saving and the Government Deficit in Italy', *this volume*.

4 Generational accounting. The case of Italy*

DANIELE FRANCO, JAGADEESH GOKHALE,
LUIGI GUISO, LAURENCE J. KOTLIKOFF
and NICOLA SARTOR

1 Introduction

Generational accounting is a new technique developed by Auerbach, Gokhale and Kotlikoff (1991) and Kotlikoff (1992) that can be used to study the effects on different generations of the government's fiscal policy. Generational accounting measures directly how much existing generations can be expected to pay, on net, to the government over their remaining lifetimes. The present value of the projected net payments by those now alive together with the government's net wealth and the present value of the projected net payments by future generations must cover the present value of government purchases/expenditures on goods and services. Generational accounting uses this equation – the government's intertemporal budget constraint – to infer the likely burden to be imposed on future generations. Specifically, generational accounting involves the projection of the present value of government spending, the calculation of the government's net wealth, and, as mentioned, the estimation of the present value of net payments to be made by current generations. The present value payments required of future generations is then determined as a residual.

Generational accounting represents an alternative to deficit accounting for purposes of understanding generational policy. Conventional deficit accounting has been criticized on a number of grounds including its failure to account for implicit government liabilities, its failure to adjust for inflation and growth, its failure to capture pay-as-you-go social security and related policies, and its neglect of policies that redistribute across generations through the change in the market price of assets.[1] While many economists have suggested adjusting the deficit to deal with these and other problems, there is a fundamental problem with deficit accounting for which no adjustment is available. This problem is the lack of an economic basis for the tax and transfer labels that are attached to government receipts and payments. Unfortunately, the deficit depends on which labels/words are chosen to describe government receipts and payments and, as such, contains large margins of arbitrariness.

For example, the government is free to label workers' social security contributions "taxes" and retirees' social security benefits "transfers"; alternatively, it is free to label these contributions "loans" to the government and to label retirees' benefits "return of principal and interest" on these "loans" plus an additional "old age tax" equal to the difference between benefits and the "return of principal plus interest" on the "loans". Using the second set of words rather than the first to describe the same economic reality may change not only the level of the reported deficit, but also the sign of its changes over time. This is not an isolated example; every dollar the government takes in or pays out might be arbitrarily labeled from an economics perspective.

Correcting the deficit for one or more of its alleged shortcomings does not, in the end, avoid its primary shortcoming — this labeling problem — and eventuate in the measure of a well-defined economic concept. Rather it simply replaces one deficit based on arbitrary labels with another (see Kotlikoff, 1989).

Generational accounting deals naturally with all of the concerns that have been raised about deficit accounting. It takes account of inflation and growth, including growth due to demographic change. It puts implicit and explicit government liabilities on an equal footing, and thus avoids the danger of missing most of generational action by considering only those liabilities labeled as official liabilities by the government. Indeed, generational accounting captures all policies that alter the generational distribution of fiscal burdens. Most importantly, generational accounting provides the answer to an important economic question, namely whether the government's course of fiscal policy, unless modified, will necessitate that future generations pay a much larger share of their lifetime incomes to the government than will current generations. Thus generational accounting exposes the generational imbalance in fiscal policy.

Italy represents one country for which there should be acute concern about the generational imbalance in fiscal policy. Italy has one of the most generous pay-as-you-go social security and welfare systems of any of the leading industrialized countries.[2] In addition, after Belgium, Italy together with Ireland has the highest ratio of officially labeled debt-to-GDP ratio among the OECD countries. Finally, its fertility rate is one of the lowest of the industrialized countries. The low Italian fertility rate implies a declining number of Italians available to shoulder Italy's huge implicit and explicit obligations.[3]

This paper develops a set of generational accounts for Italy. It indicates that there is an extremely serious imbalance in Italy's generational policy. Unless Italy makes dramatic policy changes in the near future, future generations of Italians will face lifetime net tax burdens that are much higher than the burdens facing Italians who have just been born. This estimate takes into account the fact that future Italians will have higher incomes because of economic growth. The increase in the net tax burden is, therefore, above and beyond the increase in net taxes that will arise because of growth.

The paper proceeds by first describing general features of the Italian fiscal system and Italian demographics. Section 3 describes the method of generational accounting. Section 4 details the data used in our analysis. Section 5 presents baseline generational accounts for Italy for 1990 and explores the sensitivity of the accounts to growth rate, interest rate, and fertility assumptions. Section 6 compares the Italian generational accounts with those for the U.S. Section 7 examines the factors causing the highly significant imbalance in Italian generational policy. Section 8 considers alternative methods of equalizing the growth-adjusted fiscal burden on future and current Italians, while Section 9 discusses the likely effect of such policy initiatives on Italian national saving. The final section summarizes our findings.

2   Italian fiscal policy and the Italian demographic transition

Measured relative to GDP, the Italian government is much larger than are the government sectors in the U.S. and Japan. However, the Italian government is not large when compared with governments of other continental European countries. As can be seen from Table 4.1, total government budgetary expenditures as a share of GDP are in line with those of Germany and France, but are some 15 to 20 percentage points higher than those of the U.S. and Japan. The larger expenditure-to-GDP ratio is explained almost entirely by the greater importance of social security expenditures (19 percent of GDP as compared with 12 and 10 percent in the U.S. and Japan, respectively), and of interest payments (9 percent of GDP, as compared with 5 and 4 percent in the U.S. and Japan, respectively). The ratio of tax revenue and social security contributions to GDP, while higher than in the U.S. and Japan, are in line with those observed in Germany and far lower than in France.

Transfer payments to households and firms dominate the Italian general government budget: in 1990, the social security system and interest payments constituted 58 percent of the total budget. The largest expenditure item in the Italian general government budget is public pensions (26 percent of the budget), followed by government wage and salary payments (24 percent), and interest payments (18 percent). The public pension system is based on a pay-as-you-go scheme, with contribution rates and benefits varying for private and public workers. The Italian welfare system covers other important aspects, such as universal health care assistance, unemployment compensation and a heavily subsidized education system.

Table 4.1 Comparative fiscal indicators in 1989
(as a percentage of GDP)

Item	Country				
	Italy	U.S.A.	Japan	Germany	France
Taxes *(a)*	37.8	30.1	30.6	38.1	43.8
Total outlays	51.7	37.3	32.1	45.2	49.5
Direct spending *(b)*	20.3	20.1	15.4	21.0	21.5
Transfers *(c)*	21.4	12.6	12.6	20.4	25.0
Interest payments	9.0	4.9	4.1	2.7	2.8
Deficit	10.1	1.7	–2.5	–0.2	1.2
Net debt	95.9	30.8	14.6	22.4	24.7
Social security and education *(d)*	24.0	17.3	14.8	24.1	28.4
Pensions	12.8	7.2	5.3	11.8	12.7
Health	5.4	4.4	4.8	6.4	6.8
Unemployment	0.7	0.4	0.4	1.5	2.8
Education	5.1	5.3	4.3	4.4	6.1

Sources: Social security and education: OECD (1988); other data: Computations based on OECD, *National Accounts,* 1990, and Istat, *Conti economici nazionali, Collana d'informazione,* 1990.
(a) Including social security contributions.
(b) Purchases of goods and services including investment goods.
(c) Non-interest transfers on current account.
(d) Data refer to 1985.

The Italian government raises its revenues mainly through direct taxes and payroll taxes. In 1990, each of these taxes raised 37 percent of overall revenue. The most important direct tax is the progressive personal income tax, which is applied to all income sources except for interest income. Interest income is taxed at a flat rate, currently 30 percent for bank deposits and 12.5 percent for government bonds.[4] Capital gains are taxed at a favourable rate in the case of real estate and are virtually tax exempt in the case of stocks and shares. Corporate taxes are levied at a high nominal rate (over 46 percent),[5] although generous depreciation allowances and a plethora of exemptions reduce the effective tax rate, particularly for manufacturing industries. Relative to the U.S., a substantial fraction of revenues (26 percent for Italy compared with 18 percent for the U.S.) is collected through indirect taxation, particularly the VAT and taxes on petroleum products.

Since the mid-sixties, Italian fiscal policy has been characterized by deficit spending. The absorption of government bonds into private portfolios has been eased by the large propensity to save of Italian households, an underdeveloped financial market, and, until the mid-eighties, legal restrictions on capital movements. Until the early-eighties, the growth of public debt has been damped by low, and often negative, *ex-post* real interest rates. Since 1984, however, the Italian real interest rates on government debt have exceeded Italian growth rates, putting the growth of public debt on an unsustainable path. The Italian government has laid out several medium-term plans for halting the growth of public debt, but deficit reduction has repeatedly fallen short of official targets. Although the primary deficit has been reduced since 1986, the government has been unsuccessful so far in running a primary surplus sufficiently large to compensate for interest payments and keep the public debt from growing faster than the economy.

The size and the structure of the Italian population is expected to experience substantial changes. Although the Italian population has been growing, albeit slowly, in recent years, the Italian fertility rate has been below replacement since the 1970s. The Italian total fertility rate, which was 2.7 in the mid-sixties, fell to 1.7 in 1980 and 1.3 in 1990 – one of the lowest rates among industrialized countries. The remarkably low Italian rate of fertility portends important changes in the size and distribution of the Italian population. Table 4.2 reports these projected changes based on two fertility assumptions. Under the first, the fertility rate gradually rises over the next decade to the level (around 2.1) required for replacement of the population. Under the second, the fertility rate moderately recovers from the current exceptionally low value and is assumed to equal the EC value (around 1.6 in 1991). The Italian population is projected to fall under both fertility rate scenarios. Under the first assumption (replacement rate fertility) the Italian population falls by 8 percent by the year 2050, and by 9 percent by the year 2200. Under the second assumption (fertility constant at the EC average value) the Italian population falls by 27 percent by the year 2050, and by 84 percent by the year 2200!

Both fertility assumptions imply a rapid aging of the Italian population. Currently, 17 percent of Italian males and 23 percent of females are aged 60 and older. By the turn of the century 20 and 26 percent of respectively Italian males and females will be in this age-group under both fertility assumptions.

By the year 2030 over 23 percent of the Italian male and 29 percent of female population will be 60 and older if the fertility rate rises to the replacement value, and 26 and 32 percent respectively will be 60 and older if the fertility rate remains constant at the EC average value. Since a large fraction of government's transfers are allocated to older age-groups, the maintenance of current entitlements implies that current demographic trends will put increasing pressure on government spending.

Table 4.2 Projected size and age-sex distribution of the Italian population

Age	Replacement rate fertility				Average EC fertility			
	Year							
	1990	2010	2030	2050	1990	2010	2030	2050
Fraction of males in specified age-groups								
0–17	.230	.231	.231	.245	.230	.207	.186	.181
18–25	.133	.096	.106	.109	.133	.099	.089	.093
26–49	.339	.347	.296	.321	.339	.357	.317	.312
50–59	.122	.129	.132	.118	.122	.132	.147	.151
Over 60	.173	.196	.232	.205	.173	.202	.258	.262
Total males (millions)	27.7	27.9	27.0	25.8	27.7	27.1	24.3	20.2
Fraction of females in specified age-groups								
0–17	.206	.207	.209	.222	.206	.185	.166	.160
18–25	.121	.087	.096	.100	.121	.089	.080	.082
26–49	.320	.320	.271	.295	.320	.328	.288	.280
50–59	.123	.127	.127	.114	.123	.130	.140	.142
Over 60	.228	.258	.294	.267	.228	.265	.324	.333
Total females (millions)	29.4	29.3	28.3	26.9	29.4	28.6	25.7	21.4

3 The method of generational accounting

To clarify the method of generational accounting, we write the government's intertemporal budget constraint for year t as:

$$\sum_{s=0}^{D} N_{t,t-s} + \sum_{s=1}^{\infty} N_{t,t+s} = W_t^g + \sum_{s=0}^{\infty} (1 + r)^{-s} G_{t+s} . \qquad (1)$$

The first term on the left hand side of (1) adds together the present value of the remaining lifetime net payments of all generations alive at time t. By net payments we mean all taxes paid to and all transfers received from general government (central and local government as well as independent government agencies such as the Italian Social Security System). The expression $N_{t,k}$ stands for the time t present value of remaining lifetime net payments of the generation born in year k. The second term on the left hand side of (1) adds together the present value as of time t of net lifetime payments of future generations. The right hand side consists of W_t^g, the government's net wealth in year t, plus the present value of government expenditures on goods and services. In the latter expression, G_s stands for government expenditure on public goods and services in year s, and r stands for the real pre-tax (constant) rate of return. A set of generational accounts is simply a set of values of $N_{t,k}$ divided by $P_{t,k}$ (the generation's current population size in the case of existing generations or initial population size in the case of future generations), with the property that the combined total value of the $N_{t,k}$'s adds up to the right hand side of equation (1). In our calculation of the $N_{t,k}$'s for existing generations (those whose $k \leq 1990$) we distinguish male from female cohorts, but, to ease notation, we omit sex subscripts in equations (1) and (2).

The term $N_{t,k}$ is defined by:

$$N_{t,k} = \sum_{s=\max(0,\,k-t)}^{k+D} (1 + r)^{-s}\overline{T}_{t+s,k}P_{t+s,k} \, . \qquad (4.2)$$

In expression (2) $\overline{T}_{t+s,k}$ stands for the projected average net payment to the government made in year $t+s$ by a member of the generation born in year k. By a generation's average net payment in year $t+s$ we mean the average across all members of the generation alive in year $t+s$ of payments made, such as income, payroll and indirect taxes, minus all transfers received, such as social security, welfare and unemployment insurance. The term $P_{t+s,k}$ stands for the number of surviving members of the cohort in year $t+s$ who were born in year k. For generations who are born prior to year t, the summation begins in year t. For generations who are born in year k, where $k > t$, the summation begins in year k. Regardless of the generation's year of birth, the discounting is always back to year t. In dividing the total present value payments of each generation (the $N_{t,k}$'s) by the generation's population size we are, in effect, discounting for mortality; note that dividing the term $P_{t+s,k}$ in equation (2) by the generation's base year population size forms a survival probability.

Returning to the first term in equation (1), the index s in the first summation runs from age 0 to age D, the maximum age of life. The first element of this summation is $N_{t,t}$, which is the present value of net payments of the generation born in year t; the last term is $N_{t,t-D}$, the present value of remaining net payments of the oldest generation alive in year t, namely those born in year t-D.

Equation (1) indicates the zero-sum nature of intergenerational fiscal policy. Holding the right hand side of equation (1) fixed, a decrease in the present value of net taxes paid by existing generations (a decrease in the first term on the left hand side of equation (1)) requires an increase in the present value of net taxes paid by future generations (an increase in the second term on the left hand side of (1)).

To determine the aggregate present value net payments required of future generations we simply solve equation (1) for the second term on the left hand side. While future generations, as a group, can be expected (given current policy) to pay this derived amount, there are many ways this collective burden may be allocated between those generations arriving in the future. For purposes of illustrating the size of the burden that will likely be imposed on future generations relative to that imposed on current generations, we assume that the burden on each successive generation remains fixed as a fraction of the lifetime income of that generation; that is, the absolute fiscal burden of successive generations is assumed to grow at the rate of growth of their lifetime incomes, which we take to be the rate of growth of productivity.

The construction of generational accounts involves two steps. The first step entails projecting each currently living generation's average taxes less transfers in each future year during which at least some members of the generation will be alive. The second step converts these projected average net tax payments into a present value using an assumed discount rate and taking into account the probability that the generations' members will be alive in each of the future years (i.e., we discount for both mortality and interest).

In projecting each currently living generation's taxes and transfers, we consider first their taxes and transfers in the base year, in this case, 1990. The totals of the different taxes and transfers in the base year are those reported by the Italian national accounts. In using these data we are using the same fiscal aggregates that underlie the conventionally calculated Italian general government deficit. These totals of base year taxes and transfers are distributed to the different generations according to their ages and sexes based on the 1989 Bank of Italy's Survey of Household Income and Wealth (henceforth SHIW; see for details the Methodological Appendix to this volume) and the Survey of Consumer Expenditures by Istat (henceforth CES). Future taxes and transfers by age and sex are assumed to equal their

1990 values with adjustments for growth. The calculations presented here are based on yearly projections up to year 2200. Three different interest rate and growth rate assumptions have been made, centered around our base case assumption of a 4 percent real interest rate and a 2 percent rate of productivity growth.

As mentioned, inferring the fiscal burden on future generations requires knowing not only the sum total of generational accounts of current generations, but also the government's initial net wealth position and the projected present value of the government's spending on goods and services. While in principle a measure of total net wealth is required, an estimate of net financial wealth has been used, owing to the difficulties of assessing the value of real non-marketable wealth.[6] The government's net financial wealth is estimated in a manner consistent with the general government deficit reported in the national accounts.[7] The present value of non-education and non-health government spending on goods and services is projected assuming that the *per capita* level of this spending remains constant in the future except for an adjustment for growth. We treat education and health spending differently from other government spending. These expenditures represent purchases of goods and services by the government on behalf of specific age-groups. We treat these expenditures, in effect, as additional age-specific transfer payments. That is, our estimates of the present value of net payments by current generations are net of the projected value of education and health spending on these generations.

Taxes on capital income require special treatment. Unlike other taxes, taxes on capital income may be capitalized into the value of existing (old) assets. Take, as an example, an increase in the nominal capital income tax rate in the presence of a provision that permits firms immediately to deduct from taxable income their new investment. As described in Auerbach and Kotlikoff (1987) and by other economists, this will lead to a fall in the market value of existing capital. While owners of existing capital will be hurt by the capital loss, new investors in capital will be unaffected by the increase in the nominal capital income tax. If they buy existing capital the decline in the price of that capital will just make up for the higher tax on the future income to be earned on the existing capital. If they buy new capital, the larger immediate deduction (the amount of the deduction is proportional to the tax rate) makes up for having to pay higher taxes on the future income earned on the new capital.

In this example, it would clearly be inappropriate to charge the higher capital income tax against the generational accounts of new investors (who, by the way, are typically young and middle age) rather than to the generational accounts of the owners of existing capital (who, by the way, are typically old). Instead, generational accounting ascribes to the owners of existing assets all inframarginal taxes capitalized in the price of their assets. As discussed at more length in Auerbach, Gokhale and Kotlikoff (1991), owners of existing assets can be viewed, from the perspective of generational accounting, as owning assets valued at replacement cost (rather than market value), but owe a tax equal to the value of the inframarginal taxes capitalized into the market value of the asset.

4   Sources and data construction

Figure 4.1 reports the age and sex profiles for the appropriation account of the general government, as well as those relative to private net wealth, income, consumption and the propensity to consume out of wealth. Separate profiles are derived for males and females in each of the 91 cohorts present in the SHIW. The relative profile is obtained by benchmarking individual positions against a 40-year-old male.

In order to calculate the generational accounts, the receipts listed in the appropriation account for the general government have been broken down into taxes on capital, labor and commodities, social security contributions and other revenues. To determine the aggregate amount of taxes on capital and labor income we allocate total income tax revenue to capital and labor according to their shares of national income. The payments in the appropriation account have been broken down into spending on health, education, pensions, household responsibility payments and other social security transfers, such as unemployment benefits. The aggregate 1990 values of each of these different payments and receipts are allocated by age and sex according to cross section age-sex profiles, which are assumed to be constant through time apart from an age-independent shift to account for growth in the economy. Thus, while relative receipts and payments across age groups do not vary over time, their absolute amount grows at the economy's rate of growth.

Income and consumption profiles have been computed from SHIW. As the survey records personal after tax income, the amount of labor taxes paid on this personal income was derived by applying the methodology developed in Franco and Sartor (1990). The profile for social security contributions has been derived by applying nominal social security tax rates to the estimated profile of gross-of-tax individual labor income taxes, taking into account the industry, type of worker and region of work.

Revenue from direct taxes on capital has been separated into marginal and inframarginal taxes, according to the methodology outlined in Auerbach, Gokhale and Kotlikoff (1992). The relevant tax parameters have been calculated based on estimates and data reported in Giannini (1989). We estimate that inframarginal taxes represent 36 percent of total corporate tax revenue. Marginal and inframarginal taxes on capital were imputed to each member of the cohort in proportion to her/his holdings of gross wealth (excluding real estate).

Figure 4.1

Age and sex profiles
(index number: 40-year-old male = 1)

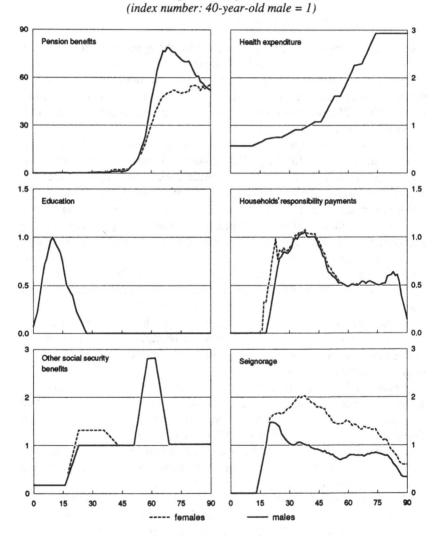

----- females   ——— males

Figure 4.1 *(cont.)*

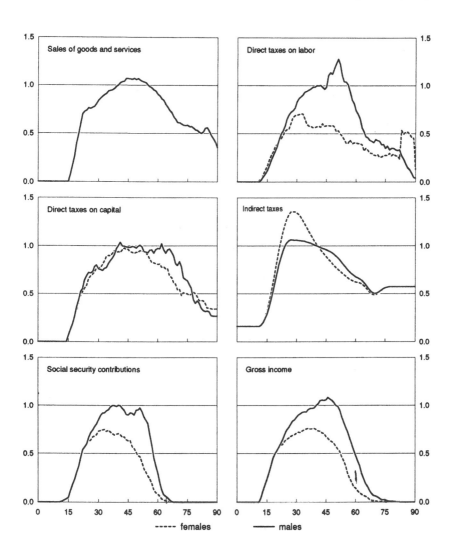

The age and sex profiles for net indirect taxes were obtained by applying nominal consumption tax rates to each of the 185 goods surveyed in the CES by Istat. In the case of excise duties, the implicit rate of taxation has been obtained by dividing the unitary tax by the average price of the good. Since

Figure 4.1 *(cont.)*

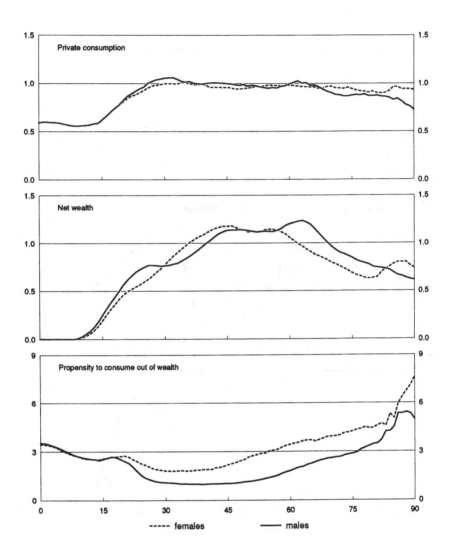

the survey records household, and not individual consumption, it was necessary to impute total household consumption of each good to each member of the household. With the exception of consumer durables and those items whose consumption is age-specific (such as toys or education fees), all consumption expenditures were imputed assuming that each member receives an equal share of total household consumption. In the case of rents, the amount imputed to young household members (aged 18 or less) was set equal to half the amount imputed to adults. Consumer durables have been imputed only to adult members of the family.

On the benefit side, the age profiles for health expenditure were obtained from hospital and ambulatory care utilization profiles and from pharmaceutical consumption profiles, as described in Franco (1992). For education, profiles were obtained using the data on the Ministry of Education's expenditure per student in each educational level (from infant school to university). Unemployment and short-term disability benefits and sick pay were imputed to citizens aged 20 to 59, assuming constant *per capita* payments. Maternity benefits were imputed to females aged 20 to 39. Severance pay provisions were imputed to citizens aged 55 to 65. In both cases, constant *per capita* payments were assumed. For pensions, profiles were obtained from the SHIW,[8] while the profiles for households' responsibility payments are those estimated by Franco and Sartor (1990).

5   Baseline generational accounts and sensitivity analysis

Tables 4.3 and 4.4 present the baseline generational accounts respectively for males and females at every fifth age for nine different combinations of productivity growth and interest rates.[9] The table assumes, perhaps optimistically, that in the year 2000 the Italian fertility rate will reach the level required to stabilize the Italian population (the replacement rate fertility assumption of Table 4.2). All amounts are in 1990 dollars.[10] The accounts indicate the average amount an individual in the specified age-sex group will pay in net taxes over the rest of her/his life. For example, assuming a real interest rate of 4 percent and a growth rate of 2 percent, the projected present value net payments of 35 year old males and females are $34,300 and $4,000, respectively. On average females pay much less labor income and social security taxes because they earn and participate less. Notice that males aged 50 and over and females aged 45 and over have negative generational accounts. They can expect to receive, in present value, more in future transfers than they can expect to pay in taxes. The size of the generational accounts first rises and then falls with age. This reflects the fact that young children are years away from their peak tax paying years, while older individuals are in or near their retirement years in which they are on the receiving end of the government's tax and transfer programs.

Table 4.3 Net payments for age-zero and future male generations
(thousands of dollars)

Generation's age in 1990	g = .015			g = .020			g = .025		
	r = .03	r = .04	r = .05	r = .03	r = .04	r = .05	r = .03	r = .04	r = .05
0	128.9	94.0	65.1	147.8	111.2	79.1	165.6	129.5	94.7
5	144.5	111.9	83.0	160.9	128.3	97.3	175.4	145.0	112.7
10	174.8	146.2	118.6	188.0	160.9	132.5	198.4	175.2	146.9
15	216.0	193.7	170.0	224.8	205.5	182.2	230.4	216.3	194.3
20	234.9	221.2	203.8	238.5	228.9	213.0	238.6	235.0	221.6
25	221.4	217.2	207.5	219.7	220.3	213.0	214.3	221.4	217.4
30	180.7	185.8	184.1	174.2	184.3	185.6	164.0	180.6	185.7
35	126.9	139.8	145.6	116.5	134.3	143.4	102.8	126.7	139.6
40	64.7	83.5	95.5	51.7	74.9	90.0	35.8	64.4	83.1
45	0.8	23.2	39.4	-13.4	12.7	31.7	-29.9	0.4	22.7
50	-64.7	-41.4	-23.0	-78.7	-52.6	-31.9	-94.4	-65.0	-41.9
55	-130.5	-109.0	-91.1	-142.9	-119.4	-99.9	-156.5	-130.8	-109.5
60	-174.0	-157.0	-142.3	-183.7	-165.4	-149.6	-194.0	-174.3	-157.4
65	-160.2	-148.5	-138.1	-166.7	-154.3	-143.3	-173.6	-160.4	-148.7
70	-125.2	-117.9	-111.2	-129.2	-121.5	-114.5	-133.4	-125.3	-118.0
75	-93.4	-89.0	-84.9	-95.8	-91.2	-87.0	-98.3	-93.5	-89.1
80	-69.2	-66.8	-64.5	-70.5	-68.0	-65.6	-71.8	-69.2	-66.8
85	-50.0	-48.9	-47.8	-50.6	-49.4	-48.4	-51.2	-50.0	-48.9
90	-9.5	-9.5	-9.5	-9.5	-9.5	-9.5	-9.5	-9.5	-9.5
Future generations	332.2	290.9	259.5	356.1	310.2	272.9	382.8	332.5	289.9
Percentage change	153.8	205.1	292.5	136.3	173.6	238.2	125.5	150.5	198.5

Table 4.4 Net payments for age-zero and future female generations
(thousands of dollars)

Generation's age in 1990	g = .015			g = .020			g = .025		
	r = .03	r = .04	r = .05	r = .03	r = .04	r = .05	r = .03	r = .04	r = .05
0	20.1	20.1	14.1	14.4	21.4	17.5	1.6	20.1	20.2
5	27.1	28.3	22.4	20.5	29.1	25.9	6.9	27.0	28.4
10	48.1	51.5	46.7	40.2	51.3	49.8	25.3	48.0	51.6
15	78.7	85.9	83.8	68.7	83.8	85.6	52.0	78.5	85.8
20	89.0	101.4	103.9	76.4	96.8	103.5	57.6	88.7	101.3
25	74.2	92.0	99.6	59.1	84.6	96.6	38.3	73.8	91.7
30	40.2	62.8	75.3	23.1	52.9	69.8	1.1	39.8	62.4
35	-0.1	25.8	42.3	-18.3	14.0	34.8	-40.7	-0.6	25.3
40	-40.6	-13.0	6.3	-58.9	-25.8	-2.7	-80.7	-41.1	-13.5
45	-78.5	-50.7	-30.1	-96.0	-63.8	-40.0	-116.2	-78.9	-51.3
50	-114.2	-88.3	-68.0	-130.0	-100.7	-77.8	-147.7	-114.7	-88.9
55	-143.6	-121.1	-102.8	-156.9	-132.0	-111.8	-171.5	-144.0	-121.6
60	-155.2	-137.5	-122.5	-165.4	-146.1	-129.9	-176.4	-155.5	-137.8
65	-140.9	-128.1	-117.0	-148.1	-134.4	-122.5	-155.8	-141.1	-128.4
70	-116.6	-108.3	-100.9	-121.2	-112.4	-104.6	-126.1	-116.8	-108.5
75	-91.2	-85.9	-81.2	-94.0	-88.5	-83.6	-97.0	-91.3	-86.1
80	-68.9	-66.0	-63.4	-70.4	-67.5	-64.7	-72.0	-69.0	-66.1
85	-49.7	-48.4	-47.4	-50.3	-49.0	-47.8	-51.0	-49.7	-48.4
90	-7.6	-7.6	-7.6	-7.6	-7.6	-7.6	-7.6	-7.6	-7.6
Future generations	51.9	62.3	56.3	34.8	59.7	60.5	3.7	51.5	61.9

Table 4.5 The composition of male generational accounts. Present values of receipts and payments
(thousands of 1990 dollars; r=.04, g=.02)

Generation's age in 1990	Payments							Receipts				
	Net payment	Direct taxes: labor	Direct taxes: capital	Indirect taxes	Social sec. contr.	Seignor-age	Other revenue	Pension benefits	Health exp.	Other soc. sec. benefits	Househ. respon. paym'ts	Educa-tion
0	111.2	75.5	9.0	48.5	126.6	0.1	13.5	60.4	31.4	8.6	3.0	58.6
5	128.3	83.4	10.0	51.8	139.9	0.1	13.1	66.8	32.1	9.2	3.3	58.6
10	160.9	92.0	11.0	55.4	154.3	0.1	12.6	73.7	32.9	9.9	3.6	44.5
15	205.5	101.3	12.9	59.2	170.1	0.1	12.0	81.4	33.6	10.7	4.0	20.5
20	228.9	107.1	17.9	60.6	179.1	0.1	11.5	90.1	34.3	11.3	4.4	7.1
25	220.3	107.1	21.1	57.6	174.4	0.1	10.8	99.7	34.6	11.3	4.3	0.7
30	184.3	101.7	21.0	52.1	159.6	0.0	10.1	110.5	34.8	11.0	4.0	0.0
35	134.3	92.4	21.0	46.1	136.5	0.0	9.4	122.4	34.5	10.6	3.5	0.0
40	74.9	79.8	22.2	39.8	107.5	0.0	8.5	135.7	34.0	10.3	2.9	0.0
45	12.7	67.2	20.7	33.5	79.8	0.0	7.7	150.5	33.4	10.0	2.3	0.0
50	-52.6	52.3	19.4	27.2	52.5	0.0	6.8	167.0	32.2	9.7	1.8	0.0
55	-119.4	37.4	17.3	21.7	25.4	0.0	5.9	185.8	30.5	9.1	1.5	0.0
60	-165.4	25.3	16.5	17.2	3.8	0.0	5.0	196.7	28.3	6.9	1.3	0.0
65	-154.3	17.4	14.9	13.4	0.1	0.0	4.1	173.7	25.3	4.1	1.1	0.0
70	-121.5	12.1	11.7	10.7	0.0	0.0	3.3	134.3	21.5	2.7	0.9	0.0
75	-91.2	8.1	8.8	8.7	0.0	0.0	2.6	98.9	17.7	2.1	0.7	0.0
80	-68.0	4.6	5.7	6.7	0.0	0.0	2.0	71.0	13.9	1.6	0.5	0.0
85	-49.4	1.9	4.2	5.0	0.0	0.0	1.5	50.0	10.5	1.2	0.3	0.0
90	-9.5	0.2	3.1	1.2	0.0	0.0	0.4	11.5	2.5	0.3	0.0	0.0
Future generations	310.2											

Table 4.6 The composition of female generational accounts. Present values of receipts and payments (thousands of 1990 dollars; $r=.04$, $g=.02$)

Generation's age in 1990	Payments							Receipts				
	Net payment	Direct taxes: labor	Direct taxes: capital	Indirect taxes	Social sec. contr.	Seignor-age	Other revenue	Pension benefits	Health exp.	Other soc. sec. benef.	Househ. respon. paym'ts	Educa-tion
0	21.4	52.2	9.0	54.6	54.1	0.1	14.1	55.4	34.7	10.2	3.4	59.1
5	29.1	57.6	9.9	58.6	59.8	0.2	13.7	61.2	35.7	11.0	3.7	59.1
10	51.3	63.6	10.9	62.9	66.0	0.2	13.3	67.7	36.8	11.9	4.1	45.1
15	83.8	68.9	12.5	67.3	72.4	0.2	12.8	74.5	37.9	12.9	4.5	20.5
20	96.8	69.4	17.4	68.7	75.9	0.0	12.3	82.2	38.9	13.7	5.0	7.1
25	84.6	66.4	20.3	64.3	71.0	0.0	11.7	90.7	39.6	13.4	4.7	0.7
30	52.9	60.6	21.2	56.3	61.2	0.0	11.0	100.1	40.1	12.8	4.4	0.0
35	14.0	52.7	21.8	47.9	48.2	0.1	10.4	110.7	40.3	12.2	3.9	0.0
40	−25.8	45.5	21.2	40.5	34.9	0.1	9.6	122.3	40.4	11.5	3.2	0.0
45	−63.8	38.5	20.1	34.3	23.2	0.1	8.8	134.6	40.2	11.2	2.7	0.0
50	−100.7	31.2	18.4	28.9	12.5	0.1	7.9	147.1	39.4	11.0	2.2	0.0
55	−132.0	24.5	16.6	24.1	4.7	0.1	7.0	159.0	37.8	10.3	1.8	0.0
60	−146.1	18.7	14.2	20.0	0.9	0.0	6.1	151.3	35.3	7.9	1.5	0.0
65	−134.4	14.4	12.4	16.2	0.1	0.0	5.1	144.7	31.7	4.9	1.3	0.0
70	−112.4	10.9	8.8	13.2	0.0	0.0	4.1	118.1	26.8	3.4	1.0	0.0
75	−88.5	7.9	7.6	10.7	0.0	0.0	3.2	92.6	21.9	2.6	0.8	0.0
80	−67.5	5.4	6.6	8.0	0.0	0.0	2.4	70.6	16.7	2.0	0.5	0.0
85	−49.0	3.5	4.8	5.7	0.0	0.0	1.7	50.9	12.1	1.4	0.3	0.0
90	−7.6	0.7	4.0	1.2	0.0	0.0	0.4	11.0	2.5	0.3	0.0	0.0
Future generations	59.7											

To better understand the numbers in Tables 4.3 and 4.4, consider Tables 4.5 and 4.6, which decompose the generational accounts into the present values of each of the various tax payments and transfer receipts. In the case of 35 year old males their generational account of $134,300 represents the difference between $305,400 in the projected present value of future taxes and $171,100 in the projected present value of future transfers. For 35 year old females their $14,000 reflects $181,200 in projected taxes in present value less $167,100 in projected transfers in present value. For 35 year old males the largest payment item is social security contributions, while for 35 year old females the largest payment item is labor income taxes. On the receipt side, the largest component for both males and females is social security pensions.

In addition to detailing the remaining lifetime payments of current generations, Tables 4.3 and 4.4 indicate in the next to last row the payment required of the generation born in 1991 assuming it, as well as all future generations, pays the same amount except for growth. If the Italian government's fiscal policy were generationally balanced, the amount Italians born in 1991 would pay would equal the amount newborns in 1990 pay times $(1+g)$, where g is the growth rate. The last row in Table 4.3 indicates the percentage difference between the amount newborns pay in 1990 times $(1+g)$ and the amount Italians born in 1991 pay under our illustrative assumption of equal growth-adjusted treatment of future Italians. Note that in the calculation of the burden on future generations we assume that the ratio of the burden on future males relative to that on future females is the same as the ratio of the accounts of newborn males to that of newborn females; i.e., we assume that in the future males will be treated by the fiscal system relative to females in the same manner as newborns are slated to be treated.

The comparison of the first and next to last rows in Table 4.3 shows a very large imbalance in the generational stance of Italian fiscal policy. For the nine combinations of interest and growth rate assumptions the percentage difference in the treatment of future Italians compared to 1990 newborn Italians ranges from 125.5 percent to 292.5 percent; i.e., depending on assumptions, future Italians will pay, in present value, somewhere between 2.3 and 4 times the amount the newborn Italians are expected to pay, given current policy. Under our base case assumptions of a 4 percent real interest rate and a 2 percent rate of growth, future Italians pay almost 3 times what 1990 newborns pay.

As the table indicates, which values one assumes for the interest rate and growth rate has an important effect on the size of the generational accounts. The extent of the generational imbalance is also quite sensitive to the growth and interest rate assumptions. The higher the interest and growth rates, the larger the absolute value of the generational accounts. Higher interest rates increase the percentage difference in accounts of current and future newborns, while higher growth rates do the opposite. Besides the sensitivity to assumptions on the interest and growth rates, the results might also be affected by other specific assumptions mainly concerning the evolution of public pensions and the uncertainty surrounding the demographic projections. As far as the first is concerned, the 1992 pension reform is not considered in the baseline accounts. This tends to overestimate the generation gap.[11] On the other hand, the figures in Table 4.3 are based on the replacement rate fertility assumption and this might underestimate the gap. If we instead calculate the burden on future generations based on the assumption of a nearly constant fertility rate (to be precise, constant age-specific fertility rates), the percentage difference in the net lifetime payments of future and newborn Italians rises from 173.6 percent to 246.6 percent. Note that changing the assumption about future fertility leaves unchanged the generational accounts of current generations.

6   Comparing the Italian and the U.S. generational accounts

It may be instructive to compare the Italian base case generational accounts with the U.S. generational accounts computed under the same interest and growth rate assumptions. Table 4.7 does just this. There are a number of interesting differences between the Italian and American accounts. First, the generational policy imbalance is much smaller in the U.S. than in Italy. The percentage difference in the treatment of future generations relative to current newborns is 173.6 percent for Italy, but only 28.0 percent for the U.S. Future Italian males (females) will pay $310,200 ($59,700) compared to $89,500 ($5,700) for future American males (females).

While future Italians pay more, young adults and middle age Italians are slated to pay less than their American counterparts. In the case of 40-year-old American males, the remaining lifetime net tax bill is over twice the corresponding bill for 40-year-old Italian males. The larger Italian generational imbalance is also reflected in the age at which net payments break even. In the case of both Italian males and females, the break-even age (viz. the age at which gross payments to the government equal benefits received) is fifteen years less than the break-even ages for American males and females. This phenomenon is largely explained by the greater generosity of the Italian pension system relative to that of the U.S. Compare, for example, the −$121,500 generational account of 70 year old Italian males with the corresponding −$47,100 generational account for 70-year-old American males.

Table 4.7 A comparison of Italian and U.S. generational accounts
(thousands of dollars; $r = .04$, $g = .02$)

Generation's age in 1990	Italian males	American males	Italian females	American females
0	111.2	62.4	21.4	4.4
5	128.3	80.7	29.1	12.1
10	160.9	116.4	51.3	36.3
15	205.5	166.9	83.8	68.8
20	228.9	200.2	86.8	94.5
25	220.3	227.3	84.6	103.6
30	184.3	223.1	52.9	100.9
35	134.3	207.8	14.0	93.5
40	74.9	191.9	–25.8	81.1
45	12.7	164.5	–63.8	61.6
50	–52.6	116.5	–100.7	35.9
55	–119.4	67.1	–132.0	3.5
60	–165.4	13.6	–146.1	–31.8
65	–154.3	–37.4	–134.4	–62.2
70	–121.5	–47.1	–112.4	–67.1
75	–91.2	–44.6	–88.5	–62.9
80	–68.0	–37.6	–67.5	–53.9
85	–49.4	–29.2	–49.0	–44.3
90	–9.5	–1.5	–7.6	–7.4
Future generations	310.2	81.5	59.7	5.7

A final interesting difference between the Italian and American generational accounts is the situation of males relative to females. While Italian policy provides older females with more net payments than does American policy, it extracts somewhat larger net payments from younger females and much larger net payments from future females.

7   Understanding the generational imbalance in Italian fiscal policy

Much of the generational imbalance in Italian fiscal policy reflects the pending demographic transition. Under the base case interest and growth rate assumptions, the percentage difference in the treatment of future and newborn Italians falls by more than half (69.7 percent compared with 173.6 percent) if the Italian population is assumed to experience no demographic change in the future. By no demographic change we mean that the number of Italians in each age-sex group in future years would equal the corresponding 1990 number of Italians.

A second very important factor in explaining the generational imbalance is the large level of the Italian public debt relative to GDP. As mentioned in Section 2, since the mid-eighties the Italian public debt is on an unsustainable path. For example, Blanchard *et al.* (1990) estimated that the gap between the actual primary balance and the level required in 1989 to avoid a debt to GDP runaway was equal to 5.2 percent of GDP. The effect of the large amount of debt on generational accounts has been estimated by assuming, counterfactually, that the Italian debt is zero. In this case, the percentage imbalance in generational policy declines from 173.6 percent to 135.1 percent. This exercise indicates that while the government's debt accounts for about one third of the imbalance in generational policy, most of the imbalance in policy has nothing to do with officially labeled government debt. This illustrates the point that sole focus on debt can be highly misleading for assessing a government's generational policy.

A third critical factor underlying the generational imbalance in policy is the scale of Italy's social security system. To see the importance of social security, suppose that pension benefits were immediately and permanently reduced by 20 percent. In this case the generational imbalance would decline from 173.6 percent to 86.9 percent.

Table 4.8 Understanding the source of generational imbalance in Italian fiscal policy (percentage difference in generational accounts of future Italians and 1990 newborns)

	(1)	(2)	(3)	(4)
	Base case	No demographic change	Zero debt	Lower social security benefits
Percentage difference	173.6	69.7	135.1	86.9
Percentage difference	(2) and (3) 43.9	(2) and (4) 23.2	(3) and (4) 54.2	(2) and (3) and (4) 0.0

Table 4.8 summarizes the effects on the generational policy imbalance of these three counterfactual experiments. It also considers alternative combinations of these experiments. If any two of the three experiments are combined, the 173.6 percent generational imbalance falls to between 23.2 percent and 54.2 percent. Thus, the generational policy imbalance is so great that even the consideration of two dramatic reversals of circumstances is insufficient to close the gap between the fiscal treatment of current and future Italian newborns. If, on the other hand, all three experiments are combined, the gap is closed.

The imbalance in generational policy exposed here has been partially explored in a number of recent studies considering the future finances of the Italian social security system. In 1986, the Treasury Technical Committee on Public Expenditure (see Franco and Morcaldo, 1986) projected a very substantial rise in the theoretical equilibrium social security tax rate (i.e., the ratio of total pension benefits to total income subject to pension contribution) for the Employee Pension Fund. Recent estimates by the National Institute for Social Security (INPS, 1991) and the State Accounting Office (Ragioneria Generale, 1991) have concurred on the seriousness of the problem. INPS projects the rate to rise from 39.5 in 1990 to 45 percent in 2010. The State Accounting Office puts the rate at 48 percent in 2010 and 57 percent in 2025.

8   Alternative tax policies to restore generational balance

An alternative way to understand the magnitude of the generational imbalance is to consider the size of the immediate and permanent increase in alternative tax rates required to restore generational balance. Consider, for example, the immediate and permanent increase in the average labor income tax rate from its current value of 12.4 percent to 21.4 percent. This huge increase is sufficient to restore generational balance. As indicated in the first column of Table 4.9, raising the income tax in this manner raises the generational accounts of all current generations. For middle age males net lifetime payments rise, in present value, by anywhere from $40,000 to $76,000. For middle age females net lifetime payments rise, in present value, by anywhere from $23,000 to $45,000. The large additional payments of these and other currently living generations permit a significant decline in the fiscal burden of future generations. In the case of males the decline is $139,200, and in the case of females it is $2,000.

Of course, raising labor income taxes is not the only way to restore generational balance. Columns two, three, and four in Table 4.9 show the changes in generational accounts if social security contributions, capital income taxes, or indirect taxes, respectively, are raised to correct the generational imbalance. While the impact on future generations is fairly similar regardless of which tax is increased, the distribution of the additional burden across current generations is quite sensitive to the choice of tax instrument. Compare, for example, rectifying the generational imbalance by

Table 4.9 Changes in generational accounts required to attain generational balance (thousands of dollars)

Tax to be increased

Ages	Labor income tax (1)	Social security contributions (2)	Capital income tax (3)	Indirect taxes (4)
Males				
0	56.5	72.5	44.5	48.1
10	68.9	88.4	54.3	55.0
20	80.2	102.6	64.0	60.2
30	76.1	91.3	61.0	51.7
40	59.9	61.6	53.3	39.5
50	39.2	30.1	40.1	27.1
60	19.0	2.2	27.1	17.1
70	9.1	0	13.3	10.6
80	3.5	0	4.6	6.7
Future generations	−139.2	−122.9	−151.3	−147.7
Females				
0	43.6	31.0	43.6	54.3
10	47.6	37.8	54.0	62.5
20	51.9	43.5	63.4	68.2
30	45.4	35.0	61.2	55.8
40	34.0	20.0	51.9	40.2
50	23.3	7.1	38.8	28.6
60	14.0	0.5	24.9	19.9
70	8.1	0	13.1	13.1
80	4.1	0	6.4	8.0
Future generations	−2.0	−6.2	−7.3	−17.5
Average net propensity to save	21.1	20.1	22.0	21.3

raising social security taxes with the alternative of raising capital income taxes. For Italians aged 60 and over the former policy involves a very small increase in their remaining lifetime payments, while the latter policy involves a significant increase. This difference simply reflects the fact that older Italians are, in the main, retired, and pay very little in social security taxes. On the other hand, they pay a significant share of capital income taxes reflecting their considerable share of total Italian wealth.

Since an immediate and permanent increase in tax rates that restores generational balance seems unlikely, Table 4.10 explores more realistic, although still quite painful initiatives that would close the gap between the treatment of future and current generations. The table shows the change in generational accounts resulting from three different policies. The first involves an equal revenue switch from social security payroll taxation to indirect taxation.[12] The second involves a 63 percent increase in income tax rates for 10 years which would lower the Italian debt to GDP ratio to about 0.6 by the turn of the century. A debt to GDP ratio of 0.6 is one of the requirements proposed by the EC for participation in the European monetary union. The third policy involves a gradual reduction in social security pension benefits. According to this policy pensions would ultimately be reduced by 20 percent, but the reduction would occur over a 10-year period, with benefits being reduced by 2 percent per year.[13]

The first policy of replacing social security payroll taxation with indirect taxation has little effect on the percentage difference in the treatment of future and newborn Italians, but it does redistribute substantial sums between males and females. Males pay a much larger share of total payroll taxes than do females, reflecting their larger share of total labor earnings. In contrast, the male share of indirect tax payments is quite close to the female share. Hence, switching from payroll to indirect taxes moves the fiscal system away from a tax paid primarily by males toward a tax paid by both males and females. In the case of 40 year old males this "revenue neutral" change in tax bases reduces their remaining lifetime net tax bill by $37,300, while it increases the bill of 40 year old females by $36,600. Future males also benefit greatly by this provision, but this gain to future generations of Italians is almost completely offset by the loss to future females.

The second policy of reducing the ratio of public debt to GDP from 0.9 to 0.6 reduces the percentage difference in the treatment of future and newborn Italians by raising the net payments of all currently alive Italians, with the exception of the newborn. The percentage gap in the treatment of future and newborn Italians is reduced from 173.6 percent to 151.7 percent. The adjustment is mainly born by middle age individuals, who are close to their peak income tax paying years.

Table 4.10 Changes in generational accounts arising from three hypothetical policies (thousands of dollars)

Ages	Switching from social security to indirect taxation (1)	Reducing debt/GDP ratio to 60 percent over 10 years (2)	Cutting social security benefits by 20 percent over 10 years (3)
Males			
0	−41.1	0.0	12.1
10	−56.5	2.0	14.7
20	−72.1	11.7	18.1
30	−67.6	17.4	22.1
40	−37.3	18.5	26.9
50	−4.4	16.3	31.8
60	26.5	9.3	27.2
70	18.9	5.4	13.4
80	11.8	2.4	4.8
Future generations	−117.3	−24.7	−67.9
Females			
0	42.3	0.0	11.1
10	45.1	3.0	13.6
20	45.3	9.6	16.4
30	38.1	11.7	20.0
40	36.6	10.5	24.2
50	38.4	8.8	27.8
60	34.4	6.0	24.2
70	23.3	4.3	14.0
80	14.2	2.7	5.8
Future generations	115.5	−4.7	−4.2
Average net propensity to save	12.6	12.3	15.4

The third policy of gradually cutting social security benefits by 20 percent is more effective than the previous one in reducing the intergenerational imbalance.[14] Its intragenerational effects are also different. This policy redistributes substantial sums from existing older Italians toward younger and future Italians. The percentage gap in the treatment of future and newborn Italians is reduced from 173.6 to 92.7 percent. 60-year-old males pay $27,200 more, while 60-year-old females pay $24,200 more. The growth-adjusted benefit to future male Italians is $67,900; it is $4,200 for future females.

9   The impact on national saving of alternative tax policies

This section considers the likely impact effects on national saving of the various fiscal policy experiments described in the previous section. Specifically, for each policy we first multiply each living generation's marginal propensity to consume out of lifetime resources by the projected policy-induced change in its account. We then sum these products across all living generations to determine the aggregate change in consumption.

Let Xc_k be the marginal propensity to consume out of lifetime wealth for a typical member of the generation born in year k, and $\Delta N^j_{t,k}$ the present value of the change in the remaining lifetime net payments of the generation born in year k induced by policy j (where j ranges from 1 to 7, corresponding to the policies described in Tables 4.9 and 4.10). Then the effect on national saving at time t when the policy is implemented, is equal to:

$$\Delta s^j = \sum_{s=0}^{D} Xc_s \, \Delta N^j_{t,t-s} \, .$$

That is, the increase in national saving is equal to the reduction in the consumption of all generations alive at time t.

To compute the marginal propensities to consume out of lifetime resources we have first estimated lifetime wealth for each individual born in year k. Our methodology is outlined in the Appendix. Under the assumption of homothetic preferences marginal and average propensities coincide and are estimated by the average ratio of current consumption of each individual in an age/sex cohort to her/his lifetime resources. The last rows of Tables 4.9 and 4.10 report the net national saving rate, as a percentage of net national product, induced by the corresponding policy. Recall that the net national saving in 1990 was around 10.2 percent of net national product. Hence, the effect of each of the policies in these tables is about to double the national saving rate.

However, since the various policies are differently distributed across age and sex, they have also different implications for the level of national savings. Thus, restoring generational balance through indirect taxation or raising taxes on capital has the largest impact on national saving, while increasing social security contributions has the smallest effect.

The policies described in Table 4.10 have, as expected, a smaller impact on national saving. In the case of switching from social security taxation to indirect taxation, national saving increases by 2.4 percentage points. It rises by 2.1 percentage points if social security benefits are reduced by 20 percent over 10 years, and it rises by 5.2 percentage points when the debt-to-GDP ratio is reduced to 0.60 in 10 years.

10   Summary and conclusion

There is a serious imbalance in Italy's generational policy. Unless major steps are taken and taken soon, future generations of Italians will be forced to pay over their lifetimes much more than the net taxes expected to be collected from current young Italians. This generational policy imbalance reflects the combination of the explicit liability to service very large amounts of government debt and the implicit liability to pay substantial sums to existing generations in the form of pension and health benefits. Were there a large projected number of future Italian workers to share these burdens, these liabilities would be less troubling. But the Italian population is rapidly aging and declining.

There are a large variety of fiscal measures that can be used to bring Italian policy into generational balance. For example, one could raise income taxes. The current average rate of taxation on total income (capital plus labor income) is 14 percent. To bring Italian policy into generational balance would require immediately and permanently raising the average income tax rate to 23 percent. Precisely which fiscal measures are taken and how quickly they are implemented will determine how the burden of adjusting to generational balance will be distributed over different cohorts of Italians. One thing, however, is clear. The longer the delay in making the adjustment to a balanced course of policy, the larger will be the generational imbalance that needs to be addressed. In our base case calculations (which do not consider the effects of the 1992 pension reform), future generations will pay almost three times more than current newborn Italians if all the adjustment is forced on future Italians. But this calculation assumes that those Italians born in the immediate future will share in the larger lifetime net tax burden. Suppose, instead, that the next 10 cohorts of Italians are left off the hook and treated in the same manner as current newborn Italians are projected to be treated. Then generations of Italians born after the turn of the century will be left with a growth-adjusted lifetime net tax bill that is almost four rather than almost three times larger than the bill facing current Italian newborns. The reform of the public pension system introduced at the end of 1992 represents a major step towards a balanced fiscal policy. It should limit the net taxes paid by future generations of Italians to less than twice those paid by current young Italians. As pointed out in Section 7, the achievement of fiscal balance requires, however, other important action.

APPENDIX

The estimation of lifetime resources and of the marginal propensity to consume

Lifetime resources at time t for an individual born in year k is the sum of non-human and human wealth. Human wealth is defined to include not only the present value of after-tax future earnings, but also the present value of social security benefits, i.e. the level of pension wealth. Of course, for a retired individual human wealth is equal to the value of pension wealth. To estimate lifetime resources we have used the 1989 SHIW, which contains information on the value of household net worth, earnings and pension income, and personal characteristics such as age, sex, years of education, occupation etc.

The overall sample of income recipients (14,552 observations) was split into two parts. The first includes only working persons aged over 16 years and below 60 (the retirement age is 55 for women); the second group includes retired people aged over 60 (55 for women) and below 91 (maximum length of life) whose income comes only from social security benefits. The pension wealth of the last group was computed by taking the present value of social security benefits on the assumption that benefits are constant up to death at the value currently observed for each single person.

To account for the rapidly increasing probability of death after average life expectancy has been reached, the discount rate in the computation of the pension wealth portion of lifetime resources has been set equal to 12 percent.

For the first group, pension wealth has been computed following the previous procedure after setting the level of social security benefits at 80 percent of the projected earnings at age 60 (see below) on the assumption that all members of the male labor force retire at 60 (55 for female members). To compute the other portion of human wealth we have first fitted a WLS regression of current earnings against a vector of demographic characteristics and a second order polynomial in age to allow for cohort effects (see Table 4.A1).

For an individual born in year k the fitted value of earnings at t is:

$$Y_{t,k} = bX_k + a(t - k) + a_1(t - k)^2$$

where X_k is the vector of characteristics of the specific individual aged t–k. Projected earnings j years ahead are computed as

$$Y_{t+j,k} = [bX_k + a(t + j - k) + a_1(t + j - k)^2] (1 + g)^j$$

Table 4.A1 Earnings function estimates *(a)*
(dependent variable: individual earnings)

Variables	Coefficients	*t*-statistics
Education	379.7	4.6
Education squared	–3.1	–0.8
Age	554.6	14.2
Age squared	–5.7	–11.2
Male	3,240.8	21.5
Married	1,374.8	6.9
Occupation:		
Operative and laborer	–4,716.3	–16.9
Clerical	–3,247.7	–10.4
Precision craft	866.1	1.7
Professional	5,398.8	8.1
Manager	11,418.7	8.9
Entrepreneur	21,005.9	9.8
Other	–7,338.2	–20.8
Sector:		
Agriculture	–4,740.8	–15.5
Industry	33.2	0.1
Services	–119.2	–0.4
North	1,192.1	6.3
South	–707.8	–3.9
Constant	2,905.8	3.2
Adjusted R^2	.78	
Standard error	507.70	
Dependent variable mean	30,633.30	
Number of observations	9,290.00	

(a) The equation has been estimated by WLS using as weights the fitted values of an OLS first stage regression. The sample of 9,290 observations is obtained excluding individuals with zero labor earnings, individuals not in the labor force or older than 65. The dependent variable is expressed in thousands of 1989 lire.

where g is the rate of growth of productivity (2 percent per year). Thus, the present value of earnings is given by

$$H_k = \sum_{i=t-k}^{60} (1 + r)^{(t-k)-i} Y_{t+i-(t-k)}$$

where r is the discount rate set at 4 percent.

For each individual lifetime wealth is then obtained adding together her/his human wealth and her/his share of the household net holdings of real and financial assets, according to the method of division defined in Section 4.

For individuals below age 16 we have assumed that they own only human wealth. The last has been computed by assuming that they enter the labor force at age 17 and taking the average human wealth of the individuals aged 17 and discounting it back appropriately. Thus, for example, for those aged 10, lifetime resources are given by $(1 + g)^7 (1 + r)^{-7} H_{17}$, where H_{17} is the average value of human wealth of working individuals aged 17.

For young dependents (aged below 28) which have not yet started to work, we have assumed that they would start working within a year and we have imputed to them the human wealth of those working individuals one year older, adjusting for growth and discounting.

Finally, given lifetime wealth and consumption for each single individual in the sample, the average and marginal propensity to consume have been computed by dividing the consumption of each single cohort (imputed according to the methodology described in Section 4) by the cohort average lifetime resources. The age pattern of the average propensity to consume out of wealth is shown in Figure 4.1 separately for males and females.

NOTES

* We wish to thank Alessandro Petretto, Guido Tabellini and Ignazio Visco for their helpful comments. Luigi Sciamplicotti provided valuable research assistance. Errors are the authors' responsibility.

1 Consider a policy which lowers the market price of an asset, such as a tax on land. Since the sellers of land are, on average, older generations and the purchasers of land, are, on average, younger generations, such a policy redistributes between the old and the young. The physical land is unchanged, but the old are forced to sell their land at a lower price to the benefit of the young purchasers of land.

2 This paper was prepared before the Italian Government, in December 1992, issued a legislative decree reforming the public pension system. The reform aims at stabilizing the ratio of spending to GDP at the 1992 level. It provides an increase in the age of retirement, a lengthening of the reference period for calculating pensionable earnings, an increase in the minimum number of years of contributions required for old-age pension entitlement. Wage indexation of pensions is replaced by price indexation. Special rules for public sector employees are to be gradually repealed. As the timing and features of the reform

were not known when the paper was prepared, the baseline generational accounts presented in Section 5 reflect the previous statutory provisions. However, in order to account for these reforms at least in part, it was decided not to consider the fact that the Italian pension system had not yet reached full maturity. This means that in the baseline accounts the ratio of pension benefits to per capita GDP is assumed to be constant at its 1990 level. This tends to underestimate the generational imbalance existing before the 1992 pension reform. The long-term effects of the 1992 reform are approximated by the third fiscal policy experiment presented in Section 8, which considers a 20 percent cut in social security benefits. The medium-term effects of the reform are in fact milder than those suggested in our experiments, in which it is assumed that the cut in social security benefits is achieved in 10 years.

3 Clearly, migration and increases in labor force participation (especially for women), might, to some extent, effectively counteract the decline in fertility. As will be seen later, to at least partly account for this possibility we will base our computations on an optimistic assumption about future fertility.

4 For a full description of the tax treatment of financial assets see Cavazzuti and Giannini (1991).

5 As from 1991, the corporate tax rate is above 47 percent.

6 The derivation of a correct measure of non-financial wealth is an extremely complex task, as it involves adjusting the general government appropriation account through the following steps: i) assessment of the market value of general government's real assets, including historic buildings and building sites as well as loss-generating public enterprises; ii) inclusion among current costs of market rents of those assets (such as government buildings) currently used by general government; iii) exclusion from revenues of profits, dividends and other incomes currently earned on assets. As far as point i) is concerned, it might be noted that the so called Commissione Cassese (a commission appointed by the Government in 1985 to estimate public sector real estate) valued government-owned land at 431 trillion lire and buildings at 220 trillion lire. These government assets thus amounted to two thirds of GDP.

7 More precisely, a measure of net financial wealth has been derived by capitalizing net interest payments (i.e., interest payments minus interest income) at the nominal interest rate before tax on newly issued government bonds (currently around 12 percent). According to this measure, the government net financial liabilities were in 1990 equal to 77 percent of GDP.

8 It should be noted that in 1990 the Italian pension system had not yet reached full maturity. The ratio of the average pension benefit to *per capita* GDP was therefore likely to increase significantly in the future.

9 As already said, the baseline generational accounts do not consider the full effects of the 1992 pension reform. See note 2.

10 The exchange rate used for calculation was 1,198 lire per dollar, the average rate in 1990.

11 See note 2.

12 More precisely, the average indirect tax rate has been increased to the level required to offset the revenue loss arising in the base year from the reduction in the social security tax rate. In the following years, revenue neutrality need not occur.

13 The 20 percent cut in the 1990 pension-to-*per capita* GDP ratio is broadly consistent with the effects of the 1992 pension reform. See note 2.

14 See note 2.

REFERENCES

Auerbach, A.J., J. Gokhale and L.J. Kotlikoff (1991). 'Generational Accounts: A Meaningful Alternative to Deficit Accounting', in D. Bradford, (ed.), *Tax Policy and the Economy*, Cambridge, MA: National Bureau of Economic Research, Vol. V.

Auerbach, A.J., J. Gokhale and L.J. Kotlikoff (1992). 'Generational Accounting: A New Approach to Understanding the Effects of Fiscal Policy on Saving', *Scandinavian Journal of Economics* **94**: 303-18.

Auerbach, A.J. and L.J. Kotlikoff (1987). *Dynamic Fiscal Policy*, Cambridge: Cambridge University Press.

Blanchard, O.J, J.C. Chouraqui, R.P. Hagemann and N. Sartor (1990). 'The Sustainability of Fiscal Policy: New Answers to an Old Question', *OECD Economic Studies* **15**: 7-36.

Cavazzuti, F. and S. Giannini (1991) (eds.). *Sistemi fiscali e integrazione europea*, Bologna: Il Mulino.

Franco, D. (1992). 'L'espansione della spesa pubblica in Italia (1960-90)", in Ente Einaudi, *Il disavanzo pubblico in Italia: natura strutturale e politiche di rientro*, Bologna: Il Mulino, Vol. I.

Franco, D. and G. Morcaldo (1986). *Un modello di previsione degli squilibri del sistema previdenziale*, Roma: Istituto Poligrafico e Zecca dello Stato.

Franco, D. and N. Sartor (1990). *Stato e famiglia*, Milano: Angeli.

Giannini, S. (1989). *Imposte e finanziamento delle imprese*, Bologna: Il Mulino.

INPS (1991), *Il nuovo modello previsionale INPS per le pensioni – Caratteristiche generali e risultati di sintesi della proiezione al 2010 del Fondo Pensioni Lavoratori Dipendenti*, Roma.

Kotlikoff, L.J. (1989). 'From Deficit Delusion to the Fiscal Balance Rule – Looking for a Sensible Way to Measure Fiscal Policy', NBER Working Paper 2841.

Kotlikoff, L.J. (1992). *Generational Accounting – Knowing Who Pays, and When, for What We Spend*, New York: Free Press.

OECD (1988). *The Future of Social Security Protection*, Paris.

Ragioneria Generale dello Stato (1991). *Fondo Pensioni Lavoratori Dipendenti. Una proiezione al 2025*, Roma: Istituto Poligrafico e Zecca dello Stato.

II

LIFE-CYCLE SAVING AND PRECAUTIONARY MOTIVES

5 Young households' saving and the life cycle of opportunities. Evidence from Japan and Italy*

ALBERT ANDO, LUIGI GUISO
and DANIELE TERLIZZESE

1 Introduction

The earnings profile appears to rise steeply with age in most countries, especially those with rapid growth such as Italy and Japan. It is therefore natural to expect that, because of the consumption smoothing principle, young people will dissave.

Using microdata for Japan and Italy, we show that families and singles both save and accumulate net worth throughout their working lives, even while they are quite young and their current incomes are lower than future incomes.

We are thus faced with the question as to why young people do not dissave. This is a shift in emphasis from recent literature, in which much effort has been devoted to devising modifications to the life-cycle theory that could accommodate the relatively low propensity to dissave by older, retired families.

The mere lack of dissaving by very young households may be explained by the presence of liquidity constraints or myopia. The ingenious interaction of liquidity constraints with uncertainty recently proposed by Deaton (1991) can, within a buffer stock context, explain a limited amount of saving; it is, nonetheless, probably inadequate to explain the significant saving by very young households with relatively low incomes.

We propose instead an explanation based on the hypothesis that, for very young households, due to the expectation of (future) consumption opportunities not available today, higher future income might be accompanied by larger needs. This creates a situation in which, at a later period, the marginal utility of income is higher even though the expected income is higher than the current income.

The increase in current consumption induced by an expected increase in future income might then be small (or even negative). According to this interpretation, consumption will then be concentrated in those periods in which the opportunities are better. In contrast with the smoothing of consumption, we obtain what might be called a "consumption lumping" principle.

Consumption lumping can also be obtained if the marginal utility is higher in the middle age because of the evolution of the family size. Attanasio and Browning (1991) show that controlling for the demographic changes within the households considerably smoothes the age consumption profile. However the close association between consumption and income at young ages still characterizes the data.

In Section 2 we present evidence that young families and individuals with relatively low current earnings who anticipate rapidly increasing future earnings nevertheless save a significant proportion of their current income. We also show that the reaction to anticipated changes in income is negligible for very young families, and that it becomes sizeable and significantly different from zero for older cohorts. We also show that the level of net worth affects consumption with a significant, positive and smaller than one coefficient, indicating that families do follow a fairly long-term plan of asset accumulation. This casts doubt on the hypothesis of myopic behavior.

In Section 3 we outline a theoretical explanation and offer two illustrative examples. We conclude in Section 4 with a general discussion in which we contrast our theoretical explanation of the young consumer's behavior with alternative explanations put forward in recent literature.

2   The saving behavior of young households: an empirical assessment

In a recent paper Carroll and Summers (1991) presented a composite and well-documented picture of consumption behavior that is difficult to square with standard versions of the permanent income or life-cycle theories. In particular, they use microdata to show that the basic implication of a simple life-cycle model is not borne out. On the contrary, there seems to be little evidence of low frequency consumption smoothing, as both young and old households dissave too little.

The behavior of the second group has been thoroughly investigated, both empirically (Ando and Kennikell, 1986; Hayashi, Ando and Ferris, 1988, among others) and theoretically (Davies, 1981; Hurd, 1989). Our focus here is on the behavior of young consumers, which is interesting for at least two reasons.

First, the predictions of the life-cycle theory at the individual level are characterized by, among other features, zero lifetime saving and negative correlation between current saving and expected future income. The main features of macrodata are positive and sizeable total saving and positive correlation between the saving-to-income ratio and the growth rate of aggregate income. The implications of the theory at the micro level and macrodata are usually reconciled with each other by aggregating consumers at different points in the life cycle. However, the effects of aggregation are unambiguous only when the preferred age pattern of consumption and the lifetime earnings profile are such that families do not dissave before retirement. If young individuals dissave significantly, the larger weight assigned to them in a growing economy by the process of aggregation could result in total saving being negatively correlated with growth. The saving behavior of young consumers is therefore crucial in assessing the consequences of aggregation for the level of total savings and its correlation with the growth of income.[1]

Second, whereas simple extensions of the life-cycle theory have been able to account for the low level of dissaving among the old, the behavior of the young has proved more difficult to rationalize. Liquidity constraints and myopia are often invoked to explain the lack of borrowing against a higher future stream of income. These hypotheses are suggestive but they are not entirely convincing (see the discussion in Section 4). We hope that greater emphasis on young people will eventually make it easier to discriminate between the alternative interpretations of saving behavior.

2.1 Descriptive evidence: high saving rate by the young and a potential sample selection bias

Table 5.1 shows saving by age for Italian and Japanese households, together with the cross-section earnings profile, which appears to be increasing with age. Given the high growth experienced by both countries, the adjustment for increases in productivity would make the two profiles extremely steep, especially at the beginning of life.[2] Consequently, the strict life-cycle theory would suggest that young consumers decumulate substantial amounts of wealth (where they have any at the beginning of their working lives) or run negative saving.

The evidence points in the opposite direction. Young households save a considerable proportion of their current income. Combining cross-section data for different years and looking at the annual change in net worth of the average household in a specific age cohort, while giving a rather different measure of net accumulation, nonetheless confirms the basic fact: in spite of steep earnings profiles young households, both in Italy and Japan, accumulate wealth.[3]

Table 5.1 Younger households' saving, disposable income, wealth accumulation and earnings by age in Italy and Japan

Age of the head of household	Italy				Age of the head of household	Japan (c)			
	Saving (a)	Annual change in wealth (b)	Disposable income	Earnings		Saving (d)	Annual change in wealth (e)	Disposable income	Earnings
20 – 23	2,744	–	21,391	15,253	20 – 24	405.2	584.4	1,640.5	1,577.1
24 – 27	3,504	9,267	23,229	17,232	25 – 29	404.6	745.9	2,252.6	2,101.9
28 – 31	5,076	12,238	27,109	20,103	30 – 34	391.4	952.5	2,943.1	2,713.9
32 – 35	6,205	10,103	29,613	23,488	35 – 39	478.3	1,090.7	3,579.1	3,251.9
36 – 39	5,611	16,387	31,786	25,505	40 – 44	586.1	1,143.4	4,044.3	3,620.7
40 – 43	7,903	9,531	33,856	26,971					

Sources: Italy: Bank of Italy Survey of Household Income and Wealth, 1987 and 1989; in thousands of 1987 lire. Japan: National Survey of Family Income and Expenditure, 1979 and 1984, Status Bureau, Government of Japan; in thousands of 1979 yen. (a) Defined as households' disposable income minus households' consumption expenditure. – (b) Annualized change in net worth between the end of 1987 and the end of 1989, in 1987 prices. – (c) These figures represent a weighted average for ordinary families (married couples, their children and other members such as retired parents), single-person households and working male adults living in another household. See also the explanation in the text on the construction of cohorts. – (d) Defined as households' disposable income minus (economic) consumption. – (e) Weighted average of the annualized change in net worth for ordinary and single-person households between the fourth quarter of 1979 and the fourth quarter of 1985, in 1979 prices, and the saving of male, working dependent adults (mostly living with their parents). For the last group, saving is defined as income minus consumption since no information on their assets and liabilities is available. This concept includes real capital gains and losses, especially on values of residential property.

A potentially important bias might arise from the fact that young consumers still living as dependents within their families do not appear as independent households in the surveys. If (for whatever reason) they tend to consume more of what they earn (or, similarly, if the young consumers who become independent are thriftier), the observed "oversaving" of the young might be a statistical illusion. Given the tendency for young consumers in both Japan and Italy to live in their parents' houses long after they start working, this sample selection problem could be important.

Before proceeding with the more elaborate analysis, we check in the simplest possible manner whether the living status of young adults makes a significant difference. Table 5.2 shows mean values of some key variables for a number of relevant groups. Our comments refer to Japan but, as can easily be seen, the same conclusions apply to Italy. Row A corresponds to pure nuclear families;[4] row B corresponds to pure nuclear families extended to include one, and only one, working dependent adult male aged 25-29[5] (extended families); and row C corresponds to a single, working adult male aged 25-29 and living alone.[6] For row B the saving-to-income ratio is .22, while for the sum of rows A and C, which represents a fictitious family comparable with that in row B, it is .15. Thus, the saving-to-income ratio is 7 percentage points higher for the extended families. The conclusion that we draw from this table is that, if anything, young working dependents save proportionately more than independent consumers of comparable age. It is thus difficult to interpret the overall behavior of young households within a standard consumption smoothing paradigm. However, the issue deserves further scrutiny, especially on the question of the response of young consumers to (expected) future changes in earnings.

2.2 Young consumers and future income changes

If many years of longitudinal data on both earnings and consumption were available it would be possible to construct measures of expected future earnings for each single consumer and test their effect on current consumption. Unfortunately, longitudinal data are not usually available for either consumption or earnings. For Italy we have access to a short panel where a sample of households were interviewed both in 1987 and 1989. This information can be usefully exploited to test for the effects of future expected income on current consumption. For Japan we do not have panel data. However, by combining cross-sectional data at different points in time it is possible to construct cohort average data for consumption and current and future earnings.

The basic idea is illustrated in Figure 5.1, which shows two cross-section patterns of earnings for individuals (heads of households) with specific

Table 5.2 Disposable income, consumption and net worth by type of household: Italy (I) and Japan (J)

	Age		Disposable income		Consumption		Net worth		Saving rate	
	I	J	I	J	I	J	I	J	I	J
A Pure nuclear families	58	52	30,880	4,611	23,947	4,029	162,140	22,104	.22	.14
B Extended families with one working adult aged 25-29	58	54	48,234	5,556	33,133	4,334	194,379	23,879	.31	.22
C Single person families aged 25-29	27	27	19,741	2,113	17,332	1,667	47,467	4,083	.12	.20
D Combined households (A+C)			50,621	6,733	41,279	5,696	209,607	26,187	.18	.15

Sources: Italy: Bank of Italy Survey of Household Income and Wealth, 1989; thousands of 1987 lire. Japan: National Survey of Family Income and Expenditure, 1979, Status Bureau, Government of Japan; thousands of 1979 yen.

characteristics (occupation, education, etc.) over all ages. Suppose that the cross-section age-earnings profile *aa* was observed in year *t*, and *bb* was observed in year *t+h* (to be specific, let *t* be 1979 and *t+h* be 1984, the two years covered by the available Japanese surveys). Suppose then that the position *p* represents the actual earnings of a group of individuals aged 35 in 1979. They will be aged 40 in 1984, and hence will occupy the position *s* in that year. We suppose this position represents, for 1979, the expected earnings five years ahead of individuals who, in 1979, occupy position *p*. Note that this group's lifetime path of earnings is considerably steeper than either *aa* or *bb*[7] and is generally quite different from the path that would be obtained by adjusting *aa* for the growth in the economy's overall productivity, represented by the distance between *q* and *s*.

Figure 5.1

Cross-section pattern of earnings

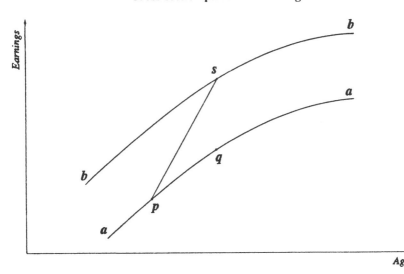

The principal problem when using a sequence of cross-section data to approximate panel data stems from the possibility that, between 1979 and 1984, the household in question changed type. For example, single persons get married, married couples divorce and so on. Since the mean income of these different household types is different, careful handling of the type changes is required in order to obtain reasonable estimates of expected future income. Clearly, the issue is of particular relevance for young consumers, who are the focus of our attention.[8]

Consider then the population of ordinary households (husband and wife, their children and perhaps other members) aged between 30 and 35 living in 1984. Let us focus our attention on the male head of each household. He could have come from one of four groups. He may have already been the head of the same household; he could have been a single person living independently; or he could have been a working dependent adult in someone else's household, most probably his parents'. The fourth possibility, a non-working dependent adult in someone else's household, can be dismissed for our purposes since there are very few non-working dependent adult males over the age of 25.

We shall refer to type i families, $i=(OF, SF, DA)$, and type j families, $j=(GOF, GSF, GDA)$, where the symbols represent respectively: ordinary families with married couples at the core, male single-person families, and working male dependent adults in 1979 (i) and 1984 (j), and G is a mnemonic for "grown". All are aged 25-29 in 1979 and 30-34 in 1984.

Figure 5.2

Households' transition paths

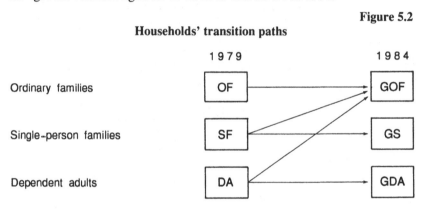

We have no information that can precisely match each type i family with a type j family. By making strong assumptions we can, however, deduce the transition probabilities. We assume, first of all, that all families in OF will move to GOF. Since the divorce rate in Japan is extremely low and the mortality rate at these ages is also low, this seems a reasonable assumption. We also assume that families in SF will be in either GSF or GOF and families in DA will be in either GDA or GOF; in other words we assume that a single person does not become a dependent adult, or a dependent adult a single person. This may not be a reasonable assumption, but without it, it would become extremely hard to proceed. The possible transition paths are illustrated in Figure 5.2. From the number of families and individuals in each group, obtained from the 1980 and 1985 Japanese censuses, we have estimated the transition probabilities, which are then used to compute the expected future earnings of each type i family. We have verified that the number of corresponding families and individuals in the samples of the National Survey of Family Income and Expenditure, multiplied by sampling ratios, approximates the census figures fairly well.

The last step was to divide the family types into smaller groups in order to construct a set of cohort means to be used in the estimation. We used occupation, location, and the number of children as classificatory variables, and managed to obtain about 70 cohorts for each age-group.

As mentioned before, we departed in this paper from the standard approach to constructing expected earnings, which adjusts the cross-section pattern of earnings of similar families for the general productivity gains over time. For each 1979 cohort the level of future expected earnings is defined as the mean earnings of the corresponding cohort in 1984, using as weights the transition probabilities computed as shown above. In other words we assume a perfect foresight forecast.

For the Italian case we proceed in a somewhat simpler way. The availability of a two-year panel for 1987 and 1989 taken from the Bank of Italy Survey of Household Income and Wealth (SHIW)[9] allows the construction of an estimate of future expected income; this is obtained taking the fitted values of a regression of earnings in 1989 against information available in 1987, including earnings in that year.[10]

2.3   Empirical findings

The regression results for Japan relating to the 1979 survey are shown in Table 5.3a. Regressions were run by dividing all the variables by earnings in 1979 (Y79). For ease of interpretation, the results are shown in the level form. The two columns refer respectively to households whose head was aged 25-29 and 30-34 in 1979.

Considering first the younger consumers, we note that the coefficient of current earnings (after the terms KID and MEM are taken into account), is .584, against the .052 for expected future earnings (denoted as EY84). Further, the coefficient of EY84 is not at all significant. This result appears to confirm the contention of Carroll and Summers (1991) and Carroll (1989) that expected future income does not have much effect on either consumption or savings.

On the other hand, the coefficient of net worth in 1979, W79, is significantly different from zero (.05, with a t-ratio of 4.58), but considerably smaller than one. This means that, in contrast with the myopia hypothesis, young consumers plan for the future, although they adjust very slowly if they find a significant gap between their current and planned patterns of asset accumulation.

Table 5.3a Dependence of younger households' consumption on current earnings, expected future earnings and net worth: Japan
(dependent variable: consumption in the 1979 survey, C79)

	Age of household's head in 1979	
	25 – 29 number of cohorts = 62	35 – 39 number of cohorts = 71
Constant	454.40 (5.17)	1,082.80 (7.15)
Y79	0.506+0.049KID+0.016MEM (2.57) (5.45) (0.38)	0.198+0.048KID+0.125MEM (2.34) (7.61) (3.78)
EY84	0.052 (.79)	0.169 (3.65)
W79	0.05 (4.58)	0.025 (2.55)
R^2	0.64	0.72
Mean of:	{ C79 = 2,517.1; KID = 1.47; MEM = 0.41 }	{ C79 = 2,880.6; KID = 1.52; MEM = 0.41 }

Legend:
   KID: Number of children aged 17 or younger;
   MEM: Number of members in the family, other than husband, wife and their children. t-statistics are reported in parentheses.

For the older age group, the coefficient of current income is considerably smaller (.294, taking into account the terms KID and MEM), and the coefficient of expected income is both large, .169, and significant. This is a clear indication that the older group takes future earnings into account in determining consumption. Net worth has a somewhat smaller coefficient, but remains an important variable in the regression.[11]

In Table 5.3b, using the 1984 survey as the reference year, we investigate the possibility that past consumption (C79) might affect current consumption in the form of habit persistence. Since only two surveys are available, we cannot construct the perfect foresight earnings forecast for the 1984 cohorts. It turns out that C79 is completely insignificant in these regressions and we conclude that, for this set of data, habit persistence is not an important factor in the determination of current consumption.

Table 5.4 reports the analogous estimates for Italy. The regressions were run by dividing all the variables by an estimate of permanent earnings[12] and inserting "transitory" earnings (measured as the difference between current and "permanent" earnings) as an additional regressor.

Table 5.3b Dependence of younger households' consumption on current earnings, past consumption and net worth: Japan
(dependent variable: consumption in the 1984 survey, C84)

	Age of household head in 1984	
	30 – 34 number of cohorts = 62	35 – 39 number of cohorts = 71
Constant	1,081.0 (5.17)	1,012.7 (3.95)
Y84	0.420+0.030KID+0.215MEM (6.08) (3.01) (2.90)	0.446+0.030KID+0.128MEM (7.34) (3.44) (1.64)
C79	–0.75 (–0.69)	–0.032 (–0.22)
W84	0.037 (4.66)	0.032 (6.25)
R^2	0.71	0.77
Mean of:	{ C84 = 2,919.4; KID = 1.54; MEM = 0.16 }	{ C84 = 3,321.8; KID = 1.52; MEM = 0.18 }

Legend:
    KID: Number of children aged 17 or younger;
    MEM: Number of members in the family, other than husband, wife and their children. *t*-statistics are reported in parentheses.

The age-classes considered differ somewhat from those used in the Japanese case because of data availability. In spite of this and of the different nature of the data used, the results appear surprisingly similar to those obtained for Japan.

For the younger age-class, expected future earnings are not statistically significant (column A1); the coefficient of wealth is instead significant and of the same order of magnitude as that for Japan, even though, given the size of the sample (only 36 observations), we do not consider this result as particularly robust. For the older age-group, the coefficient of expected future income (column A2) is sizeable (.228) and significant at the 10 percent level.

In columns B1 and B2 we report an additional specification for the two age groups that includes future expected income interacted with a dummy representing (future) changes in the job position of the head of the households; while we postpone the interpretation at these results to the end of Section 3.1, it is worth noticing that the introduction of this additional regressor decreases the effect of future income on current consumption for those who will change job position, relative to those who will not.

Table 5.4 Dependence of younger households' consumption on current earnings, expected future earnings and net worth: Italy
(dependent variable: consumption in the 1987 survey divided by permanent income)

| | Age of household's head in 1987 | | | |
| | 20 – 30 | | 31 – 40 | |
	A1	B1	A2	B2
Constant	0.009	0.009	−0.80E–03	0.30E–03
	(0.630)	(0.582)	(0.157)	(0.006)
$\bar{Y}87$	0.760	0.744	0.344	0.350
	(3.428)	(3.136)	(3.187)	(3.284)
$\tilde{Y}87$	0.692	0.695	0.407	0.381
	(4.752)	(4.660)	(4.970)	(4.681)
Y^e89	−0.139	−0.138	0.228	0.259
	(0.608)	(0.588)	(1.850)	(2.113)
$D1Y^e89$		0.037		−0.103
		(0.293)		(2.432)
W87	0.049	0.049	0.020	0.020
	(3.328)	(3.281)	(3.655)	(3.761)
AGE	−0.10E–03	−0.11E–03	0.17E–03	0.10E–03
	(0.188)	(0.187)	(1.074)	(0.898)
NCOM	−0.14E–03	−0.06E–03	0.97E–03	0.76E–03
	(0.159)	(0.007)	(0.794)	(0.627)
NKID	−0.84E–03	−0.80E–03	−2.00E–03	−1.90E–03
	(0.593)	(0.721)	(1.563)	(1.439)
EDUC	0.20E–04	0.04E–03	0.10E–03	0.10E–03
	(0.054)	(0.094)	(0.777)	(0.848)
R^2	0.698	0.699	0.433	0.453
SE	0.324	0.329	0.279	0.276
Mean of dep. variable	1.021	1.021	0.933	0.933
No. of observations	36	36	175	175

Legend:
   $\bar{Y}87$: permanent income in 1987; $\tilde{Y}87$: transitory income in 1987; Y^e89: earnings expected in 1987 for 1989; D1 = 1 for households whose head has changed job position and zero otherwise; W87: net worth at the beginning at 1987; AGE: age of the household head; NCOM: number of family members; NKID: number of children.

It is difficult to square these results with the hypothesis of myopic behavior. Simple models of consumption associated with liquidity constraints appear also to be contradicted.[13] It is interesting, in our view, that the effect of future earnings on current consumption becomes significant only for households who are at a later stage of the life cycle, albeit still relatively young. One possible explanation is that liquidity constraints, while binding for very young households, cease to be so fairly soon. In Section 3, after presenting our theoretical framework to account for the saving behavior of young households, we shall take up this issue again, arguing that the age dependency of the sensitivity to expected future income finds a natural explanation in our approach.

3   The life cycle of opportunities

In the conventional approach, economic agents are identified with a given preference relation defined over a given consumption set. Although this description is inherently static, some goods could be interpreted as being available only in the future, and the preference relation could be dependent on the state of the environment, as the description of each good involves the contingencies in which it will be consumed. However, in the absence of a complete set of markets in which, at the beginning of the agent's life, all the commodities so defined can be exchanged, it seems more natural to define not only agents' decisions but also their "identities" as being the result of a sequential process.

At the start, each agent has a preference relation involving a (usually small) set of commodities, namely those with which he is most familiar, perhaps because of his parents' behavior. But he probably does not have a clear opinion concerning other goods, certainly those not yet invented but also, and more significantly, those consumed in different socioeconomic levels. As the agent grows older and pursues his career, his position on the social ladder changes, he moves to different places and the composition of his family evolves. He becomes acquainted with new people, observes new habits and discovers new consumption patterns. Indeed, the agent's own social identity, as defined by his relationships with other people, can be said to evolve with age.

At the beginning of their working lives, individuals face a wide range of possible paths, all of which might involve not only different patterns of lifetime earnings but also a different structure of needs and preferences. As they grow older, either by choice or by chance some of the original possibilities will no longer be feasible, and each individual will eventually settle down in what might be called a "social niche". The social niche to which an individual belongs entails, to some extent, a preferred consumption structure and, for this reason, we interpret the discovery of the niche as providing the opportunity for improving consumption choices. It is then intuitive that people have an incentive to postpone some of their purchases until they have learned in which social niche they will end up.

To put it more formally, we are describing a situation in which utility is the joint product of consumption and (social) environment. The two "factors" are complementary, so that a better environment entails higher marginal utility of consumption.

In the following, rather than pursuing the analysis at the abstract level, we shall present two simple examples.

In the first model, the niche is taken to represent the position in the "social pyramid". The higher the position the better the environment: social promotion improves health conditions, raises the cultural level, boosts the self-image. The positive externalities associated with the improvements in the environment justify the assumption that social promotion entails larger utility per unit of expenditure. In the model, the social stratum the agent belongs to is made to coincide with his kind of job, which is given at the beginning of the working life but might change with age.

In the second model the social niche will be identified with the agent's "true tastes", which are unknown at the beginning of his life and are progressively discovered; the opportunity to learn about his real preferences leads the young consumer to accumulate resources for the day when, having grown up and "discovered himself", he will be able to derive greater utility from consumption. If the evolution of preferences over the life cycle is ignored, saving of young cohorts will be underestimated, or their borrowing overestimated.

In both models young consumers have something to learn (about themselves or their environment), and this knowledge can be usefully exploited in their consumption choices. Furthermore, in both models saving is motivated by the desire of flexibility in an environment where opportunities are expected for the future. Finally, both models might yield positive savings when young in circumstances where a pure life-cycle model would predict borrowing or zero savings.

3.1　The opportunity of social promotion

In the first example an individual's niche is identified with his job position. Let us suppose that the various jobs in an economy are associated with different incomes, working conditions and overall social environments.[14] They can often be ranked according to a dominance criterion, as some involve both a larger income and a more agreeable environment. For example, let us consider a mine worker and a university teacher. The switch from the former's to the latter's job, quite apart from bringing a higher income, implies a dramatic improvement in health conditions and in the cultural and social quality of life. Similar though less marked differences usually accompany the progression from a job as an unskilled worker to one as a skilled craftsman and from the latter to a managerial position, or, more generally, whenever there is a change in the type of job.

We believe it is reasonable to assume that the better the working conditions and the stronger the positive externalities generated by relationships with colleagues and by the social circle associated with a given job, the higher the utility derived from each unit of consumption (on this point, see also Arrow, 1974).

Let us take an economy in which there are two types of jobs, σ_h and σ_l, corresponding to two rungs on the social ladder (high and low respectively). σ_h dominates σ_l, since it entails both a better environment and a higher income ($y_h > y_l$). Consider also an agent whose life is divided into two periods, who consumes c_i in period i ($i=1,2$) and works, in the first period, in job σ_l. The future, however, also holds the possibility of social promotion and the agent anticipates that, with probability p, he will be offered a better job. Reflecting the idea that there is little social downgrading, we assume that the agent never drops below the social ranking from which he starts. Some partial but clear evidence supporting this assumption is presented in Table 5.5 below. Drawing from the 1989 SHIW we can compute that, in the Italian case, 80 percent of the about 600 job changes observed in the sample (over a two-year period) leads to earnings at least as high as those in the original job.

On the basis of our previous discussion, we can assume that

$$u_1(c,\sigma_h) > u_1(c,\sigma_l) \tag{1}$$

where $u(\cdot)$ is the instantaneous utility function, and the subscript on $u(\cdot)$ denotes a partial derivative.[15]

The agent then solves:

max $u(c_1,\sigma_l) + (1-p)u(c_{21},\sigma_l) + pu(c_{22},\sigma_h)$

s.t. $c_1 + s = y_l$

$c_{21} = y_l + s$

$c_{22} = y_h + s$

where s represents saving and, for the sake of simplicity, the subjective discount rate is set equal to the interest rate and both are set equal to zero. This problem, under assumption (1), will be labeled (A).

To have a benchmark, let us now consider the case in which the only difference between the two jobs is the income they offer, so that the utility function is independent of σ and assumption (1) is replaced by:

$$u_1(c,\sigma_h) = u_1(c,\sigma_l). \tag{2}$$

We shall label this modified problem as (B). It is useful to write down the first order conditions of both problems, for the sake of simplicity assuming interior solutions:

$$u_1(y_l - s,\sigma_l) = (1 - p)u_1(y_l + s,\sigma_l) + pu_1(y_h + s,\sigma_h) \tag{FOC A}$$

$$u_1(y_l - s,\sigma_l) = (1 - p)u_1(y_l + s,\sigma_l) + pu_1(y_h + s,\sigma_l). \tag{FOC B}$$

For a given p, let us call $s^*(p)$ the solution to (FOC A) and $\hat{s}(p)$ the solution to (FOC B); the latter is the one usually considered in literature. If we now take (FOC A) together with assumption (1), it is simple to prove that $s^*(p)$ is larger than $\hat{s}(p)$ and, provided that the gain from social promotion is large enough, s^* can be positive even when $\hat{s}$ is negative.

A second interesting implication of the model is that the effect on saving of an increase in future expected income can be positive and, if negative, smaller in absolute value than that found in the standard case. Indeed, suppose that expected increases in income result from an increase of the probability of the better job, σ_h. If the gain from social promotion is large, we have that:

$$u_1(y_h + s^*(p),\sigma_h) > u_1(y_l + s^*(p),\sigma_l). \tag{3}$$

If (3) is true, it is immediate from the first order conditions that an increase in p yields an increase in the optimal saving, that is $s^*(p)$ is an increasing function, whereas $\hat{s}(p)$ is clearly a decreasing one.

Suppose now that (3) is false, that is, suppose

$$u_1(y_h + s^*(p),\sigma_h) \leq u_1(y_l + s^*(p),\sigma_l) \tag{3'}$$

and assume that the marginal utility of consumption, given σ, is convex. We then have:

$$u_1(y_l + \hat{s}(p),\sigma_l) - u_1(y_h + \hat{s}(p),\sigma_l) >$$
$$u_1(y_l + s^*(p),\sigma_l) - u_1(y_h + s^*(p),\sigma_h)$$

which follows from the assumed convexity of the marginal utility of consumption and the fact that $s^*(p) > \hat{s}(p)$. Note that in the LHS we used condition (2) to substitute σ_l for σ_h. The above inequality implies that a given increase in p, say to p', yields a smaller reduction in the RHS of (FOC A) than in the RHS of (FOC B), and hence a smaller decrease in the optimal s^*, as compared with $\hat{s}$, that is

$$s^*(p) - s^*(p') < \hat{s}(p) - \hat{s}(p').$$

It is worth noticing that an increase in the expected future income arising from a larger y_h would have in this model the standard effect of reducing current saving. The different result obtained varying the probability of y_h follows from the fact that a rise in p entails, together with the income increase, an increase of the probability of the opportunity: the larger future income goes hand in hand with a better future environment for consumption, and this offsets, to some extent, the incentive to borrow out of the larger income and increase current consumption.

Table 5.5 Probability of job change and increase in earnings by age

Age	Probability of job change (a)	Probability of earnings increase (b)
< 30	11,7	78,2
30 – 34	10,4	77,9
35 – 39	5,7	83,1
40 – 65	3,9	75,4

Source: Bank of Italy Survey of Household Income and Wealth, 1989.
(a) Percent. Computed over a two-year time span.
(b) Percent. Conditional on job change.

The saving behavior that is motivated by the anticipation of future consumption opportunities, geared to the discovery of the social niche, has an intrinsic dynamics that is difficult to capture fully with the overly simple model presented here. Indeed, the discovery of the social niche is a learning process that we believe is faster at young age, slows down as the agent pursues his chosen career and virtually comes to a stop at some time in the middle of the life cycle. Some calculations made on the SHIW, though far from representing conclusive evidence, lend support to this presumption. In Table 5.5 we show the probability of changing jobs for different age classes; it peaks at young age (before age 30) with a value close to 12 percent, it falls slightly between 30 and 35 (about 10 percent), it halves between 35 and 40 and hovers a little below 4 percent thereafter. We interpret these findings as suggestive of the fact that the flow of new opportunities that the consumer can reasonably anticipate drains away as he grows older. As a result, the reaction of consumption to expected future income might be negligible at very young age, when changes in income are expected to be offset by changes in consumption opportunities; at a somewhat older age the standard life-cycle behavior would tend to prevail. As anticipated in the previous section, the age-dependence of the reaction to future income finds a natural explanation in our framework. Also, we are now in a position to provide a reasonable interpretation of the regressions presented in columns B1 and B2 of Table 5.4; these were run using a dummy, to represent future changes in job position, interacting it with expected future income. When the latter is significantly different from zero, the coefficient of the dummy is significant and negative, thereby reducing the size of the effect on current consumption of expected future earnings. Other things equal, a future change in job position leads to larger current saving; assuming that the change in job position is to some extent anticipated, this is precisely what our theory would predict.

3.2   Learning about preferences

In the second example, let us consider a consumer who lives for two periods. In each of the periods there are two goods, a and b; in the first period the consumer likes a but he is uncertain whether he likes b or not. However, he knows that, in the second period, his own tastes will settle down and he will learn whether b yields positive utility. For simplicity, we assume that the consumer has the same, certain income, y, in both periods, that the interest rate on saving is equal to the subjective discount rate and that both are equal to zero.

Also, to keep the model to the bare essentials, we arbitrarily set the price of both goods, in both periods, equal to 1 and assume a utility function separable across time units and across goods. The qualitative results do not depend on these simplifying assumptions. Formally, we have the following problem

$$\max_{\{a_1, b_1, a_{21}, a_{22}, b_2\}} U = p[u(a_1) + v(b_1)] + (1 - p)u(a_1) +$$

$$+ p[u(a_{21}) + v(b_2)] + (1 - p)u(a_{22})$$

$$\text{s.t.} \qquad a_1 + b_1 + s = y$$

$$a_{21} + b_2 \quad = y + s$$

$$a_{22} \quad\quad = y + s$$

where p is both the probability that, today, the consumer likes b and the probability that, tomorrow, his preferences will settle on liking b; s is the amount of saving. The indexing of a in the second period reflects the anticipation of learning and the usual non-negativity constraints on a and b are understood. No restriction is imposed on s (i.e., we assume a perfect capital market). Note that if we neglect the last constraint and assume $a_{21} = a_{22}$ – i.e. we exclude that learning occurs – the solution to the problem requires $s = 0$. This provides us with a convenient benchmark to be used in the assessment of the effect on saving of learning about preferences.

Using the budget constraints, we can write the FOC for the problem as

$$pu'(y + s - b_2) + (1 - p)u'(y + s) - u'(y - s - b_1) = 0 \quad \text{(i)}$$

$$pv'(b_1) - u'(y - s - b_1) \quad \leq 0 \ (= 0 \text{ if } b_1 > 0) \quad \text{(ii)}$$

$$v'(b_2) - u'(y + s - b_2) \quad \leq 0 \ (= 0 \text{ if } b_2 > 0). \quad \text{(iii)}$$

We assume that $v'(b) - u'(y - b) = 0$ has a strictly positive solution. From (ii) and (iii), for given $s \geq 0$ and for p in the interval $(0,1)$, it follows immediately that $b_2 > b_1$. If b_1 is zero for some $p > 0$ and $s = 0$, then it is zero also for the same p and $s > 0$ and we obtain, from (i), that the optimal s is positive.

Let us then assume interior solutions, and suppose that $s = 0$. Then, from (ii) we solve for the optimal b_1, say $b_1(p,y)$, and from (iii) we solve for b_2, say $b_2(y)$. Let us define

$$g(p) = pu'(y - b_2(y)) + (1 - p)u'(y) - u'(y - b_1(p,y)) \quad \text{(4)}$$

where y is understood as an argument of $g(\cdot)$. Clearly if, for given p, $g(\cdot) > 0$, the optimal value of s is positive. Before we move to identify the conditions on the utility functions that guarantee that $g(\cdot)$ is positive, let us analyze the meaning of the function $g(p)$. In the second period, the optimal choice of b_2 is zero if the consumer discovers that he does not like good b and is $b_2(y)$ otherwise. In the first period the optimal choice of b_1 is an average of these two choices, with weights, say, $1 - \gamma(p)$ and $\gamma(p)$. Indeed, the choice of b_1 trades off the cost of wasting resources – when b_1 is positive and the consumer discovers that he does not like it – with the cost of consuming too little of it. The latter is higher the larger is the marginal utility in the neighborhood of zero.

Residually, we define the optimal choices of the (random variable) $\tilde{a}_2 = [a_{21}, a_{22}]$ – conditional on the realization of the uncertain preferences – and a_1, with the latter being an average, with weights $\gamma(p)$ and $1 - \gamma(p)$, of the former, that is:

$$g(p) = pu'(a_{21}) + (1 - p)u'(a_{22}) - u'(\gamma a_{21} + (1 - \gamma)a_{22}). \quad \text{(4')}$$

The definition of $g(p)$ given by (4), or equivalently by (4'), reads then as the difference between the expected value of the marginal utility of $\tilde{a}_2$ and the marginal utility of *some* weighted average of $\tilde{a}_2$.[16]

Moving now to the analysis of the conditions under which $g(\cdot) > 0$, first of all note that $g(0) = g(1) = 0$, as $b_1(0) = 0$ and $b_1(1) = b_2$. Hence, a sufficient, though by no means necessary, condition for $g(p)$ to be positive in the interval $(0, 1)$, is that $g(p)$ be a concave function of p. In particular, given that the first two terms of $g(p)$ are linear in p, we look for the condition under which the last term, that is $h(p) = u'(y - b_1(p))$, is convex in p. Differentiating twice $h(p)$ and using (ii), it can be shown that $h(p)$ is (strictly) convex if and only if:

$$\eta_v + \eta_u > 2(\varrho_v + \varrho_u) \tag{5}$$

where ϱ is the coefficient of absolute risk-aversion and η the coefficient of absolute prudence (that is the coefficient of risk-aversion applied to the marginal utility) evaluated respectively at b for the $v(\cdot)$ and at $(y-b)$ for the $u(\cdot)$. Note that condition (5) implies that the first derivative of at least one of the two functions $u(\cdot)$ and $v(\cdot)$ is convex. It is easily verified that condition (5) is satisfied by utility functions belonging to the class of CRRA functions; the only exception is the logarithmic utility, for which the LHS of condition (5) is equal to the RHS and saving is zero for all values of p. As mentioned before (see also note 16), condition (5) is not necessary for our model to generate positive savings. The same result can be obtained with utility functions that do not satisfy (5); one interesting case is the quadratic utility function (i.e. a function with non-convex first derivative).[17]

The import of this result is that the opportunity of learning about his own preferences induces the young consumer to accumulate resources for the time when, having grown up and "discovered himself", he will be able to extract higher utility from consumption. Ignoring the evolution of preferences over the life cycle leads, as the benchmark solution shows, to underpredicting the saving of the young cohorts (or to overpredicting their borrowing).

4 Discussion

Simple versions of the life-cycle hypothesis are unable to explain fully the observed facts regarding the savings of young consumers. An amendment to the theory appears to be called for, and two main directions have been explored in literature: the possibility of liquidity constraints and that of myopic behavior. Liquidity constraints represent a somewhat obvious explanation of the relatively small amount of borrowing by the young generations, as they simply postulate that they are unable to borrow.

Although this explanation merely shifts the question one step back, since the presence of borrowing constraints should itself be theoretically justified, it does capture some important features of the actual working of markets. There are, however, grounds for doubting whether credit market imperfections are enough to explain the observed deviation of young people's behavior from that postulated by the life-cycle theory.

Firstly, taken literally, the borrowing constraint assumption would imply that agents should be "on the constraint", consuming all their income, whereas we observe non-negligible savings, even in the early part of their working lives. To be sure, Deaton (1991) has recently shown that the existence of positive savings can be made compatible with binding liquidity constraints when there is uncertainty and the consumers are either "impatient" or "imprudent".[18] Both assumptions are somewhat unusual, and their nature implies that the savings thus generated are not likely to be large.[19]

Second, and more importantly, the consumption pattern of young generations closely follows that of income in countries where the level of development of financial markets is widely different and where the incidence of liquidity constraints is therefore also likely to differ widely.

The second explanation proposed in literature, namely shortsightedness, simply implies that people do not borrow against future income, because they do not think of it. The status of this hypothesis is not clear, however. It would seem to be an interpretation superimposed on models whose structure has little to do with myopic behavior.

On the empirical side, shortsightedness is invoked to explain a low (or zero) coefficient on expected future income in regressions of current consumption (see Carroll, 1989). In the same regressions, however, current wealth appears to have a coefficient significantly different from zero and smaller than one, which is not consistent with short-sighted consumers.

In this paper we have provided evidence that young people's current consumption responds to some extent to future earnings. We have also offered an explanation of the apparently low responsiveness that preserves the forward-looking feature of the life-cycle theory. We have outlined a theory in which current savings can be interpreted as a choice of flexibility, since the existence of future opportunities may be an incentive to postpone consumption until those periods in which it yields greater utility.

The life-cycle theory starts with the notion that the temporal distribution of resources is different from the optimal allocation of consumption over the life span, and that savings are needed to reallocate resources over time. In its original version, it emphasized the feature that, by and large, earnings are less than the optimal level of consumption after retirement (and perhaps at the beginning of life) and that they tend to be more than the optimal level of consumption during the middle range of a family's life. In this paper, we have emphasized the possibility that the optimal consumption pattern may be rising more sharply than earnings at a very young age. This might lead to large savings at the beginning of working life, when earnings are relatively low, and to consumption lumping rather than consumption smoothing behavior at a relatively young age.

NOTES

* This is an enlarged and revised version of a paper, coauthored with Daniel Dorsainvil, presented at the Conference on "Saving Behavior: Theory, International Evidence and Policy Implications", Helsinki, May 1991, and published in the *Scandinavian Journal of Economics*, 94, 1992, with the title "Saving Among Young Households. Evidence from Japan and Italy". The relevant parts are here reprinted with permission. Basic computations using Japanese data and the construction of the cohort means were completed in 1986-87 at the University of Osaka, when Ando was given access to data from the 1979 and 1984 national surveys of family income and expenditure. We wish to thank Agar Brugiavini, Chris Carroll, Angus Deaton and T. Srinivasan for very helpful suggestions and the participants in the Helsinki conference for their comments. We are also grateful to Luigi Sciamplicotti for very valuable research assistance.

1 To be sure, the reference to aggregation could in principle be avoided, as both positive savings and a positive correlation with the growth rate of the economy are consistent, in general equilibrium, with a representative agent model; however, the latter seems to require a higher level of sensitivity of consumption decisions to interest rates than is usually estimated (or larger movements in interest rates than those currently observed; see also Carroll and Summers, 1991). The aggregation of consumers at different points in the life cycle thus appears the most reliable mechanism to explain the correlation between savings and growth at the macro level.

2 Assuming a rate of growth of productivity of 4 percent in Italy and 5 percent in Japan (approximately equal to the average growth of GDP per worker in the last 30 years in the two countries) the adjustment for growth would lead to a level of earnings in the highest age bracket 2.2 times as large as that in the youngest age bracket in Italy, and 2.6 times that in Japan.

3 The larger estimate for saving implied by the change in net worth is due partly to capital gains on housing, which were substantial in both Japan and Italy between the two years used to construct the figures in the table.

4 That is either couples, possibly with non-working children, or one of the remaining members of a former couple with non-working children.

5 In most cases the additional working dependent adult is the daughter or son of the head of the household, though we allow for all other possible cases. For Japan only households with male dependent adults were selected.

6 To correct for a possible bias in the saving propensity due to the age of the pure nuclear families being lower than that of the extended families, for Italy we randomly draw a subsample from the pure nuclear families that has the same (head of household's) age distribution as that observed among the extended families. For Japan, we select pure nuclear families in the age bracket 50-54, approximately matching the average age of the extended families.

7 The movement from position p to position s consists of two components. The first, from s to q, is the age effect, which might include improvements in skills and, therefore, an increase in productivity that cannot be distinguished from other effects of age. The second component of the movement, from q to s, is the productivity increase specific to calendar year, and is common to all members of the work force, regardless of age. An empirical distinction between these two reasons for a change in earnings could be important since changes due to calendar year productivity increases are more likely to be subject to surprises. Thus, the distinction is potentially useful in assessing the explanation of the correlation between savings and growth observed in fast-expanding economies based on a "surprise" element.

8 A similar problem, arising when older people merge into one of their children's households, was tackled by Hayashi *et al.* (1988).

9 The Bank of Italy SHIW collects information on a random sample of about 8,000 Italian households. A subset of the 1987 total sample was interviewed again in 1989 and forms the panel component (1,208 households). Further details on the survey are given in the Methodological Appendix to this volume.

10 Our procedure has the shortcoming that it covers only a horizon of five years in the case of Japan and two years in the case of Italy. For the young groups with which we are dealing here, the relevant expected earnings should cover the major portion of their working life of some 30 years or so.

11 To assess whether the impact on consumption of changes in earnings due to calendar year increases in productivity differs from that of changes due to the age effect, according to the classification made in note 6, we ran a regression splitting EY84 into these two components. Unfortunately, this distinction was possible only for the younger group; in this case both components turned out to be not significantly different from zero.

12 Permanent earnings are identified with the fitted values of a Weighted Least Squares regression against a vector of family characteristics including a polynomial in age. Notice that, by construction, the "transitory" component of earnings is given by the residuals of this regression; hence, as in King and Dicks-Mireaux (1982), it might include also a permanent component.

13 A positive effect of future expected income on current consumption might be consistent with the presence of liquidity constraints in Deaton's model, in which the anticipation of higher future income reduces the need for precautionary saving.

14 The idea of a strict connection between a consumer's job position and his social niche, i.e. his social status, is emphasized by Solow (1990).

15 We assume that the agent's utility is directly dependent on his position on the social ladder. Alternatively one might assume that utility depends only on goods, some of which are not marketable but can be acquired through status. A similar approach is taken by Cole, Mailath and Postlewaite (1992), who also emphasize the interaction between agents' social status and savings decisions in a general equilibrium context.

16 Note that the weights used to compute the expected value of the marginal utility of $\tilde{a}_2$, p and $(1-p)$, are not necessarily the same as $\gamma(p)$ and $(1-\gamma(p))$. Since we want to prove that $g(\cdot)$ is positive, we would like the ratio $\gamma(p)/p$ to be small enough. How small is "small enough" clearly depends on the curvature of the marginal utility. If the latter is convex (as customarily assumed in the precautionary saving literature) then $\gamma(p)/p=1$ is sufficient to have positive savings, but we can have the same result provided that $\gamma(p)/p$ does not exceed 1 by too much. If, on the contrary, the marginal utility is concave, the function $\gamma(p)/p$ should be appropriately smaller than 1 for the model to generate positive saving. All this means that there is no hope to derive a reasonably weak sufficient condition for positive savings independent from the assumption made on the marginal utility: any condition that is sufficient for a function displaying a concave derivative is likely to be far too strong when referred to a function with convex derivative.

17 Positive saving is obtained for all values of p in the interval $(0,1)$ provided that income is well within the interval of definition of the quadratic utility.

18 The role of prudence is not directly examined by Deaton, but a simple extension of his argument to a model with finitely lived consumers establishes the claim.

19 In Deaton's simulations the amount of saving that can be generated is generally less than 1 percent of (mean) income, a relatively small amount when compared with the actual saving of young households. We must, however, note that sizeable savings by the young can be obtained if imperfections in the market for consumption loans are coupled with imperfections in the market for mortgages (Artle and Varaiya, 1978). Saving for the future purchase of a house can also be interpreted within our framework, with no constraints assumed for the credit markets. It can be shown that there is an incentive to increase current saving, postponing the purchase of a house, if (a) home ownership enhances the marginal utility of consumption; (b) there are transaction costs in the secondary market for houses; (c) there is uncertainty about future income streams but learning takes place.

REFERENCES

Ando, A. and A.B. Kennickell (1987). 'How Much (or Little) Life Cycle Is There in Micro Data? The Cases of the United States and Japan', in R. Dornbusch, S. Fischer and J. Bossons (eds.), *Macroeconomics and Finance. Essays in Honor of Franco Modigliani*, Cambridge, MA: MIT Press.

Arrow, K.J. (1974). 'Optimal Insurance and Generalized Deductibles', *Scandinavian Actuarial Journal* 1: 1-42.

Artle, R. and P. Varaiya (1978). 'Life Cycle Consumption and Homeownership', *Journal of Economic Theory* **18**: 38-58.

Attanasio, O. and M. Browning (1991). 'Consumption over the Life Cycle and over the Business Cycle', CEPR Meeting, Madrid, June.

Carroll, C. (1989). 'Uncertain Future Income, Precautionary Saving and Consumption', MIT, mimeo.

Carroll, C. and L.H. Summers (1991). 'Consumption Growth Parallels Income Growth: Some New Evidence', in B. D. Bernheim and J. B. Shaven (eds.), *National Saving and Economic Performance*, Chicago: University of Chicago Press.

Cole, H.L., G.J. Mailath and A. Postlewaite (1992). 'Social Norms, Saving Behavior and Growth', *Journal of Political Economy* **100**: 1092-125.

Davies, J.B. (1981). 'Uncertain Lifetime, Consumption and Dissaving in Retirement', *Journal of Political Economy* **89**: 561-77.

Deaton, A. (1991). 'Saving and Liquidity Constraints', *Econometrica* **59**: 1221-48.

Hayashi, F., A. Ando and R. Ferris (1988). 'Life Cycle and Bequest Savings', *Journal of the Japanese and International Economies* **2**: 450-91.

Hurd, M.D. (1989). 'Mortality Risk and Bequests', *Econometrica* **57**: 779-813.

King, M. and L-D.L. Dicks-Mireaux (1982). 'Asset Holdings and the Life Cycle', *Economic Journal* **92**: 247-67.

Solow, R.M. (1980). *The Labor Market as a Social Institution*, Cambridge, MA: Basil Blackwell.

6 Dissaving by the elderly, transfer motives and liquidity constraints*

ALBERT ANDO, LUIGI GUISO
and DANIELE TERLIZZESE

1 Introduction

The stripped-down version of the life-cycle model implies that older consumers should start decumulating assets right after retirement at a rate sufficient to achieve zero wealth by the time of death. Of course, this extreme pattern of behavior only obtains under highly restrictive assumptions, such as lack of uncertainty about the time of death, the absence of health uncertainty and the absence of a bequest motive. Relaxing these assumptions might still lead to decumulation of assets as households get older, though at a slower rate.

Several studies, for various countries, provide evidence on this issue.[1] By and large, there does appear to be asset decumulation by the elderly though at a much lower rate than would be implied by a life-cycle model without uncertainty or bequests. Thus, as is pointed out by Ando and Kennickell (1987), the traditional characterization of the no-uncertainty-no-bequests life-cycle model is clearly rejected by the data. While there is a fair consensus on this statement, there is much less agreement on the reason for the observed slowness of decumulation. As already mentioned, two main explanations have been proposed: the precautionary saving induced by (uninsurable) uncertainty about the time of death or by the possibility of major catastrophes in old age that require large outlays; and the desire to pass part of the accumulated assets on to one's heirs. Discriminating between these two possibilities is important, as the first is fully consistent with the life-cycle theory and its implications for aggregate saving, while the second might impose significant departures from that model.[2] Ando (1985) and Hayashi, Ando and Ferris (1988) find that in Japan the elderly dissave and argue that the observed dissaving is not due to life-cycle consumption smoothing but to substantial *inter vivos* transfers. In contrast, Hurd (1987, 1989) argues the absence of a bequest motive in the U.S., finding that elderly households potentially having a bequest motive, i.e. those with independent adult children, dissave proportionally more than those without children. Thus, the slow rate of decumulation of the elderly would be due to mortality risk.

In this paper we reconsider the issue of wealth decumulation by the elderly and assess the presence of a transfer motive, drawing on Italian data. As we will show, if there are incentives to anticipate bequests well before the time of death, owing, for instance, to the existence of borrowing constraints on the children, Hurd's test might have little power in discriminating among alternative explanations of the slow decumulation by the elderly.

We start in Section 2 discussing a potential weakness of tests of the bequest motive based on the relative speed of wealth decumulation of elderly households with and without potential heirs. That is, they fail to recognize that when liquidity constraints are likely to be relevant, *inter vivos* transfers might be an alternative to *post mortem* bequests. We argue that to assess the existence of a bequest motive, or more generally of a transfer motive, one should look at the entire pattern of wealth accumulation and decumulation.

Accordingly, we document in Section 3 the pattern of wealth accumulation and decumulation by Italian households, drawing on the 1989 Bank of Italy Survey of Household Income and Wealth (SHIW). Italy, in this respect, may well be an ideal case, with its typically strong family ties and the widespread belief that the bequest motive is important. On the other hand, as documented by Guiso, Jappelli and Terlizzese (1994b) and by Maccan, Rossi and Visco (1994), liquidity constraints due to the imperfect working of the consumption loan and mortgage markets are widespread, which makes it worthwhile to anticipate bequests to the time when the liquidity constraint is binding. The use of cross-section data to make inferences on the pattern of wealth over age of a representative household can be highly misleading unless proper account is taken of the fact that households of different ages are also different households and that households' behavior might differ substantially according to composition. Thus, we adjust for differences in productivity among cohorts and deal with the issue, first raised by Shorrocks (1975), of the wealth-mortality correlation. We also discuss adjustments for several sources of bias, including the merging of elderly individuals into younger households and, more importantly for the Italian case, the tendency of young consumers to live in their parents' houses long after they start working. The main result here is that some decumulation appears to take place, roughly after retirement, though at a slow rate. However, while according to wealth data the elderly decumulate assets, saving as gauged by income and consumption data is persistently positive at all ages after retirement. While this finding, as argued by Hayashi *et al.* (1988), is consistent with *inter vivos* transfers to the younger generations, we also observe that this discrepancy may be partly due to differential capital gains and losses on financial assets and liabilities induced by inflation.

We then rely, in Section 4, on the pattern of wealth and savings documented in Section 3 to test the existence of a transfer motive, examining its implications for the pace of wealth accumulation and decumulation. In Section 5 we offer additional evidence on the presence of a transfer motive, based on information on life insurance purchases and on the relative economic condition of parents and independent working children. Section 6 brings several loose ends together and concludes.

2   Testing the existence of a bequest motive

A possible way to assess the existence of a bequest motive is to contrast the behavior of households with and without a potential bequest motive, that is households with and without children. Exploiting this idea, Hurd (1987, 1989) examines panel data on wealth and consumption from the U.S. Retirement History Survey and concludes that elderly households with living children decumulate faster than those without.[3] He interprets his results as evidence against the presence of a bequest motive.[4] But this interpretation can be granted only if, as Hurd assumes, bequests take place at the death of the donor. This imposes a severe restriction on the timing of the transfer. In assessing the presence of a bequest motive one should recognize that bequests are transfers between generations and allow for the possibility that they might take place before the death of the donor. As a result, it might well be that those with a stronger bequest or transfer motive actually decumulate faster than those with a weaker motive. For instance, as argued by Cox (1990), if young households are subject to liquidity constraints, their parents have a strong incentive to anticipate planned bequests to the time when the borrowing constraint is binding. Therefore the observed decumulation of wealth could reflect transfers from the older to the younger generation. Thus, Hurd's finding that elderly households with living children decumulate more than those without cannot be taken as conclusive evidence against the bequest motive; it might in fact be interpreted as evidence in favor of the existence of a transfer motive.

Laitner (1993) studies the interaction between liquidity constraints and intergenerational transfers in a general equilibrium, overlapping generations model with altruistic consumers. Looking at stationary equilibria, he shows that the presence of liquidity constraints might give rise to substantial *inter vivos* transfers from parents to their children, while at the same time younger households might accumulate faster in anticipation of their intention to make a transfer later in life.

This suggests that to assess the existence of a bequest motive, or more generally of a transfer motive, one should look at the entire pattern of wealth accumulation and decumulation. The accumulation behavior of working parents with dependent children can be contrasted with that of households without children. If a transfer motive is present, the former should accumulate wealth faster than the latter; at a later stage, when children become independent adults and some of them are liquidity-constrained, parents with non-dependent children will rapidly decumulate assets to provide their children with liquidity.

Before tackling these issues directly in Section 4, we now document the wealth accumulation and decumulation behavior of Italian households.

3 The age pattern of wealth

The first column of Table 6.1 shows the cross-section pattern of wealth over age. The data used are drawn from the 1989 Survey of Household Income and Wealth (SHIW), which contains detailed data on households' characteristics, earnings, income from capital, and financial and real assets.[5] It also contains information on the age and economic status of any children living outside the parents' house, which will be exploited further on.

Table 6.1 Age-wealth profile

Age	Number of households	Net worth (a)	Ratio of net worth to permanent income	Index of net worth (b)	Index of net worth-to-permanent income ratio (c)
under 30	567	76.0	1.56	1.00	1.00
30-39	1,489	113.8	2.46	1.49	1.58
40-49	1,804	161.7	3.61	2.12	2.31
50-59	1,769	187.6	4.80	2.47	3.08
60-64	816	174.7	6.91	2.30	4.43
65-69	710	146.7	7.40	1.93	4.74
70-74	387	103.9	6.25	1.37	4.01
75-79	380	101.7	6.41	1.34	4.10
over 79	239	94.9	7.96	1.25	5.10

(a) Millions of 1989 lire.
(b) Net worth at age "under 30"=1.
(c) Ratio of net worth to permanent income at age "under 30"=1.

Wealth appears to increase rapidly with age up to the age-class 50-59 when it reaches a peak; it declines thereafter, with most of the decumulation taking place in the 15 years after retirement (age 60 for men and 55 for women). Wealth flattens subsequently, before declining substantially at very old ages. From these data one cannot, however, conclude for wealth decumulation by the elderly. As noted by Shorrocks (1975), the study of the age-wealth relationship on the basis of cross-sectional data could be misleading. Examining individuals of different ages observed at a single point in time in order to extract information on the behavior of a typical individual over age can distort the behavioral pattern of the typical individual (household) unless proper account is taken of at least two factors.

First, in a growing economy individuals belonging to different cohorts also belong to different vintages of productivity and hence of lifetime resources. Thus, if growth is sufficiently rapid wealth decumulation will appear in the cross-sectional data even if none is present in the longitudinal profile.

Second, since survival probability is likely to be correlated with wealth, the mean wealth of older cohorts overstates the wealth of the typical individual. This effect, of course, tends to offset the cohort effect. Thus, to exploit cross-section data to illuminate the age pattern of wealth of the average individual, proper adjustments need to be made for cohort effects and the wealth-mortality correlation.

3.1   The growth-adjusted profile

The second column of Table 6.1 shows the growth-adjusted profile. The adjustment is made by dividing net worth by a measure of permanent income that incorporates cohort effects (see the Appendix for the details on the construction of permanent income). The adjustment for growth has substantial effects: first of all, the peak in wealth is reached after retirement, in the age-class 65-69; second, the decumulation appears to take place only after age 69; third, in the 10 years following the peak in wealth only 13 percent of net worth is decumulated while the unadjusted figures show a decumulation of about 40 percent. However, the observed slowness of decumulation might be due to the sample bias induced by the negative correlation between wealth and mortality. Thus, before reaching firm conclusions one needs to tackle this issue.

3.2   Adjusting for the wealth-mortality correlation

As noted by Shorrocks (1975), the adjustment for the wealth-mortality correlation is potentially important. Clearly its empirical relevance depends on the extent of the effect of wealth on the probability of death. Unfortunately data on the wealth and characteristics of the deceased are not generally available. The panel component[6] of the 1989 SHIW does have information on those interviewed in 1987 who died between 1987 and 1989, but the size of the sample is too small to allow a reliable estimate of the correlation between wealth and mortality. However, some information is available from census data, and this can be used to estimate the wealth-mortality relationship. Table 6.2 displays the probability of death for various types of household computed by the Italian National Institute of Statistics (Istat) according to economic status and age of the deceased. Based on a set of criteria (see note *(b)* to the table), households are classified in increasing order of affluence from Type 1 to Type 5.

The main feature, perhaps a surprising one, is that while there is a clear negative relation between the indicator of economic status and the probability of death at younger ages, there is little (if any) correlation at ages above retirement. In the age groups 65-69 and 70-74, the probability of death is initially increasing with the indicator of the economic condition of the household and declines only for the most well-off.

Indeed, in these age groups mortality is lower for Type 1 households than for Type 5. This suggests that insofar as the classification of households by type is a monotonic function of wealth, the Shorrocks composition adjustment might have little effect on the age-wealth pattern after retirement since one should adjust the weights of households at both ends of the wealth distribution upwards.

To assess whether the indicator of family type is a good proxy for wealth or income, we have classified the families in the SHIW using the methodology followed by Istat and we have identified the five family types (see, again, note *(b)* to Table 6.2). For each family type and age of the household head we have computed mean wealth. The results are shown in Table 6.2, with average income in parentheses. There is a very strong positive correlation between the family type indicator and both mean wealth and income, so the negative correlation between mortality and family type at young and middle ages carries over in terms of wealth and income. However, for the age-groups past retirement it is confirmed that the poorest households have a lower probability of death than the richest.[7]

Using these figures and assuming that the mortality ratios are constant across age within each age class, it is possible to adjust the age-wealth profile for the correlation between wealth and mortality. This entails rescaling the weights of the family-wealth groups with their survival ratio. The result of this adjustment is reported in the last row of the table. Not surprisingly, the effect on the profile is negligible. While the estimate of the mean level of

Table 6.2 Wealth and mortality correlation. Age of the deceased and average wealth and income of his family (a)

Family type	Age 30-44 Prob. of death	Age 30-44 Wealth (income)	Age 45-54 Prob. of death	Age 45-54 Wealth (income)	Age 55-64 Prob. of death	Age 55-64 Wealth (income)	Age 65-69 Prob. of death	Age 65-69 Wealth (income)	Age 70-74 Prob. of death	Age 70-74 Wealth (income)
1	1.297	85.8 (25.5)	2.766	124.0 (29.1)	4.275	147.2 (26.8)	7.353	123.2 (23.1)	11.837	130.3 (21.8)
2	0.850	88.8 (24.9)	2.285	143.1 (31.4)	5.055	149.4 (35.1)	9.735	215.6 (35.3)	14.776	137.7 (36.4)
3	0.469	144.4 (34.7)	1.700	193.8 (46.3)	4.342	182.8 (46.4)	9.307	217.4 (47.0)	14.393	141.5 (34.0)
4	0.381	142.3 (40.1)	1.580	198.9 (49.9)	4.012	223.2 (50.7)	8.370	266.1 (55.9)	13.273	192.7 (44.7)
5	0.310	183.7 (49.8)	1.339	339.0 (66.1)	3.758	399.4 (66.2)	8.093	286.3 (61.0)	12.083	290.9 (58.0)
Total	0.447	139.6	1.797	190.6	4.458	195.3	8.923	197.2	13.669	157.7
Mortality ratio:										
– richest	0.650		0.745		0.8043		0.907		0.884	
– poorest	2.365		1.539		0.959		0.887		0.685	
Adjusted wealth		137.6		189.1		193.4		195.8		156.0

Sources. Figures on the probability of death by family type are taken from Istat, *La mortalità differenziale secondo alcuni fattori socio-economici. Anni 1981-82*, Roma, 1990.

(a) The probabilities are computed dividing the number of deaths over the period November 1, 1981, to April 30, 1982, by the resident population at the end of October 1981 in each age-class-family-type combination. The figures in the table are multiplied by 1,000.

(b) Households are classified in the five groups according to the following procedure. First of all four indicators of the economic status of the household are selected; they are: i) average education of the members of the household of the deceased with completed education; ii) occupation of each household member of working age (i.e. with age less than 75 and not yet retired, and older than 14, excluding students); iii) number of earners among those of working age; iv) presence of unemployed persons in the household. For each criterion a score in the interval 0-1 is assigned, and the scores for the four criteria are added together. This assigns a total score to each household. A score equal to 1 is given to the household characteristic which ranks highest. Taking education as an example, if a member of the household is a university graduate he is given score 1; if he has a secondary school diploma he is given a score equal to 13/17, where 13 is the number of years of schooling for a secondary school diploma, and 17 for a university degree. A similar procedure is followed for the other criteria. On the basis of the total score, households are divided into quintiles, with type 1 belonging to the first quintile, type 2 to the second and so on.

wealth at each age class is reduced, its pattern over age is unchanged. Thus we can conclude that at least in the Italian case, but probably for other countries as well, this adjustment is likely to be of little importance. Accordingly we ignore it.

3.3   Adjusting for household composition

It is important to notice that in the computation of the age-wealth profiles presented in Table 6.1 one overlooks two possible sources of bias, arising from the fact that the age pattern of household wealth could reflect the pattern of saving of individuals living together but at very different points in the life cycle. The first type of problem, noticed by Ando (1985) and Hayashi *et al.* (1988), relates to extended families. If extended families are widespread, as in Japan, wealth decumulation of the elderly may be substantially underestimated since households with elderly individuals do not appear as such in the sample. This problem is likely to be much less significant in Italy.

Table 6.3 Income, consumption and wealth by family type

Family type	Number of house- holds	Age of house- hold's head	Dispos- able income *(a)*	Consump- tion *(a)*	Net worth *(a)*	Propen- sity to save
Nuclear households	6,780	52	34.1	26.1	140.8	0.21
Extended households	358	49	46.9	33.0	190.6	0.30
Other	1,136	47	28.8	22.0	110.9	0.24

(a) Millions of 1989 lire.

Table 6.3 reports information on the structure of Italian households by type. Extended households differ substantially in terms of accumulated assets and propensity to save, but only 4.3 percent of the households in the sample are extended in the sense of dependent parents living with their children.[8] Further evidence on this phenomenon is given in Table 6.4, which reports information on elderly people moving in and out of their children's family based on data from the panel component of the 1989 SHIW. The probability of an extended family forming over a two-year period is around 2 percent. However, there is only a slightly lower probability of an elderly parent's leaving his children's house or of an extended family dissolving. In both cases, movements in wealth and disposable income are considerable; as they move in or out, these elderly persons bring not only their income but their assets with them. Nor is the merging phenomenon confined to poor parents. Rather, the income of such entrants is higher than average income in the survey. However, given the small number of extended families in the sample it is unlikely that adjusting for them will have a significant effect on the age-wealth profile; in fact, taking it into account increases wealth decumulation only slightly.

Table 6.4 Movement of older relatives into and out of younger households

		Number of house- holds	Age of house- hold's head	Age of older relative	Net worth *(a)*		Disposable income *(a)*	
					1987	1989	1987	1989
Entrants	1987	16	51	78	213.7	321.1	32.7	50.5
	1989	7	51	77	99.5	155.6	21.7	37.8
Leavers	1987	13	42	73	290.5	65.3	50.5	27.6
	1989	7	40	67	278.2	100.5	35.9	18.2

Source: 1987 and 1989 SHIW (panel respondents).
(a) Millions of 1989 lire.

The second possible source of bias relates to the presence of young workers still living with their parents, or of multiple-earner households with earners of different generations. In Italy, children tend to live with their parents long after they start working, in the meantime accumulating assets before becoming independent (or in order to do so). Ando, Guiso and Terlizzese (1994) found that young dependent workers are likely to build considerable wealth, so that the accumulation of the young could compensate for the decumulation by their parents. To allow for this possibility, we limit our analysis to the sample of pure nuclear households, i.e. households with husband and wife (if present) and non-working dependent children (if present).[9]

The first column of Table 6.5 reports the age-wealth profile for this adjusted sample, which comprises 5,405 households out of the original sample of 8,274. The adjustment proves particularly important. The ratio of wealth to permanent income now peaks at age 65-69 and declines smoothly thereafter. In the ten years following the peak, 18 percent of total wealth is decumulated. The annual rate of decumulation is 1.68 percent. Thus, people are likely to die still holding considerable amounts of wealth.

Table 6.5 Age-wealth profile: pure nuclear households

Age	Number of households	Net worth (a)	Ratio of net worth to permanent income	Index of net worth (b)	Index of net worth-to-permanent income ratio (b)	Saving rate (c)
under 30	377	76.6	1.51	1.00	1.00	0.17
30-39	1,170	115.0	2.44	1.50	1.62	0.19
40-49	1,267	164.3	3.86	2.14	2.56	0.21
50-59	909	179.2	5.92	2.34	3.92	0.21
60-64	484	158.3	8.31	2.07	5.50	0.23
65-69	465	128.9	8.64	1.68	5.72	0.26
70-74	288	91.3	6.95	1.08	4.60	0.25
75-79	286	87.4	7.07	1.19	4.68	0.22
over 79	159	71.6	6.25	0.93	4.14	0.21

(a) In millions of 1989 lire.
(b) Wealth at age "below 30"=1.
(c) As a ratio to disposable income.

3.4   Wealth decumulation and the conventional measure of saving

A puzzling feature of the evidence on wealth decumulation based on the analysis of the age-wealth profile is that it is not confirmed by the data on saving, if the latter is defined as the difference between income and consumption. The last column of Table 6.5 shows that for the sample of pure nuclear households the saving rate is positive for all age-groups, albeit slightly declining in old age as predicted by the life-cycle theory. Part of the difference between the two measures of saving presumably stems from sample selection bias[10] and from the likelihood that the survey underestimates household consumption more seriously than income. However, reasonable adjustments to consumption and income can hardly account for saving rates as high as 20 percent.[11] Further, this inconsistency between savings measured by changes in net worth and savings measured by income and consumption is not specific to Italy. Hayashi *et al.* (1988) show that the same problem arises in the Japanese case. Data on income and consumption from the Consumer Expenditure Survey and on net worth from the Survey of Consumer Finances, reported by Ando and Kennickell (1987), can be used to show that qualitative similar results also hold for the U.S. data.

These figures, as Hayashi *et al.* (1988) argue, could be consistent with saving by the elderly together with intergenerational transfers from the older to the younger generation. This interpretation might also explain the rapid accumulation of wealth by younger households that is reflected in the wealth data, which, again, does not square with savings as measured by income and consumption data (Ando *et al.*, 1994).

An alternative explanation of this inconsistent pattern exhibited by saving measured as change in net worth and as income minus consumption is based on the distortion induced in the conventional measure of saving by the presence of inflation and of financial assets whose value is fixed in nominal terms. If a family owns a significant amount of financial assets, inflation would reduce the family's net worth, and saving measured as the change in net worth would reflect this fact, but saving measured as income minus consumption would not. Similarly, if a family is carrying a debt fixed in nominal terms, under inflation it acquires capital gains.[12]

Furthermore, these capital gains and losses might not be evenly distributed among households of various types. If younger households (between ages 30 and 40) are more likely to hold debt (associated mainly with recent acquisition of houses) and older households (over 60 years old), on the other hand, having paid off mortgages have accumulated significant amounts of financial assets, then under inflation younger households make significant capital gains on their financial liabilities while older households incur capital losses on their financial assets. Thus, if nominal interest payments and receipts are included in the income of these households and capital gains and losses on their financial liabilities and assets are not accounted for, a substantial overestimation of saving for older households and a corresponding underestimation for younger households may result from the conventional definition of saving as income minus consumption. These biases will not be present in the measure of saving defined as the change in net worth, provided that real assets are valued at market value.

On the other hand, suppose that the relative price of houses increases significantly from one year to the next. Such real capital gains will accrue uniformly to all homeowners regardless of their other asset-liability position. Such capital gains will also be missed by the measure of saving as conventionally defined as income minus consumption, while the alternative measure of the change in net worth will capture them provided that the market value is accurately caught.

Given these possibilities, the mere fact that older people's net worth position declines more than the rate accounted for by saving defined as income less consumption, and that younger people's net worth increases by more than their saving can justify, does not conclusively imply the presence of *inter vivos* transfers.

In view of this ambiguity in the interpretation of the cause of the discrepancy between the change in net worth and income minus consumption for various age-groups, we present below a number of elements that do not directly depend on this discrepancy but nevertheless tend to indicate the presence of intergenerational transfers.

If some elderly families act on their bequest motive but actual transfers of resources take place during their lifetime as well as at the time of their death, then the implication would be that elderly households with a transfer motive decumulate their wealth faster than households without it. This is precisely the result obtained by Hurd with reference to the U.S., using panel data from the Retirement History Survey and by Börsch-Supan (1992) using the Socio-Economic Panel for Germany.[13] Both Hurd and Börsch-Supan interpret their results as evidence against the existence of a bequest motive. As we argued in Section 2, however, this interpretation is correct only if bequests are constrained to take place on the death of the donor. But if credit market imperfections are significant, intergenerational transfers might be targeted towards liquidity-constrained young households and be effected well before the death of the donor. *Inter vivos* transfers would in this case effectively counteract credit market imperfections. On this hypothesis, Hurd's test might have little power to assess the existence of a transfer motive. Yet it would still be the case that during their accumulation phase households with a transfer motive should, on average, accumulate wealth faster than those without.

4   Transfer motives and the pattern of wealth accumulation

This section presents a formal test of the foregoing propositions. The idea is to contrast the accumulation of wealth by households with children (and thus with a potential transfer motive) with that by childless households.

Thus, if a transfer motive is present, one would expect to find that other things being equal, households with young dependent children accumulate more rapidly than those with no children. On the other hand, households with independent working children might, at some stage, decumulate faster than households without children in order to help ease a binding liquidity constraint.

To perform our test we assume, as in King and Dicks-Mireaux (1982), that the (log of the) ratio of wealth to permanent income can be expressed as a piecewise linear function of age and of the indicator for the presence of a transfer motive, aside from a set of variables measuring: i) households' characteristics (sex, education and geographical location), to allow for household heterogeneity and variation in tastes; ii) perceived income risk, to account for precautionary accumulation of assets; iii) participation in the labor market by elderly households to allow for non-declining earnings profiles. In summary, we estimate an equation of the form

$$\log(w/y)_i = \sum_{j=1}^{8} \theta_j da_{ji} + \beta X_i + \gamma_1 h_{di} A_i + \gamma_2 h_{ci} D_i + \delta f_i D_i + \varepsilon_i \quad (1)$$

where i is the index of the households, w denotes accumulated wealth, y is a measure of permanent income, the da_j variables are segments of the age spline and X is a vector of characteristics. The other variables in the equation will be defined shortly. The first four terms of the spline (da_1, da_2, da_3, da_4) refer to the following age intervals: under 30, 30-39, 40-49, 50-59. In light of the typical pattern of wealth accumulation in a life-cycle model, we identify the accumulation phase with the age interval 30-59. The remaining four terms (da_5, da_6, da_7, da_8 standing for the intervals 60-69, 70-74, 75-80 and over 80) cover the decumulation phase.[14] The indicator for the presence of a potential transfer motive is given by the variables h (mnemonic for heirs); h_d is a dummy variable equal to 1 if the household is in the accumulation phase and has dependent children and zero otherwise; h_c is equal to 1 if the household is in the decumulation phase and has independent children; it is zero otherwise. The θ_j's, β, γ_1, γ_2 and δ are parameters while ε is an error term.

To perform our test we interact the h dummy with the age spline. The variable A_i is a segment of the spline in the age interval 30-59, while D_i is a segment corresponding to age above 69, i.e. past the peak in the ratio of wealth to permanent income as shown in Table 6.5. Under the assumption that a transfer motive is present, the first interaction term, which refers to households with dependent children in their accumulation phase, should be positive. The second interaction term, for households with independent children whose head is over 69, should be negative. Finally, to account for differential perceived mortality of singles and couples, we introduce a further interaction term between the age spline after retirement and an indicator for household type, f, taking value 1 for single-person households.[15]

4.1 Empirical results

For the reasons given in Section 4 we restrict the sample to pure nuclear households, with only the husband and wife being allowed to be income recipients. All households with additional income recipients have been rejected. Thus, extended households are not included in the final sample.

Table 6.6 OLS estimates. Dependent variable: logarithm of the ratio of net worth to permanent income (number of observations: 5,138)

Variables	(1)	(2)	(3)	(4)
da_1	0.072	0.057	0.056	0.068
	(2.030)	(1.597)	(1.590)	(1.895)
da_2	0.090	0.090	0.090	0.086
	(8.549)	(8.634)	(8.669)	(7.931)
da_3	0.038	0.042	0.041	0.030
	(4.047)	(4.467)	(4.416)	(2.827)
da_4	0.039	0.054	0.056	0.055
	(4.195)	(5.668)	(5.836)	(5.302)
da_5	0.018	0.021	0.019	0.021
	(1.541)	(1.856)	(1.670)	(1.702)
da_6	−0.026	−0.011	−0.007	0.008
	(−0.891)	(−0.362)	(−0.226)	(0.267)
da_7	−0.066	−0.044	−0.026	0.009
	(−1.936)	(−1.287)	(−0.726)	(0.222)
da_8	−0.079	−0.058	−0.025	0.018
	(−2.255)	(−1.643)	(−0.600)	(0.378)
Resident in the North		−0.060	−0.064	−0.063
		(−1.074)	(−1.147)	(−1.114)
Resident in the South		−0.047	−0.056	−0.056
		(−0.842)	(−1.015)	(−1.018)
Male		0.294	0.242	0.243
		(4.417)	(3.252)	(3.254)
Primary school		0.119	0.114	0.107
		(2.061)	(1.963)	(1.845)
High school		0.275	0.266	0.248
		(4.585)	(4.431)	(4.102)
University degree		0.555	0.545	0.520
		(6.800)	(6.676)	(6.333)
Older worker		1.421	1.414	1.43
		(1.639)	(1.630)	(1.652)
Income variability			0.106	0.103
			(2.126)	(2.046)
fD			−0.020	−0.011
			(−1.836)	(−1.768)
$h_d A$				0.010
				(2.052)
$h_c D$				−0.022
				(−1.516)
h_d				−0.200
				(−1.870)
Constant	−2.39	−2.42	−2.41	−2.637
	(−2.393)	(−2.430)	(−2.425)	(−2.641)
Adjusted R^2	0.128	0.142	0.143	0.144
Log-likelihood	−9,362.49	−9,320.75	−9,317.47	−9,313.80

Moreover, the choice of the logarithmic specification for equation 1 results in the exclusion of those households with zero or negative net worth (257 households after selecting pure nuclear households).

The results of the estimation of equation (1) are given in Table 6.6. The first column reports a simple regression of the log of the ratio of wealth to permanent income against the age spline alone, which just reproduces the pattern described in Table 6.5. Wealth is accumulated at decreasing rates up to the age bracket 60-69, while there appears to be decumulation thereafter, at rates increasing with age. The annual rate of decumulation is estimated at 3.7 percent for age-group 70-74 and 6.1 percent in the higher age-group. The second column introduces a set of variables to control for variation in tastes and households' characteristics. Households with higher education hold more assets and the same is true for households headed by men, but the basic picture remains unaltered: though the size and significance of the coefficients of the age dummies after retirement is somewhat reduced, they are still negative and increasing in absolute value with age.

In the third column we further allow for differential mortality and other effects. The coefficient of the f variable, interacted with the age spline during the decumulation phase, has the expected negative sign; its size implies that a large part of the decumulation observed in the total sample after retirement is accounted for by singles, who as "households" have a higher perception of mortality than couples. The specification in column (3) also includes a dummy variable to account for income uncertainty (1 for those households that report that they expect their income in the next five years to be unstable). Its coefficient is positive and significantly different from zero, implying that wealth accumulation is affected by precautionary saving. This finding confirms a similar result obtained by Guiso, Jappelli and Terlizzese (1994a) using a direct measure of earnings uncertainty.

Finally, column (4) reports the results of our test. The h_d dummy has been interacted with the A variable, corresponding to the age-groups 30-39, 40-49 and 50-59. The results are interesting in several respects. First of all the coefficient of the interaction term between the h_d variable and these three terms of the age spline has the positive sign implied by the existence of a transfer motive; households with dependent children that are in their accumulation phase accumulate at a rate about 1 percent higher than households of the same age without children. Since, moreover, households with children also have more current needs, their average wealth might be expected to be, *ceteris paribus*, lower than that of households without children. This suggests adding to the regression the dummy variable h_d alone. Its coefficient is significant and, as expected, negative: on average the ratio of wealth to permament income of households with children is 20 percent lower than that of households without dependent children.[16]

Secondly, the interaction between the dummy for households with independent children, h_c, and the age spline after retirement, D, is negative though it is significant only at the 12 percent level of confidence. Other things being equal, after retirement households with independent children decumulate 2.2 percentage points faster than those without children.

These results are consistent with the existence of a transfer motive and with *inter vivos* transfers to the younger generation to relieve liquidity constraints or other adverse contingencies. Clearly, to be helpful these transfers must be well timed. Thus, one would expect that the rate of asset decumulation is highest when liquidity constraints are most likely to bind or family needs to arise. In the 1989 survey we have no direct information on liquidity-constrained households; however, one can use the 1987 SHIW to compute the average age of the households that are liquidity-constrained. Using the definition adopted by Guiso and Jappelli (1994), the average age of liquidity-constrained households (excluding the retired) is 43 if discouraged borrowers are included and 40 if only households that have been denied credit are considered. Given that the generation gap is about 29 years and that fertility ranges from age 29 to 37 (see note 14), the decumulation induced by intergenerational transfers should be highest in the age interval 69-77. Using the estimates reported in column 4, it turns out that the average rate of decumulation for households with independent children is 1.4 and 1.3 percent per year in the age-classes 70-74 and 75-79 respectively and only 0.4 percent afterwards.[17]

Households without a transfer motive accumulate less rapidly before retirement but continue to accumulate even thereafter. A possible interpretation is that the elderly and their children may conclude mutually beneficial informal pacts to insure themselves against, respectively, major disasters or the fear of catastrophic illness in old age, and the possibility of being denied credit in the loan market or other similar contingencies when younger. The observed decumulation, then, would correspond to the insurance payout from the older to the younger generation. Households without children have no such pact at their disposal and have to resort to precautionary saving.

5   Additional evidence on the bequest motive

The evidence provided in the previous section is consistent with consumers having a bequest motive and anticipating the transfer to the time when it is most valuable. However, it is also consistent with the absence of a bequest motive and with transfers motivated only by reciprocity between parents and their children, whereby parents agree to transfer money to children when an adverse event occurs or a particular need arises in exchange for help or assistance in case of need.

Discriminating between these two possibilities is beyond the scope of this paper.[18] However, we can shed some further light on the presence of a bequest motive by looking at the age profile of insurance purchases by households with and without a potential bequest motive.

5.1   Evidence based on life insurance

Additional evidence of the bequest motive can be obtained by looking at the age pattern of life insurance. If a bequest motive is present, parents facing life uncertainty have an incentive to purchase life insurance in order to assure sufficient income to their descendants. Fischer (1973), extending the previous work of Yaari (1965), shows that even if insurance is not actuarially fair, life insurance will be taken out if the weight attached to the utility from leaving a bequest is sufficiently high. Thus, concern for their descendants makes consumers more likely to purchase life insurance. Further, since as Yaari emphasized the concern for bequests is likely to be hump-shaped because the importance of leaving inheritances is greatest when the consumer dies in middle age, the probability of buying life insurance will also be hump-shaped.

Table 6.7 offers some support for the bequest motive. It reports the proportion of households holding life insurance at various ages. The first column refers to the total sample. The proportion with life insurance rises initially with age up to age 40-49 and declines rapidly thereafter; after age 65-69 very few households hold life insurance.

This pattern reproduces very closely the theoretical simulations of Fischer (1973), where life insurance purchases increase to around age 40 and decline thereafter, possibly becoming negative at old ages, when (fair) annuities become a dominant form of holding assets. The second and third columns of Table 6.7 report the age pattern of insurance for households with and without children. Although the shape of the life insurance profile is quite similar, households with dependent children are more likely to purchase life insurance. While life insurance holdings are only slightly larger for very young households with dependent children, they significantly exceed the purchase of life insurance by households without children at older ages. This can be interpreted as *prima facie* evidence of the existence of a bequest motive. However, the result might depend on differences in tastes and characteristics of the two types of households. A proper test of the effect of the bequest motive (as measured by the presence of children) on the purchase of life insurance must take account of these differences.

Table 6.7 Age profile of life insurance holding *(a)*

Age	Total sample	Households without dependent children	Households with dependent children
under 30	13.6	13.0	14.3
30-39	19.8	15.2	21.4
40-49	20.1	15.4	20.6
50-59	15.2	11.5	16.1
60-64	9.6	7.0	12.0
65-69	5.8	3.8	9.2
70-74	2.1	1.0	5.2
75-79	1.8	0.6	7.0
over 79	1.7	1.1	3.6

(a) Life insurance holding is a dummy variable equal to 1 if the household holds life insurance and zero otherwise; the data in the table thus represent the proportion of households with life insurance in each specified age-class.

Let y_i be the latent variable for the insurance purchase decision of the i-th household. When $y_i > 0$ the bequest motive is strong enough to make it worthwhile purchasing life insurance. We assume that it depends linearly upon a vector of variables z which includes a polynomial in age, a set of demographic variables to account for differences in tastes and the dummy for the presence of dependent children as an indicator of the bequest motive:

$$y_i^* = \beta z_i + u_i$$

where β is a vector of coefficients and u_i an error term.

Let y_i be a dummy variable taking value 1 if household i purchases life insurance and zero otherwise. Then

$$\text{prob}(y_i = 1) = \text{prob}(y_i^* > 0) = \text{prob}(u_i > -\beta z_i).$$

Assuming u_i is normally distributed, the vector of parameters β can be estimated (up to a constant of proportionality) by maximum likelihood. The results of the probit estimates are displayed in Table 6.8. Column (1) reports the results of a simple model where the vector z includes only a third order polynomial in age and the proxy for the bequest motive (dependent children).

Table 6.8 Probit estimates: purchase of life insurance

(dummy equal to 1 if the household holds life insurance, zero otherwise; t-statistics in parentheses)

Variables	(1)	(2)	(3)	(4)
Age	0.163	0.130	0.167	0.166
	(3.674)	(2.829)	(3.596)	(3.594)
Age^2	–0.28E–02	–0.21E–02	–0.29E–02	–0.29E–02
	(–3.136)	(–2.279)	(–3.099)	(–3.125)
Age^3	0.13E–04	0.89E–05	0.14E–04	0.14E–04
	(2.189)	(1.466)	(2.324)	(2.391)
h_d	0.230	0.246	0.171	0.155
	(5.135)	(4.924)	(3.299)	(2.979)
h_c			0.103	
			(1.863)	
Household characteristics:				
Males		0.19E–02	–0.029	0.050
		(0.025)	(–0.367)	(–0.638)
Living in the North		–0.059	–0.092	–0.083
		(–1.269)	(–1.960)	(–1.768)
Living in the South		–0.282	–0.229	–0.230
		(–5.771)	(–4.614)	(–4.624)
Married		0.186	0.147	0.157
		(2.555)	(2.004)	(2.141)
Years of education		0.046	0.037	0.036
		(10.816)	(8.475)	(8.148)
Permanent income			0.61E–02	0.59E–05
			(7.977)	(7.582)
Condition of independent children (a)				
Much better				–0.303
				(–1.895)
Better				–0.106
				(–1.217)
The same				0.191
				(2.824)
Worse				0.317
				(2.633)
Much worse				0.346
				(1.486)
Constant	–3.825	–3.892	–4.542	–4.471
	(–5.508)	(–5.417)	(–6.238)	(–6.162)
Sample size	8,161	8,161	8,161	8,161
Life insurance holders	1,139	1,139	1,139	1,139
Likelihood at binomial	–3,298.5	–3,298.5	–3,298.5	–3,298.5
Final likelihood	–3,103.9	–3,015.9	–2,982.9	–2,972.0

(a) The economic condition of each independent child is identified with integers from 1 to 5, corresponding to five groups, from the "much better" to the "much worse". The average economic condition of independent children is computed taking the mean condition and rounding it to the closest integer. This integer then identifies one of the five groups in the table.

The coefficient of the h_d variable is positive and significant, while the probability of purchasing insurance rises until around age 40 and declines thereafter. This regression just summarizes the data shown in Table 6.7. Adding a set of demographic variables as in column (2) leaves the coefficient of the h_d variable and its significance unchanged; purchasing insurance is more likely for households not living in the North or in the South but in Central Italy, for households headed by a man, for married couples and households with higher education.

As Fischer (1973) points out, one of the major reasons for the purchase of life insurance is the fact that the death of the head of the family involves the loss of a primary source of income. Further, the loss is greater the higher is the expected future income associated with the household's head. This implies that households which have higher permanent income are also more likely to buy insurance. To take this into account we add to the specification our measure of permanent income. The results in column (3) of Table 6.8 support this conjecture. Permanent income has a positive and highly significant effect on the probability of life insurance purchase.[19]

The specification in column (3) includes as an additional regressor the dummy for the existence of independent children. If a bequest motive is present, one might expect this variable too to affect the probability of purchasing life insurance. Its coefficient is positive but lower than that of the indicator for dependent children, perhaps because, as is suggested by Yaari (1965), the bequest motive is stronger when children can only rely on parents' resources. Since we have information on the economic condition of independent children relative to that of their parents, we can test whether a life insurance purchase is more likely when children are relatively poorer than parents. The regression in the last column of Table 6.8 replaces the dummy variable for the existence of independent children with five dummies for the average economic condition of the independent children when they are present. While the existence of independent children who are in a better or much better condition than their parents lowers the probability of life insurance purchases, the probability of purchasing life insurance is higher for independent children who are in the same or in worse economic conditions. Further, the effect on the probability is highest for independent children who are much worse off, and decreases monotonically to turn negative when the parents' economic condition is worse than that of their children.

These results support the view that households have a bequest motive and that bequests or transfers are more likely to be effected the poorer the children are relative to the parents as predicted by models with altruistically linked consumers.[20] It is true, however, that a large number of households with dependent children or with independent but poor children do not purchase life insurance. While the share of households with children in worse economic conditions than their parents is only 8.4 percent, that of households with dependent children is certainly much higher (62 percent); yet only 13 percent of the households in the sample have life insurance policies.

In part, this could be due to life insurance costs exceeding fair premiums and in part to households having accumulated enough assets in the form of bequeathable wealth; but it is also likely that some households simply do not conform to the prediction of a model with a bequest motive. This would indeed be consistent with the relatively small share of households reporting the desire to leave a bequest as a primary reason for saving.[21]

6 Conclusions

We have documented the pattern of wealth accumulation and decumulation of Italian households over the life cycle. Although the evidence contradicts the strict life-cycle model of saving, it is not necessarily inconsistent with versions of that model extended to accommodate a transfer motive, life length uncertainty and the risk of catastrophes in old age. Households accumulate fast, at rates above 7 percent per year, when young. They appear to decumulate after retirement but at rates consistent with substantial amounts of wealth left as bequests even after some of it has been transferred *inter vivos*. Our test for the transfer motive shows that before retirement households with children tend to accumulate somewhat faster than childless households. After retirement, most of the observed decumulation is accounted for by households with independent children; households without children, perhaps because of fear of catastrophes, continue to accumulate assets. Finally, other indirect evidence suggests that the resource gap between parents and independent children leaves enough room for transfers to be operative, while evidence based on life insurance is consistent with the bequest motive model, in that households with still dependent children or independent children who are economically worse off than their parents are more likely to hold life insurance policies.

APPENDIX

The construction of permanent income

To compute the permanent income of the household we have used the overall sample of income recipients in the 1989 SHIW (14,552 observations). This sample was then split into two parts. The first includes only working persons over age 16, while the second includes only retired people. The permanent income of retired persons is proxied with their pension income. To compute the permanent income of working consumers we proceed as follows. Let $Y(\tau, j)$ denote the earnings of individual j of age τ. We assume that individual earnings can be expressed as a function of a vector Z of individual characteristics (education, occupation, sector, regional location and family size), a quadratic function of age $\phi(\tau)$ and a zero-mean disturbance u

$$Y(\tau, j) = Z\beta + \phi(\tau) + u.$$

Normal earnings, not adjusted for cohort effects, are then defined as

$$Y_p(\tau, j) = Z\hat{\beta} + \hat{\phi}(\tau) + 0.5\hat{u}$$

where the hats denote the estimated values from a Generalized Least Squares regression, using as weights the residuals from a first-stage OLS regression.

Human wealth of individual j of age τ_0 is then computed as

$$H(\tau_0, j) = \sum_{k=1}^{R_j - \tau_0} \left[Y_p(\tau_0 + k, j) \right] \left(\frac{1+n}{1+r} \right)^k$$

where $Y_p(\tau_0 + k, j)$ is the projected value of normal earnings from the previous equation, R_j is the retirement age of member j and n and r represent, respectively, the rate of growth of productivity and the rate of interest. Retirement age is assumed to be 65 for husbands and 55 for wives; the annual rate of interest is assumed to be equal to 5 percent and the rate of productivity growth to 2.5 percent.

The permanent income of individual j is defined as the annualized value of his human wealth. From this, the permanent income of the household is obtained as the sum of the permanent income of its income recipients.

NOTES

* We wish to thank Tullio Jappelli for very helpful discussion and valuable suggestions.

1 Modigliani (1988) and Kotlikoff (1988), in their debate on the role of intergenerational transfers, provide a summary of the literature and an assessment of the empirical evidence. Overall, it appears that some asset decumulation takes place but at a much slower speed then that implied by the stripped-down version of the life-cycle model. Brugiavini (1987) reaches the same conclusion using Italian cross-sectional data. She finds that some decumulation of assets takes place after retirement but at speeds inconsistent with the simple life-cycle model. Ando and Kennickell (1987) point out that in the U.S. the pace of wealth decumulation is too slow to be accounted for by death uncertainty alone.

2 A bequest motive does not necessarily hamper the aggregate implications of the life-cycle theory. Provided that the fraction of the total lifetime resources allocated to bequests depends on the donor's position in the distribution of income and not on the level of resources in his possession, the well-known form of the aggregate consumption function as a linear, homogeneous function of labor income and wealth is left unchanged. This feature was first observed by Modigliani and Brumberg many years ago. See Modigliani (1986) for a review of issues related to this point.

3 A similar result is obtained by Börsch-Supan (1992) using the Socioeconomic Panel for Germany, while Ohtake (1991) using cross-sectional data for Japan finds that elderly households with living children dissave significantly less that households without children.

4 Even accepting that there is no bequest motive, it is not clear why elderly households with living children should decumulate faster than those without. On this point, Hurd provides no interpretation.

5 A full description of the SHIW is provided by Brandolini and Cannari in the Methodological Appendix to this volume.

6 The panel component is a sample of 1,208 families already interviewed in 1987. See the Methodological Appendix for details.

7 Some additional evidence on the wealth-mortality correlation is available for Japan. Using 1985 and 1990 data on mortality by age and on average income in 47 Japanese regions, we found that while there is some negative correlation between income and mortality at ages before 60, the correlation disappears or even changes sign at older ages. These results are consistent with the Italian data and suggest that ignoring the Shorrocks adjustment in constructing wealth, income and consumption profiles from cross-sectional data is not likely to alter the results significantly. For the U.S., we have assembled from the census and vital statistics data similar to those for Japan, separated by race. The result suggests that there is little correlation between income and mortality at any age. However, for the U.S., variation in mean income among states is rather too small for the results to be reliable, requiring further work with more detailed data.

8 The dominance of "nuclear" households in the Italian economy is not a recent phenomenon. Rather, as documented by Federici (1984), by the 19th century it was already the main form of family organization.

9 Limiting our investigation to "nuclear" families may introduce additional biases if the presence and absence of young working adults is systematically related to some characteristics of the host family, such as income, wealth, and the average propensity to save. However, there is no way to obtain any information on such a possibility from any known data base, since it would require extremely detailed accounts of household finances separated into activities of individuals.

10 For example, suppose that on average families incur significant expenses when the head of the family dies or becomes incapacitated and the family is taken in by a younger household. If this occurs during spring and the survey is conducted later in the year, then since the family no longer exists the expense in question

will not be registered as part of consumption, but the reduction in net worth from the previous year will be recorded.

11 In the Methodological Appendix to this volume, Brandolini and Cannari show that SHIW data underestimate both consumption and income, with underestimation of consumption exceeding that of income by 5 percentage points.

12 This observation, of course, is well known, and it has become a common practice in handling aggregate data to adjust income to reflect capital gains and losses due to inflation. In the survey data, however, the measurement of households' financial assets and liabilities appeared to be particularly poor, so that for most purposes it seemed better not to adjust income. On the other hand, the underestimation of financial assets and liabilities appears to be reasonably uniform over the entire sample and does not seem to change dramatically from one year to the next, so that the change in net worth probably contains significant information about the saving of the family in the period, certainly on its sign if not on the amount.

13 Börsch-Supan shows that Hurd's result holds also using data from the PSID.

14 The average age of marriage for men in Italy is 27, with the first child born at age 29 (see Istat, *Sommario di statistiche storiche 1926-1985*, Roma, 1986). Assuming that fertility is on average completed at age 37, children become independent when the parent is in the age bracket 56-64.

15 In principle one should interact the f dummy with the entire age spline. In practice the effect of perceived mortality at younger ages must be negligible given the low value of the probability of death.

16 Notice, however, that the overall effect of the presence of dependent children is to increase the *level* of net worth at all ages in the accumulation phase.

17 Another implication of liquidity constraints is that the rate of wealth accumulation should be lower when liquidity constraints are most likely to be binding; in our case this should occur around age 40. The estimates in Table 6.7 show that the annual rate of wealth accumulation drops from 8.5 percent in the 30-39 age-group to 3.0 percent at 40-49 and rises to 5.5 percent at age 50-59. This is consistent with the presence of binding liquidity constraints around age 40.

18 Cox (1987) and Cox and Rank (1992) perform tests to discriminate between transfers motivated by exchange and by altruism.

19 The same results obtain if instead of the measure of permanent income one includes a set of occupational dummies as proxies of future income. The coefficient of the occupational dummies is higher for occupations that are likely to deliver higher permanent income, such as managers and entrepreneurs.

20 If the decision to leave a bequest or make a transfer is a decision to increase the utility of the beneficiary at the expense of the utility of the donor, then given equal concern of parents for their children's welfare, a transfer will be more likely, the lower the resources of the beneficiary with respect to those of the donor. In general, in a growing economy new generations are better off, on average, than previous generations. Thus, one would expect the scope for

transfers to decrease as the rate of growth of the economy rises. Among the households with independent children, in 57 percent of the cases, children are reported to have a much better (19 percent) or better (38 percent) economic condition. For 35 percent the economic condition of the independent children is about the same, and in only 8 percent of the cases are children worse or much worse off than their parents. This distribution seems to indicate that there is scope for a transfer to become operative surely in 8 percent of the cases but probably in no more than 43 percent of the households with living independent children, which corresponds to 18 percent of the households in the total sample.

21 In Italy, as in other countries, only a small share of households report that bequests are an important reason for saving. See Barca, Cannari and Guiso (1994).

REFERENCES

Ando, A. (1985). 'The Saving of Japanese Households: A Micro Study Based on Data from the National Survey of Family Income and Expenditure 1974 and 1979', Department of Economics, University of Pennsylvania, mimeo.

Ando, A. and A.B. Kennickell (1987). 'How Much (or Little) Life-Cycle Is There in Micro Data? The Cases of the United States and Japan', in R. Dornbush, S. Fischer and J. Bossons (eds.), *Macroeconomics and Finance. Essays in Honor of Franco Modigliani*, Cambridge, MA: MIT Press.

Ando, A., L. Guiso and D. Terlizzese (1994). 'Young Households' Saving and the Life Cycle of Opportunities. Evidence from Japan and Italy', *this volume*.

Barca, F., L. Cannari and L. Guiso (1994). 'Bequests and Saving for Retirement. What Impels the Accumulation of Wealth?', *this volume*.

Börsch-Supan, A. (1992). 'Saving and Consumption Patterns of the Elderly. The German Case', *Journal of Population Economics* 5: 289-303.

Brugiavini, A. (1987). 'Empirical Evidence on Wealth Accumulation and the Effects of Pension Wealth: An Application to Italian Cross-Section Data', Discussion Paper 20, London School of Economics, Financial Markets Groups.

Cox, D. (1987). 'Motives for Private Income Transfers', *Journal of Political Economy* 95: 508-46.

Cox, D. (1990). 'Intergenerational Transfers and Liquidity Constraints', *Quarterly Journal of Economics* 105: 187-217.

Cox, D. and M.R. Rank (1992). 'Inter-Vivos Transfers and Intergenerational Exchange', *Review of Economics and Statistics* 74: 305-14.

Deaton, A. (1991). 'Saving and Liquidity Constraints', *Econometrica* 59: 1221-48.

Federici, N. (1984). *Procreazione, famiglia, lavoro della donna*, Torino: Loescher.

Fischer, S. (1973). 'A Life Cycle Model of Life Insurance Purchases', *International Economic Review* 14: 132-52.

Guiso, L. and T. Jappelli (1994). 'Intergenerational Transfers and Capital Market Imperfections: Evidence from a Cross-Section of Italian Households', *this volume*.

Guiso, L., T. Jappelli and D. Terlizzese (1994a). 'Earnings Uncertainty and Precautionary Saving', *this volume*.

Guiso, L., T. Jappelli and D. Terlizzese (1994b). 'Why Is Italy's Saving Rate so High?', *this volume*.

Hayashi, F., A. Ando and R. Ferris (1988). 'Life Cycle and Bequest Savings', *Journal of the Japanese and International Economies* 2: 450-91.

Hurd, M.D. (1987). 'Saving of the Elderly and Desired Bequests', *American Economic Review* 77: 298-312.

Hurd, M.D. (1989). 'Mortality Risk and Bequests', *Econometrica* 57: 779-813.

King, M.A. and L-D.L. Dicks-Mireaux (1982), 'Asset Holding and the Life Cycle', *Economic Journal* 92: 247-67.

Kotlikoff, L.J. (1988). 'Intergenerational Transfers and Saving', *Journal of Economic Perspectives* 2: 41-58.

Laitner, J. (1993). 'Long-Run Equilibria with Borrowing Constraints and Altruism', *Journal of Economic Dynamics and Control* 17: 65-96.

Maccan, L., N. Rossi and I. Visco (1994). 'Saving and Borrowing Constraints', *this volume*.

Modigliani, F. (1986). 'Life Cycle, Individual Thrift and the Wealth of Nations', *American Economic Review* 76: 297-313.

Modigliani, F. (1988). 'The Role of Intergenerational Transfers and Life Cycle Saving in the Accumulation of Wealth', *Journal of Economic Perspectives* 2: 15-40.

Ohtake, F. (1991). 'Bequest Motives of Aged Households in Japan', *Ricerche Economiche* 45: 283-306.

Shorrocks, A.F. (1975). 'The Age-Wealth Relationship: A Cross-Section and Cohort Analysis', *Review of Economics and Statistics* 57: 155-63.

Yaari, M.E. (1965). 'Uncertain Lifetime, Life Insurance and the Theory of the Consumer', *Review of Economic Studies* 32: 137-50.

7 Earnings uncertainty and precautionary saving*

LUIGI GUISO, TULLIO JAPPELLI
and DANIELE TERLIZZESE

1 Introduction

The idea that people accumulate assets to face unexpected drops in income dates back to Friedman (1957). Later studies by Leland (1968), Sandmo (1970) and Drèze and Modigliani (1972) stated the theoretical conditions about preferences under which an increase in uninsurable risk leads to higher saving. Recent research has further sharpened the theory of precautionary saving. Zeldes (1989), Caballero (1990) and Weil (1993) have extended the two-period framework used by earlier authors to multi-period models and established that the amount of precautionary saving increases in response to an increase in the variance of the shocks of the income generating process and in its degree of persistence. Kimball (1990) has shown that if people have decreasing prudence, precautionary saving declines as individual wealth rises.

Precautionary saving has several empirical and policy implications. Zeldes (1989) points out that precautionary saving may explain some of the consumption "puzzles", such as the excess sensitivity of consumption to anticipated income fluctuations, the growth of consumption even in the presence of low real interest rates and the slow rate of wealth decumulation of the elderly. If uncertainty affects consumer behavior, government insurance programs and tax policies may reduce individual risks and may increase welfare (Barsky, Mankiw and Zeldes, 1986). Since generation specific risks may be offset by a chain of intergenerational transfers, a finding that consumers react strongly to uncertainty would therefore question not only the quadratic utility model, but Barro's (1974) dynastic model as well.

Most of these discussions have proceeded in an empirical vacuum. There is almost no evidence on the importance of precautionary saving. Invariably, empirical studies must face a fundamental problem: how should one measure the subjective uncertainty of future income fluctuations? Since this variable is unobservable, research to date relied on simulations or on indirect proxies for risk. While useful, both approaches have serious drawbacks. Simulations performed by Skinner (1988), Zeldes (1989), and Caballero (1991) have shown that with realistic parameter values, earnings uncertainty can generate a substantial amount of saving and wealth. For example, Skinner (1988) and Caballero (1991) find that earnings uncertainty alone may account for as much as 60 percent of U.S. households' net worth. But these simulation results depend on maintained assumptions about preferences and the process that generates income. More importantly, simulations do not test whether people actually respond to risk as predicted by the theoretical models.

Econometric tests that use indirect proxies for risk run into a number of different problems. Time series studies rely on proxies that reflect aggregate risk only. As noted by Kimball (1990), individual risks – that are likely to be the main determinants of precautionary saving – tend to wash out in the process of aggregation. At the cross-sectional level, proxies for risk are almost invariably correlated with other consumer attributes, and it is impossible to distinguish whether they are truly measuring risk or capturing some other effect. More fundamentally, indicators of risk are subject to a problem of self-selection. Households in risky categories may have chosen to belong to that category simply because they are less risk-averse, in which case their average propensity to save might not be higher than that of the average household. This problem casts doubt on Friedman's (1957) original approach – recently replicated by Skinner (1988) – based on occupational dummies to classify households in different risk categories.

To avoid these shortcomings in assessing the empirical relevance of precautionary saving, and given the unobservable nature of households' perceived uncertainty, there is no alternative but to rely upon direct survey information on the households' subjective assessment of specific risks.[1] Our empirical approach to precautionary saving was shaped by these considerations. A question on the subjective probability distribution of earnings in the 1989 Bank of Italy Survey of Household Income and Wealth (SHIW)[2] was therefore included. In principle, this survey allows us to assess the effect of uncertainty on consumption and wealth accumulation in a way that is free from the problems that plague empirical studies based on indirect measures of risk.

Our analysis is subject to one important qualifier. What matters for saving decisions is human wealth uncertainty. The available data, however, provide information only on the probability distribution of earnings one year ahead. Thus, in order to estimate the effect of uncertainty on consumption and wealth accumulation we need to make two assumptions: (i) the degree of persistence in the income generating process is identical for all households; (ii) the probability distribution from which earnings are drawn is time-invariant. While restrictive, we provide evidence that the first assumption is not a bad description of the data, at least not enough to cast serious doubts on our main findings. The second is a maintained hypothesis and rules out jumps in the income generating process. It implies, for example, that uncertainty is age-independent. The paper is organized as follows. Section 2 briefly reviews the theory of precautionary saving. Section 3 describes the 1989 SHIW and the self-reported measure of earnings uncertainty. Sections 4 and 5 report the empirical tests of the effect of uncertainty on consumption and wealth accumulation. Section 6 explores the validity of our maintained assumption, i.e. that the persistence of earnings is the same across individuals, and Section 7 the implications of our results for the explanation of some of the consumption puzzles. Section 8 summarizes our main findings and their implications for current research. The Appendix contains information about the survey and the definitions of the variables used in the empirical tests.

2   The theoretical model

In this section we briefly review a model of precautionary saving with earnings uncertainty. Following Caballero (1990) and Weil (1990), we assume that the household maximizes a time-separable utility function over an infinite horizon and that the within-period utility function is exponential, with constant degree of absolute prudence equal to θ.[3] We further assume that after-tax labor income y follows the stochastic process:

$$y_t = \gamma y_{t-1} + (1 - \gamma)\hat{y} + \varepsilon_t \tag{1}$$

which combines a deterministic component $\hat{y}$ and a stochastic component ε, identically and independently distributed with zero mean and variance σ^2. The parameter γ measures the degree of persistence of the innovations in income.

The consumer chooses a sequence of consumption values to maximize the expected value of utility under the budget constraint $w_t = Rw_{t-1} + y_t - c_t$, where w_t is end-of-period wealth, c_t is consumption and R the interest factor, assumed to be constant. The problem is then:

$$\max \quad -\frac{1}{\theta} \, \mathrm{E} \sum_{i=0}^{\infty} \beta^i \exp(-\theta c_{t+i})$$

$$\text{s.t.} \quad w_t = Rw_{t-1} + y_t - c_t$$

$$y_t = \gamma y_{t-1} + (1 - \gamma)\hat{y} + \varepsilon_t.$$

It can be shown that the solution to this problem has two parts. The first part is the certainty-equivalence level of consumption, the second can be identified with precautionary saving. In the case where the interest rate is equal to the discount rate ($\beta R = 1$):

$$c_t = \frac{R - 1}{R - \gamma}\left(y_t + \frac{1 - \gamma}{R - 1}\hat{y} + w_{t-1}\right) - \frac{\Pi}{R} \tag{2}$$

where:

$$\Pi = \frac{R - \gamma}{\theta R} \log \left[E \exp\left(-\frac{\theta R}{R - \gamma}\varepsilon\right)\right]. \tag{3}$$

The first term in equation (2) is the optimal level of consumption when income is certain and equal to $E(y_t)$. The term Π is the precautionary component of saving. When the income shock is normally distributed, this term reduces to:

$$\Pi = \frac{\theta R}{R - \gamma}\sigma^2 \tag{3'}$$

which increases with the variance of the shock σ^2, the degree of earnings persistence γ, and the degree of prudence θ.

Caballero (1991) considers the finite-life version of the exponential utility model assuming that labor income follows a random walk, and derives the implications for wealth accumulation: the higher the risk, the higher the amount of assets accumulated by prudent consumers at each stage of the life cycle.

Exponential utility, though analytically convenient, is restrictive. It implies that the sensitivity of consumption to uncertainty, measured by the degree of prudence, is independent of the level of individual resources. Kimball (1990) argues convincingly that, like risk aversion, prudence declines with wealth. People who have already accumulated substantial assets may choose to respond less to sudden drops in earnings than those with little assets. Unfortunately, closed-form solutions for consumption can be obtained only in the case of exponential utility, where prudence is constant. However, the intuition behind equation (2) is more general. Provided that prudence is positive, uncertainty lowers the optimal level of current consumption and increases the level of assets that individuals choose to hold.

In Sections 4 and 5 we test these predictions of the theory of precautionary saving, that is that uncertainty lowers consumption and raises wealth accumulation. We will also test the assumption that the effect of uncertainty does not depend on the level of households' resources (constant prudence). In the next section we describe the data and the self-reported measure of uncertainty used in this study.

3   The data and the self-reported measure of uncertainty

In this paper we use the most recent wave of the Bank of Italy Survey of Household Income and Wealth (SHIW), referring to the year 1989.

The 1989 SHIW contains detailed information about income, wealth, consumption and a series of demographic characteristics of 8,274 households divided into two groups: (i) a random sample of 7,066 households interviewed for the first time at the beginning of 1990; (ii) 1,208 households which were also interviewed at the beginning of 1988 (the panel component of the SHIW). The overall sample is representative of the Italian resident population, as shown by a comparison of population and sample means of selected demographic variables (see for details the Methodological Appendix in this volume). Balance-sheet items are reported as of December 31 of 1989, while income and consumption refer to the year 1989.

The 1989 SHIW included two new questions regarding the probability distribution of the rate of growth of nominal earnings and inflation for the year following the survey. Every income recipient was asked to attribute weights, summing to 100, to given intervals of inflation and nominal earnings increases one year ahead.[4] These two marginal distributions are then used, following the procedure illustrated below, to measure the subjective uncertainty of real earnings in 1990.

We assume that the variance of household earnings can be proxied by the variance of the earnings of the head of the household.[5] To obtain an estimate of the variance we proceed as follows. Let z denote the percentage growth rate of nominal earnings, π the rate of inflation and x the rate of growth of real earnings. The variables x, z and π are three stochastic variables that satisfy the identity:

$$z = x + \pi.$$ (4)

With obvious notation, the variance of z can be expressed as:

$$\sigma_z^2 = \sigma_x^2 + \sigma_\pi^2 + 2\varrho\sigma_x\sigma_\pi.$$ (5)

We wish to recover the variance of x, σ_x^2.

From the survey we have information about σ_z and σ_π. However, in order to use equation (5) we need to make an assumption about the value of ϱ, the correlation coefficient between the rate of growth of real earnings x and the rate of inflation π. For given ϱ, equation (5) can be solved for σ_x, giving:

$$\sigma_x = -\varrho\sigma_\pi \pm \sqrt{\sigma_z^2 - (1 - \varrho^2)\sigma_\pi^2} \ . \tag{6}$$

Since σ_z and σ_π can be either positive or equal to zero, there are four possible cases: each defines a sample region in Table 7.1. The analysis of these cases, together with the condition that $\sigma_x > 0$, helps in identifying the value of ϱ.

Table 7.1 Inflation and earnings uncertainty

Group 1: 980 households	Group 2: 673 households
$\sigma_z^2 = 0, \ \sigma_\pi^2 = 0$	$\sigma_z^2 > 0, \ \sigma_\pi^2 = 0$
$\Rightarrow \sigma_x^2 = 0$	$\Rightarrow \sigma_x^2 = \sigma_z^2$
Group 3: 172 households	**Group 4: 1,084 households**
$\sigma_z^2 = 0, \ \sigma_\pi^2 > 0$	$\sigma_z^2 > 0, \ \sigma_\pi^2 > 0$
$\Rightarrow \sigma_x^2 = \sigma_\pi^2$	$\Rightarrow \sigma_x^2 = (\sigma_z + \sigma_\pi)^2$

Consider first the group of households that has point expectations for both inflation and the rate of growth of earnings, i.e. $\sigma_z^2 = 0$ and $\sigma_\pi^2 = 0$. Here the value of ϱ is immaterial, and from equation (6) we immediately obtain that $\sigma_\pi^2 = 0$. A second group of households has point expectations about inflation $(\sigma_\pi^2 = 0)$ but not about earnings $(\sigma_z^2 > 0)$. Equation (6) implies that in this case the variance of real earnings must be equal to the variance of nominal earnings, i.e. $\sigma_x^2 = \sigma_z^2$.

A third group of households has point expectations about earnings $(\sigma_z^2 = 0)$ but not about inflation $(\sigma_\pi^2 > 0)$. In this case equation (6) reduces to:

$$\sigma_x = -\varrho\sigma_\pi \pm \sqrt{(\varrho^2 - 1)\sigma_\pi^2} \ . \tag{7}$$

The only solution to equation (7) that is both real and positive can be obtained by setting $\varrho = -1$, implying $\sigma_x^2 = \sigma_\pi^2$.

A fourth group is uncertain about both earnings and inflation ($\sigma_z^2 > 0$ and $\sigma_\pi^2 > 0$). As we shall see below, one of the main findings of this paper is that earnings uncertainty is small. Thus, we are interested in generating the largest possible estimate of the variance, since any lower measure would strengthen our results. We therefore concentrate on the larger solution, corresponding to the plus sign in equation (6), which is decreasing in ϱ.[6] Choosing $\varrho = -1$ yields the largest possible estimate of the variance that is consistent with the data.[7] Thus, in this case we set $\sigma_x^2 = (\sigma_z + \sigma_\pi)^2$.

Finally, the variance of the level of real earnings σ^2 can be obtained by noting that next year's income, as perceived by the household, is $y_{t+1} = y_t(1 + x)$, where y_t is labor income in the year of the survey. Thus, $\mathrm{var}(y_{t+1}) \equiv \sigma^2 = y_t^2 \sigma_x^2$.

Table 7.2 displays the frequency distribution of the ratio between the subjective standard deviation and current earnings (σ/y). More than one third (34 percent) of those surveyed hold point expectations about expected real earnings one year ahead. For almost two thirds of the sample the standard error is less than 2 percent of current earnings. The remaining third display a measure of uncertainty that in the majority of cases does not exceed 5 percent of current earnings.

Table 7.2 Frequency distribution of the ratio of the subjective standard deviation to the mean of earnings in selected classes

σ/y (%)	Number of observations in the sample	Frequency (%)
0	980	33.7
0 – 0.5	302	10.4
0.5 – 1.5	752	25.6
1.5 – 2.5	532	18.4
2.5 – 3.5	173	6.0
3.5 – 4.5	88	3.0
4.5 – 6.5	63	2.2
6.5 – 10.0	13	0.5
10.0 – 15.0	6	0.2
mean: 1.15	2,909	100.0

The magnitude of the figures in Table 7.2 contrasts considerably with the size of uncertainty generally assumed in the literature on precautionary saving. In fact, most simulations assume values of the standard error of earnings shocks between 10 and 20 percent of the level of earnings.[8] Estimates of uncertainty obtained with U.S. panel data under the hypothesis that earnings follow a univariate stochastic process yield values between 5 to 10 times higher than what we find in the survey.[9]

There are three possible explanations that may account for the differences between the self-reported measure of earnings uncertainty and the standard errors of earnings found in U.S. panel data. First, it is possible that part of the variability in income in panel data is due to measurement errors. For instance, Pischke (1990) shows that accounting for these measurement errors may reduce by 10 to 20 percent the estimate of the standard error of earnings shocks.

A second possibility is that Americans face more earnings uncertainty than Italians. In the absence of better measures, the income distribution might be a useful index to compare earnings risk across countries: a more unequal distribution might signal higher chances of very bad and very good income draws. In the Appendix we compare the income distribution implied by the 1989 Italian Survey and by the 1983-86 Survey of Consumer Finances (Tables 7.A2 and 7.A3). The main insight of this comparison is that the distribution of income is less equal in the U.S. than in Italy, but not by a very large extent. If income distribution is indeed correlated with earnings risks across countries, the difference between the self-reported measure of uncertainty used in this study and the estimates of uncertainty found in econometric studies of U.S. households may in part be attributed to the fact that Italian households live in a less risky environment.

The third and more important element to be considered is that the error of the time series process for earnings estimated with panel data is not the same as the uncertainty faced by individuals. Stochastic processes of earnings estimated with panel data overestimate the "true" uncertainty to the extent that households have better information about their earnings prospects than the econometrician.

The discrepancy between our measure of uncertainty and that obtained in panel studies could therefore be ascribed to households' forecasts being conditional on a much larger set of variables than those observed by the econometrician.[10] A comparison of our measure of uncertainty and the indicators of risk most commonly adopted by other authors is instructive. Many of the characteristics of households with lower uncertainty (Table 7.3, column (2)) are not dramatically different from those with higher uncertainty (Table 7.3, column (3)). Yet, among the latter, young households,

Table 7.3 Sample characteristics for varying levels of earnings uncertainty and regression of uncertainty on characteristics

Variables	Total sample	Low uncertainty $(\sigma/y < 3\%)$	High uncertainty $(\sigma/y \geq 3\%)$	Coefficients of the regression $\sigma/y = x\beta + \varepsilon\ (a)$	t-statistics
	(1)	(2)	(3)	(4)	(5)
Demographics					
Male	0.91	0.91	0.91	0.198E–3	0.175
Married	0.84	0.85	0.81	–0.206R–2	–1.980
Family size	3.39	3.40	3.38	–0.547E–4	–0.087
Number of children	1.44	1.43	1.44	0.952E–4	0.141
Education	10.47	10.30	11.04	0.122E–3	1.675
Age	42.88	43.25	41.66	–0.585E–4	–2.110
Occupation					
Operative and laborer	0.27	0.29	0.22	–0.215E–4	–2.659
Clerical	0.34	0.35	0.31	–0.286E–2	–3.674
Precision craft	0.10	0.09	0.13	–0.550E–3	–0.534
Professional	0.07	0.06	0.08	–0.644E–3	–0.544
Manager	0.03	0.03	0.04	–0.442E–3	–0.422
Entrepreneur	0.02	0.02	0.01	–0.197E–2	–0.931
Self-employed	0.16	0.15	0.20		
Other	0.01	0.01	0.01	–0.108E–2	–0.258

Table 7.3 (cont.)

Variables	Total sample	Low uncertainty ($\sigma/y < 3\%$)	High uncertainty ($\sigma/y \geq 3\%$)	Coefficients of the regression $\sigma/y = x\beta + \varepsilon$ (a)	t-statistics
	(1)	(2)	(3)	(4)	(5)
Sector					
Agricultural	0.04	0.05	0.03	−0.254E-2	−1.817
Industry	0.25	0.25	0.23	0.479E-3	0.620
Services	0.44	0.43	0.47	0.439E-3	−0.010
Public administration	0.27	0.27	0.27		
Regional location					
North	0.46	0.48	0.38	−0.752E-5	−0.010
Centre	0.16	0.17	0.16		
South	0.38	0.35	0.46	0.319E-2	4.134
Constant				0.146E-1	6.61
Income and balance sheet (b)					
Earnings	33.24	33.18	33.44		
Permanent earnings	31.86	31.86	31.87		
Consumption	30.95	30.58	32.18		
Net worth	204.38	201.85	212.69		
Av. prop. to consume (c)	0.79	0.79	0.79		
Number of observations	2,909	2,229	680	2,909	
Adjusted R^2				0.019	

(a) The mean of the dependent variable in column (4) is 0.0115. Excluded attributes from the regression are: self-employed, resident in the Centre and employed in the public sector. − (b) Expressed in millions of 1989 lire. − (c) As a percentage of disposable income.

professionals, managers and residents in Southern regions are relatively more numerous. Also the self-employed face higher uncertainty, in line with the commonly adopted assumption that this is a "high" risk category.[11]

Households with higher education may report a higher value of uncertainty simply because they understand the survey questions better than households with little education. However, on average, households with high uncertainty have only one year of schooling more than households reporting lower uncertainty. A regression of (σ/y) on the sample characteristics (column (4) in Table 7.3) shows that education has a small coefficient and is significantly different from zero only at the 10 percent level. On the other hand, the regression confirms that self-employed and households living in the South tend to report a higher variance.

The difference between the values displayed in Table 7.3 and those assumed in simulation studies or found in panel data is substantial, even if one takes into account the three reasons why the self-reported measure may differ from the econometric estimates. One may even be inclined to question the validity of the survey responses altogether. Our only rebuttal is that the responses about the inflation variable are highly plausible. Unlike individuals' earnings, inflation is an aggregate variable, and can be verified *ex-post*. The average expected inflation in the sample is 7 percent, which is quite close to that predicted in 1989 for 1990 by the most sophisticated econometric models. Nor does the mean hide numerous implausible extreme values. Actually, for more than 50 percent of the sample the entire probability distribution for inflation is bunched between 5 and 7 percent. Finally, as already pointed out, the self-reported measure of uncertainty correlates with the risk categories that *a priori* are thought to be most subject to risk and is not explained by the fact that only households with higher education understand the survey questions. Thus, we regard our measure of uncertainty as a reliable indicator of individual risks.

4   The effect of earnings uncertainty on consumption

As shown in Section 2, the appropriate measure of uncertainty is human-wealth uncertainty, which depends, in turn, on the variance of the one-period shocks to income and on the persistence of the disturbance. The more persistent the shocks, the greater the uncertainty faced by the individual. In the cross-section we lack a measure of persistence, but if the degree of persistence is the same for all households, knowledge of one-period-ahead uncertainty is sufficient to estimate the amount of precautionary saving. Accordingly, we assume that individual incomes follow a process with idiosyncratic variance but common persistence (in Section 6 we offer some evidence corroborating this assumption).

4.1 Development of the empirical model

To test for the presence of precautionary saving we estimate three specifications of the consumption function. As mentioned in Section 2, only in the case of constant absolute risk aversion an explicit closed-form solution for optimal consumption can be derived. In this special case individual consumption is the sum of two components. The first is a fraction λ of the certainty-equivalence level of lifetime resources L, where L is the sum of human wealth and non-human wealth; the second is the precautionary component, which, under the assumption of normality, is proportional to the variance of the earnings shocks:

$$c_i = \lambda L_i - \mu \sigma_i^2 \tag{8}$$

where i indexes households. The problem of this specification derived from exponential utility is that it constrains the degree of prudence to be constant.

Since deviations from absolute risk aversion utility functions may result in non-linearities, we also estimate a second-order Taylor expansion of a general consumption function that includes quadratic and interaction terms between lifetime resources L and the measure of uncertainty. The advantage of this specification is that it does not constrain the degree of prudence to be constant. But this unrestricted specification does not guarantee that the effect of uncertainty on consumption decreases with lifetime resources, as implied by the hypothesis of decreasing prudence.

A tighter use of Taylor series expansion is suggested by Skinner (1988). Assuming a constant relative risk aversion utility function, he approximates the solution of the consumer's intertemporal maximization problem taking a second-order expansion of the Euler equations.[12] The insight of Skinner's approximation can be captured in a two-period, simplified version of his multi-period model.[13] In this case the approximation to the first-period consumption function is:

$$c_{i1} = L_{i1}/\cdot\left\{1 + \left[1 + \frac{\phi\sigma^2}{E(L_{i2})^2}\right]^{1/\theta}\right\} \tag{9}$$

where $\phi = \delta(\delta+1)/2$, δ is the degree of relative risk aversion, E is the expectation operator, and the expectation for time 2 is conditional on information as of time 1.[14]

The important insight of equation (9) is that the effect of uncertainty on consumption depends on the amount of total resources at risk, i.e. the variance of earnings is scaled by the expectation of lifetime resources. In order to capture the interaction of uncertainty and individuals' resources, we also estimate the following consumption equation:

$$c_i = \lambda L_i - \mu \sigma_i^2 / L_i^\alpha. \tag{10}$$

The parameter α measures the sensitivity to the level of non-human wealth exhibited by the reaction to uncertainty. If $\alpha = 0$, equation (10) reduces to the case of constant absolute prudence (equation (8)). If $\alpha > 0$, the effect of uncertainty on consumption declines with households' total resources. This decline is faster the higher the value of α.

4.2   Sample selection and empirical results

The original sample of the 1989 SHIW numbers 8,274 households. We exclude all households in which the head is not in the labor force or reports zero earnings in 1989. Since older households may spend down accumulated precautionary saving, we also exclude households in which the head is older than 65 (further restricting the sample to those younger than 55 does not change the results). After these exclusions the sample shrinks to 5,347 households. A sizeable fraction of these households (2,419) did not answer the questions concerning the probability distribution of income and inflation. Excluding also households with negative net worth (19 observations) the sample shrinks further to 2,909 observations (this is the sample whose characteristics are reported in Table 7.3).[15]

For entrepreneurs and some managers, most income is property income. The effect of capital income uncertainty on consumption – in particular, the effect of interest rate uncertainty – is theoretically ambiguous (Sandmo, 1970). Since we do not want to bias the test against the presence of precautionary saving, we also exclude 159 managers and entrepreneurs. This reduces the sample further to 2,750.

To reduce heteroscedasticity, all variables are divided by permanent earnings. Following King and Dicks-Mireaux (1982), these are defined as normal annual earnings adjusted for cohort effects. The procedure used in constructing this variable is described in the Appendix.[16] Transitory earnings are defined as the difference between permanent earnings and current earnings. Human wealth is the product of permanent earnings and the age of the household to retirement, assumed to be 65.[17] Lifetime resources are the sum of households' net worth and the constructed measure of human wealth. Since assets and liabilities are measured at the end of the period, we proxy beginning-of-period net worth by subtracting 1989 savings from end-of-period net worth.

To take into account the effects of differences in preferences and family composition on the propensity to consume, we add a set of demographic variables to the regressors. After dropping non-significant variables, the estimated consumption function includes age, education and family size. The dependent variable is the ratio of consumption of non-durables and services divided by permanent earnings.

The results of the three specifications of the consumption function are reported in Table 7.4a. All estimated equations explain a large fraction of the variability of the ratio of consumption to permanent earnings (the adjusted R^2 is around 0.45 in all specifications). In all cases the estimated coefficient of permanent earnings is higher than that of transitory earnings.

Column (1) reports the specification with constant prudence. The coefficient of σ^2 is small and not significantly different from zero. Column (2) adds the interaction term between σ^2 and total resources.[18] In this case the two coefficients have opposite signs, and are both significantly different from zero. The effect of earnings uncertainty, however, becomes negative for high values of wealth.

In column (3) of Table 7.4a we constrain the interaction term between resources and uncertainty to be consistent with the hypothesis of decreasing prudence. The coefficient a is computed by a grid search maximizing the value of the likelihood function; its estimated value is 1.2.[19]

The effect of uncertainty is again statistically significant. Evaluating this effect at the sample means of permanent earnings, wealth and variance, we find that the shortfall of consumption in response to uncertainty is 0.14 percent of permanent earnings. This effect tends to zero as the level of wealth increases.

Overall, the coefficients in Table 7.4a indicate that the effect of uncertainty on consumption is rather small. The specification of column (2) clearly rejects the assumption of constant prudence. The likelihood ratio test between the specification of column (3) and the specification with constant prudence yields a value of 5.80, as opposed to a theoretical value of a $\chi^2(1)$ of 3.84: the restriction $a = 0$ is rejected at the 5 percent confidence level.

One possibility to account for a small effect of uncertainty on consumption is that the family provides earnings' insurance, either by intergenerational transfers or by transfers within the family (Kotlikoff and Spivak, 1981). While it is hard to test for the former effect, it is possible to test for the latter by restricting the sample to households with one income recipient. It is indeed plausible that households with two or more income earners pool their risks and are better insured than isolated households.

Table 7.4a   Consumption function estimates. Total sample *(a)*
(dependent variable: ratio of non-durable consumption to permanent earnings)

Variables	Constant prudence	General specification	Decreasing prudence *(b)*	Means of variables *(c)*
	(1)	(2)	(3)	(4)
Permanent earnings	0.632 (29.61)	0.614 (28.82)	0.630 (29.63)	1.000
Transitory earnings	0.560 (37.03)	0.544 (35.72)	0.566 (38.68)	0.027
Net worth	0.010 (15.98)	0.009 (15.00)	0.010 (15.86)	6.146
σ^2	0.398E–1 (0.32)	–1.111 (–5.29)		0.012
$\sigma^2 L$		0.143E–2 (6.82)		12.642
σ^2/L^α			–281.0 (–2.43)	0.49E–05
Age	0.021 (1.31)	0.034 (2.15)	0.024 (1.55)	1.520
Family size	0.812 (6.70)	0.789 (6.57)	0.792 (6.53)	0.118
Education	0.290 (6.71)	0.285 (6.65)	0.291 (6.75)	0.351
Constant	1.282 (1.45)	1.354 (1.55)	1.278 (1.45)	0.036
Adjusted R^2	0.452	0.461	0.453	
Standard error	0.295	0.293	0.295	
No. of observations	2,750	2,750	2,750	
Log-likelihood	–542.8	–519.6	–539.9	

(a) With respect to the sample of Table 7.3, we exclude 159 managers and entrepreneurs. Consumption, income, wealth and earnings' variance are expressed in millions of 1989 lire. The mean of the dependent variable is 0.983. Asymptotic *t*-statistics are reported in parentheses.

(b) The value of α that maximizes the likelihood function is 1.2.

(c) All variables are divided by permanent earnings.

Table 7.4b Consumption function estimates. Sample of households with one income recipient *(a)*
(dependent variable: ratio of non-durable consumption to permanent earnings)

Variables	Constant prudence	General specification	Decreasing prudence *(b)*	Means of variables *(c)*
	(1)	(2)	(3)	(4)
Permanent earnings	0.814 (15.10)	0.787 (14.53)	0.802 (14.90)	1.000
Transitory earnings	0.666 (29.61)	0.642 (27.42)	0.662 (30.56)	−0.003
Net worth	0.010 (11.09)	0.009 (10.48)	0.010 (11.03)	6.338
σ^2	−0.296 (−1.82)	−1.102 (−3.91)		0.012
$\sigma^2 L$		0.149E−02 (3.49)		8.848
σ^2/L^α			−330.0 (−2.70)	0.66E−05
Age	0.016 (0.84)	0.025 (1.30)	0.019 (1.02)	1.870
Family size	0.608 (4.09)	0.600 (4.05)	0.592 (3.98)	0.140
Education	0.130 (1.98)	0.129 (1.97)	0.129 (1.96)	0.433
Constant	−0.103 (−0.09)	0.135 (0.12)	0.066 (0.06)	0.045
Adjusted R^2	0.515	0.519	0.516	
Standard error	0.305	0.304	0.305	
No. of observations	1,311	1,311	1,311	
Log-likelihood	−301.1	−295.0	−299.9	

(a) With respect to the sample of Table 7.3, we exclude 159 managers and entrepreneurs and 1,459 households with more than one income recipient. Consumption, income, wealth and earnings' variance are expressed in millions of 1989 lire. The mean of the dependent variable is 1.039. Asymptotic *t*-statistics are reported in parentheses.
(b) The value of α that maximizes the likelihood function is 1.2.
(c) All variables are divided by permanent earnings.

The results for this restricted sample of 1,311 households are reported in Table 7.4b. The main difference with respect to the estimates of Table 7.4a is that the coefficient of σ^2 in the constant prudence specification (column (1)) is negative and significant at the 10 percent level. In the specification of column (3) the coefficient of the uncertainty variable is also larger than the corresponding coefficient in Table 7.4a, indirectly supporting the hypothesis that families share risks. Even if at sample means the effect of uncertainty is estimated to be 0.22 percent of permanent earnings, 50 percent higher than in the whole-sample estimates, its impact on consumption remains small.[20]

In Table 7.5 we report the frequency distribution of the effect of uncertainty on saving for the specification that is consistent with decreasing prudence. We note: (i) precautionary saving declines as the ratio of total resources to permanent earnings increases; (ii) the magnitude of precautionary saving is of some importance (greater than 0.5 percent of permanent earnings) for a small proportion of the sample; (iii) the frequency distribution of households with more than one income recipient is more concentrated towards smaller values of precautionary saving than the distribution of households with one income recipient.

Table 7.5 Precautionary saving for varying levels of lifetime resources

Precautionary saving (as a percentage of permanent earnings)	Total sample estimates (a)		Sample of households with one income recipients (a)	
	% of cases	L/Y_p	% of cases	L/Y_p
(1)	(2)	(3)	(4)	(5)
0	33.1	29.1	32.7	31.0
0 – 0.05	34.9	25.2	31.4	28.3
0.05 – 0.1	10.8	23.6	11.7	24.9
0.1 – 0.5	17.0	20.7	18.7	22.6
0.5 – 1.0	2.6	21.2	3.0	21.9
1.0 – 2.0	1.0	18.5	1.4	19.7
> 2.0	0.6	17.8	1.1	18.8
Effect at sample means	0.14	29.4	0.22	31.2

(a) See Tables 7.4a and 7.4b for the definition of the sample and of the empirical specifications. Y_p denotes permanent earnings.

The amount of precautionary saving that we find in the data is not inconsistent with that computed in theoretical simulations. Caballero (1990), assuming an exponential utility function with relative degree of prudence equal to 1, an AR(1) process for income and a coefficient of variation of the stochastic component of income equal to 10 percent, presents simulation results for varying levels of persistence. When the AR coefficient is equal to 0.8, the effect of uncertainty is slightly larger than 0.01 percent. When the AR coefficient is increased to 0.95, the effect rises to 0.1 percent. Substantial effects of uncertainty arise only when the income shocks persist for a long time; and in particular, when income is difference stationary.

5 Earnings uncertainty and wealth accumulation

If uncertainty increases savings, it will increase also assets accumulation. In principle, savings and wealth are linked through the intertemporal budget constraint, and calculating the impact of uncertainty on saving or net worth should be equivalent. In practice, however, measured saving and net worth are not constrained to obey the intertemporal budget constraint. Besides the well-known problem that differences in net worth may differ from saving flows because of capital gains, in a cross-section saving and net worth result from rather different sources of information. Saving is computed as the difference between disposable income and consumption, while net worth results from the aggregation of numerous and detailed questions about households' balance sheets.[21]

Thus, testing whether uncertainty affects wealth accumulation provides an independent test of the theory of precautionary saving and a check of the validity of the findings of the previous section. It also allows us a direct computation of the contribution of precautionary savings due to earnings uncertainty to total wealth accumulation.

The life-cycle hypothesis implies a non-linear relationship between the ratio of wealth to permanent earnings and age. Extending the work of King and Dicks-Mireaux (1982), we posit the following relation for the ratio of wealth to permanent income:

$$\ln(W/Y_p) = f(\text{Age}, \sigma^2, X) + u \tag{11}$$

where Y_p is permanent earnings, X is a vector of variables which influences the age-wealth relationship and u is an error term.[22] The vector X will include permanent income if preferences are non-homothetic (King and Dicks-Mireaux, 1982). The relation between age and net worth is modelled using a piece-wise linear function: the rate of wealth accumulation is assumed to be constant within years brackets until retirement (this function is described in the Appendix). As our sample excludes households with heads over 65, we do not deal with the issue of wealth decumulation of the elderly after retirement. In addition to age and uncertainty, we introduce a set of additional variables which may alter the age-wealth profile via tastes and family needs (number of children, family size and regional location).

Column (1) of Table 7.6 shows the basic specification where wealth depends only on age and uncertainty. The ratio of wealth to permanent earnings increases until retirement at an average yearly rate of roughly 4 percent, except for households in the age bracket 45 to 54, where wealth accumulation is considerably smaller. The effect of uncertainty is statistically significant: at sample means, it is equal to 1.82 percent of net worth (roughly 10 percent of permanent earnings).[23] In levels, the amount of assets accumulated in response to earnings uncertainty is estimated to be 3.7 million lire, corresponding to almost $3,000.[24]

The second regression of Table 7.6 introduces additional variables. Large families and residents in Central regions possess greater wealth than that implied by the basic specification, while the number of children, given family size, reduces wealth.

In the third regression of Table 7.6 we further add the interaction of uncertainty with age and the logarithm of permanent earnings as separate regressors. The coefficient of the interaction term is negative, a finding that is consistent with the hypothesis that uncertainty affects more strongly the behavior of young households who have not yet accumulated enough assets to cushion against bad draws of income. This finding is therefore again consistent with decreasing prudence.

The results of column (3) also indicate that the higher is permanent income, the higher is the ratio of wealth to permanent income, thus rejecting homotheticity. Non-homotheticity is also consistent with the failure of certainty equivalence, thus indirectly supporting the theory of precautionary saving. But in all cases the estimated effect of uncertainty is basically unaffected and precisely estimated.

Overall, the results of this section are remarkably consistent with the results of the previous section and shed further light on the magnitude and pattern of the effect of uncertainty over the life cycle. In Section 4 we estimate that precautionary saving is equal to 0.14 percent of permanent earnings. The sample average age to retirement is 20 years. Cumulating these savings one obtains a value of the ratio of wealth held for precautionary reasons to permanent earnings that is close to the 1.82 percent contribution to wealth accumulation implied by the estimates of column (1) in Table 7.6.

Table 7.6 Effect of earnings uncertainty on wealth accumulation
(dependent variable: logarithm of the ratio of net worth to permanent earnings)

Variables (a)	(1)	(2)	(3)	Means of variables (4)
Age less than 25	0.013 (0.13)	0.027 (0.28)	0.003 (0.03)	23.984
Age 25 to 34	0.049 (4.12)	0.053 (4.43)	0.049 (4.09)	8.968
Age 35 to 44	0.040 (5.02)	0.044 (5.49)	0.047 (5.85)	6.255
Age 45 to 54	0.006 (0.73)	0.005 (0.63)	0.004 (0.56)	2.983
Age 55 to 64	0.043 (3.09)	0.037 (2.65)	0.037 (2.61)	0.543
σ^2/Y_p	0.15E–02 (3.50)	0.15E–02 (3.45)	0.59E–02 (2.84)	12.372
$\sigma^2\,\text{Age}/Y_p$			–0.95E–04 (–2.29)	549.140
No. of children		–0.167 (–3.37)	–0.071 (–1.38)	1.427
Family size		0.093 (2.27)	–0.022 (–0.50)	3.383
Resident in the North		–0.103 (–1.78)	–0.156 (–2.73)	0.455
Resident in the South		–0.045 (–0.75)	0.039 (0.63)	0.382
Log (Y_p)			0.464 (6.12)	10.287
Constant	0.240 (0.10)	–0.169 (0.07)	–4.114 (–1.75)	1.000
Adjusted R^2	0.080	0.084	0.098	
Standard error	1.052	1.049	1.041	
No. of observations	2.750	2.750	2.750	
Log-likelihood	–4,037.5	–4,028.8	–4,006.0	

(a) The mean of the dependent variable is 1.288. The definition of the age spline is given in the Appendix. Asymptotic *t*-statistics are reported in parentheses.

6   Persistence and implications

So far, we have maintained the assumption that the degree of persistence of the income shocks is the same (at least in mean) for all households. Since our estimates might be biased if this assumption were not valid, in this section we provide some evidence about the differences in the degree of persistence among households in the sample.

Ideally, we would need a long panel to address this issue properly. However, in the present context, we are mainly interested in testing whether the degree of persistence varies across households. For this purpose we can draw some inferences using a two-year panel, i.e. merging the information of the 1989 SHIW with that provided by the 1987 SHIW. As mentioned in Section 3, one of the features of the 1989 SHIW is that it contains a small panel component of 1,208 households who were interviewed also in 1987. Thus, for these households we have information on earnings and demographic characteristics at two points in time.

If we exclude households whose head is not in the labor force, and households who experienced major changes in status and family composition between 1987 and 1989, we are left with a sample of 603 households. This sample can be partitioned into four groups, according to the occupation of the head: operatives and laborers, clerical workers, professionals and self-employed. These groups represent 85 percent of the 603 panel observations. The other groups are too small to provide reliable estimates.

Since we only have two observations for each household (in 1987 and in 1989), the only process that we can estimate is an AR(1) process. We assume that income, in deviations from its mean, follows the process $y_{jt} = \gamma_j y_{jt-1} + \varepsilon_{jt}$, where γ measures the degree of persistence of the shocks ε, and j indexes each group of households ($j = 1, 2, 3, 4$). Lagging this expression one period, and substituting the result in the previous equation, we get:

$$y_{jt} = \gamma_j^2 y_{jt-2} + \eta_{jt}, \quad \text{where} \quad \eta_{jt} = \varepsilon_{jt} + \gamma \varepsilon_{jt-1}. \tag{12}$$

In Table 7.7 we report the results of estimating equation (12) in logarithms and in levels.[25] In the first three groups the differences in the estimated γ_j are not statistically significant. The degree of persistence varies in fact from 0.73 to 0.76 when the specification is in logarithms, and from 0.80 to 0.82 when it is in levels. For professionals the estimated γ is 10 points higher than in other groups in the log-specification, but only 3 points higher in the specification in levels. On the whole, the assumption that the degree of persistence is the same for all households is not unreasonable. The patterns of Table 7.7 cannot substantially affect the results presented in Sections 4 and 5.

Table 7.7 Estimates of the degree of persistence of household earnings, by occupation of the head *(a)*

	Operative and laborer (1)	Clerical (2)	Self-employed (3)	Professional (4)
Log specification	0.756	0.739	0.730	0.848
Level specification	0.804	0.808	0.815	0.835
Number of observations	214	165	114	42

(a) All estimated coefficients are significant at the 1 percent level.

7   Implications for consumption puzzles

Skinner (1988) and Zeldes (1989) have pointed out that precautionary saving may explain, at least partly, the empirical failure of the permanent income hypothesis. As in many other countries, several recent studies indicate that in Italy consumption growth is correlated with lagged disposable income and expected income and that consumption growth has been high even in the presence of low real interest rates. Guiso, Jappelli and Terlizzese (1994), using aggregate annual data, regress the growth rate of consumption on the expected growth rate of disposable income and a measure of the expected real interest rate and find that the coefficient of disposable income growth is about 0.6.[26] Given that we estimate that precautionary saving is small, it is not surprising that our results cannot account for this failure, as we show below.[27]

Assuming $\beta R = 1$, constant prudence and normally distributed earnings shocks, the first-order condition of the consumer maximization problem in Section 2 is:

$$\frac{\Delta c}{c} = \frac{\theta c}{2} \frac{\sigma^2}{c^2}. \tag{13}$$

In this special case, consumption grows only if there is uncertainty ($\sigma^2 > 0$), to an extent that depends on the degree of relative risk aversion θc. Equation (13) is the base for the claim that precautionary saving may be responsible for consumption growth even when the real interest rate is low. Approximating average consumption by average permanent earnings, our results give us the opportunity to evaluate equation (13) at sample means and check what it implies for consumption growth.

The ratio of the (average) variance to the square of (average) consumption is equal to 0.04 percent. The constant prudence specification in Table 7.4b implies that precautionary saving, i.e. the term $\theta/(R-\gamma)$ in equation (2), is equal to 0.3. Assuming that $\gamma = 0.75$, a number that is consistent with the results reported in Table 7.7, and that the real interest rate is 4 percent, the implied value of θ is 0.09. The sample mean of consumption is 30. Thus relative risk aversion, θc, is about 3. This implies that consumption growth in excess of the growth implied by the certainty equivalence model of consumption is a modest 0.06 percent per year.

Even a value of θ as high as 0.5 (which implies an implausible degree of relative risk aversion of 15) accounts for a growth in consumption of less than 0.1 percent per year, a far cry from the average consumption growth of 3 percent per year recorded in Italy in the last three decades.

8   Conclusions

The main contribution of this paper to the literature on precautionary saving is to test the theory using a self-reported measure of uncertainty of future earnings. On the whole, the results indicate that subjective earnings uncertainty affects the level of saving in the direction predicted by the theory and in a way that is consistent with decreasing prudence. At sample means, the results indicate that, on average, precautionary saving accounts for 2 percent of households' net worth; in level, this implies that households hold a non-negligible amount of assets (almost $3,000) to protect themselves from bad income draws. The estimates also imply reasonable values of the coefficient of relative risk aversion.

However, the results also suggest that earnings uncertainty, i.e. the source of uncertainty most frequently studied in the theoretical literature, fails to explain a large fraction of saving and wealth accumulation. Our results imply that earnings uncertainty is not, at least in the context of the Italian economy, a viable explanation for the empirical failure of the permanent income hypothesis.

One possible interpretation of our results is that we fail to find a large effect of precautionary saving because households are informally linked by risk-sharing arrangements. Since our evidence suggests that precautionary saving is only slightly higher for single income earners than for households with two or more income earners, this interpretation must imply that risk sharing takes place through networks that pool income risks from different households, rather than within the same household. In the present paper we have not tested for this effect, but we regard it as an interesting topic for future research.

Finally, we wish to stress that the results of this paper do not cast doubts on the importance of precautionary saving per se. Survey respondents, in

Italy and elsewhere, consistently indicate that saving for emergencies is one of the main reasons for saving. Future empirical studies may reveal that, beside earnings uncertainty, other important types of risk, such as health and mortality risks, are important determinants of saving.

APPENDIX

This Appendix provides a comparison of the income variance and distribution in the 1989 Survey of Household Income and Wealth and in the U.S. 1983-86 Survey of Consumer Finances, details on the data set and definitions of the variables employed in this study. The construction of permanent earnings is described in the second part of the Appendix.

Table 7.A1 **Means and standard deviations of income and wealth in the 1983 SCF and in the 1989 SHIW**

	1989 SHIW	1983 SCF
Disposable income		
mean (μ_y)	35.5	25.7
standard deviation (σ_y)	29.4	29.0
σ_y/μ_y	0.83	1.13
Net worth		
mean (μ_w)	173.2	71.6
standard deviation (σ_w)	307.4	166.5
σ_w/μ_w	1.77	2.32

Sources: For Italy the statistics refer to the sample of 8,274 households of the 1989 SHIW. The numbers are in millions of 1989 lire. For the U.S. we have used the 1983 SCF and selected the sample of 3,692 households (excluding the sample of high-income respondents). Numbers for the U.S. are in thousands of 1982 dollars.

1   The 1989 Bank of Italy Survey of Household Income and Wealth (SHIW) and the 1983-86 Survey of Consumer Finances

Because of its sample design and its collection of detailed wealth statistics, the 1989 SHIW is similar to the 1983-86 Survey of Consumer Finances (SCF). The SCF is representative of the U.S. population (Avery and Kennickell, 1988, pp. 30-31). We provide a comparison of the income variance and distribution of the 1989 SHIW and the 1983-86 SCF. Table 7.A1 indicates that for both disposable income and net worth the ratio of the standard deviation to the sample mean is lower in Italy than in the

U.S. Table 7.A2 reports the distribution of income in the two surveys. The share of aggregate family income received by the highest decile is 33 percent in the U.S. and 25.2 percent in Italy. That received by the lowest decile is 1 percent in the U.S. and 2.7 percent in Italy.

Table 7.A2 Share of family income deciles: a comparison between the 1983 SCF and the 1989 SHIW *(a)*

| Income decile | 1989 SHIW | | | 1983 SCF |
	Average income *(b)* (1)	% of families (2)	% of income (3)	% of income (4)
Lowest	13.5	25.8	2.7	1
Second	22.2	15.7	4.3	3
Third	28.0	12.4	5.5	4
Fourth	33.9	10.3	6.5	5
Fifth	39.8	8.8	7.7	7
Sixth	45.4	7.7	9.1	8
Seventh	52.9	6.6	10.8	10
Eigth	62.5	5.6	12.7	13
Ninth	78.1	4.5	15.7	16
Highest	125.9	2.8	25.2	33

(a) Data sources: The numbers in columns (1), (2) and (3) are based on the sample of 8,274 households of the 1989 SHIW. The source for the income distribution in the U.S. is Avery *et al.* (1984), Table 2, p. 681.
(b) In millions of 1989 lire.

2 Variables definition

Inflation uncertainty. Question: "In this table we have indicated some classes of inflation. We are interested in knowing your opinion about inflation twelve months from now. Suppose now that you have 100 points to be distributed between these intervals (a table is shown to the person interviewed). Are there intervals which you definitely exclude? Assign zero points to these intervals. How many points do you assign to each of the remaining intervals?"

For this and the following variable the intervals of the table shown to the person interviewed are the same. The intervals are:

> 25 percent; 20-25 percent; 15-20; 13-15; 10-13; 8-10; 7-8; 6-7; 5-6; 3-5; 0-3, less than 0. In case it is less than zero, the person is asked: "How much less than zero? How many points would you assign to this class?"

Earnings uncertainty. Question: "We are also interested in knowing your opinion about labor earnings or pensions twelve months from now. Suppose now that you have 100 points to be distributed between these intervals (a table is shown to the person interviewed). Are there intervals which you definitely exclude? Assign zero points to these intervals. How many points do you assign to each of the remaining intervals?"

Head of the household. If the person who would usually be considered the head of the household (i.e., the husband or the father) has migrated or works abroad, the head of the household is the person who is responsible of the economic activity of the family.

Age of the head of the household. Question: "Where were you born and in which year?" In the wealth regressions we choose the following spline function for age:

Age (1) = Age if Age <24,   Age(1) = 24 otherwise,
Age (2) = Min(Age–24, 10) if Age > 24,   Age(2) = 0 otherwise,
Age (3) = Min(Age–34, 10) if Age > 34,   Age(3) = 0 otherwise,
Age (4) = Min(Age–44, 10) if Age > 44,   Age(4) = 0 otherwise,
Age (5) = Min(Age–54, 10) if Age > 54,   Age(5) = 0 otherwise,
Age (6) = Age–64 if Age > 64,   Age(6) = 0 otherwise.

Household size. Total number of persons in the family. Persons include head, spouse (whether married or not married), children, other relatives, and non-relatives living in the household.

Education of the head of the household. Question: "Education of household's head". Responses: (5) no education; (6) completed elementary school (5 years); (7) completed second grade (8 years); (8) completed high school (13 years); (9) completed college degree (17 to 19 years); (0) post-graduate education (more than 20 years of education). The variable has been recoded according to the values given in parentheses. For the highest class we have assumed a value of 20 years of education.

Marital status of the head of the household. Question: "Marital status of household's head". Responses: (1) Married (includes couples living together); (2) never married; (3) separated and divorced; (4) widowed.

Occupation of the head of the household. Question: "Main occupation of household's head". Responses: (1) operative and laborer; (2) clerical; (3) precision craft; (4) professional; (5) manager; (6) entrepreneur; (7) self-employed; (8) other.

Sector of occupation of the head of the household. Question: "Main sector of occupation of household's head". Responses: (1) agricultural; (2) and (3) industry; (4) public administration; (5), (6) and (7) services.

Region of the country. Question: "Residence of the household". Responses: North (Piemonte, Valle D'Aosta, Liguria, Lombardia, Trentino, Friuli, Veneto, Emilia-Romagna); Center (Marche, Umbria, Toscana, Lazio); South (Abruzzi, Molise, Campania, Basilicata, Puglia, Calabria, Sicilia, Sardegna).

Labor earnings of household. Question: "How much did you earn from your labor activity net of all taxes and contributions in 1989?" This question is asked to each member of the household, whether it is employed or self-employed. The variable used in the estimation is the sum of net of taxes labor earnings of the household. The variable refers to the year 1989.

Consumption of household. Sum of the expenditures on non-durable consumption items (food consumption, entertainment, education, clothes, medical expenses, housing repairs and additions). Durable consumption (vehicles, furniture and appliances, art objects) is not included in the definition of consumption. The variable refers to the year 1989.

Household net worth. Sum of household's liquid assets (checking accounts, saving accounts, money market accounts, certificates of deposits), financial assets (stocks, government bonds, other bonds), property and business, net of household liabilities (debt owed on credit cards, on car loans, other forms of consumer debt, and mortgages on houses, properties and additions). The variable is measured at the end of 1989.

3   The construction of permanent earnings

We estimate permanent earnings on a sample of 5,347 households, excluding households whose head is not in the labor force or older than 65. To compute permanent earnings we proceed as follows. Denote by $Y(\tau)$ the earnings of a household of age τ. We assume that permanent earnings of this household at age τ can be expressed as:

$$Y(\tau) = Z\beta + \phi(\tau)$$

where Z is a vector of household (or head) characteristics, and $\phi(\cdot)$ is a quadratic function of age. We estimate this regression proxying Z with age, education, gender, marital status, occupation, regional location, family size and number of income earners.

To account for heteroscedasticity, we estimate the equation by Generalized Least Squares, using as weights the residuals from a first-stage OLS regression. The final estimates are reported in Table 7.A3.

Assuming that the maximum age at which people work is 65 years, the estimated permanent earnings at age τ_0 is:

$$Y_p(\tau_0) = (65 - \tau_0 + 1)^{-1} \sum_{\tau=\tau_0}^{65} [Zb + f(\tau)] \left(\frac{1+n}{1+r}\right)^{(\tau-\tau_0)}$$

where b and f indicate, respectively, the estimated coefficients of β and ϕ reported in Table 7.A4. The parameters n and r represent, respectively, the rate of growth of productivity and the rate of interest. Assuming that $r = n$, the expression reduces to:

$$Y_p(\tau_0) = Zb + (65 - \tau_0 + 1)^{-1} \sum_{\tau=\tau_0}^{65} f(\tau).$$

The second term can be computed using the fact that, by the mean value theorem, there exists a $\tau^*(\tau_0)$ such that:

$$f[\tau^*(\tau_0)] = (65 - \tau_0 + 1)^{-1} \sum_{\tau=\tau_0}^{65} f(\tau).$$

Table 7.A3 Earnings function estimates *(a)*
(dependent variable: total household's earnings)

Variables	Coefficients (1)	*t*-statistics (2)	Means of variables (3)
Education	0.524	5.62	9.800
Education squared	0.003	0.64	115.66
Age	0.246	3.03	43.03
Age squared	−0.002	−2.42	1953.7
Male	1.449	3.27	0.905
Married	2.851	6.93	0.847
Family size	0.387	2.98	3.436
No. of children	0.517	2.73	1.457
No. of income earners	10.120	35.70	1.671
Occupation			
Operative and laborer	−5.165	−11.62	0.322
Clerical	−3.568	6.82	0.299
Precision craft	2.120	2.50	0.083
Professional	12.390	6.75	0.028
Manager	5.983	5.76	0.065
Entrepreneur	18.456	7.32	0.016
Other	−6.130	−3.72	0.001
Sector			
Agriculture	−3.485	6.81	0.053
Industry	−0.476	1.14	0.254
Services	0.223	0.63	0.446
North	2.425	6.03	0.400
South	−1.628	−4.36	0.385
Constant	−1.868	0.98	1.000
Adjusted R^2	0.344		
Standard error (%)	5.830		
Dependent variable mean	31.388		
Observations	5.347		

(a) The sample of 5,347 observations is obtained excluding households with zero labor earnings, households where the head is not in the labor force or older than 65. The dependent variable is expressed in millions of 1989 lire. The following attributes are excluded from the regression: self-employed, resident in Central Italy, employed in the public sector.

Having determined the value of $\tau^*(\tau_0)$ as a function of the estimated coefficients and of τ_0, permanent earnings are then computed as:

$$Y_p(\tau_0) = Zb + f[\tau^*(\tau_0)].$$

Human wealth is the product of permanent earnings and the age of the household to retirement. Transitory earnings are defined as the difference of permanent earnings and current labor earnings.

NOTES

* This paper was originally published in the *Journal of Monetary Economics*, 2 (1992) and is here reprinted with permission. Thanks for helpful suggestions go to Fumio Hayashi. Sean Craig, Larry Kotlikoff, Marco Pagano, Steffen Pischke, Nicola Rossi, Ignazio Visco, and participants in seminars in Helsinki, Madrid, Milano and Roma provided useful comments. We also thank Luigi Sciamplicotti for extensive research assistance. Any remaining errors are the authors' responsibility. Tullio Jappelli acknowledges financial support from C.N.R.

1 In the words of Kotlikoff (1989, page 30): "Pinning down empirically the extent of precautionary saving will require new surveys that examine two issues: first, the nature of the implicit family insurance agreement and, second, the extent of subjective uncertainty. This latter issue has been thoroughly finessed in the precautionary saving literature by simply assuming the nature of subjective probabilities." This paper takes a modest step towards addressing these issues.

2 The SHIW is a survey representative of the Italian population run every two years by the Bank of Italy. See for details the Methodological Appendix to this volume.

3 Kimball (1990) defines absolute prudence as the ratio between the third derivative and the second derivative of the within-period utility function. If utility is exponential absolute prudence coincides with absolute risk aversion.

4 The wording of these questions is reported in the Appendix. The intervals are the same for the two variables. They are: > 25 percent; 20-25; 15-20; 13-15; 10-13; 8-10; 7-8; 6-7; 5-6; 3-5; 0-3; < 0. The size of the classes was intentionally smaller in those classes which, *a priori*, were thought to include the majority of the observations.

5 Thus, we only use the probability distributions that can be derived from the answers of heads of households. This procedure is certainly correct for all households with only one income recipient. We show below that limiting the analysis to these households does not affect our main conclusions. Our procedure yields a biased measure of the "true" measure of uncertainty to an extent that depends on both risk sharing schemes within the family and on the stochastic process that generates the incomes of the family members other than the head of the household.

6 The observations falling in the fourth group can be further partitioned into $\sigma_z^2 \geq \sigma_\pi^2$ and $\sigma_z^2 < \sigma_\pi^2$ (581 and 503 households respectively). In the first case

there is no ambiguity for the choice of the solution in equation (6), since the only positive solution corresponds to the plus sign.

7 Alternatively, assuming that ϱ is the same for all individuals, one could use the result for the third group, and set $\varrho = -1$.

8 Skinner (1988), Caballero (1990, 1991) and Carroll (1991) in their simulations assume that the standard error of the shock to labor income is between 10 and 20 percent.

9 For instance, Hall and Mishkin (1982) and MaCurdy (1982), using the Panel Survey of Income Dynamics, obtain estimates on the order of 20 percent.

10 The estimates of uncertainty in Table 7.2 are slightly downward biased because in computing the variances of earnings and inflation we have ignored the variance within the intervals. This effect could be of some importance only in those cases where the answers are concentrated in the extreme intervals, i.e. the wider intervals. Where the concentration of responses is greatest, i.e in the central classes which are only 1 percentage point wide, the bias is actually very small. Even assuming that the probability distribution within the interval is uniform, the effect on the estimated standard deviation of earnings would amount to 0.3 percentage points of current earnings.

11 For instance, Friedman (1957) and Skinner (1988) assume that the self-employed are a "high-risk" group.

12 Skinner's (1988) work is more suited to the estimation of Euler equations, because the consumption function that he derives involves a forward-looking representation of lifetime uncertainty that is difficult to implement empirically with cross-sectional data.

13 Equivalently, we might consider Skinner's model under the simplifying assumption that the ratio of current income to lifetime resources is constant over age. This would yield an equation slightly more complex, but similar, to equation (9) in the text.

14 Note that the expectation involves, as Skinner recognizes, the value of consumption that appears on the left-hand side. Thus, equation (9) is not, strictly speaking, a closed-form solution.

15 In Table 7.3 we show that education and uncertainty do not covary significantly within the sample. But respondents might be on average richer and more educated than non-respondents. In this case the estimates would be affected by sample selection bias. We have therefore estimated a probit equation for respondents using the set of variables in Table 7.3, and the consumption function by the Generalized Tobit estimator.The coefficient of the Mill's ratio was not significantly different from zero, and the values of the other parameters were almost identical to those reported in Tables 7.4a and 7.4b.

16 Our empirical results are unaffected if we exclude from the estimation of permanent earnings and from the consumption function estimates households with less than 5 million lire of earnings.

17 The calculation of human wealth assumes that the real rate of interest is equal to the rate of productivity growth (see the Appendix).

244   Luigi Guiso, Tullio Jappelli and Daniele Terlizzese

18 We have also introduced quadratic terms in uncertainty and total resources. The implied effect of uncertainty on consumption is very similar to that displayed in column (2).

19 Note, however, that the likelihood is relatively flat around the estimated value of a.

20 Also in this case the value of a that maximizes the likelihood function is 1.2.

21 In the previous section we proxy beginning-of-period net worth by subtracting to wealth 1989 savings. In the tests presented in this section, instead, there is no need for this adjustment.

22 We use logs in order to reduce heteroscedasticity. However, the results using the ratio of wealth to permanent income, rather than the log of the ratio, yield results that are very similar to those reported in Table 7.6.

23 Regression (1) in Table 7.6 implies that the percentage contribution of uncertainty to total wealth is $1-[1/\exp(b\sigma^2/Y_p)]$, where b is the estimated coefficient of the uncertainty term.

24 This result is very similar if the variance of earnings is entered in levels, rather than being scaled by permanent earnings.

25 We have included in each equation a set of demographic variables (age, gender, regional location and sector of activity) to account for individual differences. Note that the error of the estimated equation, η, is autocorrelated. However, it is uncorrelated with ε_{jt-2}, and therefore the estimate of γ is consistent.

26 Jappelli and Pagano (1989) also find high excess sensitivity in Italian aggregate consumption data.

27 Given that we do not test for the effect of mortality risk on saving, we cannot address the issue of the slow wealth decumulation by the elderly.

REFERENCES

Avery, R.B. and A.B. Kennickell (1988). '1983-86 Survey of Consumer Finances: Technical Manual and Codebook', Washington, DC: Board of Governors of the Federal Reserve System.

Avery, R.B., G. Elliehausen, G.B. Canner and T.A. Gustafson (1984). 'Survey of Consumer Finances', *Federal Reserve Bulletin* **70**: 679-92.

Barro, R.J. (1974). 'Are Government Bonds Net Wealth?', *Journal of Political Economy* **82**: 1095-118.

Barsky, R.B., G.N. Mankiw and S.P. Zeldes (1986). 'Ricardian Consumers with Keynesian Propensities', *American Economic Review* **76**: 676-91.

Caballero, R. (1990). 'Consumption Puzzles and Precautionary Savings', *Journal of Monetary Economics* **25**: 113-36.

Caballero, R. (1991). 'Earnings Uncertainty and Aggregate Wealth Accumulation', *American Economic Review* **81**: 859-71.

Carroll, C.D. (1991). 'Buffer Stock Saving and the Permanent Income Hypothesis', Board of Governors of the Federal Reserve System, Economic Activity Section Working Paper 114.

Drèze, J.H. and F. Modigliani (1972). 'Consumption under Uncertainty', *Journal of Economic Theory* **5**: 308-35.

Friedman, M. (1957). *A Theory of the Consumption Function*, Princeton: Princeton University Press.

Guiso, L., T. Jappelli and D. Terlizzese (1994). 'Why Is Italy's Saving Rate so High?', *this volume*.

Hall, R.E. and F. Mishkin (1982). 'The Sensitivity of Consumption to Transitory Income: Estimate from Panel Data on Households', *Econometrica* **50**: 461-81.

Jappelli, T. and M. Pagano (1989). 'Consumption and Capital Market Imperfections. An International Comparison', *American Economic Review* **79**: 1088-105.

Kimball, M.S. (1990). 'Precautionary Saving in the Small and in the Large', *Econometrica* **58**: 53-73.

King, M. and L-D.L. Dicks-Mireaux (1982). 'Asset Holdings and the Life-Cycle', *Economic Journal* **92**: 247-67.

Kotlikoff, L.J. (1989). *What Determines Saving?*, Cambridge, MA: MIT Press.

Kotlikoff, L.J. and A. Spivak (1981). 'The Family as an Incomplete Annuities Market', *Journal of Political Economy* **89**: 372-91.

Leland, H. (1968). 'Saving and Uncertainty: The Precautionary Demand for Saving', *Quarterly Journal of Economics* **82**: 465-73.

MaCurdy, T.E. (1982). 'The Use of Time Series Processes to Model the Error Structure of Earnings in a Longitudinal Data Analysis', *Journal of Econometrics* **18**: 82-114.

Pischke, S. (1990). 'Individual Income, Incomplete Information and Aggregate Consumption', Princeton University, mimeo.

Sandmo, A. (1970). 'The Effect of Uncertainty on Savings Decisions', *Review of Economic Studies* **37**: 82-114.

Skinner, J. (1988). 'Risky Income, Life Cycle Consumption and Precautionary Saving', *Journal of Monetary Economics* **22**: 237-55.

Weil, P. (1993). 'Precautionary Savings and the Permanent Income Hypothesis', *Review of Economic Studies* **60**: 367-83.

Zeldes, S.P. (1989). 'Optimal Consumption with Stochastic Income: Deviations from Certainty Equivalence', *Quarterly Journal of Economics* **104**: 275-98.

8 Risk sharing and precautionary saving*

LUIGI GUISO and TULLIO JAPPELLI

1 Introduction

The recent theoretical literature has explored the effect of uncertainty on saving and asset accumulation. In principle, precautionary saving may explain some of the discrepancies between the predictions generated by the standard life-cycle model (without uncertainty) and the empirical evidence. For instance, life-span uncertainty may account for the fact that the rate of wealth decumulation after retirement is much slower than that predicted by the standard life-cycle model (Davies, 1981; Hurd, 1989); earnings uncertainty may explain the excess sensitivity of consumption to expected income fluctuations (Zeldes, 1989; Caballero, 1990); the interaction between borrowing constraints and earnings uncertainty may explain why consumption tracks income so closely over the individual life cycle (Deaton, 1991); the increase in social and private insurance arrangements may account for the reduction in private saving rates that took place in the eighties in most industrialized countries (Kotlikoff, 1989; Auerbach and Kotlikoff, 1989).

Simulations run by Skinner (1988), Zeldes (1989) and Caballero (1991) with reference to income risk suggest that precautionary saving may form a large share of total life-cycle saving. At the empirical level, however, very few studies have been devoted to establishing the existence of a precautionary motive for saving and on measuring its magnitude. Moreover, the few available empirical findings yield only mixed support for the theory. Friedman (1957) found that households in more risky occupations save more than those in safer occupations, but his finding is not supported by the more recent evidence provided by Skinner (1988). Carroll and Samwick (1991) use the history of household incomes in the PSID to construct a proxy for the variance of lifetime earnings and find that earnings uncertainty explains a large part of asset accumulation. Guiso, Jappelli and Terlizzese (1994), using a self-reported measure of uncertainty from the 1989 Bank of Italy Survey of Household Income and Wealth, find a positive but weak relation between saving or net worth and the variance of the subjective probability distribution of households' earnings.

A common approach of these papers is that they consider the effect of earnings uncertainty on saving treating households as isolated individuals. The intent of the present paper, by contrast, is to provide a test of earnings uncertainty based on the idea that individuals can insure themselves against some of the fluctuations in earnings – as well as other risks – by forming households. As has been shown by Kotlikoff and Spivak (1981) and more recently by Mace (1991) and Cochrane (1991), risk sharing arrangements within the household may go a long way towards substituting for formal insurance markets.

The idea behind our empirical test is to compare the consumption behavior of households with different number of earners. Households with multiple incomes are more easily protected against income shocks than those with sole breadwinner: the formers' need for precautionary saving is lower. Thus, according to the theory of precautionary saving, the saving rate of households with one income recipient should be higher than that of households with multiple earners.

Section 2 summarizes the assumptions required to generate precautionary saving and the conditions under which risk sharing reduces the risk of each income earner in the household. Section 3 presents the data, which are drawn from the 1987 Bank of Italy Survey of Household Income and Wealth (SHIW), and Section 4 develops the empirical model. The results, presented in Section 5, support the theory of precautionary saving. Other things being equal, households with two incomes display a higher average propensity to consume (APC) and a lower marginal propensity to consume (MPC) out of lifetime resources than single-income households.

One possible explanation of these findings that cannot be ruled out in principle is that the average propensity to consume of households with two income earners is higher than that of households with one income earner because the former group spends a larger share of their income on market-produced goods and services. Section 6 furnishes additional evidence to sort out competing explanations for the observed behavior.

In Section 7 we comment on the implications of our results for the understanding of the evolution of the private saving rate, both over time and between countries. In Italy, the dramatic rise in the women's participation rate may well have contributed to the parallel reduction in saving that has taken place over the past two decades. Since the female participation rate varies widely across countries (Graham, 1987; Modigliani, 1990), our findings may also help to explain international differences in saving rates. Section 8 concludes.

2   Risk sharing, uncertainty and saving

The theoretical conditions under which precautionary saving arises in response to uncertainty were originally explored by Leland (1968), Sandmo (1970) and Drèze and Modigliani (1972) using two-period models. Skinner (1988), Zeldes (1989) and Caballero (1990) have generalized these early results to multi-period models. The main conclusion of this theoretical literature is that when income risk is uninsurable and utility is time-separable, earnings uncertainty increases saving and wealth accumulation if the third derivative of the utility function is positive: a sufficient condition is that absolute risk aversion be non-increasing with wealth.

If this condition is met, an increase in income risk implies an increase in precautionary saving. Further, for any given value of the concavity of the utility function, the effect of risk on saving increases with the convexity of the marginal utility. In analogy with the Arrow-Pratt measure of absolute risk aversion, Kimball (1990) has introduced a measure of the strength of precautionary saving, the ratio between the third derivative and the second derivative of the utility function, $p(w) = -v'''(w)/v''(w)$, where $v(\cdot)$ is the second-period utility index and w is the household's wealth. For small risks, precautionary saving is proportional to $p(w)$.

The index $p(w)$ is the degree of absolute prudence. Since prudence varies with wealth, precautionary saving can be higher or lower depending on whether prudence is decreasing or increasing with wealth. Kimball (1990) and Weil (1990) argue that decreasing prudence is a plausible property of utility functions. For instance, proper risk aversion implies decreasing prudence.[1]

Figure 8.1 summarizes the effect of an increase in income risk on consumption. The line CC is the consumption function if prudence is constant, while the curve DD depicts consumption as a function of wealth if absolute prudence is decreasing. An increase in risk shifts the consumption function downwards, because a greater amount of lifetime wealth is needed to sustain the same level of consumption. Alternatively, given wealth, current consumption must fall to allow for precautionary saving. If absolute prudence is constant, the shift in consumption is independent of the level of wealth. The broken line $C'C'$ indicates that at each level of wealth the ratio of consumption to wealth falls, while the marginal propensity to consume is unaffected.

If, however, prudence is a decreasing function of wealth, the precautionary premium, i.e the amount of additional wealth needed to finance the certainty equivalence level of consumption, falls as wealth rises

(Kimball, 1990). In this case the consumption function is non-linear in wealth, and an increase in risk shifts the consumption function to the line $D'D'$. As in the previous case the average propensity to consume falls; but with decreasing prudence the marginal propensity to consume increases at each level of consumption. The intuitive reason is that an increase in wealth has two effects: it raises permanent income, and it makes the consumer feel more secure. Both effects stimulate consumption.

Figure 8.1

**The effect of income risk on the average
and marginal propensity to consume**

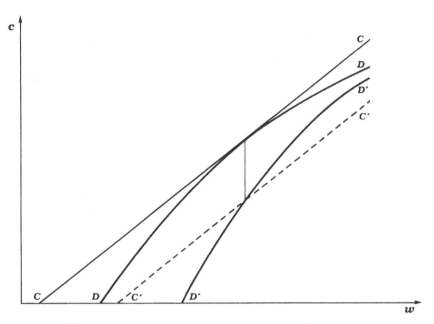

The idea that uncertainty stimulates saving is intuitive, but it proves surprisingly difficult even to test for the existence of precautionary saving, let alone quantify it. The main reason is that the driving variable in precautionary saving, i.e. subjective individual uncertainty about future events, is not observable. Simulations such as those by Kotlikoff and Spivak (1981), Skinner (1988) and Zeldes (1989) suggest that precautionary saving may be important, but they rely heavily on the parametrization of the income, health or mortality risks.

Time series tests have little power to investigate the amount of precautionary saving. The main problem here is aggregation: precautionary saving may be a response to specific individual risks rather than to aggregate risk; and aggregate measures of risk mainly reflect aggregate uncertainty. Using cross-sectional data, some authors have relied on sample separation rules to test whether the average propensity to consume is lower for some population groups. For instance, Friedman (1957) and Skinner (1988) test whether farmers and the self-employed – presumably riskier occupations – tend to consume less than individuals in other occupations.

There are three main problems with this type of test. First, there is no evidence that perceived income uncertainty is actually greater for farmers and the self-employed than for other groups. Second, even assuming that the ordering of income risks is correct, there is a problem of self-selection: if prudence is correlated with risk aversion, and less risk-averse individuals choose the more risky occupations, they may actually consume more than those in safer occupations. Third, the empirical tests do not distinguish between the average and the marginal propensity to consume out of wealth. Yet as Figure 8.1 shows, this distinction is important; with decreasing prudence the effect of risk on the MPC and on the APC takes opposite signs. Failure to distinguish the two effects may bias the results towards accepting the null hypothesis of absence of precautionary saving.

To gauge the potential effect of uncertainty empirically, we propose a new test based on the idea that households with more than one income earner insure part of the risk associated with each individual income. Thus, if the family provides insurance against income risk, the need for precautionary saving is attenuated. It is easy to show that the pooling of different risks reduces the risk of each participant, even if the individual risks are positively correlated.

Given two random variables u_1 and u_2, identically distributed with mean zero, variance σ_u^2 and correlation coefficient ϱ, the random variable z, obtained as a linear combination of u_1 and u_2 with weight $1/2$, has variance $\sigma_z^2 = (1 + \varrho)\sigma_u^2/2$. If $\varrho < 1$, then $\sigma_z^2 < \sigma_u^2$.

Households benefit from risk sharing even when the risks are not identically distributed. Suppose that u_1 and u_2 have positive correlation coefficient ϱ, but different variances σ_1^2 and $k^2\sigma_1^2$ respectively, with $k > 1$.

Let z_1 and z_2 be two random variables obtained as a linear combination of u_1 and u_2

$$z_1 = \beta u_1 + (1 - \beta)u_2 \qquad 0 < \beta < 1$$

$$z_2 = (1 - \beta)u_1 + \beta u_2.$$

The variance of z_1 is then

$$E(z_1^2) = [\beta^2 + (1 - \beta)^2 k^2 + 2\beta(1 - \beta)\varrho k]\sigma_1^2. \tag{1}$$

If $\varrho < 1/k$, the value of β that minimizes $E(z_1^2)$ is

$$\beta = \frac{k(k - \varrho)}{1 + k(k - 2\varrho)}. \tag{2}$$

This value of β implies that $E(z_1^2) < \sigma_1^2$ and that $E(z_2^2) < k^2\sigma_1^2$. Thus, if the value of ϱ does not exceed the root of the ratio between the lowest and the highest variance, there exists a combination of risks such that the transformed individual risk is smaller than the original risk.

This discussion makes it clear that the conditions under which risk sharing is mutually beneficial are quite general, not restricted only to the case of independently and identically distributed risks.[2] The remainder of this paper is given over to describing the data set and an empirical framework that can test whether multiple-earner households do in fact save less than single-income households.

3 Data and sample

To implement the test, we use the 1987 Survey of Household Income and Wealth (SHIW), which is a representative survey of the Italian population carried on in the Spring of 1988 by the Bank of Italy.[3] To separate the effect of risk from other effects, we restrict the sample in several directions; most importantly, we exclude all but nuclear families (i.e., households consisting of a couple and their children, if any). Singles are excluded in order to control for economies of scale in consumption. The reason for this becomes apparent if we compare two households, a married couple with both spouses working and a single. Two factors are at work. First, a voluminous literature on equivalence scales has demonstrated that there are substantial economies of scale in the consumption of durables and non-durables. Second, risk sharing within the household may reduce earnings uncertainty. The first factor tends to reduce the APC of the couple with respect to that of the single person, while the second tends to increase it.

We also exclude extended families, i.e. those with more than two income earners. Apart from the problem of economies of scale, the reasoning here is that it is difficult to determine who is the decision-making unit (or, indeed, units).

Finally, we exclude households in which the head is older than 55, the age at which earnings peak, on average. As suggested by Skinner (1988), we do not want to bias the results by neglecting the fact that the elderly are likely to spend down accumulated precautionary savings. We also want to isolate the effect of income risk from that of mortality and health risks.

The final sample contains 3,156 couples with or without dependent children. In all cases the head of the household is taken to be the man – hereafter referred to as the 'husband' – and in all cases the man is in the labor force and has labor income of more than 5 million lire in 1987. In 44 percent of the households the woman – hereafter, the 'wife' – is also in the labor force.

The income variable refers to earnings only, for both salaried and self-employed workers. Lifetime resources are computed as the sum of non-human and human wealth. The latter is estimated by discounting the sum of an estimate of expected future earnings over the remaining working life, adjusting for cohort effects (see the Appendix for details). Since non-human wealth is measured at the end of 1987, we subtract from wealth 1987 savings. This measure of wealth differs from initial net worth since savings do not include 1987 capital gains, so that the non-human wealth indicator is only an approximation of beginning-of-period net worth.

As theory suggests, we subtract purchases of durable goods from the definition of consumption. This measure of consumption should also reduce the extent by which our results will be affected by the substitution between market and home production. If the wife elects to work outside the home, the value of time spent in the production of home-produced goods rises (Becker and Ghez, 1975); accordingly, expenditure on goods produced in the market might increase also. As this substitution effect may affect the interpretation of our results, it is treated further in Section 6.

Table 8.1 reports the sample means of selected variables for the whole sample, and separately for the sample of two-income and single-income households (1,384 and 1,772 respectively). The ratio of consumption to lifetime wealth is slightly higher in the single-income group. However, the characteristics of the two groups are different. First, the average number of children in single-income households is twice as high. Second, while the absolute levels of earnings and wealth in single-income households are lower than in two-income households (21.2 million lire versus 33.5 for earnings, and 96.6 versus 127.4 for wealth), the wealth-income ratio is higher (4.56 as against 3.80). Third, single-income households are less well educated, less likely to live in the North or in Central Italy and more likely to be headed by a self-employed worker, by an operative and by a laborer. Thus, a proper test of the proposition that two-income households have a higher APC and a lower MPC requires controlling for all relevant factors.

Table 8.1 Sample means for selected variables

	Total sample	Two-income households	Single-income households
Husbands' characteristics			
Earnings	20.80	20.40	21.20
Age	40	41	41
Years of education	11	12	10
Occupation:			
Operative and laborer	0.34	0.28	0.39
Clerical and precision craft	0.34	0.43	0.27
Self-employed	0.26	0.22	0.30
Employed in:			
Industry	0.33	0.29	0.36
Services	0.33	0.31	0.34
Public sector	0.30	0.37	0.25
Wives' characteristics			
Proportion working	0.44	1.00	0.00
Earnings of those working	–	13.05	–
Age	37	37	36
Years of education of those working	–	12	–
Occupation:			
Operative and laborer	0.12	0.28	0.00
Clerical and precision craft	0.25	0.57	0.00
Self-employed	0.04	0.10	0.00
Employed in:			
Industry	0.07	0.17	0.00
Services	0.12	0.27	0.00
Public sector	0.23	0.52	0.00
Households' characteristics (a)			
Living in the North or in Central Italy	0.58	0.70	0.49
Number of children	2.13	1.40	2.71
Consumption	21.60	24.80	19.10
Earnings	26.60	33.50	21.20
Non-human wealth	112.20	127.40	96.60
Lifetime wealth	855.60	1,025.30	723.10
Non-human wealth/earnings	4.22	3.80	4.56
Consumption/earnings	0.81	0.74	0.90
Consumption/lifetime wealth	0.025	0.024	0.026
Number of observations	3,156	1,384	1,772

(a) Consumption, earnings and wealth are expressed in millions of 1987 lire.

4   The empirical model

We assume that household consumption can be approximated by a linear function of lifetime resources, risk, family size and age.[4] The proxy for risk is a dummy variable F that is assigned the value of 1 if the wife works and 0 if not. To capture the effect of risk on the marginal propensity to consume, the variable F is also interacted with lifetime wealth, w. The resulting consumption function for individual i is

$$c_i = \beta_0 + \beta_1 w_i + \beta_2 F_i + \beta_3 F_i w_i + \delta z_i + u_i \qquad (3)$$

where c denotes consumption and w lifetime wealth; z is a vector of variables that includes family size, age and age squared of the head of the household; u is an error term. The Certainty Equivalent model implies that $\beta_2 = \beta_3 = 0$. The theory of precautionary saving suggests instead $\beta_2 > 0$. The hypothesis of decreasing absolute prudence suggests that the effect of risk is a decreasing function of household resources, i.e. $\beta_3 < 0$.

Before turning to the estimation, we must address a problem of endogeneity of the regressors in equation (3). One could assume that the wife's decision to work, and how much to work, is independent from household consumption and estimate equation (3) by ordinary least squares. But in reality the two decisions, i.e. how much to consume and how to allocate time between home and market production, may be taken simultaneously. If F, the dummy variable for working wife, is indeed endogenous, the ordinary least square estimates of the parameters of equation (3) are inconsistent. To allow for the potential endogeneity of F, we proceed in two steps. We first model the wife's decision to work or not. Assume the wife decides to work if

$$R_i - R_i^* \geq \varepsilon_i \qquad (4)$$

where R indicates the real wage of the wife, R^* her reservation wage and ε a stochastic term. The variable R^* is unobservable; however, if R^* can be expressed as a linear function of a vector of observable variables W, i.e. if $R_i^* = \lambda' W_i$, we can define the following indicator for the latent variable R^*

$$\begin{aligned} F_i &= 1 \qquad \text{if } R_i - \lambda' W_i \geq \varepsilon_i \\ F_i &= 0 \qquad \text{otherwise.} \end{aligned} \qquad (5)$$

Assuming that the error term ε is normally distributed with zero mean and unit variance we obtain consistent estimates of the parameters of equation (5) and of the Mill's ratio. Using the inverse Mill's ratio in equation (3), we obtain consistent estimates of the parameters β_0, β_1, β_2, β_3 and δ.

5 Empirical results

Table 8.2 reports the estimates of the probability of the wife's working (equation (5)). We specify the wife's decision to work as a function of demographic characteristics of wives (age, region of residence), proxies of permanent income of husbands (age, education and occupation dummies) and four variables measuring the number and age of children in the household.

Table 8.2 Probit estimates: probability of wife working

Variables (a)	Estimated coefficients	t-statistics	Means of variables
Age of wife	0.167	3.95	36.80
Age of wife squared	−0.002	−3.46	1,411.80
Years of education of husband	0.088	3.23	10.70
Years of education of husband squared	−0.002	−1.42	135.60
Age of husband	−0.024	−0.51	40.40
Age of husband squared	0.10E−03	0.17	1,689.40
Occupation of husband:			
Operative and laborer	0.135	2.02	0.34
Clerical and precision craft	0.266	4.24	0.34
Professional, manager or entrepreneur	−0.037	−0.30	0.04
Husband employed in:			
Agriculture	−0.132	−0.99	0.39
Industry	−0.182	−2.89	0.33
Services	−0.157	−2.56	0.33
No. of children	−0.162	−4.49	1.58
No. of children less than 3 years old	−0.001	−0.16	0.43
No. of children less than 6 years old	−0.136	−0.18	0.21
Average age of children	−0.006	−0.11	6.90
North and Central Italy	0.426	8.51	0.58
Constant	−3.500	−5.24	1.00
Number of wives working	1,384		
Sample size	3,156		
Likelihood at binomial	−2,163.7		
Final likelihood	−1,967.4		

(a) Dependent variable = 1 if the wife is employed, 0 otherwise. Excluded dummies are: self-employed, public sector, resident in the South.

The binomial, unconditional estimate is 44 percent. The conditional probability is a decreasing function of the number and age of children. Wives are also less likely to work if they live in the South and if the husband is self-employed. Since the purpose of the first-stage probit estimation is to provide an instrument for the second stage estimation, the interpretation of the probit coefficients is not essential to the validity of the test of precautionary saving.

The estimated coefficients of the consumption function are displayed in Table 8.3. To reduce heteroscedasticity, all the variables in equation (3) are divided by lifetime wealth. The order of magnitude of the coefficient of lifetime wealth (0.025) is consistent with the life-cycle model. Family size positively affects the average propensity to consume, whereas the age coefficients indicate that the ratio of consumption to lifetime wealth is concave in age.

Table 8.3 Generalized tobit estimates
(dependent variable: ratio of non-durables consumption to lifetime wealth)

Variables (a)	Linear effect of risk		Non-linear effect of risk (b)	
	Estimated coefficients	t-statistics	Estimated coefficients	t-statistics
Lifetime wealth (w)	0.025	31.60	0.019	34.57
F	6.040	17.67		
Fw	−0.24E−02	2.03		
$\exp(-aw)$			−145.240	−19.41
$F\exp(-aw)$			103.661	22.71
Family size	0.390	4.32	0.210	2.55
Age of husband	0.854	6.42	0.704	5.47
Age of husband squared	−0.003	−1.77	−0.001	−0.62
Constant	−31.771	−11.16	−17.386	−6.17
Mill's ratio	−0.004	−6.04	−0.004	−13.91
Mean of dependent variable	0.029		0.029	
Adjusted R^2	0.638		0.655	
Standard error	0.008		0.008	
Number of observations (n)	3,156		3,156	
$F(k, n-k)$	793.6		856.2	

(a) All variables are divided by lifetime wealth.
(b) The value of a that maximizes the likelihood function is 0.5.

Table 8.4 Effect of risk on the average and marginal propensities to consume out of lifetime wealth

A. Effect computed on the basis of the coefficients of Table 8.3

Lifetime wealth (a)	APC(F=1) – APC(F=0)		MPC(F=1) – MPC(F=0)	
	Linear specification	Non-linear specification	Linear specification	Non-linear specification
200	0.0270	0.0367	–0.0024	–0.0180
300	0.0180	0.0200	–0.0024	–0.0100
400	0.0130	0.0130	–0.0024	–0.0070
500	0.0100	0.0093	–0.0024	–0.0050
700	0.0060	0.0056	–0.0024	–0.0030
850	0.0047	0.0042	–0.0024	–0.0021
1,000	0.0040	0.0033	–0.0024	–0.0020
1,500	0.0016	0.0018	–0.0024	–0.0010
3,000	–0.0003	0.0006	–0.0024	–0.0003

B. Effect computed on the basis of the coefficients of Table 8.5

Lifetime wealth (a)	APC(F=1,T=0) – APC(F=0,T=1)		MPC(F=1,T=0) – MPC(F=0,T=1)	
	Linear specification	Non-linear specification	Linear specification	Non-linear specification
200	0.0100	0.0084	–0.0014	–0.0040
300	0.0060	0.0046	–0.0014	–0.0020
400	0.0040	0.0030	–0.0014	–0.0015
500	0.0030	0.0021	–0.0014	–0.0011
700	0.0020	0.0013	–0.0014	–0.0007
850	0.0013	0.0009	–0.0014	–0.0005
1,000	0.0010	0.0008	–0.0014	–0.0004
1,500	0.0001	0.0004	–0.0014	–0.0002
3,000	–0.0006	0.0001	–0.0014	–0.0001

(a) Millions of 1987 lire.

The average propensity to consume of households with two income earners (F=1) is substantially higher than that of single-income households (F=0). The coefficient of the interaction term between F and w is negative and significantly different from zero, so that the effect of risk on consumption depends on the level of total wealth, as implied by decreasing prudence. Evaluated at sample means, the differences between the two APCs and the two MPCs is 0.005 and –0.0024, respectively. If the sample separation rule is indeed correlated with income risk, these results support the theory of precautionary saving.

Since the distribution of wealth is highly skewed, it is preferable to compare APC and MPC at various levels of household resources. The upper panel of Table 8.4 reports the differences for a number of levels of lifetime wealth. As predicted by the theory, the difference in APC narrows as total resources rise. Although the numbers in Table 8.4 are small in absolute value, they indicate that at sample mean the effect of risk pooling on the consumption of two-income households is 3.54 million lire, or 10.6 percent of earnings.

One problem with this linear specification is that if prudence is decreasing in wealth, the effect of a reduction in risk on consumption becomes negative at high levels of w. In fact, the estimated effect of a reduction in risk on APC turns negative when w exceeds 2,500 million lire, somewhat more than twice the mean value of lifetime wealth of two-income households.

There are two possible solutions to this problem. The first is to impose a constraint on the parameters of the consumption function such that the effect of risk is zero for high levels of w. This is equivalent to constraining $\beta_2 + \beta_3 w^* = 0$, where w^* is a given (arbitrary) value of lifetime wealth. If one chooses a value of w^* equal to 3,000 million lire, the constraint cannot be rejected by a Wald test at the 1 percent level of significance. Under this restriction the difference in APC is similar to the unconstrained case. However, in this case the estimated MPC is constant.

A second approach replaces equation (3) with a specification such that APC and MPC differences tend to zero as wealth tends to infinity

$$c_i = \beta_0 + \beta_1 w_i + \beta_2 \exp(-\alpha w_i) + \beta_3 F_i \exp(-\alpha w_i) + \delta z_i + u_i \qquad (6)$$

where α represents the sensitivity of prudence with respect to wealth. The presence of precautionary saving now implies $\beta_3 > 0$ and $\alpha > 0$ if prudence is decreasing in wealth. Since equation (6) is non-linear in the parameters, we estimate α by a grid search that maximizes the value of the likelihood function.

The estimated coefficients of equation (6) are reported in the third column of Table 8.3. The coefficient of the interaction term between F and w is positive and highly significant. The estimated value of α is 0.5, and the restriction $\alpha = 0$ is strongly rejected (the likelihood ratio test yields a value of 116). The pattern of the age variable resembles that for the linear specification, while the coefficient of family size is lower.

As shown in the upper panel of Table 8.4, at the mean value of w the effect of risk on APC is only slightly smaller than in the linear specification.

However, in the non-linear specification the APC difference tends to zero as household resources increase. More importantly, the difference in MPC, which was constrained to be constant in the linear specifications, decreases with household resources and tends to zero as these become large. This pattern is consistent with the hypothesis that prudence is decreasing in wealth.

6 Additional issues

Our results are open to the objection that equation (3) implicitly assumes that the marginal utility of consumption does not depend on wives' and husbands' decisions to work or working hours; that is, that in the utility function of the household, consumption and leisure are separable goods. But if the two decisions are simultaneous, the variable F may actually be proxying for leisure in the utility function, and have little or nothing to do with risk.

A second related issue is that when the real wage rate of the wife rises, so does the value of time spent in non-market activities, e.g. in the production of home-produced goods (Becker and Ghez, 1975). As time at home becomes more costly, purchases of market-produced goods might also increase. The substitution of market-produced goods for home-production has its strongest effects on durables (appliances and cars), but also affects some non-durables, such as housekeeping, laundry and food. If this substitution effect is strong, the findings set forth in the previous section could be attributed to the fact that the APC of two-income households is higher because they have an incentive to substitute market-production for home-production; they could not, accordingly, be regarded as evidence of precautionary saving.

In the present section we attempt to discriminate between these alternative interpretations of our results on the basis of econometric evidence and information on the consumption shares of specific items, such as child care and dining out, that are likely to be substitutes for home production.[5]

To address the identification problem we add to equation (3) a dummy variable that takes the value of 1 if both husband and wife are school-teachers employed by the government.[6] Since their earnings are almost perfectly correlated, pooling does not reduce earnings uncertainty, so we can assume that the coefficient of this dummy captures the substitution effect between leisure and consumption. The importance of precautionary saving is then measured as the difference between the dummy F and the dummy for teachers T, i.e. we make the (non-testable) identification assumption that in one group of the sample, school-teachers, there is no risk sharing.

Table 8.5 Generalized tobit estimates with dummies for teachers *(a)*
(dependent variable: ratio of non-durables consumption to lifetime wealth)

Variables *(b)*	Linear effect of risk		Non-linear effect of risk *(c)*	
	Estimated coefficients	*t*-statistics	Estimated coefficients	*t*-statistics
Lifetime wealth (w)	0.025	31.43	0.019	34.59
F	6.060	17.69		
Fw	–0.24E–02	–2.01		
$\exp(-\alpha w)$			–145.787	–19.44
$F\exp(-\alpha w)$			104.040	22.73
T	–2.306	–1.50		
Tw	0.14E–02	0.95		
$T\exp(-\alpha w)$			–23.69	–1.37
Family size	0.393	4.34	0.211	2.56
Age of husband	0.853	6.40	0.706	5.49
Age of husband squared	–0.003	–1.76	–0.001	–0.63
Constant	–31.775	–11.16	–17.422	–6.19
Mill's ratio	–0.004	–5.97	–0.004	–13.88
Mean of dependent variable	0.029		0.029	
Adjusted R^2	0.637		0.655	
Standard error	0.008		0.008	
Number of observations (n)	3,156		3,156	
F(k, n–k)	617.1		749.4	

(a) The dummy T is 1 if both husband and wife are school or university teachers, 0 otherwise.
(b) All variables are divided by lifetime wealth.
(c) The value of α that maximizes the likelihood function is 0.5.

The results are reported in Table 8.5. The pattern of the coefficients of T is the opposite to that of F, but the coefficients are not very precisely estimated, possibly because the sub-sample of teachers counts only 52 couples. In the lower panel of Table 8.5 we report an estimate of the effect of risk sharing assuming that the coefficients of the additional dummies enables us to identify the effect of leisure on consumption. We subtract the APC of teachers – computed setting $F=1$ and $T=1$ in Table 8.5 – from that of the group in which the wife is in the labor force and at least one of the spouses is not a teacher – i.e. setting $F=1$ and $T=0$.

The effect of risk sharing on consumption is substantially lower than that estimated on the basis of Table 8.3 and reported in the upper panel of Table 8.4: for instance, at sample means, the effect of risk pooling on precautionary saving is now estimated to be 0.87 million lire according to the linear specification (2.7 percent of earnings) and 0.74 million lire (2.2 percent of earnings) according to the non-linear specification.

As far as the substitution between home and market production is concerned, we first note that, in addition to the substitution effect in production, there is also a substitution effect in consumption that works in the opposite direction, i.e. reducing expenditure in the market. If the wife works, there is less time left for consumption activities, and the demand for market produced goods falls. Becker and Ghez (1975) show that market consumption will rise only if the substitution effect in production outweighs that in consumption, so the problem may not be serious after all.[7] Furthermore, our measure of consumption excludes expenditures on durables, thus limiting to non-durables the source of ambiguity in the results.

The Becker and Ghez hypothesis suggests that when the opportunity cost of working is high, the wife does not join the labor force. In particular, when there are young children, the wife's time spent at home is relatively valuable. Thus, if the wife works even when young children are present in the family, one would expect a great deal of substitution between home-production and consumption (e.g. in the form of child care services).

We therefore add to equation (3) a dummy variable for the presence of children under 3 years of age, and interact this dummy with F, the variable indicating whether the wife is in the labor force. Under the theory of substitution between home and market production, one would expect a positive coefficient of this interaction term, because having young children and being in the labor force should increase market consumption. However, we find just the opposite.[8] The dummy for young children is negative and not significantly different from zero, the interaction term is negative and significant at the 5 percent level and all other coefficients have the same signs, magnitude and significance levels.[9] Similar results are obtained when households with children either under 3 years of age or under 6 years of age are excluded from the sample.

Finally, some information is available on the spending items that are most likely to reflect the substitution between time and consumption. The SHIW unfortunately lacks detailed expenditure categories, so we must rely on the annual consumer survey by Istat, which lacks information on earnings, assets and several demographic characteristics, but contains highly detailed information on spending.[10]

Table 8.6 Saving, growth, labor force participation and share in consumption of selected expenditure categories, 1966-1988

	66–70	71–75	76–80	81–85	86–88
Consumption share of expenditure on:					
Domestic services and laundry:					
2 members	–	1.6(*a*)	1.4	1.3	1.1(*c*)
4 members	–	1.3(*a,b*)	1.2(*b*)	1.3	0.9(*c*)
Dining out:					
2 members	–	4.8(*a*)	4.7	4.8	4.5(*c*)
4 members	–	4.2(*a,b*)	4.1(*b*)	4.5	4.1(*c*)
Net private saving rate	17.9	15.4	13.1	10.0	12.7
Rate of growth of GDP	6.2	3.1	4.3	1.8	3.1
Labor force participation rate between age 20 and 59:					
Men	91.2	90.2	90.8	89.8	88.3
Women	30.0	31.2	39.4	44.8	49.0
Married men	–	–	–	94.0	93.3
Married women	–	–	–	39.2	43.0
Percentage of households with:					
Single income earner	–	–	61.0(*d*)	59.9	58.7(*c*)
Two income earners	–	–	32.0(*d*)	33.3	34.4(*c*)
More than two income earners	–	–	7.0	6.8	6.9

Sources: Consumption shares: Istat, *Indagine sui consumi delle famiglie,* various years. Rate of growth of national income and net private saving rate, adjusted for inflation: Pagliano and Rossi (1992). Labor force participation rate: Istat, *Annuario di statistiche del lavoro, Indagine sulle forze di lavoro* and *Bollettino mensile di statistica,* various years. Households by income recipients: from 1978 to 1981, Istat, *Annuario delle forze di lavoro,* various years; from 1982 to 1987, Istat, *La distribuzione quantitativa del reddito in Italia nelle indagini sui bilanci di famiglia,* Collana d'informazione, 1979.
(*a*) 1975.
(*b*) 4 and 5 members.
(*c*) 1986-1987.
(*d*) 1978-1980.

We collect data from 1975 to 1987 on the share of total consumption going to domestic services and laundry and to dining out (see Table 8.6). Since the survey lacks information on income earners, we break these shares down by family size.[11] The two shares are fairly small and quite stable over time. But over the same time period the women's labor force participation rate rose by over 10 percentage points.

While the evidence of this section is anything but conclusive, it indicates that substitution between market and non-market activities and between leisure and consumption cannot be the entire explanation of the difference in APC of households with different number of income earners.

7 Macroeconomic implications

This section examines the possible relevance of our analysis to the reduction in the private saving rate that has been observed in the Italian economy and to international differences in saving rates.

The slowdown in economic growth from an annual average of 6.2 percent in the late sixties to 2.3 percent in 1981-88 is often cited as the main factor underlying the substantial reduction (more than 5 percentage points) in the Italian private saving rate (see Table 8.6). However, other factors have also been at work, such as the decline in population growth, the increase of social security benefits and the development of credit markets.

We suggest that an additional factor may have been the very rapid increase in the women's participation rate, from 30 to 49 percent in the past decade and a half, while the men's participation rate has held more or less unchanged.[12] In fact, we find that when the increase in the female participation rate is accompanied by a rise in the proportion of multiple-income households, the precautionary component of saving declines.[13] The extent of this reduction depends on the sensitivity of saving to risk, as well as on the change in family composition. In practice, the share of multiple-earner households has increased by 3 percentage points over the past decade.[14] This implies that our results may possibly account for only a small part of the decline in private saving.

The reduction in saving and the increase in the women's participation have occurred in all industrialized countries, although not at the same time or to the same extent. While demographics, income growth and fiscal policy are usually thought to be the main determinants of the cross-country variation in saving rates, Graham (1987) and Modigliani (1990) have found that other things being equal, there is a strong negative correlation between the labor force participation rate of women and the saving rate. For instance, the Scandinavian countries, with female participation rates higher than 70 percent, also exhibit relatively low saving rates. In Belgium, Italy and the Netherlands the pattern is just the opposite. The present paper offers one possible explanation for this correlation.

8 Conclusions

Uncertainty over the future is very widely considered to be an important determinant of savings. So far, however, empirical studies have not succeeded in isolating the precautionary motive from the life cycle and the bequest motives for saving. In this paper we test the theory of precautionary saving in response to earnings uncertainty with an approach that differs from those adopted by the previous literature. Theory suggests that risk sharing reduces precautionary saving. Thus, we compare the consumption choices of households with different numbers of income earners.

The empirical results bear out the theoretical predictions. Other things being equal, households with two income earners have an average propensity to consume out of lifetime wealth that is about 0.1 percentage points higher than single-income households; this implies that risk pooling leads to an increase in consumption of roughly 2.5 percent of current earnings. In principle, the substitution between time and consumption and between home and market production may account for the results. However, econometric evidence and data on the share in consumption of items that are likely to be close substitutes for home production fail to support this hypothesis.

If an increase in the female participation rate reduces precautionary saving, our results could explain part of the reduction in the overall saving rate experienced by the Italian economy. And as the rise in women's labor force participation and the decline in saving have been observed virtually throughout the industrialized world, these findings may be relevant to an explanation of international disparities in saving.

More generally, this paper suggests that precautionary saving is a phenomenon worth studying, and that households may respond to other, and perhaps more important, risks. It is possible that changes in other sources of uncertainty may have contributed to the fall in the saving rate in Italy. In particular if, as seems likely, the shift from the turbulent seventies to the more stable eighties has brought a reduction in individual uncertainty, then precautionary saving may have declined. Plausible as this conjecture is, it is impossible at the moment to support it with direct evidence.

APPENDIX

1   Definition of variables

Head of the household. The head is always the male, who in all cases is in the labor force.

Household size. Total number of persons in the family: head, spouse (including common-law wives), children, other relatives, and non-relatives living in the household. Households with income earners other than the head and the spouse are excluded.

Education of the household's head and of the spouse. Responses: (5) no education; (6) completed elementary school (5 years); (7) completed junior high school (8 years); (8) completed high school (13 years); (9) completed university degree (17 to 19 years); (0) post-graduate education (more than 20 years of education). The variable has been coded according to the values given in parentheses. For the highest class we assume a value of 20 years of education.

Occupation of the household's head and of the spouse. Responses: (1) operative or laborer; (2) and (3) clerical and precision craft; (4), (5) and (6) professional, manager and entrepreneur; (7) self-employed.

Sector of occupation of the household's head and of the spouse. Responses: (1) agricultural; (2) and (3) industry; (4) public sector; (5), (6) and (7) services.

Residence of the household. Responses: North or Central Italy (Piemonte, Valle D'Aosta, Liguria, Lombardia, Trentino, Friuli, Veneto, Emilia-Romagna, Marche, Umbria, Toscana, Lazio); South (Abruzzi, Molise, Campania, Basilicata, Puglia, Calabria, Sicilia, Sardegna).

Consumption of household. Sum of expenditures on non-durable consumption items in 1987 (food consumption, entertainment, education, clothes, medical expenses, housing repairs and additions). Durable consumption (vehicles, furniture and appliances, art objects) is not included in the definition of consumption.

Earnings of the household's head and of the spouse. Question: How much did you earn from your labor activity net of all taxes and contributions in 1987? This question is asked to each member of the household, whether employed or self-employed. Household earnings are defined as the sum of net of taxes earnings of the household's head and the spouse.

Household net worth. Sum of household's liquid assets (checking accounts, savings accounts, money market accounts, certificates of deposit), financial assets (equities, government bonds and corporate bonds), property and business assets, net of liabilities (debt owed on credit cards, on car loans, other forms of consumer debt, and mortgages on houses, properties and additions). The variable is measured at the end of 1987.

Household lifetime wealth. Sum of human wealth and household net worth. The former is the discounted value of the sum of the head's and spouse's earnings projected until retirement, and is defined below.

2   The construction of human wealth

To compute human wealth we proceed as follows. Denote by $Y(\tau,j)$ the earnings of a household member j of age τ. In the sample j is either the husband or the wife, if employed. We assume that individual earnings can be expressed as a function of a vector Z of individual characteristics (education, occupation, sector, regional location and family size), a quadratic function of age $\Phi(\tau)$ and a normally distributed disturbance u

$$Y(\tau,j) = Z\beta + \Phi(\tau) + u.$$

Normal earnings, not adjusted for cohort effects, are then defined as

$$Y_p(\tau,j) = Z\hat{\beta} + \hat{\Phi}(\tau) + 0.5\hat{u}$$

where the hats denote the estimated coefficients from a Generalized Least Squares regression, using as weights the residuals from a first-stage OLS regression. The earnings function estimates are reported in Tables 8.A1 and 8.A2 for husbands and wives, respectively.

Human wealth of individual j of age τ_0 is then computed as

$$H(\tau_0, j) = \sum_{k=1}^{R_j - \tau_0} Y_p(\tau_0 + k, j) \left(\frac{1 + n}{1 + r}\right)^k$$

where $Y_p(\tau_0 + k, j)$ is the projected value of normal earnings from the previous equation, R_j is the retirement age of member j and n and r represent, respectively, the rate of growth of productivity and the rate of interest. Retirement age is assumed to be 65 for husbands and 55 for wives; the rate of interest is assumed to be equal to the rate of productivity growth.

Table 8.A1 Generalized least squares estimates, 1 (a)
(dependent variable: earnings of the husband)

Variables	Estimated coefficients	t-statistics	Means of variables
Years of education	1.486	6.89	10
Years of education squared	−0.014	−1.65	133
Age	0.685	3.71	44
Age squared	−0.005	−2.58	2,042
Occupation of the husband:			
Operative and laborer	−11.858	−20.88	0.33
Clerical and precision craft	−12.291	−22.31	0.30
Professional, manager or entrepreneur	1.056	1.03	0.05
Husband employed in:			
Agriculture	−2.493	−2.51	0.06
Industry	3.919	6.98	0.34
Services	2.387	4.32	0.32
Family size	0.125	0.68	3.60
North and Central Italy	1.540	3.56	0.61
Constant	−5.682	−1.39	1.00
Adjusted R^2	0.277		
Number of observations	5,122		
Dependent variable mean	23.100		

(a) The dependent variable is expressed in millions of 1987 lire. Excluded dummies are: self-employed, employed in the public sector, resident in the South.

Table 8.A2 Generalized least squares estimates, 2 (a)
(dependent variable: earnings of the wife)

Variables	Estimated coefficients	t-statistics	Means of variables
Years of education	0.566	3.47	11
Years of education squared	–0.004	–0.62	142
Age	0.536	3.70	39
Age squared	–0.005	–2.89	1,632
Occupation of the wife:			
Operative and laborer	–3.919	–20.88	0.32
Clerical and precision craft	–2.273	–22.31	0.54
Professional, manager or entrepreneur	3.836	1.03	0.07
Wife employed in:			
Agriculture	–3.161	–2.51	0.04
Industry	1.634	6.98	0.17
Services	1.574	4.32	0.27
Family size	–0.317	0.68	3.54
North and Central Italy	0.892	3.56	0.71
Constant	–2.318	–1.39	1.00
Adjusted R^2	0.193		
Number of observations	1,912		
Dependent variable mean	13.779		

(a) The dependent variable is expressed in millions of 1987 lire. Excluded dummies are: self-employed, employed in the public sector, resident in the South.

NOTES

* An earlier version of this paper was presented to the Meeting of the European Economic Association, Cambridge, August 28-30, 1991. We thank Guglielmo Weber for helpful suggestions. Any errors are the responsibility of the authors. Tullio Jappelli acknowledges financial support from C.N.R.

1 A utility function is 'proper' if the addition of an undesirable risk does not make desirable an undesirable independent risk (Pratt and Zeckhauser, 1987).

2 We do not deal with the problem of determining optimal risk sharing within a household. This would be relevant only if the family maximized a function – say, the sum – of individual utilities, and not the utility of the sum of individual consumptions.

3 The 1987 SHIW provides detailed information on labor income, consumption of durables and non-durables, tangible and financial wealth and several

demographic characteristics of a random sample of 8,027 households. See the Methodological Appendix to this volume for details about the SHIW and the Appendix to this chapter for the definition of the variables used in this chapter.

4 A closed-form solution for optimal consumption can be obtained only by assuming that the utility function is exponential (see, for instance, Caballero, 1990). Weil (1993) has generalized this to a class of two-level utility functions with constant elasticity of intertemporal substitution and a constant coefficient of absolute risk aversion. In both cases, the effect of uncertainty is separable and additive with respect to that of human and non-human wealth. However, constant absolute risk aversion also implies constant absolute prudence. It follows that an increase in income risk lowers the APC, but leaves the MPC unaffected. Even if the hypothesis that prudence is decreasing in wealth is plausible, utility functions with decreasing prudence do not yield a closed-form solution for optimal consumption when income is uncertain. Thus, several authors suggest linear approximations to the optimal consumption rule under uncertainty (e.g. Skinner, 1988).

5 Note, however, that the results would still carry the implication that an increase in the female participation rate reduces the saving rate, albeit through a different channel (see Section 7).

6 This group in Italy faces virtually negligible uncertainty: in practice, government employees cannot be laid off, and salary depends only on seniority.

7 Carroll and Summers (1991, pp. 21-22) compare the age-consumption profile for a number of countries, concluding that the substitution between consumption and time is not a viable explanation for the association between income and consumption throughout the life cycle.

8 For brevity these results are not reported and are available upon request.

9 We choose to test for the effect of children under 3 years of age because Italian law contains several provisions that apply to working women until the child is 3. Repeating the estimation with dummies for children under 6 – i.e. under school age – or with both dummies does not change the pattern of results.

10 See Istat, *Indagine sui consumi delle famiglie.*

11 It would be most useful to compare the consumption shares of families with one and two income earners, but this information too is lacking. However, as the female participation rate has increased dramatically over the past 10 years, under the theory of substitution between time and consumption one should observe an increase in the consumption of goods that are close substitutes of home-production (for given family size). The numbers in Table 8.6 do not support this hypothesis.

12 These figures are all the more telling, in that the women's participation was roughly constant from the late fifties to the mid seventies.

13 A similar point was recently made by Summers and Carroll (1987), who observe that in the United States the increase in two-income households may have reduced income uncertainty and, in turn, precautionary and aggregate saving. In the United States the percentage of married women in the labor force rose from 30.5 in 1960 to 54.6 in 1986. However, data from the 1972 Consumer

Expenditure Survey indicate that the APC of married couples is 77.9 percent for two-income, and 81.2 percent for single-income households. Thus, Summers and Carroll dismiss the changing composition of households as a viable explanation for the decline in the U.S. saving rate. But the characteristics of the two groups of households are different. Vickery (1979), using the same data set, found that holding other variables constant, households with two-income earners have a higher APC.

14 Given the increase in the female participation rate, the change in the household composition by number of income earners is rather small. Part of the explanation is that over the same period the number of married couples in the labor force declined by 6 percentage points (from 74.5 percent in 1978 to 68.5 percent in 1988).

REFERENCES

Auerbach, A.J. and L.J. Kotlikoff (1989). 'Demographics, Fiscal Policy, and U.S. Saving', NBER Working Paper 3150.

Becker, G.S. and G. Ghez (1975). *The Allocation of Time and Goods over the Life-Cycle*, Chicago: University of Chicago Press.

Caballero, R. (1990). 'Consumption Puzzles and Precautionary Savings', *Journal of Monetary Economics* **25**: 113-36.

Caballero, R. (1991). 'Earnings Uncertainty and Aggregate Wealth Accumulation', *American Economic Review* **81**: 859-71.

Carroll, C. and L.H. Summers (1991). 'Consumption Growth Parallels Income Growth: Some New Evidence', in B. D. Bernheim and J. B. Shaven (eds.), *National Saving and Economic Performance*, Chicago: University of Chicago Press.

Carroll, C. and A.A. Samwick (1991). 'The Nature and Magnitude of Precautionary Saving', Board of Governors of the Federal Reserve System, mimeo.

Cochrane, J. (1991). 'A Simple Test of Consumption Insurance', *Journal of Political Economy* **99**: 957-76.

Davies, J.B. (1981). 'Uncertain Lifetime, Consumption, and Dissaving in Retirement', *Journal of Political Economy* **89**: 561-77.

Deaton, A. (1991). 'Saving and Liquidity Constraints', *Econometrica* **59**: 1221-48.

Drèze, J.H. and F. Modigliani (1972). 'Consumption under Uncertainty', *Journal of Economic Theory* **5**: 308-35.

Friedman, M. (1957). *A Theory of the Consumption Function*, Princeton: Princeton University Press.

Graham, J.W. (1987). 'International Differences in Saving Rates and the Life-Cycle Hypothesis', *European Economic Review* **31**: 1509-29.

Guiso, L., T. Jappelli and D. Terlizzese (1994). 'Earnings Uncertainty and Precautionary Saving', *this volume*.

Hurd, M.D. (1989). 'Mortality Risk and Bequests', *Econometrica* **57**: 779-813.

Kimball, M.S. (1990). 'Precautionary Saving in the Small and in the Large', *Econometrica* **58**: 53-73.

Kotlikoff, L.J. (1989). *What Determines Saving?*, Cambridge, MA: MIT Press.

Kotlikoff, L.J. and A. Spivak (1981). 'The Family as an Incomplete Annuities Market', *Journal of Political Economy* **89**: 372-91.

Leland, H. (1968). 'Saving and Uncertainty: The Precautionary Demand for Saving', *Quarterly Journal of Economics* **82**: 465-73.

Mace, B.J. (1991). 'Full Insurance in the Presence of Aggregate Uncertainty', *Journal of Political Economy* **99**: 928-56.

Modigliani, F. (1990). 'Recent Declines in the Saving Rate: A Life Cycle Perspective', *Rivista di politica economica* **80** (English version): 5-42. (Also in M. Baldassari, L. Paganetto and E.S. Phelps, *World Saving, Prosperity and Growth*, New York: St. Martin's Press, 1993.)

Pagliano, P. and N. Rossi (1992). 'The Italian Saving Rate: 1951 to 1990 Estimates', in *Income and Saving in Italy: A Reconstruction*, Temi di discussione 169, Banca d'Italia.

Pratt, J.W. and R.J. Zeckhauser (1987). 'Proper Risk Aversion', *Econometrica* **55**: 143-54.

Sandmo, A. (1970). 'The Effect of Uncertainty on Savings Decisions', *Review of Economic Studies* **37**: 82-114.

Skinner, J. (1988). 'Risky Income, Life Cycle Consumption and Precautionary Saving', *Journal of Monetary Economics* **22**: 237-55.

Summers, L.H. and C. Carroll (1987). 'Why Is U.S. National Saving so Low?', *Brookings Papers on Economic Activity* **2**: 607-42.

Vickery, C. (1979). 'Women's Economic Contribution to the Family', in R. Smith (ed.), *The Subtle Revolution*, Washington, DC: Urban Institute.

Weil, P. (1990). 'Equilibrium Asset Prices with Undiversifiable Labor Income Risk', Harvard University, Harvard Institute of Economic Research Discussion Paper 1507.

Weil, P. (1993). 'Precautionary Saving and the Permanent Income Hypothesis', *Review of Economic Studies* **60**: 367-83.

Zeldes, S.P. (1989). 'Optimal Consumption with Stochastic Income: Deviations from Certainty Equivalence', *Quarterly Journal of Economics* **104**: 275-98.

III

BORROWING CONSTRAINTS,
INTERGENERATIONAL TRANSFERS AND BEQUESTS

9 Saving and borrowing constraints*

LIVIO MACCAN, NICOLA ROSSI
and IGNAZIO VISCO

1 Introduction

Recent research on the evolution of the Italian saving rate has suggested that capital market imperfections are among the probable explanations for the high rate of saving in Italy. Reasonable as it is, the borrowing constraints hypothesis[1] can only be accepted or rejected on empirical grounds. In the case of Italy, Jappelli and Pagano (1988), Guiso and Jappelli (1994) and Guiso, Jappelli and Terlizzese (1994) have attempted to evaluate the impact of capital market imperfections on households' saving decisions and have substantiated their claims by means of a number of empirical tests designed to assess the effect of credit market imperfections on the saving behavior of Italian households.[2]

Their work relies crucially on exogenously given criteria to identify liquidity-constrained consumers. For example, in Jappelli and Pagano (1988), the sample selection rule (i.e. the arbitrary threshold above which liquidity constraints are supposed to operate) coincides with a propensity to save below 15 percent. Alternatively, they rely (along with Guiso and Jappelli, 1994) on direct information (available in the Bank of Italy Survey of Household Income and Wealth, SHIW) regarding consumers turned down (or expecting to be turned down) in the market for consumer credit. Finally, to assess the impact of mortgage market imperfections Guiso *et al.* (1994) assume that homeowners are not constrained in the mortgage market.

In the first case, the arbitrary threshold level focuses exclusively on liquidity constraints in a narrow sense, i.e. those giving rise to single-period planning horizons. In the second case, the direct information misses all borrowing constraints arising in the mortgage market. In the third case, so long as the consumption behavior of homeowners reflects past borrowing constraints the sample selection rule could be misleading. In short, rather than providing a genuine estimate of the extent of liquidity constraints, the available evidence concerns their sample distribution conditional on exogenously given selection criterion. However, the macroeconomic impact of capital market imperfections depends crucially on their diffusion in terms of the number of households involved and their aggregate consumption. Moreover, the use of exogenously given criteria to identify borrowing constraints prevents a thorough assessment of the impact of economic policy on their distribution across households. Needless to say, this somewhat impairs the usefulness of otherwise interesting information.

Mariger (1986, 1987) recently suggested a methodology to assess the extent and nature of borrowing constraints without reference to direct external indicators. The theoretical reference framework is given by the intertemporal model initially discussed in Yaari (1965) and extended to allow for endogenous liquidity constraints.[3] The present paper takes an intermediate view and proposes, in Section 2, a life-cycle consumption model with endogenously determined restricted borrowing for a fraction of the population. The model is applied, in Section 3, to the microeconomic information contained in the Bank of Italy SHIW for the year 1987. Section 4 summarizes the main results and Section 5 concludes.

2   Consumers' behavior and borrowing constraints

Let the household's intertemporal preferences be defined over the vector $c_t = (c_t, c_{t+1}, ..., c_T)$ of all consumption levels between periods t and T, and let the same preferences be represented, under certainty, by the following additive function (Modigliani and Ando, 1957):

$$u(c_t^T) = \sum_{j=t}^{T}(1 + \varrho)^{t-j}[\gamma^{-1}f_j^{1-\gamma}c_j^\gamma] \qquad (\gamma < 1, \ \gamma \neq 0) \quad (1)$$

where t and T denote the current and terminal period of the household's planning horizon,[4] ϱ is the constant rate of intertemporal preference, and $(1 + \varrho)^{t-j}$ the subjective discount factor to be applied to utility expected in period j; f_j indicates the "effective" family size, i.e. the household size adjusted for family composition:

$$f_j = [d_j + \lambda_1(1 - d_j)]n_j^a + \lambda_2 n_j^i + \lambda_3 n_j^f + \lambda_4 n_j^g + \lambda_5 n_j^o$$

$$(j = t, \ t + 1, ...,T) \quad (2)$$

where j is the age of the head of the household, d_j is an indicator function equal to one if $j < 65$ and to zero otherwise, n_j^a denotes the number of main adults (parents) in the household in period j ($n_j^a \leq 2$), n_j^i, n_j^f and n_j^g denote the number of children in different age-groups in period j. Finally, n_j^o denotes the number of other members of the household, in period j. In equation (2), the parameter λ_1 represents a proportionality factor (an equivalence scale) converting old people into adults of less than 64 years of age. Similarly, λ_2, λ_3, λ_4 and λ_5 convert children of different ages and other members into equivalent adults, allowing for different needs of households with children in different age-groups.[5] In the following, three age-groups will be accounted for: 0-5, 6-14 and 15-19. "Other members of the household" will therefore include children over 19.

To define the optimal consumption plan that allows for borrowing constraints, it is assumed that the consuming unit maximizes (1) under an intertemporal budget constraint which, in the generic period i, takes the following form:

$$a_i = (1 + r)^{i-t}\left[a_t + \sum_{j=t}^{i-1}(1 + r)^{t-j}(y_j - c_j) \right] \geq b_i$$

$$(i = t + 1, ..., T + 1) \qquad (3)$$

where a_t and y_t denote, respectively, the household's net wealth at the beginning of period t and its net non-interest income in the same period, and r is the (constant) real net rate of return.

In (3), b_i indicates the minimal level of net worth to be held by the household in period i of its life cycle.[6] In Mariger (1986, 1987) it is assumed that the lower limit to net wealth is given by the household's equity in real assets (houses, durables and business property):

$$b_i = \min\left[\left(a_t^r + \sum_{j=t}^{i} e_j \right), (\theta a_t^{nr}) \right]$$

$$(i = t + 1, ..., s; \ 0 \leq \theta \leq 1) \qquad (4)$$

where a_t^r denotes the household's equity in real assets, a_t^{nr} denotes the current value of the household's real assets and e_j is the mortgage payment due in year j according to the mortgage contract signed in year t. The household is therefore assumed to accumulate equity in real assets according to a well defined mortgage schedule until it owns the fraction θ of its net wealth. To put it differently, (4) implies that a simple non-negativity constraint holds on the household's net wealth whenever the latter consists entirely of financial assets. As soon as real assets enter the household portfolio and a collateral exists, the borrowing constraint is partially relaxed and limited borrowing is allowed for. Notice that if the constraint happens to be binding in period $T+1$ only, then θ indicates the fraction of real wealth that the household intends not to consume.[7]

This assumption is certainly appropriate in the U.S. setting, where the incidence of owner occupied dwellings reaches a peak early in the life cycle. In Italy, by contrast, the pattern of housing tenure increases slowly with age: at age 32, only 40 percent already have a house, and another 30 percent will buy (or inherit) one later in life.[8] In this case, the borrowing constraint (4) could underestimate the hardship of young households who do not yet own a house but want or have to buy one in the future. In this paper it has therefore been assumed that the constraint could take separate forms for homeowners (b_i^h) and for non-homeowners (b_i^n), so that, in the former case,

$$b_i^h = b_i \tag{5}$$

as given by (4), and, in the latter,

$$b_i^n = \pi_i \phi a_i^{nr} \qquad (i = t + 1, \ ..., \ s; \ 0 \leq \phi \leq 1) \tag{6}$$

where π_i is the cumulative probability of buying a house in period i conditional on not having already bought one, ϕ is the downpayment, as a percentage of the value of the real assets a_i^{nr} to be bought at time i, and it is implicitly assumed that the house is the only real asset available.[9] Equation (6) suggests that, far from experiencing a simple non-negativity constraint on financial assets, non-homeowners are actually forced to accumulate them in order to meet the time-varying downpayment requirement (in expected value). Notice that equation (5), by contrast, allows homeowners to borrow up to $(1 - \theta)$ of the value of the house.[10]

Note that, if $-\infty = b_i(\forall i)$ and $a_{T+1} \geq b_{T+1} \equiv 0$, the problem defined by the objective function (1) and the budget constraint (3) reproduces the well known standard life-cycle setting. On the contrary, if the borrowing constraint is binding, in at least one period, the household's behavior could be substantially altered and the life-cycle planning horizon of length $T-t$ could be substituted by a number of single period or multiperiod planning horizons with lengths less than $T-t$.

Clearly, in the present setting, the case of single-period planning horizons (usually characterized by average propensities to consume near unity and typically applicable to unemployed people or young households) is just one of the possible outcomes. Other alternatives can easily be envisaged: (i) multiperiod horizons of households whose consumption plan embodies an initially rising and subsequently declining household size but whose intertemporal resources cannot be moved freely across periods in order to match the household's consumption profile; (ii) multiperiod horizons of households intending to buy a durable that involves a substantial downpayment. Finally, (iii) with uncertain lifetimes, one should also take into account the case of single-period or short multiperiod planning horizons of retirees whose consumption path, far from being constant, is downward sloping on account of their decreasing life expectancy.

Mariger (1986) has discussed at length the case in which the constraint (3) happens to be binding in the generic period s $(t < s < T)$, and he has characterized the solution as $c_t^{*s} = (c_t^*, c_{t+1}^*, ..., c_s^*)$, indicating a procedure for selecting the cutoff point s. In particular, it can be shown that the cutoff point s can be found by searching for the maximum s that minimizes current (optimal) consumption c_t^*. Given s, the subsequent cutoff point can be found by reconsidering the optimum problem (1)-(3) where, however, $t = s$ and $i = s+1, s+2, ..., T$. Finally, for each s, c_t^{*s} is none other than the solution to the optimum problem (1)-(3) where $T = s$ and $-\infty < b_i < \infty (\forall i < s)$. Hence, for a generic household,

$$c_t^* = \beta_t \left[a_t + \sum_{j=t}^{s} (1 + r)^{t-j} y_j - (1 + r)^{t-s-1} b_{s+1} \right] \qquad (\forall\ t \leq s) \quad (7)$$

where

$$\beta_t = f_t / \left(f_t + \sum_{j=t+1}^{s} \psi^{j-t} f_j \right) \qquad (8)$$

for $s > t$, and $\beta_t = 1$ for $s = t$. Since

$$\psi = (1 + r)^\gamma / (1 + \varrho)^{1/(1-\gamma)} \qquad (9)$$

in (8) the denominator denotes the discounted sum of effective household members over the interval $[t,s]$. Hence, equation (8) indicates that, through time, consumption parallels the time path of effective household size.

Note that, in the presence of uncertainty, it would not be possible to derive a closed-form solution to the household's optimum problem.[11] However, an approximate solution is available if we assume, as in Mariger (1986), that: (i) actuarially fair insurance is available to insure net labor income in each future period against the possibility that an earner might die while other members are still alive, and (ii) the family behaves as if the expected family composition in each future period will be realized with certainty. In practice, this implies (i) increasing the discounting of future labor earnings as the probability of their realization decreases,[12] and (ii) replacing f_i by its mathematical expectation conditional on the information set available at time t, $E_t(f_i)$.[13]

In the present case, the borrowing constraint (6) is a source of additional difficulties. Quite clearly, the decision on whether, when and how to buy a house should be part of the consumer's optimization problem. However, allowing explicitly for an endogenous tenure profile over the life cycle would substantially increase the overall complexity of the model. In particular, the empirical analysis, which is already far from straightforward, would be greatly affected by such an extension. Therefore, tenants will be assumed to behave as if expected house ownership $E_t(a_t^{nr})$ in each future period could be realized with certainty.

3   The empirical analysis

The empirical analysis therefore relies on the following description of a generic household's behavior:

$$c_t = \beta_t \left\{ a_t + \sum_{j=t}^{s}(1 + r)^{t-j}y_j - \mu - (1 + r)^{t-s-1}\left[\delta^h \min\left(a_t^r + \sum_{j=t}^{s} e_{j,\theta}a_t^{nr} \right) \right. \right.$$

$$\left. \left. + (1 - \delta^h)\pi_t\phi E_t(a_t^{nr}) \right] \right\} + \varepsilon_t \qquad\qquad (\forall\ t \le s) \quad (10)$$

where the parameter μ allows for systematic measurement errors in life-cycle wealth,

$$\beta_t = \left\{ 1 + \sum_{j=t+1}^{s} \psi^{j-t}\left[(d_j + (1 - d_j)\lambda_1)E_t(n_j^a) + \lambda_2 E_t(n_j^i) + \lambda_3 E_t(n_j^f) \right. \right.$$

$$\left. \left. + \lambda_4 E_t(n_j^g) + \lambda_5 E_t(n_j^o) \right] \right\} \Big/ \left[(d_t + (1 - d_t)\lambda_1)n_t^a + \lambda_2 n_t^i \right.$$

$$\left. + \lambda_3 n_t^f + \lambda_4 n_t^g + \lambda_5 n_t^o \right]^{-1} \qquad\qquad (s > t) \quad (11)$$

and δ^h is a dummy variable equal to 1 for homeowners and zero otherwise.

The model is completed by the condition endogenizing the cutoff point s:

$$s = \left[\max\ k \mid c_{t,1}^{*k} \le c_{t,1}^{*l} \right] \qquad\qquad (t \le (k,l) \le T) \quad (12)$$

where $c_{t,1}^{*s}$ denotes the first element in the vector $c_t^{*s} = (c_t^*, c_{t+1}^*, ..., c_s^*)$.

The parameters ψ and μ are allowed to vary linearly with the level of education of the head of the household.[14] Allowing a limited variation in β and μ accounts for two distinct phenomena. On the one hand, there is a strong presumption that misreporting of information on wealth tends to be positively correlated with the household's level of resources. On the other hand, Mariger's (1986, 1987) findings suggest that tastes may vary systematically with the level of education. In particular, the present formulation allows the rate of time preference to depend on the level of education.[15]

In equation (10), ε_t is an additive stochastic term assumed to be normally distributed with zero mean and constant variance,[16] and orthogonal to the regressors. Notice that the model (10)-(12) is non-linear in the parameter vector $(\theta, \psi, \lambda, \mu)$.[17] However, the main source of problems in the estimation of model (10)-(12) does not come from its non-linearity, but from the dependence of optimal consumption on the cutoff point s given in (12), which depends in turn on the parameter vector, as well as on the full matrix of regressors. Naturally, given the above assumptions on ε_t and given s, a non-linear least squares estimator of the parameter vector is readily available. Estimation was therefore carried out iteratively and a few iterations usually proved sufficient to reach a maximum of the objective function.

The estimation of the parameter vector exploits the microeconomic information available in the 1987 Bank of Italy SHIW (see the Methodological Appendix to the volume). To ease the computational constraint, and to allow for some behavioral heterogeneity, observations on 7,170 households[18] were classified by geographic region (North-west,[19] North-east,[20] Center,[21] South,[22] Islands[23]).

The estimation of the model requires data on households' current and expected composition, current and expected net labor income, current and expected retirement income, current net real and financial wealth and consumption. Since the Survey does not provide information on future variables, most variables had to be constructed. The additional maintained hypotheses (described in detail in Appendix A) involved in the estimation of such variables should be carefully accounted for when evaluating the empirical results.

Table 9.1 presents parameter estimates for the five regions (along with their heteroscedasticity-corrected standard errors) and allows some initial comments. Most parameters turn out to be precisely estimated and of an order of magnitude compatible with *a priori* information. The main exception is provided by the estimates of the elements of λ in the Islands, whose standard errors, however, are such that the implied equivalence scale is never significantly different from that prevailing in the rest of the country. In particular, with the exception of this region, adults over 65 are equivalent, for consumption purposes, to about 0.7 young adults.[24] As far as other members of the household are concerned, the general pattern of equivalence scales is common across regions. Children in the 0-5 age band are equivalent, for consumption purposes, to 0.3-0.7 young adults in Northern and Central Italy, while children in the 6-14 and 15-19 age-groups weigh substantially less on the household budget. Other adults are equivalent, for consumption purposes, to 0.3-0.5 young adults.

Table 9.1 Parameter estimates of the consumption function with liquidity constraints

	North-west	North-east	Center	South	Islands
θ	0.673	0.751	0.784	0.539	0.538
	(0.075)	(0.061)	(0.071)	(0.142)	(0.119)
ψ_1	1.002	0.946	1.003	1.012	1.017
	(0.009)	(0.029)	(0.009)	(0.011)	(0.012)
ψ_2	1.000	0.994	0.994	0.999	1.008
	(0.007)	(0.008)	(0.006)	(0.008)	(0.009)
ψ_3	0.993	0.988	0.992	1.000	1.018
	(0.004)	(0.005)	(0.004)	(0.005)	(0.008)
ψ_4	0.997	1.006	1.004	1.016	1.034
	(0.005)	(0.005)	(0.004)	(0.007)	(0.009)
ψ_5	0.985	0.969	0.981	0.995	0.999
	(0.005)	(0.006)	(0.005)	(0.006)	(0.007)
ψ_6	0.985	1.000	1.013	1.007	1.019
	(0.006)	(0.008)	(0.007)	(0.010)	(0.009)
λ_1	0.692	0.723	0.610	0.672	1.039
	(0.089)	(0.093)	(0.065)	(0.124)	(0.303)
λ_2	0.558	0.267	0.745	−0.012	1.932
	(0.175)	(0.207)	(0.159)	(0.153)	(0.853)
λ_3	−0.011	0.114	0.444	0.438	4.553
	(0.250)	(0.226)	(0.229)	(0.239)	(2.043)
λ_4	0.386	0.159	0.313	0.257	3.338
	(0.218)	(0.152)	(0.182)	(0.198)	(1.467)
λ_5	0.363	0.529	0.409	0.251	0.049
	(0.182)	(0.267)	(0.177)	(0.150)	(0.705)
μ_1	−19.559	−15.558	−15.657	−20.043	−22.309
	(1.414)	(1.846)	(1.115)	(1.043)	(1.461)
μ_2	−28.825	−25.933	−24.120	−27.989	−27.923
	(1.461)	(1.093)	(0.908)	(0.847)	(1.439)
μ_3	−34.107	−28.000	−29.732	−30.446	−32.071
	(1.118)	(1.426)	(1.278)	(0.798)	(1.439)
μ_4	−34.610	−37.884	−33.045	−34.354	−40.985
	(1.836)	(2.536)	(1.731)	(2.037)	(3.225)
μ_5	−47.596	−35.875	−29.110	−37.350	−41.929
	(4.518)	(4.766)	(2.514)	(4.232)	(6.742)
μ_6	−57.703	−487.319	−304.628	−23.751	−71.774
	(20.439)	(197.750)	(95.847)	(42.877)	(2.084)
R^2	0.519	0.569	0.519	0.462	0.408

The point estimates of μ show a positive relationship with the level of education, thereby suggesting a systematic underestimation of life-cycle wealth for richer households. The extent of the underestimation is, however, limited. On average, it amounts to about 30 percent of average real and financial wealth.[25] Finally, the estimates of θ suggest that households do not apparently intend to consume between one half and three quarters of the real component of their total assets (as measured by their housing equity). In the next section, it will be shown that unrestricted borrowing mostly characterizes homeowners. Hence, the estimated θ's are to be interpreted as indicating precautionary asset accumulation or a bequest motive.

For a given rate of intertemporal preference ϱ and for a given level of education, the estimates of ψ imply an estimate of the intertemporal elasticity of substitution, $[1/(1 - \gamma)]$. Given equation (8), we obtain:

$$\frac{1}{1 - \gamma} = \frac{\ln[\psi(1 + r)]}{\ln[(1 + r)/\varrho]}. \tag{13}$$

Table 9.2 presents estimates of the intertemporal elasticity of substitution (and related asymptotic standard errors) by region, level of education and selected values of the rate of intertemporal preference, ϱ. The estimates turn out to be reasonable and, to a large extent, well determined, and suggest that the response of consumers to interest rate changes could be more pronounced than is usually expected.

Interestingly, Table 9.2 points to a non-negligible degree of heterogeneity across regions and education levels. Households living in Southern Italy and in the Islands show a consistently larger than average intertemporal elasticity of substitution, as do households with a poor level of education. Given equation (13) and the implied positive relationship between the intertemporal elasticity of substitution and the rate of time preference, the evidence presented in Table 9.2 could be read to imply, for a given elasticity of intertemporal substitution, a negative relationship between the rate of time preference and the level of income (as proxied by the level of education and geographical location). This finding, which parallels Lawrance's (1991), is particularly relevant in the present setting. If capital market imperfections are non-negligible (as will be suggested in the next section) impatient individuals may refuse careers that lead to high wages after a period of training and choose jobs with flat wage paths. Hence a negative correlation between time preference and permanent income results. Alternatively, and in our opinion more plausibly, the above result may be seen to confirm a time-honored sociological argument on attitudes to the deferment of consumption.

282   Livio Maccan, Nicola Rossi and Ignazio Visco

Table 9.2 Intertemporal elasticity of substitution

	North-west	North-east	Center	South	Islands
			$\varrho = 0.00$		
Level of education:					
None	1.068	-0.890	1.105	1.394	1.574
	(0.320)	(1.027)	(0.292)	(0.369)	(0.404)
Primary school	0.999	0.786	0.803	0.963	1.254
	(0.249)	(0.269)	(0.213)	(0.256)	(0.295)
High school	0.760	0.575	0.724	1.014	1.610
	(0.142)	(0.157)	(0.125)	(0.159)	(0.281)
Diploma	0.908	1.189	1.124	1.534	2.118
	(0.162)	(0.166)	(0.121)	(0.220)	(0.302)
College	0.487	-0.051	0.365	0.830	0.976
	(0.182)	(0.210)	(0.166)	(0.216)	(0.225)
Graduate school	0.480	1.007	1.431	1.243	1.628
	(0.205)	(0.264)	(0.247)	(0.339)	(0.285)
			$\varrho = 0.02$		
Level of education:					
None	3.237	-2.697	3.347	4.225	4.770
	(0.968)	(3.111)	(0.886)	(1.118)	(1.223)
Primary school	3.027	2.380	2.432	2.916	3.799
	(0.754)	(0.815)	(0.644)	(0.774)	(0.893)
High school	2.302	1.744	2.193	3.073	4.877
	(0.431)	(0.477)	(0.378)	(0.481)	(0.851)
Diploma	2.751	3.603	3.405	4.648	6.417
	(0.491)	(0.502)	(0.366)	(0.667)	(0.915)
College	1.476	-0.155	1.105	2.515	2.957
	(0.553)	(0.635)	(0.504)	(0.655)	(0.682)
Graduate school	1.454	3.050	4.337	3.765	4.931
	(0.621)	(0.798)	(0.747)	(1.026)	(0.863)

It should be noted that the above estimates are based on a sample from which observations were eliminated only when the relevant data was missing. In contrast with a fairly common practice, all the available information was used in the estimation process and (with the exception of the geographic location) no sample selection was made beforehand. To assess its performance, the model estimated on the basis of the whole sample was therefore compared with the results of estimations based on specific subsamples (defined by tenure class, occupational sector, age of the head of the household, etc.). F-tests were computed indicating that the null hypothesis of structural homogeneity among subsamples could not generally be rejected.

As a partial exception to the previous statement, dependent workers turned out to differ from the rest of the sample. In particular, their estimated θ's proved significantly lower than the average, which also includes self-employed and retired workers. However, the overall empirical results and their implications in terms of liquidity constraints are only marginally affected if the restricted subsample is taken into consideration. In the rest of this paper, we shall therefore discuss the empirical results based on the full sample.[26] Nevertheless, to allow a complete understanding of the results, Appendix B reports the full set of results based on the truncated sample.

The sample was also not purged to avoid major cases of possible underreporting (in particular, households receiving income from self-employment or farming). Mariger (1986) pointed out that, in the present context, measurement errors could be negligible. Nevertheless, in order to assess the performance of the model in this respect, Hausman's (1978) test for measurement errors was computed assuming labor income to be measured with error. The relevant normally distributed test statistics rejected the hypothesis of contemporaneous correlation between the errors and the named regressor in three out of five regions for customary confidence levels.[27]

4 Planning horizons and borrowing constraints

Figures 9.1 and 9.2 and Tables 9.3 and 9.4 revert to the central theme of this paper and provide an estimate of single-period planning horizons (in other words, liquidity constraints). As it turns out, 1,976 households (out of 7,170, i.e. 27.6 percent) appear to experience single period planning horizons. The extent of liquidity constraints is least in the North-west of Italy (24.3 percent) and greatest in the South (31.0 percent). As Figure 9.1 and Table 9.3 show, slightly more than one third of liquidity-constrained households are headed by persons aged 31-45 (731 households out of 1,976). Younger households account for slightly more than 4 percent of the liquidity-constrained households while households headed by retired workers (aged 61 or over) account for more than 30 percent of the total. Finally, the distribution of liquidity constraints by sex, education and occupation of the head-of-household and by household size is apparently dominated by the distribution of these characteristics in the sample.

However, the distribution of liquidity constraints should not be confused with their incidence. As Figure 9.2 and Table 9.4 show, about 39 percent of households whose heads are over 75 appear to experience single-period planning horizons. The incidence is slightly lower (34 percent) for household heads in their thirties and early forties. Interestingly, the pattern is not homogeneous throughout the country. Liquidity constraints tend to be concentrated among the elderly in Northern and Central Italy, while they tend to prevail in younger households in Southern Italy and the Islands. Throughout the country, the incidence of liquidity constraints among households headed by females is almost double that among households headed by males. Moreover, it decreases markedly as the level of education rises, the fall being much sharper in the North-western and North-eastern regions. Interestingly, a clear-cut distinction between self-employed heads and dependent workers shows up only in the South and in the Islands, while liquidity constraints tend to prevail among large households. Finally, it should be noted that liquidity constraints are experienced exclusively by non-homeowners. In all regions, nearly all liquidity constraints refer to tenants with right of redemption or renters *tout-court*.

Figure 9.1

Age distribution of liquidity constraints by region
(single-period planning horizons, 1987)

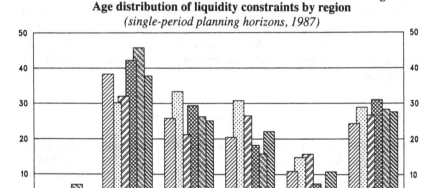

Head count is, however, not very informative. The crucial information is given by the proportion of total consumption attributable to liquidity-constrained households. This is seen to vary between 14.9 percent in North-west Italy and 22.5 percent in the South, averaging 18.3 throughout Italy, despite the higher propensity to consume of liquidity-constrained households (about 0.95 compared with an average propensity to consume of around 0.77). This is not to imply, though, that liquidity-constrained households uniformly show very large propensities to consume. On the contrary, a substantial fraction of liquidity-constrained households (between 25 and 50 percent) actually save a fair amount of their current income. Most tenants, in particular, are forced to do so by the tenure choice profile implied by equation (6).

Table 9.3 Distribution of liquidity constraints by household characteristics and region (1987, in percent)

	North-west	North-east	Center	South	Islands	Italy
Head's age:						
Under 31	4.5	3.9	4.5	2.8	7.1	4.3
31-45	38.3	30.2	32.0	42.2	45.8	37.8
46-60	25.8	33.4	21.3	29.4	26.3	25.1
61-75	20.5	30.8	26.5	18.2	15.8	22.1
Over 75	10.9	14.8	15.7	7.4	5.0	10.8
Head's sex:						
Male	65.4	58.0	63.3	81.8	74.2	69.4
Female	34.6	42.0	36.7	18.2	25.8	30.6
Head's education:						
None	9.0	12.8	13.6	15.2	17.9	13.3
Primary school	35.0	49.8	45.1	37.2	34.6	39.8
High school	36.3	23.9	23.1	30.7	28.3	29.4
Diploma	14.8	10.2	12.9	13.6	14.2	13.3
University	4.9	3.3	5.2	3.4	5.0	4.3
Head's occupation:						
Self-employed	41.2	55.7	51.2	45.4	35.8	45.9
Dependent worker	58.8	44.3	48.8	54.6	64.2	54.1
Household's size:						
1	23.4	27.2	26.8	11.0	13.3	20.0
2	26.0	27.9	27.0	13.6	12.5	21.5
3	21.9	21.0	20.7	16.7	23.3	20.3
4	21.9	16.4	20.7	30.5	34.6	24.7
5 and over	6.8	7.5	4.7	28.3	16.3	13.5

These results should be contrasted with the findings of Jappelli and Pagano (1988) and Guiso and Jappelli (1994) which rely on exogenously given criteria to identify liquidity-constrained consumers. Jappelli and Pagano (1988) apply Hayashi's (1985) methodology to Italian data. Setting the sample selection rule (i.e. the threshold above which liquidity constraints are supposed to operate) at a propensity to save below 15 percent, they estimate the difference between the propensity to consume of liquidity-constrained households and the average propensity to consume at about 10 percentage points.[28] It has, however, been convincingly argued that if the differences between the Italian and U.S. samples are taken into account, the results could be substantially altered and the relevance of liquidity constraints reduced (Marotta, 1988).

Figure 9.2

Incidence of liquidity constraints by age and region
(single-period planning horizons, 1987)

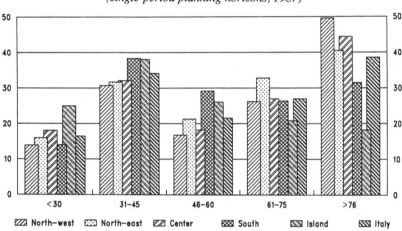

On the basis of direct information (available in the 1987 Bank of Italy SHIW) on consumers turned down (or expecting to be turned down) in the credit market, both Jappelli and Pagano (1988) and Guiso and Jappelli (1994) conclude that 15.6 percent of the household population (or 1,249 households out of 8,027) can be considered as liquidity-constrained (i.e., with desired consumption exceeding available resources). Again, the propensity to consume of constrained households is some 10 percentage points above the average. By comparing the compositions of constrained and unconstrained subsamples (thereby implicitly arriving at measures such as those reported in Table 9.4), Guiso and Jappelli observe that liquidity constraints mostly affect young households (under 30), non-homeowners and households with a lower level of education.

As already mentioned, in the first case, the arbitrary threshold level focuses exclusively on liquidity constraints in the strict sense, i.e. on the case of single-period planning horizons coinciding with higher than average propensities to consume.[29] In the second case, however, the direct information misses all borrowing constraints arising in the mortgage market. Moreover, out of 1,249 constrained households, only 55 (less than 1 percent of the sampled households) had actually applied for a loan and been refused credit, the remaining 1,194 households having not applied for a loan because they expected their application to be rejected. It is open to question whether "discouraged borrowers" should be regarded as straightforward evidence of binding constraints at work. The present estimates make only partial reference to direct external indicators and generate consumption time paths endogenously, which accommodate both single-period and multiperiod planning horizons. Moreover, single-period planning horizons are not confined to cases of propensities to consume near unity, but can also arise in the event of forced saving toward downpayment. As a result, if the different sample selection rules are properly accounted for, an under-estimation of the extent of liquidity constraints and a somewhat different composition of those constraints should come as no surprise.

Table 9.4 Incidence of liquidity constraints by household characteristics and region (1987, in percent)

	North-west	North-east	Center	South	Islands	Italy
Overall	24.3	28.9	26.7	31.0	28.3	27.6
Head's age:						
Under 31	13.9	16.0	18.1	14.0	25.0	16.5
31-45	30.7	31.7	32.1	38.4	38.1	34.1
46-60	16.8	21.3	18.2	29.2	26.1	21.5
61-75	26.2	32.8	27.0	26.4	20.8	27.0
Over 75	49.6	40.5	44.4	31.5	18.2	38.9
Head's sex:						
Male	20.4	24.3	22.7	30.8	27.3	24.8
Female	38.6	39.4	38.6	31.6	32.0	36.6
Head's education:						
None	46.9	52.0	35.1	37.1	34.1	39.2
Primary school	30.9	34.7	31.9	34.0	31.4	32.6
High school	28.2	30.4	30.6	40.0	35.2	32.3
Diploma	14.8	14.6	15.7	20.7	19.3	16.8
University	9.8	11.2	14.4	11.0	13.6	11.6
Head's occupation:						
Self-employed	22.4	28.2	26.5	27.1	19.8	25.1
Dependent worker	25.9	29.9	26.9	35.2	27.3	30.1
Household's size:						
1	46.2	43.0	44.9	36.6	33.7	42.3
2	25.0	31.6	27.3	22.3	17.6	25.3
3	17.3	23.4	21.8	27.6	30.4	22.4
4	21.7	21.8	24.8	32.7	32.8	26.8
5 and over	23.2	25.6	12.6	36.1	26.9	28.1

The present setting, however, does more than merely identify consumers who are currently liquidity-constrained (single-period planning horizons). It also makes it possible to detect consumers who expect to be constrained in the future (multiperiod planning horizons). To clarify this point, Tables 9.5-9.9 present, by region, the distribution of households by age of household's head and length of the planning horizon. The age information in each cell refers to the average age of the head of household in the period under observation while bold characters in each section of the tables indicate the head's approximate age in the last period of the current planning horizon. Moreover, for each cell, the tables report the cell's weight in terms of aggregate consumption and its average propensity to consume. In reading Tables 9.5-9.9 it is crucial to recall that, in the present model, the cutoff point is determined endogenously so as to ensure that the time path of household consumption satisfies the intertemporal budget constraint, given the household's preferences and composition. As a result, single-period planning horizons show up whenever current resources are relatively small in relation to lifetime resources. This does not imply, however, that liquidity-constrained households should necessarily be characterized by a propensity to consume equal to one.

For example, from Table 9.5 (top left) it can be inferred that in the North-west region there are 65 liquidity-constrained young households (that is 3.1 percent of the sample) whose consumption, given an average propensity to consume (apc) of 1.1, amounts to 2.6 percent of the aggregate consumption of the sample. The heads of these households are, on average, 31 years old and, obviously, their current planning horizon, being a single period one, will expire before they reach 35 years of age. We also observe (bottom right) that 38.4 percent of the households sampled actually present planning horizons lasting for more than 50 years and account for more than 45 percent of the aggregate consumption in the sample. The heads of households are on average 40 years old, the average propensity to consume is around 0.63 and their planning horizons are expected to expire when the head of household is 85 or over. Between the two extremes, a wide variety of combinations can be observed. However, though, figures naturally tend to cluster below the main diagonal where older households and shorter planning horizons prevail. In particular, in Tables 9.5-9.9, the figures relating to households whose planning horizons extend, in all likelihood, to the end of the life cycle have been set in italics. They amount to between two thirds and three quarters of the sample.

A glance at Tables 9.5-9.9 indicates that short multiperiod planning horizons are not very frequent. Setting aside the short planning horizons of old households, less than 2 percent of the households sampled have horizons that extend for only a few years. Among these, constraints associated with family composition are seldom observed.

Table 9.5 North-west. Household distribution by age of the head and length of the planning horizon (number of observations: 2,105)

	Length of the planning horizon (in years)					
	1	2-10	11-30	31-50	> 50	Total
Age: (<35)	31	23				31
% of expenditure	2.631	0.049				2.680
% of households	3.088	0.048				3.135
apc	1.150	1.202				1.150
Age: (36-45)	39	30	26			39
% of expenditure	5.177	0.076	0.197			5.450
% of households	6.556	0.143	0.095			6.793
apc	0.799	0.724	0.942			0.800
Age: (46-55)	49		30			48
% of expenditure	3.782		0.042			3.824
% of households	5.701		0.095			5.796
apc	0.732		0.406			0.726
Age: (56-65)	60	59	48			59
% of expenditure	1.452	0.290	0.223			1.964
% of households	2.423	0.285	0.190			2.898
apc	0.971	1.143	1.007			0.990
Age: (66-75)	69	63	58			68
% of expenditure	2.268	0.222	0.127			2.617
% of households	3.753	0.143	0.143			4.038
apc	1.099	1.016	0.893			1.089
Age: (76-85)	79	74	60	48		72
% of expenditure	1.404	0.121	1.184	0.366		3.001
% of households	2.423	0.095	0.998	0.238		3.705
apc	1.274	1349	0.967	0.793		1.166
Age: (>85)	87	80	*75*	*59*	*40*	50
% of expenditure	0.222	0.111	*5.922*	*29.125*	*45.009*	80.389
% of households	0.380	0.048	*6.366*	*28.361*	*38.432*	73.587
apc	1.440	1.088	*1.034*	*0.600*	*0.634*	0.660
Total	52	55	71	58	40	51
% of expenditure	16.937	0.868	7.695	29.491	45.009	100.00
% of households	24.323	0.760	7.886	28.599	38.432	100.00
apc	0.948	1.067	1.014	0.602	0.634	0.734

Table 9.6 North-east. Household distribution by age of the head and length of the planning horizon (number of observations: 1,054)

	Length of the planning horizon (in years)					
	1	2-10	11-30	31-50	> 50	Total
Age: (**<35**)	32	28				31
% of expenditure	3.074	0.467				3.541
% of households	3.131	0.285				3.416
apc	1.066	1.002				1.060
Age: (**36-45**)	40	32	25			39
% of expenditure	4.373	0.168	0.349			4.889
% of households	6.072	0.190	0.285			6.546
apc	0.724	0.437	1.134			0.734
Age: (**46-55**)	49		31			49
% of expenditure	3.197		0.320			3.517
% of households	4.744		0.190			4.934
apc	0.719		0.760			0.720
Age: (**56-65**)	60	57	52			59
% of expenditure	1.942	0.635	0.388			2.965
% of households	3.131	0.569	0.380			4.080
apc	0.864	0.969	0.901			0.882
Age: (**66-75**)	70	64	53			68
% of expenditure	4.470	0.388	0.969			5.828
% of households	7.400	0.380	0.759			8.539
apc	1.070	1.208	1.029			1.072
Age: (**76-85**)	80	74	65	48		75
% of expenditure	2.439	0.184	1.863	0.150		4.636
% of households	3.795	0.190	1.328	0.095		5.408
apc	1.256	0.885	1.219	0.902		1.228
Age: (**>85**)	87	89	*76*	*60*	*39*	54
% of expenditure	0.393	0.228	*10.770*	*25.524*	*37.709*	74.624
% of households	0.664	0.190	*11.480*	*25.142*	*29.602*	67.078
apc	1.196	1.136	*0.991*	*0.651*	*0.653*	0.717
Total	57	56	71	60	39	54
% of expenditure	19.889	2.070	14.659	25.674	37.709	100.00
% of households	28.937	1.803	14.421	25.237	29.602	100.00
apc	0.944	0.977	1.012	0.652	0.653	0.795

Table 9.7   Center. Household distribution by age of the head and length of the planning horizon (number of observations: 1,427)

	Length of the planning horizon (in years)					
	1	2-10	11-30	31-50	> 50	Total
Age: (<35)	31	29				31
% of expenditure	3.135	0.113				3.248
% of households	2.943	0.070				3.013
apc	1.055	0.877				1.051
Age: (36-45)	39	33	25			39
% of expenditure	5.079	0.207	0.047			5.333
% of households	6.237	0.070	0.140			6.447
apc	0.738	0.904	0.498			0.734
Age: (46-55)	49		28			49
% of expenditure	2.633		0.062			2.695
% of households	4.064		0.070			4.135
apc	0.648		0.873			0.652
Age: (56-65)	60	58	51			59
% of expenditure	2.934	0.809	0.385			4.148
% of households	4.415	0.561	0.350			5.326
apc	0.876	0.929	1.119			0.898
Age: (66-75)	69	62	57			67
% of expenditure	2.646	0.592	1.053			4.290
% of households	4.205	0.491	0.771			5.466
apc	1.023	1.173	0.882			1.016
Age: (76-85)	79	74	61	49		72
% of expenditure	2.636	0.260	2.095	0.270		5.261
% of households	3.994	0.210	1.682	0.280		6.167
apc	1.117	1.476	1.059	0.697		1.094
Age: (>85)	89		*76*	*60*	*39*	54
% of expenditure	0.520		*9.642*	*28.516*	*36.369*	75.046
% of households	0.841		*10.652*	*27.610*	*30.343*	69.446
apc	1.107		*0.988*	*0.671*	*0.652*	0.716
Total	55	59	71	60	39	54
% of expenditure	19.582	1.980	13.283	28.785	36.369	100.00
% of households	26.699	1.402	13.665	27.891	30.343	100.00
apc	0.895	1.093	0.988	0.671	0.652	0.774

Table 9.8 South. Household distribution by age of the head and length of the planning horizon (number of observations: 1,737)

	Length of the planning horizon (in years)					
	1	2-10	11-30	31-50	> 50	Total
Age: (**<35**)	32					32
% of expenditure	3.540					3.540
% of households	3.339					3.339
apc	1.322					1.322
Age: (**36-45**)	40	30	26			39
% of expenditure	7.785	0.098	0.092			7.975
% of households	9.499	0.230	0.173			9.902
apc	0.805	0.578	0.591			0.796
Age: (**46-55**)	49					49
% of expenditure	5.857					5.857
% of households	7.599					7.599
apc	0.727					0.727
Age: (**56-65**)	59	57	46			58
% of expenditure	3.075	0.074	0.244			3.393
% of households	3.972	0.058	0.230			4.260
apc	0.940	1.222	1.016			0.948
Age: (**66-75**)	69	67				69
% of expenditure	2.958	0.005				2.964
% of households	3.685	0.058				3.742
apc	1.223	0.162				1.206
Age: (**76-85**)	79	75	60			77
% of expenditure	1.763	0.050	0.401			2.214
% of households	2.476	0.058	0.345			2.879
apc	1.281	0.586	1.192			1.256
Age: (**>85**)	89	90	*77*	*60*	*39*	52
% of expenditure	0.258	0.465	*8.521*	*26.050*	*38.763*	74.057
% of households	0.403	0.403	*8.693*	*25.792*	*32.988*	68.279
apc	1.360	1.998	*1.036*	*0.660*	*0.642*	0.711
Total	51	68	74	60	39	52
% of expenditure	25.237	0.692	9.259	26.050	38.763	100.00
% of households	30.973	0.806	9.442	25.792	32.988	100.00
apc	0.954	1.305	1.033	0.660	0.642	0.785

Table 9.9 Islands. Household distribution by age of the head and length of the planning horizon (number of observations: 847)

	Length of the planning horizon (in years)					
	1	2-10	11-30	31-50	> 50	Total
Age: (<35)	31	25				31
% of expenditure	5.545	0.149				5.694
% of households	4.959	0.236				5.195
apc	1.492	1.020				1.471
Age: (36-45)	39	34	30			39
% of expenditure	8.399	0.439	0.491			9.328
% of households	9.445	0.472	0.590			10.508
apc	0.861	0.669	0.613			0.838
Age: (46-55)	49	41	35			48
% of expenditure	3.788	0.105	0.232			4.124
% of households	5.313	0.118	0.236			5.667
apc	0.705	0.593	0.594			0.698
Age: (56-65)	59		52			59
% of expenditure	2.771		0.175			2.946
% of households	4.132		0.118			4.250
apc	0.899		1.306			0.910
Age: (66-75)	69		50			67
% of expenditure	1.986		0.282			2.268
% of households	2.952		0.354			3.306
apc	1.280		1.267			1.279
Age: (76-85)	78	68	61	50		71
% of expenditure	1.073	0.165	0.738	0.537		2.513
% of households	1.299	0.118	0.708	0.118		2.243
apc	1.364	1.252	1.012	0.768		1.215
Age: (>85)	92	91	*77*	*61*	*39*	53
% of expenditure	0.134	0.215	*12.053*	*22.839*	*37.885*	73.126
% of households	0.236	0.118	*11.452*	*24.557*	*32.468*	68.831
apc	2.187	2.093	*1.056*	*0.605*	*0.591*	0.681
Total	48	43	72	61	39	51
% of expenditure	23.695	1.073	13.970	23.376	37.885	100.00
% of households	28.335	1.063	13.459	24.675	32.468	100.00
apc	1.025	0.962	1.033	0.606	0.591	0.781

It should be noted, however, that this is to a large extent an artifact of the specific form of the borrowing constraint for tenants. If a simple non-negativity constraint is taken instead, as in Mariger (1986, 1987), a substantial number of short multiperiod horizons shows up from the model estimates (about 10 percent of the households sampled, most of them elderly) while single-period planning horizons are considerably reduced. Clearly, the length of the planning horizon should not be confused with the situation of the household at time t. Hence, this result should not be taken to imply that "currently" constrained households disappear if, in contrast to equation (6), no forced accumulation plan is assumed. Since multiperiod planning horizons still imply that current consumption is different from that prevailing under unrestricted borrowing, constrained households would be reduced only partially and would still account for a substantial fraction of the sample. In particular, currently constrained households would amount, on average, to about 15 percent of the sample, reaching 23 percent in the North-east region and falling to 8 percent in the North-west one.

A formal test of the two competing non-nested models is therefore in order. While they both dominate a simple life-cycle representation with unrestricted borrowing, a formal comparison by means of a simple non-nested J test suggests that both models should be rejected in favor of a composite artificial alternative. We therefore stick, on *a priori* grounds, to the present model with the proviso, however, that the results shown in this paper should be considered as an upper limit. Quite clearly, though, the implications of the above transcend the present paper and overshadow much of the literature on liquidity constraints by pointing out that still little is known about saving behavior under restricted borrowing.

5 Concluding remarks

The empirical results reported in this paper suggest that liquidity constraints are indeed an important feature of the Italian economy. Depending on the model specification, it is estimated that restricted borrowing affects between one sixth and one fourth of the population. If due care is taken of a number of differences in the underlying empirical analysis, this finding is roughly in agreement with the conclusions of Jappelli and Pagano (1988) and Guiso and Jappelli (1994). The present results also permit an analysis of the role of short multiperiod planning horizons which cannot be detected by other methodologies relying on indirect indicators of borrowing restrictions.

The composition of liquidity constraints and their incidence on specific segments of the population, however, differ somewhat from those observed by Jappelli and Pagano (1988), and Guiso and Jappelli (1994). Again, this is partly due to the sample selection rules adopted in the analysis. It is true, however, that the present paper highlights the importance of liquidity constraints for the elderly more than do previous papers. With regard to other segments of the population, the conclusions are more disappointing: in this paper, as in earlier literature, the actual extent and distribution of liquidity constraints turn out to be highly model-dependent, suggesting that further efforts should be devoted to modeling the saving behavior of liquidity-constrained households.

APPENDIX A

The data

Household composition. For each household in the sample the time path (in the household life cycle) of the following variables was reconstructed: (i) number of main adults (usually parents) in the household (n_t^a), (ii) number of children in the three age-groups (0-5, n_t^i, 6-14, n_t^f, and 15-19, n_t^g), and (iii) number of other adults (n_t^o).

The number of main adults in a household (usually two) is a decreasing function of time, owing to a non-zero (and increasing with age) probability of death. Mortality tables (Istat, 1987) by age and sex were used to define the time profile (in the life cycle) of this variable, excluding divorces for married couples and new marriages for single parents.

The time profile of children in the three age-groups mentioned above assumes, for simplicity, a zero mortality rate. It should be noted that, given the role played by young families, the possibility of new births was allowed for by carefully reconstructing a fertility table by age and family composition, based on the work of Livi Bacci and Santini (1969). For simplicity, only women over 25, without children, were assumed to have a child in families where both parents are present.

Children over 20 were counted as "other adults" along with all the other members of the household (mostly elderly). However, while the elderly are subject to a standard mortality rate, children over 20 are subject to the mortality rate as well as to an "exit rate" which, on the basis of available information (Bonato, 1985), differs by age, sex and household composition and is assumed to be unity at age 35.

Life-cycle wealth. Life-cycle wealth in the time interval $[t, s]$ is defined as follows:

$$w_t^s = a_t + y_t + \sum_{j=1}^{n_t^l} \sum_{i=t+1}^{t+1+m_j} y_{ij}^l (1 + r)^{t-1} + \sum_{j=1}^{n_t^p} \sum_{i=t+1}^{s} y_{ij}^p (1 + r)^{t-1} \qquad (A.1)$$

where $m_j = \max[0, \min(35 - n_{tj})]$ if the income recipient is a son and $m_j = s - t$ otherwise. In equation (A.1) n_{tj} is the age of the j-th income recipient in period t; n_t^l is the number of household members earning labor income in period t; n_t^p denotes the number of household members receiving a pension (old age or disability) in t; a_t is the household net worth at the beginning of period t; y_t indicates household disposable income in period t; y_{ij}^l represents the labor income earned in period i by the j-th recipient; y_{ij}^p is the pension transfer received in period i from the j-th recipient. The net real interest rate, r, is assumed to be given and equal to 3 percent per annum.

The definitions of real assets and of disposable income follow the Survey's guidelines. Financial assets are not directly provided in the Survey and have been estimated by capitalizing the interest flow reported in the Survey with the 1987 average rate of return on households' financial assets. Expected labor income profiles up to the age of retirement for each adult in the sample have been generated assuming (i) that annual hours worked will remain constant until retirement, (ii) that the ratio of an individual's hourly wage to the average hourly wage of the appropriate age-sex-education cell will remain constant, and (iii) that average hourly wages for each cell will grow at an annual growth rate of 3 percent. It should be outlined that these hypotheses were applied to the reconstruction of labor income profiles for both dependent and self-employed workers.

Dependent and self-employed workers have been considered separately in the estimation of retirement income in order to account fully for the different institutional settings. It has been assumed that up to one half of social security wealth is indistinguishable from other forms of wealth in its effect on consumption. It is worth noting, however, that preliminary experiments indicated a fairly flat likelihood over the plausible range of the parameter measuring the replacement effect. Indeed, the results reported in the main text are very similar to those obtained in a one-for-one replacement.

Minimal net worth. In the definition of the minimal allowable equity in real assets (equation (4)), two mortgage schedules were adopted. The first, for durable goods, is a five-year mortgage schedule. The second, for housing and business property, is a fifteen-year mortgage.

With regard to the expected downpayment (equation (6)), the conditional probability of buying a house is derived from the age distribution of first-time buyers as in the 1987 Bank of Italy SHIW. The percentage downpayment is fixed at 50 percent and the value of the house is equal to the average value of houses bought by first-time buyers in the relevant age band.

APPENDIX B

The subsample of dependent workers

Table 9.B1 reports the parameter estimates for the five regions and their heteroscedasticity-corrected standard errors as derived from the subsample of dependent workers. The restricted subsample contains 1,163 observations from the North-west, 452 from the North-east, 691 from the Center, 836 from Southern Italy and, finally, 413 from the Islands. It should be noted that testing for measurement errors indicates that these seem, as expected, to be confined entirely to self-employed workers. By comparison with the whole sample, dependent workers apparently intend not to consume a lower fraction (between zero and one half) of their real wealth. Moreover, the proportionality factor converting old people into adults of less than 64 years of age tends to be lower in the subsample of dependent workers, while no definite pattern emerges for equivalence scales concerning children of different ages and other members of the households.

The intertemporal elasticity of substitution is presented in Table 9.B2. In comparison with the evidence presented in Table 9.2, Table 9.B2 suggests a much weaker negative relationship between the rate of time preference and the level of income as proxied by the level of education, while the geographical location still seems to work in the same direction as in Table 9.2.

The distribution and incidence of liquidity contraints by household characteristics and regions are presented in Tables 9.B3 and 9.B4. If the estimation is carried out on the subsample of dependent workers liquidity-constrained households total to 39.7 percent in the Islands and 27.8 percent in Central Italy and average to 32.0 percent throughout Italy. If due care is taken of the different sample composition, their distribution and incidence generally parallel those of the full sample.

As for the estimates based on the full sample, the extent and distribution of liquidity constraints turn out to be highly model dependent. If the non-negativity constraint (5) is imposed on tenants, liquidity constraints almost vanish. They average about 2 percent throughout Italy, reaching a maximum of 6.8 percent in the Islands and a minimum of 0.2 percent in the South.

Table 9.B1 Parameter estimates of the consumption function with liquidity constraints. Subsample of dependent workers

	North-west	North-east	Center	South	Islands
θ	0.517 (0.102)	0.329 (0.118)	0.223 (0.125)	0.283 (0.106)	−0.047 (0.253)
ψ_1	0.982 (0.004)	0.994 (0.020)	0.993 (0.008)	1.043 (0.116)	0.999 (0.012)
ψ_2	0.998 (0.005)	0.993 (0.006)	0.979 (0.005)	0.996 (0.005)	0.993 (0.007)
ψ_3	0.988 (0.004)	0.988 (0.005)	0.989 (0.003)	1.000 (0.006)	0.991 (0.006)
ψ_4	1.009 (0.003)	1.002 (0.003)	1.000 (0.003)	1.013 (0.004)	1.001 (0.005)
ψ_5	0.993 (0.005)	0.982 (0.006)	0.978 (0.004)	0.994 (0.005)	0.989 (0.006)
ψ_6	1.000 (0.007)	0.996 (0.009)	1.006 (0.015)	1.016 (0.008)	1.088 (0.023)
λ_1	0.175 (0.050)	0.437 (0.081)	0.578 (0.133)	0.357 (0.089)	0.680 (0.276)
λ_2	0.585 (0.137)	0.243 (0.166)	0.269 (0.121)	0.316 (0.142)	0.627 (0.368)
λ_3	0.320 (0.191)	−0.091 (0.200)	0.045 (0.120)	0.367 (0.223)	0.533 (0.335)
λ_4	0.598 (0.174)	0.043 (0.156)	0.233 (0.124)	0.355 (0.175)	0.643 (0.345)
λ_5	0.284 (0.123)	0.196 (0.181)	0.125 (0.110)	0.404 (0.155)	0.683 (0.343)
μ_1	−35.388 (3.256)	−31.683 (2.479)	−26.338 (3.118)	−32.476 (2.750)	−29.570 (2.394)
μ_2	−37.918 (2.000)	−36.184 (1.517)	−34.573 (1.317)	−31.840 (0.790)	−34.460 (2.023)
μ_3	−35.188 (1.059)	−32.190 (1.419)	−31.243 (1.361)	−32.114 (0.798)	−31.230 (1.334)
μ_4	−39.196 (1.797)	−36.391 (2.616)	−33.429 (1.574)	−34.677 (1.621)	−42.034 (2.776)
μ_5	−38.526 (3.759)	−27.699 (3.706)	−30.742 (2.925)	−33.856 (3.981)	−39.796 (8.375)
μ_6	−47.966 (6.681)	−214.852 (124.082)	−183.496 (265.016)	−42.936 (5.831)	−4,018.180 (2,693.450)
R^2	0.565	0.667	0.514	0.507	0.615

Table 9.B2 Intertemporal elasticity of substitution. Subsample of dependent workers

	North-west	North-east	Center	South	Islands
			$\varrho = 0.00$		
Level of education:					
None	0.387	0.805	0.907	2.410	0.960
	(0.129)	(0.695)	(0.274)	(0.423)	(0.402)
Primary school	0.946	0.768	0.288	0.855	0.759
	(0.181)	(0.196)	(0.178)	(0.168)	(0.240)
High school	0.922	0.585	0.634	1.007	0.685
	(0.124)	(0.170)	(0.110)	(0.193)	(0.207)
Diploma	1.313	1.066	0.996	1.432	1.048
	(0.099)	(0.117)	(0.109)	(0.147)	(0.179)
College	0.752	0.379	0.235	0.783	0.630
	(0.158)	(0.214)	(0.155)	(0.159)	(0.213)
Graduate school	1.015	0.865	1.206	1.543	3.838
	(0.232)	(0.289)	(0.520)	(0.278)	(0.719)
			$\varrho = 0.02$		
Level of education:					
None	1.173	2.439	2.749	7.302	2.908
	(0.390)	(2.107)	(0.829)	(1.282)	(1.218)
Primary school	2.865	2.327	0.873	2.591	2.299
	(0.547)	(0.593)	(0.539)	(0.569)	(0.729)
High school	2.792	1.771	1.921	3.052	2.076
	(0.377)	(0.516)	(0.333)	(0.584)	(0.626)
Diploma	3.977	3.228	3.018	4.339	3.176
	(0.299)	(0.356)	(0.329)	(0.445)	(0.541)
College	2.278	1.149	0.713	2.372	1.909
	(0.479)	(0.648)	(0.468)	(0.483)	(0.645)
Graduate school	3.076	2.620	3.653	4.674	11.630
	(0.704)	(0.877)	(1.574)	(0.842)	(2.179)

Table 9.B3 Distribution of liquidity constraints by household characteristics and region. Subsample of dependent workers (1987, in percent)

	North-west	North-east	Center	South	Islands	Italy
Head's age:						
Under 31	7.8	10.7	9.4	3.9	14.0	8.3
31-45	56.1	61.4	59.9	63.0	59.1	59.7
46-60	34.6	27.1	30.2	32.5	25.0	31.0
Over 61	1.5	0.7	0.5	0.6	1.8	1.1
Head's sex:						
Male	82.4	77.9	79.2	96.1	89.6	86.0
Female	17.6	22.1	20.8	3.9	10.4	14.0
Head's education:						
None	1.5	2.9	2.1	4.5	8.5	3.6
Primary school	26.0	34.3	29.7	33.1	27.4	29.8
High school	47.5	37.1	37.0	39.0	40.9	27.2
Diploma	18.2	19.3	20.8	19.2	18.9	19.1
University	6.6	6.4	10.4	4.2	4.3	6.2
Household size:						
1	9.6	10.7	12.5	1.6	3.0	7.1
2	18.5	14.3	16.1	5.2	7.9	12.5
3	29.6	30.0	29.7	14.0	25.0	24.8
4	32.8	30.7	33.3	42.1	45.1	36.7
5 and over	9.6	14.3	8.3	38.0	18.9	19.0

Table 9.B4   Incidence of liquidity constraints by household characteristics and region. Subsample of dependent workers (1987, in percent)

	North-west	North-east	Center	South	Islands	Italy
Overall	28.8	31.0	27.8	36.8	39.7	32.0
Head's age:						
Under 31	19.1	23.8	21.4	16.7	45.1	23.2
31-45	38.4	40.2	38.0	45.8	45.8	41.4
46-60	22.7	24.1	20.5	33.0	29.5	25.3
Over 61	17.2	6.7	4.8	5.7	27.3	10.8
Head's sex:						
Male	27.3	29.3	26.0	38.0	39.3	31.4
Female	39.1	38.8	37.4	20.7	43.6	36.6
Head's education:						
None	55.5	57.1	26.7	45.2	66.7	49.4
Primary school	34.9	38.4	31.3	43.0	46.9	38.1
High school	36.7	39.4	36.0	46.5	50.4	40.7
Diploma	18.1	21.4	18.9	26.1	26.3	21.4
University	17.7	14.5	23.5	15.5	15.6	17.8
Household's size:						
1	50.8	42.9	52.2	25.0	50.0	46.6
2	26.1	27.0	26.7	20.8	29.5	25.9
3	23.1	26.8	25.9	30.0	44.6	27.1
4	32.9	31.2	29.8	39.1	41.1	35.1
5 and over	32.0	41.7	17.0	43.2	35.6	36.0

NOTES

* We would like to thank Albert Ando, Daniele Franco, Luigi Guiso, Marco Pagano, Dino Rizzi and Daniele Terlizzese for their most helpful comments and criticisms and Giampaolo Lopez and Renato Serafini for their help in handling the data. Nicola Rossi gratefully aknowledges partial financial support from the Italian National Research Council. The usual disclaimer applies.
1 For recent surveys see Deaton (1992, Ch. 6) and Meghir and Weber (1993).
2 Jappelli and Pagano (1989) provide evidence on the extent of liquidity constraints based on aggregate national accounts data. As Deaton (1991) has observed, such evidence cannot be unambiguously interpreted as suggesting the presence (or absence) of capital market imperfections.
3 See also Kennickell (1984, Ch. 4) and Ando and Kennickell (1987).

4 Notice that period $T+1$, when the head of the household is no longer living, may coincide with the birth of a new household.

5 The λ's affect the time path of consumption, leaving life-cycle resources unchanged. In particular, λ_1 is likely to shift expected consumption downward when the head of the household reaches 65.

6 In the following it will be assumed that b_i ($\forall$ i) is non-stochastic.

7 This is not to say that θ measures the extent of intentional intergenerational transfers. Lifetime uncertainty would cause the family to accumulate precautionary asset reserves as well.

8 On the peculiarities of the Italian mortgage market, see Beltratti and Fornero (1990), and Guiso et al. (1994).

9 Other forms of real wealth for which a downpayment could, in principle, be required are therefore neglected.

10 It should be clearly understood that constrained and unconstrained households are assumed to share identical preferences and an identical time path for the household's labor income. They differ only in regard of the budget constraint. As long as liquidity-constrained households present a more rapidly rising labor income profile, the above assumption (which characterizes most, if not all, of the literature on the subject) may lead to an understatement of the extent of liquidity constraints.

11 It should be recalled that Yaari's (1965) model does not apply to a multiple-person family.

12 Hence, T should be interpreted as the maximum age with non-zero probability of survival.

13 It is implicitly assumed here that uncertain lifetimes do not involve any additional risk for the household.

14 The following education levels have been considered: (i) none, (ii) primary school, (iii) high school, (iv) diploma, (v) college, (vi) graduate school.

15 Interestingly in the present work, any attempt to let θ vary with the level of education (or with other household characteristics) met with failure.

16 Following White (1980), the variance-covariance matrix of parameter estimates presented below allows for heteroscedasticity.

17 Notice that π_i and ϕ are not parameters to be estimated. On the construction of the expected downpayment variable see Appendix A.

18 It should be noticed that the present sample is nine times larger than Mariger's (1986, 1987) original sample of families surveyed in the 1964 U.S. Survey of Changes in Financial Characteristics of Consumers.

19 Piemonte, Valle d'Aosta, Lombardia, Liguria. Number of observations: 2,105.

20 Veneto, Trentino-Alto Adige, Friuli-Venezia Giulia, Emilia-Romagna. Number of observations: 1,054.

21 Toscana, Umbria, Marche, Lazio, Abruzzi, Molise. Number of observations: 1,427.

22 Campania, Puglia, Basilicata, Calabria. Number of observations: 1,737.

23 Sicilia, Sardegna. Number of observations: 847.

24 In the present setting, this result should imply an age-dependent structure of preferences. However, as Mariger (1987) has suggested, it could also be taken to imply non-separability between consumption and leisure. In particular, $\lambda_1 < 1$ would indicate a relationship of substitutability.

25 It reaches 35 percent in the Islands and falls to 27 percent in the Western region.

26 The simulation exercises referred to in Rossi and Visco (1994) are also based on the full-sample estimation. It is worth emphasizing that, were the simulation exercises based on the truncated sample, the results would not change appreciably.

27 In particular, the test statistics turned out to be equal to −4.4 (West), −0.4 (East), 1.1 (Central), 8.5 (South) and −0.2 (Islands).

28 The estimates are based on the 1984 Bank of Italy SHIW.

29 Altig (1988), in reviewing Mariger's (1986) book, suggests that the arbitrary threshold model (proposed by Hayashi 1985) can be interpreted as a reduced form version of Mariger's structural model, provided that both include the same variables. Thus, as long as the identifying assumptions embodied in the structural model are not at variance with the data and insofar as short planning horizons coincide with higher than average propensities to consume, one should expect the quantitative results of the two models to agree. In the present case, a straightforward comparison is made impossible by the fact that Jappelli and Pagano (1988) and the present work are based on different samples. Jappelli and Pagano (1988) relied on the 1984 Bank of Italy SHIW while we refer to the 1987 edition of the same Survey. Moreover, as in Hayashi (1985), Jappelli and Pagano (1988) exclude the self-employed and households with heads over 65 or employed in agriculture. If the same sample selection criterion were adopted in the present setting, the liquidity-constrained elderly would obviously disappear, but the results would still tend to diverge on account of the nature of the threshold level. Single-period planning horizons also characterize households (with heads in their thirties and early forties) accumulating resources to meet the downpayment on the purchase of a house. Hence, a larger diffusion of liquidity constraints and a somewhat different composition result.

REFERENCES

Altig, D. (1988). 'Econometric Analysis of Consumption Behavior and Fiscal Policy. A Review Essay', *Journal of Monetary Economics* 22: 155-64.

Ando, A. and A.B. Kennickell (1987). 'How Much (or Little) Life Cycle Is There in Micro Data? The Cases of the United States and Japan', in R. Dornbusch, S. Fischer and J. Bossons (eds.), *Macroeconomics and Finance. Essays in Honor of Franco Modigliani,* Cambridge, MA: MIT Press.

Beltratti, A. and E. Fornero (1990). 'Acquisto dell'abitazione, motivo ereditario e tasso di risparmio in Italia', in E. Fornero and O. Castellino (eds.), *Formazione e impiego della ricchezza delle famiglie,* Torino: Fondazione Giorgio Rota.

Bonato, A.L. (1985). 'Ricostruzione retrospettiva dell'uscita dei figli dalla famiglia di origine', Padova: Università degli Studi, unpublished dissertation.

Deaton, A. (1991). 'Saving and Liquidity Constraints', *Econometrica* 59: 1221-48.

Deaton, A. (1992). *Understanding Consumption*, Oxford: Clarendon Press.

Guiso, L. and T. Jappelli (1994). 'Intergenerational Transfers and Capital Market Imperfections. Evidence from a Cross-Section of Italian Households', *this volume*.

Guiso L., T. Jappelli and D. Terlizzese (1994). 'Why Is Italy's Saving Rate so High?', *this volume*.

Hayashi, F. (1985). 'The Effect of Liquidity Constraints on Consumption: A Cross-Sectional Analysis', *Quarterly Journal of Economics* 100: 183-206.

Hausman, J.A. (1978). 'Specification Tests in Econometrics', *Econometrica* 46: 1251-71.

Istat (1987). 'Tavole di mortalità della popolazione italiana per regione: 1979-1983', *Note e Relazioni* 1.

Jappelli, T. and M. Pagano (1988). 'Consumo, indebitamento delle famiglie e razionamento del credito', *Giornale degli economisti e annali di economia* 47: 545-73.

Jappelli, T. and M. Pagano (1989). 'Consumption and Capital Market Imperfections: An International Comparison', *American Economic Review* 79: 1088-105.

Kennickell, A.B. (1984). 'An Investigation of Life Cycle Savings Behavior in the United States', Philadelphia: University of Pennsylvania, unpublished Ph. D. dissertation.

Lawrance, E.C. (1991). 'Poverty and the Rate of Time Preference: Evidence from Panel Data', *Journal of Political Economy* 99: 54-77.

Livi Bacci, M. and A. Santini, (eds.) (1969). *Tavole di fecondità della donna italiana secondo le generazioni di appartenenza*, Firenze: Università degli Studi, Dipartimento Statistico.

Mariger, R.P. (1986). *Consumption Behavior and the Effects of Government Fiscal Policies*, Cambridge, MA: Harvard University Press.

Mariger, R.P. (1987). 'A Life-Cycle Consumption Model with Liquidity Constraints: Theory and Empirical Results', *Econometrica* 55: 533-57.

Marotta, G. (1988). 'Comments on 'Liquidity Constrained Households in an Italian Cross-Section'', by T. Jappelli and M. Pagano', mimeo.

Meghir, C. and G. Weber (1993). 'Testing for Liquidity Constraints on Household Survey Data', mimeo.

Modigliani, F. and A. Ando (1957). 'Tests of the Life Cycle Hypothesis of Savings: Comments and Suggestions', *Bulletin of the Oxford University Institute of Statistics* 19: 99-124.

Rossi, N. and I. Visco (1994). 'Private Saving and the Government Deficit in Italy', *this volume*.

White, H. (1980). 'A Heteroskedasticity-Consistent Covariance Matrix Estimator and a Direct Test for Heteroskedasticity', *Econometrica* 48: 817-38.

Yaari, M.E. (1965). 'Uncertain Lifetime, Life Insurance, and the Theory of the Consumer', *Review of Economic Studies* 32: 137-50.

10 Durables and non-durables consumption: evidence from Italian household data*

AGAR BRUGIAVINI and GUGLIELMO WEBER

1 Introduction

Much empirical analysis of consumption and saving decisions abstracts from the existence of durable goods. Yet consumer durables represent an important part of the personal sector, wealth and decisions to purchase and sell durables have a major impact on overall consumer expenditure (and contribute to its marked pro-cyclical nature).

One reason for the relative neglect of consumer durables may be that satisfactory data are hard to come by. Aggregate purchase data are normally available but no information is usually provided that allows to distinguish between changes in the number of consumers who own and changes in the average stock owned. Also, no direct information is available on the value of the stock. Hence, few studies have taken the representative agent paradigm down the path of modeling consumption in durable goods (one exception is Dunn and Singleton, 1986). Furthermore, household-level data do not normally contain information on durables, beyond ownership and (at best) net purchases. This severely limits the scope for microeconometric research.

The ideal data set for the econometric analysis of durable goods consumption is a long panel, with high-quality information on all types of expenditure and retrospective questions concerning durable purchases and sales. Such a data set does not exist, and indeed is unlikely ever to exist: detailed questions on expenditure normally involve filling in diaries, and this is time-consuming. The ideal data set would likely suffer from serious attrition problems.

The data set available to us is the Italian cross-section from the 1987 Bank of Italy Survey of Household Income and Wealth (SHIW), which includes questions on one group of durable goods, transport equipment, plus some retrospective questions on past purchases, detailed information on current credit availability, purchases of non-durable goods, income and socio-demographic characteristics. The cross-sectional nature of the data limits the scope of our analysis: age and cohort effects cannot be separated; uncertainty cannot be fully taken into account.

In this paper we ask the following question: how can we model the trade-off between durable and non-durable goods? In particular, is this trade-off strongly influenced by the availability of consumer credit? And is this influence distinguishable in practice from a high degree of heterogeneity in preferences?

The paper is organized as follows: Section 2 describes the data, and sets out the major stylized facts that our theoretical model should explain. Section 3 derives some first-order conditions that can be used in estimation and discusses the effects of borrowing restrictions on the decision to purchase consumer durables. Section 4 deals with identification and estimation issues, while Section 5 presents empirical results and Section 6 draws some conclusions.

2   The data and some stylized facts

The SHIW covers some 8,000 households, and has been run on a rather regular basis for well over two decades. The survey on which this paper is based was conducted in 1988 and contains a particularly rich array of questions on financial and non-financial wealth in 1987. Detailed questions were asked not only about durable expenditure, but also about the value of vehicles, of the housing stock, and of other valuables. The data also contain information about financial wealth, both in discrete form (possession, or otherwise, of specified assets) and in value terms (the data used in the present paper are those adjusted for non- and underreporting).[1] Finally, much is asked about credit availability: for those who applied for consumer credit, we know whether they were successful, and at what terms. For the others, we even know why they chose not to apply.

In our application, we concentrate on the choice between non-durables consumption and vehicle services consumption. The latter variable we assume to be proportional, for vehicle owners, to the value of the vehicle stock. Vehicle services are particularly attractive on two grounds: they are a well-defined yet sizable commodity, and the sample information on vehicles is particularly detailed (with a high response rate). In the sample, 7,655 households provide valid answers to the question: How much was your vehicle stock worth? Of these 5,830 are strictly positive.[2] The average stock value for vehicle owners was 11.15 million lire (about $10,000 at 1987 prices) with a standard deviation of 12.92 million.

In Figure 10.1 we plot the average value of the stock against the age of the head of household. This type of variable is what one normally uses on aggregate data, where the total stock value (somehow imputed) is expressed in *per capita* terms. There is a pronounced hump over the life cycle, with a sudden decrease around retirement age (which is 60 for most men in Italy). However, Figures 10.2 and 10.3 suggest that much of the action in later years comes from decreased ownership levels: once ownership is controlled for, the post-retirement drop is less strong. The mid-fifties peak is, however, more marked.

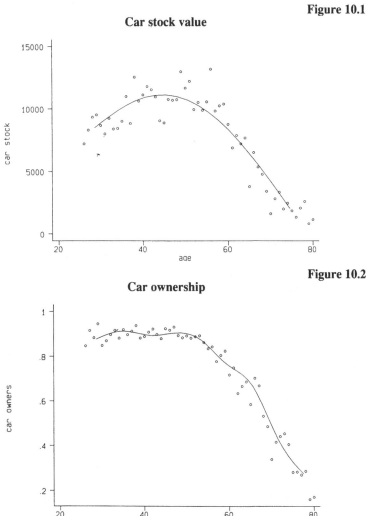

Figure 10.1
Car stock value

Figure 10.2
Car ownership

Figure 10.3

Car stock value given ownership

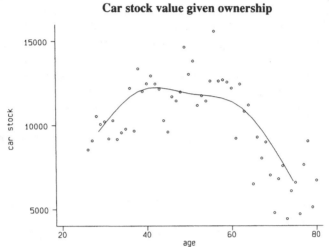

The drop in ownership after retirement seems mostly due to a decrease in the number of purchases during the year (from about 20 percent to less than 10 percent on average, as shown in Figure 10.4). Few people report selling their cars, and even fewer report an outright sale (i.e., no purchase of a replacement vehicle). This is a puzzling feature often found in micro data sets (like the British FES and the American CEX). Either owners forget having very old, hardly usable cars, or else they fail to report selling them for scrap. (Another possibility is that they let their grandchildren use them!) Finally, the average value of purchases declines very gently with age.

A final picture is of some interest. In Figure 10.5 we plot the average expenditure on non-durables and the average vehicle stock value against age. The two variables correlate very strongly – the correlation coefficients of their averages by age is 0.88, but even in the raw data their simple correlation exceeds 0.53. Part of this correlation will be due to wealth effects (age and cohort effects are not separately identified here), while some may reflect shifts in life-cycle preferences (due to changes in demographic characteristics, say). Finally, some could be due to inability to borrow.

In order to investigate the effect of borrowing ability on the relationship between durables and non-durables consumption, we constructed two credit-market indicators. The first (*cred1*) takes value 1 if the household was refused credit or did not apply for it in the expectation of a denial ("discouraged borrowers"). (This is similar to the variable used by Jappelli, 1990, and has a sample mean of 3.46 percent. See also Jappelli and Pagano, 1988.) The second (*cred2*) takes value 1 if the household did borrow funds towards a vehicle purchase (it has a sample mean of 1.21 percent).

Figure 10.4
Proportions of car purchases and sales

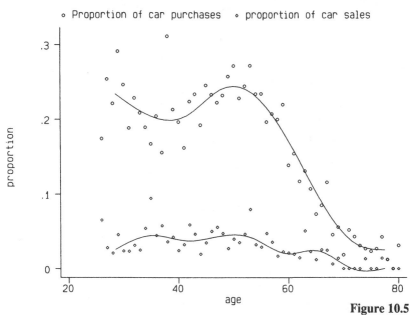

Figure 10.5
Expenditure on non-durables and car stock *(a)*

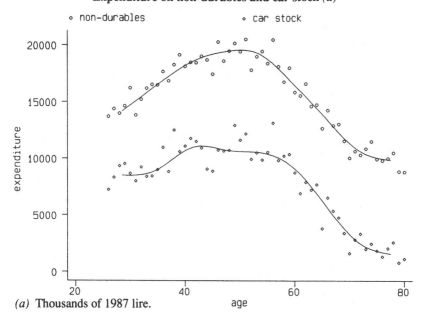

(a) Thousands of 1987 lire.

If we run a simple OLS regression for vehicle owners of the logarithm of the vehicle stock on the logarithm of non-durables consumption and *cred1*, we obtain (standard errors in parentheses):

$$\ln(stock) = -2.167 + 1.133 \ln(consumption) - .3599 \, cred1$$
$$(.266) \quad (.0274) \qquad\qquad (.080)$$

Number of observations = 5,830　$R^2 = 0.234$.

Hence, the inability to borrow reduces the stock of vehicles, for a given level of non-durables consumption (or *vice versa*!). If we introduce the ability to borrow against vehicles in the equation, we find:

$$\ln(stock) = -2.180 + 1.133 \ln(consumption) - .3482 \, cred1 + .7229 \, cred2$$
$$(.265) \quad (.0273) \qquad\qquad (.080) \qquad (.107)$$

Number of observations = 5,830　$R^2 = 0.241$

which again suggests the potential importance of credit availability in this trade-off. We obtained very similar results when household size was included in the regressions run. Whether this type of correlation is of economic interest or simply a statistical artifact will be established by estimating a structural model.

These are the stylized facts that our model should be able to predict:

i) Expenditure on non-durable goods and the value of the vehicle stock strongly correlate over the life cycle. This correlation is also present (but to a lesser extent) within age-groups (i.e., controlling for age-cohort effects);

ii) The operation of credit markets appears to be important. Households that are denied credit own less vehicle stock, for a given level of non-durables consumption. Households that have access to collateralized credit own more;

iii) The effects described in i) and ii) persist when household size is controlled for.

However, we stress that our "stylized facts" could well be due to other factors such as simultaneity bias, sample selectivity bias, preference heterogeneity, or functional form misspecification.

3　A theoretical framework

The decision to purchase a durable good is inherently dynamic. Hence we need to set up the analytical representation in a forward-looking, dynamic context. The life-cycle approach seems the most suitable: therefore we assume that the h-th consumer solves the following optimization problem (h superscripts are omitted for notational convenience):

$$\max E_t \left[\sum_{\tau=t}^{L} \frac{u_\tau(c_\tau, S_\tau)}{(1 + \varrho)^\tau} \right] \tag{1a}$$

s.t.

$$A_\tau = (1 + r_{\tau-1}) A_{\tau-1} + Y_\tau - p_\tau c_\tau - v_\tau d_\tau \tag{1b}$$

$$A_\tau \geq \phi_0 + \phi_1 v_\tau S_\tau \qquad \tau = t, ..., L - 1 \tag{1c}$$

$$S_\tau \geq 0 \qquad \tau = t, ..., L \tag{1d}$$

$$A_L \geq 0 \tag{1e}$$

$$S_{t-1}, A_{t-1} \quad \text{given} \tag{1f}$$

$$S_\tau = (1 - \delta)S_{\tau-1} + d_\tau \qquad \tau = t, ..., L \tag{1g}$$

where we implicitly assume the existence of an aggregate non-durable good ("non-durables") and of just one durable good, and the following notation applies:

c_τ = non-durable good in period τ
S_τ = stock of the durable good at the end of period τ, in efficiency units
A_τ = net liquid assets at the end of period τ
r_τ = interest rate on liquid assets in period τ
y_τ = labor income in period τ
p_τ = price of the non-durable good in period τ
v_τ = price of the durable good in period τ (per efficiency unit)
d_τ = quantity of the durable good purchased in period τ (in efficiency units)
δ = depreciation rate of the durable good
ϱ = time preference parameter.

Equation (1b) is the standard asset accumulation constraint. By using equation (1g) we can substitute out d_τ:

$$A_\tau = (1 + r_{\tau-1})A_{\tau-1} + y_\tau - p_\tau c_\tau - v_\tau(S_\tau - (1 - \delta)S_{\tau-1}) . \tag{1b'}$$

This model differs from the standard neoclassical model of durables consumption in the introduction of the borrowing constraint (1c). Thus, not only do we assume that net wealth cannot fall below a certain threshold, but we also allow for the possibility that this threshold depends on the value of the stock of durables itself. In other words, S_τ acts as collateral via the ϕ_1 coefficient. Inspection of (1c) reveals that ϕ_1 should be negative, and will normally be less than unity in absolute value if S_τ is less than fully collateralized. Note also that ϕ_1 may well be a function of observable characteristics (type of occupation, household composition, home ownership, etc.).

The rest of the constraints of the optimization problem are standard. Note, however, the non-negativity condition (1d): as the durable good is not essential for survival, but negative holdings are not feasible (barring home production), we must allow for the possibility that some consumers may perceive the zero lower limit to their stock as a binding constraint.

The first-order conditions of this optimization problem are:

$$\frac{\partial u_t}{\partial c_t} = \lambda_t p_t \tag{2a}$$

$$\frac{\partial u_t}{\partial S_t} = \lambda_t v_t - E_t \left[\frac{\lambda_{t+1}(1 - \delta)v_{t+1}}{1 + \varrho} \right] + \mu_t \phi_1 v_t - \eta_t \tag{2b}$$

$$E_t \left[\frac{\lambda_{t+1}(1 + r_t)}{1 + \varrho} \right] = \lambda_t - \mu_t \tag{2c}$$

$$\mu_t(A_t - \phi_0 - \phi_1 v_t S_t) = 0 \qquad\qquad \mu_t \geqq 0 \quad \text{(2d)}$$

$$\eta_t S_t = 0 \qquad\qquad\qquad\qquad \eta_t \geqq 0. \quad \text{(2e)}$$

When liquidity constraints are ignored, equations (2a) and (2c) can be combined to produce an estimable dynamic equation for non-durables consumption (as in Hansen and Singleton, 1982, for example). The presence of (possibly binding) liquidity constraints invalidates this procedure. However, an estimable equation can be derived, by using (2b) to substitute μ_t out of (2c) (this is the approach taken by Alessie, Devereux and Weber, 1992, who extend to durable goods the framework proposed by Alessie, Melenberg and Weber, 1988).

When credit market information is available, either equation (2b) or equation (2c) can be estimated over the subsample of consumers who are not currently affected by the liquidity constraint (as is argued by Zeldes, 1989, for an equation like (2c)). This could be our case, given that we have plenty of information on credit status and financial wealth, but we are still faced with the problem that both equations involve quantities dated t and t+1. If we want to use this approach in our application, we need to eliminate quantities dated $t+1$ from the estimable equation.

A simple way is to use equation (2c) to substitute λ_{t+1} out of equation (2b). This, however, requires assuming that λ_{t+1} is uncorrelated with both v_{t+1} and r_t, given information dated t. A sufficient condition for this to hold is that both v_{t+1} and r_t are known at time t. On these assumptions, we obtain:

$$\frac{\partial u_t(c_t, S_t)}{\partial S_t} = \frac{\partial u_t(c_t, S_t)}{\partial c_t} \frac{v_t^*}{p_t} + \mu_t \left(\phi_1 v_t + \frac{1-\delta}{1+r_t} v_{t+1} \right) - \eta_t \quad (2b')$$

where $v_t^* = v_t - v_{t+1}(1 - \delta)/(1 + r_t)$, i.e., the user cost.

This equation can be estimated on cross-sectional data, as long as consumers face an identical price for the durable good (i.e., v_{t+1} is not individual-specific), and sample separation information is available on both credit-market status and durables ownership. This we take to be our case.

Equation (2b') lends itself to an intuitive interpretation. For non-liquidity-constrained consumers the c-S trade-off is fully captured by the user cost relative to the price of non-durables. However, for liquidity-constrained consumers other considerations come into play: if S_t has a poor role as collateral, such consumers will shun the durable good in favor of non-durables, and *vice versa* when S_t is "fully collateralized". In analytical terms, the former case corresponds to the inequality:

$$-\phi_1 < \frac{v_{t+1}(1 - \delta)}{v_t(1 + r_t)}$$

i.e., to the case in which lenders allow S_t to be used as collateral for less than its end-of-period discounted value. The latter case corresponds to the inequality being reversed, i.e. to lenders giving the stock of the durable good a positive signaling role of credit worthiness.

4 Estimation issues

In order to estimate an equation like (2b') on cross-sectional data, we need to specify a functional form for preferences. We choose the following extended translog direct utility function (see Meghir and Weber, 1992):

$$u^h(c_t, S_t) = a_1^h S_t + a_2^h \ln S_t + a_3(\ln S_t)^2 + b_1^h c_t + b_2^h \ln c_t$$
$$+ b_3(\ln c_t)^2 + \gamma \ln c_t \ln S_t \quad (3)$$

where:

$$a_1^h = \varepsilon^h$$

$$b_1^h = \omega^h$$

$$a_2^h = a_{2,0} + a_2'z^h$$

$$b_2^h = b_{2,0} + b_2'z^h$$

with z^h a k vector of socio-demographic characteristics, ε^h and ω^h two idiosyncratic error terms (random preferences) and a_2, b_2 vectors of coefficients with $a_2' = [a_{2,1}, a_{2,2}, ..., a_{2,k}]$, $b_2' = [b_{2,1}, b_{2,2}, ..., b_{2,k}]$. This utility function is flexible enough to accommodate a high degree of non-homotheticity, and, via its demographic-dependent parameters, of preference heterogeneity.

Flexibility in preference specification is an important requirement in our context. Given the wide variety of behavior at the individual level, an inflexible functional form would imply a poor fit for many households at the tails of the wealth and income distribution. Hence the error term would depend on the very variables that are likely to most affect the shadow price of the net wealth constraint, μ_t. In this case, if in estimating a relation like:

$$\frac{\partial u_t(c_t, S_t)}{\partial S_t} = \frac{\partial u_t(c_t, S_t)}{\partial c_t} \frac{v_t^*}{p_t}$$

for the subsample of car owners, one found violations of the tests for overidentifying restrictions, this would not necessarily imply that μ_t is non-zero for some consumers. However, given that the term involving μ_t can be either negative or positive, identification of (2b') requires that we specify some exogenous criterion to separate possibly constrained consumers from the rest.

We assume the error term (which reflects unaccounted-for heterogeneity) to be uncorrelated with age, household composition, income and financial wealth variables, but we explicitly acknowledge its effect on both non-durable and durable goods consumption by treating all variables involving transformations of S and c as endogenous in the estimation. The exclusion of financial variables from (2b'), at least for the unconstrained group, provides the necessary restrictions for identification.

The chosen functional form rules out zero consumption of either c or S. We reconcile this restriction with our data (where zero vehicle stock is often reported) as follows: all households consume some transport services. For those who do not own a vehicle, or whose vehicle stock is worth very little (less than 500,000 lire, i.e. about $400), transport services are misclassified (public transport is included in c). For the remaining households, public transport is of negligible importance, and transport services are proportional to the value of the stock.[3] Hence we estimate (2b') on the subsample of vehicle owners, but correct for selectivity bias by standard econometric methods (the probit estimates for vehicle ownership are reported in Appendix A).

5 Results

Our estimates of equation (2b'), given the utility function in (3), are reported in Table 10.1. The first column presents estimates which refer to the whole sample of vehicle owners. The second column refers instead to the subsample of households who satisfy the following criteria: they are not poor (i.e., their financial wealth is above the first quartile), they were not denied credit (*cred1*=0) and they did not receive credit for the purchase of vehicles (*cred2*=0). The first two criteria are self-explanatory. For the third, we want to rule out those households who may be borrowing against purchases of the durable good in order to alleviate the severity of their borrowing limit (see our theoretical model above).

All variables involving c, S or their transformations were instrumented, to correct for simultaneity bias due to random preferences. The full list of both explanatory variables and instruments is given in Appendix B. Instruments involve a number of financial variables, further demographic indicators and their interactions with financial indicators, plus some variables which reflect (albeit imperfectly) previous years' vehicle purchases and sales. The equation also contains a Mill's ratio, which corresponds to the probit estimates reported in Appendix A: it is worth noting that some explanatory variables in that equation (locational dummies, logarithm of total income) are not included in the instrument list, thus giving the Mill's ratio genuine additional variability.

Neither equation is rejected by the Sargan test of overidentifying restrictions, even though there is a noticeable decrease in the test statistic in going from the full sample to the subsample. Estimates of the demographic invariant parameters are little affected by the sample choice, while some of the demographic interactions (entering a_2 and b_2) change by larger and more significant amounts (see the estimates of $b_{2,12}$, $a_{2,2}$, $a_{2,10}$, $a_{2,12}$, e.g.). However, a formal test of parameter equality across the two samples is unlikely to reject the null. As argued by Jappelli (1990), sample selection criteria based on financial wealth end up selecting out many unconstrained households, and therefore reduce the power of statistical tests of structural stability.

Another way to gauge the presence of liquidity constraints is to use the subsample parameter estimates to evaluate the value of the term involving μ_t (see equation 2b') for those households who own vehicles but are potentially liquidity-constrained (i.e., for the 987 households included in the "full sample" but excluded from the "subsample").

Table 10.1   **Relation between expenditure on non-durable goods and the stock of durables** (instrumental variable estimates; dependent variable: ln c)

Coefficients (a)	Demographic variables	Full sample	Subsample of vehicle owners
		Estimates (b)	Estimates (b)
$b^*_{2,0}$		1.802 (0.366)	1.918 (0.344)
$a_{2,0}$		1.124 (0.107)	1.133 (0.104)
a_3		0.223 (0.022)	0.208 (0.025)
γ		−0.113 (0.045)	−0.098 (0.054)
γ^*		−0.720 (0.078)	−0.708 (0.089)
$b^*_{2,1}$	YOUNG	−0.174 (0.221)	−0.236 (0.248)
$b^*_{2,2}$	AGE	−0.071 (0.047)	−0.085 (0.045)
$b^*_{2,3}$	OLDWIFE	0.032 (0.228)	0.038 (0.193)
$b^*_{2,4}$	OLDCOUPLE	0.068 (0.249)	−0.115 (0.229)
$b^*_{2,5}$	HUSBWORK	−0.176 (0.121)	−0.192 (0.118)
$b^*_{2,6}$	NKIDS	0.002 (0.050)	−0.021 (0.051)
$b^*_{2,7}$	KIDS20	0.020 (0.051)	0.039 (0.055)
$b^*_{2,8}$	MC	0.050 (0.083)	0.009 (0.089)
$b^*_{2,9}$	NEARN	−0.046 (0.030)	−0.047 (0.030)
$b^*_{2,10}$	SOUTH	0.115 (0.059)	0.153 (0.061)
$b^*_{2,11}$	INVALID	−0.696 (1.105)	1.090 (0.034)
$b^*_{2,12}$	EDUC	−0.075 (0.062)	−0.120 (0.059)
$b^*_{2,13}$	SECJOB	−0.104 (0.131)	−0.177 (0.124)
$b^*_{2,14}$	CENTR	−0.024 (0.085)	−0.003 (0.077)
$b^*_{2,15}$	INDUST	0.062 (0.052)	−0.080 (0.055)

Table 10.1 *(cont.)*

Coefficients *(a)*	Demographic variables	Full sample	Subsample of vehicle owners
		Estimates *(b)*	Estimates *(b)*
$a_{2,1}$	YOUNG	−0.058 (0.081)	−0.090 (0.101)
$a_{2,2}$	AGE	−0.022 (0.014)	−0.027 (0.014)
$a_{2,3}$	OLDWIFE	−0.000 (0.058)	0.008 (0.050)
$a_{2,4}$	OLDCOUPLE	0.026 (0.067)	−0.026 (0.066)
$a_{2,5}$	HUSBWORK	−0.059 (0.035)	,0.062 (0.036)
$a_{2,6}$	NKIDS	0.002 (0.014)	−0.006 (0.016)
$a_{2,7}$	KIDS20	0.005 (0.015)	0.013 (0.018)
$a_{2,8}$	MC	0.016 (0.025)	0.003 (0.029)
$a_{2,9}$	NEARN	−0.015 (0.010)	−0.016 (0.010)
$a_{2,10}$	SOUTH	0.036 (0.019)	0.050 (0.021)
$a_{2,11}$	INVALID	−0.172 (0.266)	0.393 (1.051)
$a_{2,12}$	EDUC	−0.024 (0.023)	−0.041 (0.022)
$a_{2,13}$	SECJOB	−0.032 (0.046)	−0.064 (0.046)
$a_{2,14}$	CENTR	−1.004 (0.029)	0.003 (0.027)
$a_{2,15}$	INDUST	0.022 (0.017)	0.029 (0.019)
Mill's ratio		0.010 (0.033)	0.007 (0.037)
Sargan test		29.2457	26.309
Degrees of freedom		30	29
Number of observations		5,587	4,600

(a) b_3^* is normalized to unity. All starred coefficients are the product of the user cost (v^*) and the corresponding unstarred coefficients. For a description of the explanatory and instrumental variables used see Appendix B.

(b) Standard errors are reported in parentheses.

On the subsample of vehicle owners, equation (2b') can be written as:

$$\frac{\partial u_t(c_t, S_t)}{\partial S_t} = \frac{\partial u_t(c_t, S_t)}{\partial c_t} \frac{v_t^*}{p_t} + \mu_t\left(\phi_1 v_t + \frac{1 - \delta}{1 + r_t} v_{t+1}\right)$$

$$= \frac{\partial u_t(c_t, S_t)}{\partial c_t} \frac{v_t^*}{p_t} + \mu_t^*.$$

Table 10.1 contains all the terms needed to evaluate the marginal utility of c and S. If we now simulate the equation on the "constrained" subsample, we can evaluate a composite term which involves both the random preference error, ω (say) and μ^*. By construction, ω is orthogonal to the instruments, hence it can be removed by projecting $(\omega + \mu^*)$ on the instruments and taking the fitted value.

By this method, we obtain an estimate of μ^*, which can be regressed against credit and demographic variables, to try to establish who the liquidity-constrained households are, and what effect the constraint has on their durables/non-durables trade-off. This is done by means of several regressions reported in Table 10.2. In column (1) we see that *cred1* has a positive, significant impact on μ^*, while *cred2* has a negligible one. Thus, for *cred1* we can confirm the finding reported in Section 2: other things being equal, credit-constrained households consume less of the durable good. However, the strong effect found in simple-minded regressions for *cred2* effectively disappears once a more structural approach is adopted, thus suggesting that it may have been a statistical artifact. Column (3) shows that this type of result comes out much stronger if we concentrate on "poor" households (some of the households included in the "potentially constrained subsample" because they meet the *cred2*=1 condition have high wealth). In column (2) we look at the effect of demographic characteristics on μ^* (age and regional indicators), while columns (4) and (5) do the same for the "poor" subsample. The most noticeable effect is the differential impact of age: for young consumers μ^* is on average smaller. Even in the most general specification (5) *cred1* has a positive and significant effect on the multiplier while, other things being equal, young consumers are more easily offered credit for a vehicle purchase.

Figures 10.6 and 10.7 provide a graphical illustration of the μ^*'s. Figure 10.6 presents a histogram of μ^*: for most "potentially constrained" consumers μ^* is close to zero. This is not surprising, given our conservative selection rules, whereby households are classified as non-liquidity constrained if they consider themselves not credit-rationed and are relatively wealthy. However, the histogram reveals that for some households μ^* is far from zero. In view of the regression results presented in Table 10.2, we

Table 10.2 Explaining the Kuhn-Tucker multiplier *(a)*
(OLS regressions; dependent variable: $\mu_t v_t \, [\phi_1 + (1 - \delta)v_{t+1}/(1 + r_t)v_t]$)

Variables	(1)	(2)	(3)	(4)	(5)
Constant	.164	−.079	.165	−.073	−.261
	(.052)	(.102)	(.052)	(.108)	(.076)
cred1	.231	.248	.518	.518	.202
	(.128)	(.126)	(.175)	(.173)	(.081)
cred2	.034	.081	.190	.261	.137
	(.158)	(.157)	(.385)	(.379)	(.181)
SOUTH		.195		.182	−.407
		(.093)		(.104)	(.076)
YOUNG		−.321		−.520	−.773
		(.148)		(.161)	(.076)
AGE4065		.283		.332	.202
		(.099)		(.107)	(.054)
KIDS20					.238
					(.041)
KIDSY					.965
					(.078)
MC					.465
					(.079)
OO					−.488
					(.083)
INVALID					9.311
					(.191)
WORKW					−.408
					(.049)
SECJOB					−1.152
					(.154)
HOMESIZE					.005
					(.001)
PREV1					.211
					(.041)
KIDSY-EARN					−.057
					(.006)
KIDS20-EARN					−.005
					(.002)
MC-EARN					−.015
					(.004)
SOUTH-EARN					−.261
					(.076)
Number of observations	987	987	834	834	834
R^2	0.003	0.031	0.011	0.055	0.804
Mean of dependent variable	0.202	0.202	0.213	0.213	0.213

(a) Columns (1) and (2) refer to the whole sample of potentially liquidity-constrained (for whom either *cred1* = 1, or *cred2* = 1, or financial wealth is low), columns (3), (4) and (5) concentrate on households whose financial wealth is low.

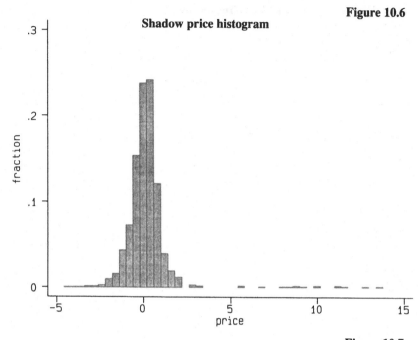

Figure 10.6

Shadow price histogram

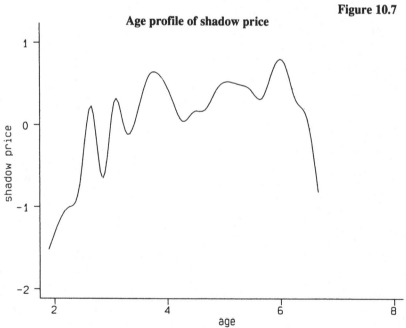

Figure 10.7

Age profile of shadow price

expect the μ^* distribution to vary significantly across age groups. Therefore, in Figure 10.7 we plot the mean of μ^* by age of the head of the household. This picture reveals quite clearly that μ^* is negative for younger households, and positive for older ones.[4] This is consistent with the hypothesis that lenders offer higher credit limits to younger customers, with a view to establishing a long-term business relation, but are reluctant to offer good credit terms to older customers.

Figure 10.8

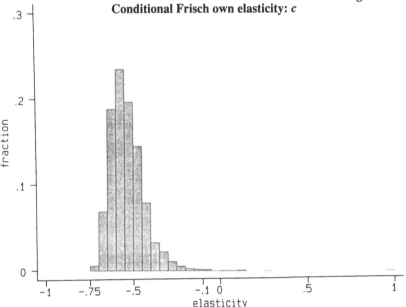

Conditional Frisch own elasticity: c

Finally, Figures 10.8 and 10.9 plot conditional own-price elasticities for both c and S. An attractive, if arbitrary, way to interpret these elasticities is as intertemporal elasticities of substitution (this is equivalent to ruling out general monotonic transformations of our "within period" utility function).[5] If we follow this path, and therefore label these price elasticities as "Frisch", we can see that Italian consumers appear more willing to engage in intertemporal substitution when we use vehicle stock equations, rather than non-durables consumption ones. Unconditional own-price elasticities (still of the λ-constant type, barring monotonic transformations of the utility function) and the budget elasticity for S are reported in Figures 10.10-10.12. It is perhaps surprising to note that for most consumers the stock of vehicles is a necessity, and therefore non-durable goods are a luxury (out of a composite budget, defined as the sum of the vehicle stock and purchases of non-durable goods).

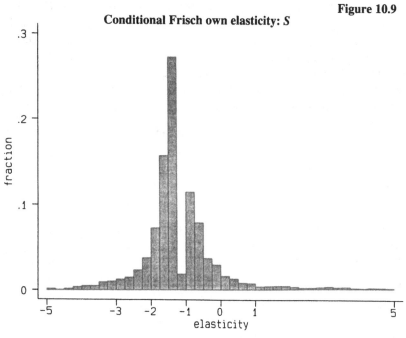

Figure 10.9

Conditional Frisch own elasticity: S

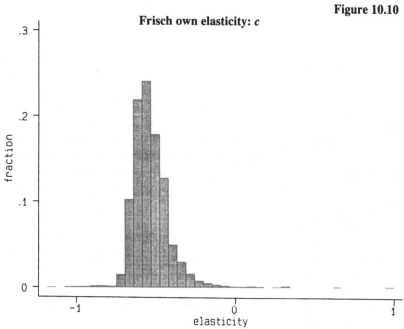

Figure 10.10

Frisch own elasticity: c

Figure 10.11

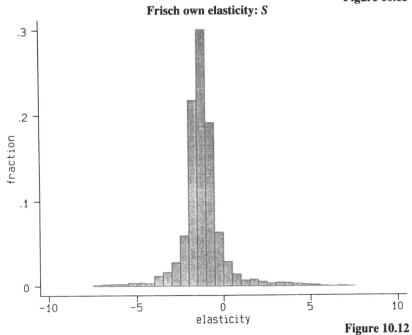

Frisch own elasticity: *S*

Figure 10.12

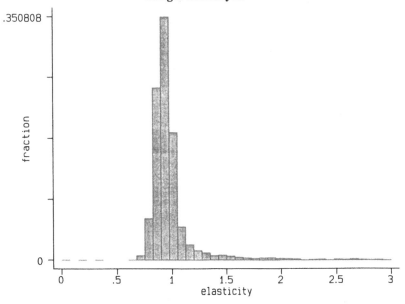

Budget elasticity: *S*

6   Conclusions

In this paper, we have tackled the issue of the effects of credit constraints on durable goods consumption. We have shown that, if the borrowing limit facing forward-looking consumers depends on the value of the collateral, i.e. on the resale value of the stock of durables, then the trade-off between the consumption of durable and non-durable goods is affected by liquidity constraints. In particular, if the extra credit made available for purchasing an extra unit of a durable good is less than the present value of its future resale value, then liquidity-constrained consumers will be induced to purchase less of that durable good and more non-durables (and *vice versa*, if the extra credit exceeds that amount).

On the basis of this theoretical model, we have derived an equation which can be estimated on cross-sectional data, and shown what type of violations to expect from credit-constrained households. In our empirical application, we have used a large survey of Italian households, which contains high quality consumption, income and financial wealth data, as well as some direct questions on access to credit and the value of the stock of vehicles. We have specified a highly flexible utility function, estimated preference parameters on the subsample of unconstrained consumers, and then evaluated the shadow price of the borrowing restrictions for potentially liquidity-constrained households. Our results suggest that households who are denied credit normally purchase fewer vehicles. However, for younger households the opposite effect prevails. This is consistent with the hypothesis that lenders offer higher credit limits to younger customers, with a view to establishing a long term business relation.

In future work, we shall attempt to evaluate whether our results are robust to the presence of adjustment costs for the stock of durables. Given the cross-sectional nature of our data, we can only try simple exercises, such as estimating the equation on a subsample of consumers who have recently purchased a vehicle, and test for parameter equality with the full sample result. The relatively high proportion of current or recent purchases in our data (about one fourth of households) gives us hope that adjustment costs may have a relatively small impact.

APPENDIX A

Table 10.A1 Probit equation estimates *(a)*
(dependent variable: vehicle ownership)

Variables	Coefficients	*t*-statistics
CONSTANT	−5.413	−9.34
YOUNG	−0.130	−1.08
AGE4065	0.088	0.90
AGE65+	0.314	2.25
AGE	−0.027	−3.73
AGESQ	−0.001	−2.76
OLDWIFE	−0.195	−2.10
WIDOW	−0.910	−9.45
OLDCOUPLE	−0.245	−3.06
HUSBWORK	−0.025	−0.28
NPENSIO	−0.266	−4.53
NUMP	0.007	0.02
LOGINC	0.672	12.15
CITY	−0.579	−3.71
TOWN	−0.083	−1.27
NKIDS	−0.050	−1.78
KIDS20	0.152	3.78
KIDSY	−0.058	−1.03
MC	0.291	5.19
NEARN	0.148	3.56
SOUTH	0.137	3.03
OO	−0.699	−4.35
SELF	−0.232	−4.09
EDUC	0.121	2.37
WORKW	0.041	0.90
SECJOB	0.042	0.28
SHDEP	0.379	6.72
SHTIT	−0.285	−0.86
SHOBB	0.209	1.05
INVALID	0.245	0.83
FINWEALTH	−0.005	−2.62
AGE-CITY	0.007	2.54
AGE-SHTIT	0.019	3.61
AGE-OO	0.007	2.46

Table 10.A1 *(cont.)*

Variables	Coefficients	t-statistics
SHAREHOLDER	0.364	2.50
BONDHOLDER	–0.267	–2.65
HOMESIZE	0.001	1.94
HOMEVALUE	0.004	1.02
POSWEALTH	0.586	9.47

Measures of fit:

Likelihood ratio χ^2:	3491.2451
Percent correctly predicted:	85.8393
Maddala's pseudo R-square:	0.3662

Table of observed and predicted outcomes:

	Predicted		
Observed	Zero	One	Total
Zero	1,287	782	2,069
One	302	5,284	5,586
Total	1,589	6,066	7,655

Normality statistics: *(b)*

Skewness:	45.8161
	(6.635)
Kurtosis:	19.1255
	(6.635)
Normality:	47.0976
	(9.210)

(a) Vehicle ownership indicator = 1 if vehicle stock value exceeds 500,000 lire.
(b) 1 percent significance level in parentheses.

APPENDIX B

The list of variable names used in the main regression of Table 10.1 is as follows:

YOUNG	= dummy: the head of the household has age below 30
AGE	= age of the head of the household
OLDWIFE	= dummy: the wife has age above 65
OLDCOUPLE	= dummy: the household is composed of an old couple (65+)
HUSBWORK	= dummy: head of the household working
NKIDS	= number of children
KIDS20	= dummy: presence of children older than 20
MC	= dummy: married couple
NEARN	= number of earners in the household
SOUTH	= dummy: southern regions and islands
INVALID	= dummy: head of the household is invalid
EDUC	= dummy: head of the household has higher education
SECJOB	= dummy: head of the household has a second job
CENTR	= dummy: household lives in the center of city or town
INDUST	= dummy: head of the household works in industrial sector

The instrumental variables used for the regression are:

YOUNG, AGE4065 (dummy: age between 40 and 65), AGE65+ (dummy: age above 65), AGE, AGESQ (age squared), OLDWIFE, OLDCOUPLE, HUSBWORK, NUMP (number of unemployed members of the household), CITY (living in a city), TOWN (living in a town), CENTR, NKIDS, KIDS20, KIDSY (dummy:children below age 6), MC, NEARN, SOUTH, OO (dummy: owner occupied house), SELF (dummy: head of the household is self-employed), AGRI (dummy: head of the household works in agricultural sector), PAMM (dummy: head of the household is civil servant), INDUST, INVALID, EDUC, WORKW (dummy: working wife), SECJOB, SHDEP (share of liquid assets as percentage of total financial wealth), SHTIT (share of government bonds and other bonds), BONDHOLDER (dummy: ownership of government bonds), SHAREHOLDER (dummy: ownership of shares), FINWEALTH (financial wealth), HOMEVALUE (value of the first house), POSWEALTH (dummy: positive total wealth), HOMESIZE (size of the first house in square meters), PREV1 (amount paid in 1987 for car purchases previous to 1987), PREV2 (amount outstanding in 1987 of car purchases previous to 1987), MILL'S ratio, EARN (earnings from employment), YSELF (earnings from self-employment). Interacted variables: AGE-CITY, AGE-SHTIT, AGE-OO, AGE-CENTR, P-KIDS20, P-KIDSY, P-MC, P-NEARN, P-SOUTH, P-OO, P-SELF, P-INDUST, P-EDUC, P-WORKW, E-KIDS20, E-KIDSY, E-MC, E-NEARN, E-SOUTH, E-OO, E-SELF, E-INDUST, E-EDUC, E-WORKW, where "P-" indicates the variable (PREV1+PREV2) and "E-" indicates the variable "earnings from employment".

The probit equation also includes: LOGINC (log of income), NPENSIO (number of pensioners), SHOBB (share of non-government bonds) and WIDOW (dummy: head of the household is widowed).

NOTES

* We are grateful for comments made by Andrea Bollino and Giuseppe Marotta. We also thank Margherita Borella for skillfully preparing the data. Cindy Miller provided outstanding editorial assistance. The early stages of this research took place at the Institute for Fiscal Studies (under the ESRC Functioning of Markets Initiative, project W102251009), where we received much support and advice, and benefited from discussions with Rob Alessie, Orazio Attanasio and Costas Meghir. We are also grateful for comments from seminar audiences at University College London, ZEW (Mannheim), ESEM92 (Brussels) and Cambridge but remain responsible for any errors. Guglielmo Weber thanks Olivetti SpA for providing financial support towards his IGIER fellowship (1991-92).

1 See the Methodological Appendix to this volume for a detailed description of the Bank of Italy survey. For details on the adjustment of financial assets for non- and underreporting – by means of a statistical matching procedure on the SHIW and the sample of BNL customers – see Cannari *et al.* (1990).

2 In fact, the number of valid responses is even higher. However, for a few households other key variables had a missing value.

3 Public transport is relatively cheap and of low quality in most Italian cities. It is normal for Italian car-owners to drive to work every day.

4 The curve in Figure 10.7 is smoothed by means of cubic spline interpolation, allowing for 10 flex points. This procedure reduces the influence of outliers, except at the extremes of the age distribution (where the underlying sample size is much reduced). In our discussion, we therefore disregard the left and right tails of the plot.

5 For instance, the conditional elasticity of non-durable consumption is defined as $\partial \log c / \partial \log p$ keeping λ and S constant. Simple computations show that this equals $(\partial u / \partial c)(c \partial^2 u / \partial c^2)$, which is (–) the elasticity of intertemporal substitution for a given S if u is the utility index which enters lifetime utility, as defined in equation (1a). Meghir and Weber (1992) provide derivations of elasticity formulae for the extended direct translog utility function, and discuss their interpretation in greater detail.

REFERENCES

Alessie, R., M. Devereux and G. Weber (1992). 'Intertemporal Consumption, Durables and Liquidity Constraints: A Cohort Analysis', University of London, Institute for Fiscal Studies, mimeo.

Alessie, R., B. Melenberg and G. Weber (1988). 'Consumption, Leisure and Earnings-Related Liquidity Constraints: A Note', *Economics Letters* 27: 101-4.

Cannari, L., G. D'Alessio, G. Raimondi and A.I. Rinaldi (1990). 'Le attività finanziarie delle famiglie italiane', Temi di discussione 135, Banca d'Italia.

Dunn, K.B. and K.J. Singleton (1986). 'Modeling the Term Structure of Interest Rates under Non-Separable Utility and Durability of Goods', *Journal of Financial Economics* **17**: 27-56.

Hansen, L.P. and K.J. Singleton (1982). 'Generalized Instrumental Variables Estimation of Nonlinear Rational Expectations Models', *Econometrica* **50**: 1269-86.

Jappelli, T. (1990). 'Who Is Credit Constrained in the U.S. Economy?', *Quarterly Journal of Economics* **105**: 219-34.

Jappelli, T. and M. Pagano (1988). 'Consumo, indebitamento delle famiglie e razionamento del credito', *Giornale degli economisti e annali di economia* **47**: 545-73.

Meghir, C. and G. Weber (1992). 'Intertemporal Non-Separability or Borrowing Restrictions? A Disaggregate Analysis Using a U.S. Panel', UCL and IFS, mimeo.

Zeldes, S.P. (1989). 'Consumption and Liquidity Constraints: An Empirical Investigation', *Journal of Political Economy* **97**: 305-46.

11 Intergenerational transfers and capital market imperfections. Evidence from a cross-section of Italian households*

LUIGI GUISO and TULLIO JAPPELLI

1 Introduction

It is a commonly held opinion that individuals are strongly motivated to develop non-market institutions to overcome, at least in part, market deficiencies. In a recent paper, Arnott and Stiglitz (1991) point out that where there is no market for insurance, individuals are prompted to develop unambiguously beneficial informal markets. They conclude that such informal markets, as those provided by arrangements within the family, are more likely to exist and to improve welfare in economies with less developed financial markets. In this paper we explore the validity of this general principle, in connection with the smoothing of consumption by individuals over their lifetimes.

According to modern theories of consumption, efficient capital markets are needed if the consumer is to be able to borrow against future income to finance current consumption. However, as Stiglitz and Weiss (1981) have shown, adverse selection and moral hazard may prevent people from borrowing the desired amount. The existence of such liquidity constraints may have important implications, especially in the context of the debt neutrality proposition (Barro, 1974), the optimality of progressive taxation (Hubbard and Judd, 1986), and the effectiveness of transitory tax levies.

In principle, borrowing constraints could be offset by a chain of operative intergenerational transfers targeted towards liquidity-constrained households. However, bequests are almost certain to be timed incorrectly: only chance can ensure that they occur precisely when liquidity constraints are binding. On the other hand, transfers between living people, in the form of either intergenerational gifts or loans, may compensate more effectively for financial market imperfections and relieve consumers from borrowing constraints.

In order to study the extent to which *inter vivos* transfers overcome capital market imperfections, we present a simple model able to describe the pattern of such transfers across generations. One way to model intergenerational transfers is to assume that transfers originate from middle-aged individuals and flow towards both the younger and the older generations. Since the income profiles are hump-shaped and human capital is illiquid, the young are more likely to be liquidity-constrained and to receive transfers. Loan repayment occurs when the consumer is in his middle age, and is directed towards the previous generation, which is now older. In Section 2, after discussing the main features of the model, we derive comparative static results relating the transfer decision of the donor to the recipient's current and future endowments.

We test the main theoretical prediction of the model exploiting a data set in which both liquidity-constrained households and transfer recipients are directly observable. This enables us to quantify the importance of *inter vivos* transfers, to describe some of the characteristics of transfer recipients, and to test whether transfers are targeted towards liquidity-constrained households. The data set, described in Section 3, is drawn from a recent survey of Italian households. The Italian economy provides an ideal case to study the connection between private transfers and capital market imperfections because there is a strong presumption that Italian households face tight liquidity constraints.

In Section 4 we comment on the results of a logit model relating the probability of receiving a transfer to an indicator of liquidity-constraints and to other economic and demographic variables that are observable in the cross-section. The results indicate that private transfers help to ease the effect of capital market imperfections. Indeed, we find that private transfers are mainly targeted towards households which do not have access to credit markets. The average size of such transfers is large enough to enable at least some consumers to move closer to the unconstrained optimal consumption path. However, we also find that many who are liquidity-constrained receive no transfers. In 1987, out of 1,249 households which reported to be liquidity-constrained, only 106 received transfers. Thus a substantial number of liquidity-constrained households remains even after transfers have been made. Section 5 summarizes our conclusions.

2 A model of intergenerational transfers

We consider a simple model with ovelapping generations and altruistic consumers. The model accounts for transfers to the younger as well as to the older generation. A similar theoretical structure has been used by Altig and

Davis (1989) to study the implications for fiscal policy and aggregate savings of the interaction between borrowing constraints and intergenerational altruism.

2.1   Assumptions

Each individual (household) lives for three periods during which he is "young", "middle-aged" and "old" respectively. At the end of the third period he dies and is replaced by an identical new consumer.

Let c_{it} and e_{it} be the consumption and income of a member of generation t when he is of age i ($i = 1, 2, 3$). Income derives from inelastically supplying one unit of labor with a hump-shaped productivity profile: thus $e_{1t} < e_{2t} > e_{3t}$ for all values of t. Consumption smoothing leads to optimal consumption by the young, c^*, to exceed current labor income e_{1t}. We further assume that the younger generation cannot borrow against future labor income because of capital market imperfections. The assumption that young households are denied credit is analytically convenient. As will be seen in Section 3, it also captures an important aspect of the actual working of the credit market.

Following Jaffee and Russell (1976), this assumption can also be justified in the following way. Children belong to one or two types: "honest" children, who will honor their commitments, and "dishonest" ones who will not, if the gain from defaulting exceeds its cost. Everyone knows his type, but banks do not. This information asymmetry implies that credit rationing may arise as an optimal response of financial intermediaries and that, at the pooling equilibrium some children will be denied loans.[1] On the other hand, parents have superior information and know their children type. On the basis of this information they decide whether to make a loan or not.

We also assume that children are altruistic with respect to their parents. Thus, even if dishonest children might find it optimal to default on bank loans, altruism implies that implicit contracts within the family are self-enforcing. Even without altruism, parents with control over their wealth until their very end might use an inheritance threat as an enforcement leverage over their children (Kotlikoff and Spivak, 1981). In this paper we assume that altruism with respect to the older generation is sufficiently strong to enforce informal contracts.

From these assumptions, it follows that first-period consumption is constrained by disposable income, $e_{1t} + \tau_{t-1}$, where τ_{t-1} is a transfer received from generation $t-1$. The transfer is in the form of a gift or a loan. Loans are payed back in the next period. During his remaining life the consumer can borrow or lend freely at the constant rate of interest r.[2] An alternative is to assume that all generations face borrowing constraints. As will be seen, if the earnings profile of the representative consumer is sufficiently hump-shaped, the main predictions of the model are the same.

At age 2 the individual transfers τ_t to the younger generation, spends R_{t-1} to pay back the loans received when young and makes gifts g_t to the old generation (i.e., to generation $t-1$). During the third period of his life, the individual consumes all available resources, i.e. savings from the previous period, s_{2t}, gifts received from the next generation, g_{t+1}, loan repayments, R_t, and his third period income, e_{3t}. The sequence of budget constraints faced by the generation t household is

$$c_{1t} = e_{1t} + \tau_{t-1} \tag{1}$$

$$c_{2t} + g_t + \tau_t + R_{t-1} + s_{2t} = e_{2t} \tag{2}$$

$$c_{3t} = e_{3t} + (1 + r)s_{2t} + g_{t+1} + R_t. \tag{3}$$

Combining the second- and the third-period budget constraints into a single equation we obtain:

$$c_{2t} + \frac{c_{3t}}{1+r} + \tau_t - \frac{R_t}{1+r} + R_{t-1} + g_t = e_{2t} + \frac{e_{3t}}{1+r} + \frac{g_{t+1}}{1+r}. \tag{2'}$$

A generation t household derives utility directly from lifetime consumption according to the time-separable utility function

$$u_t = u(c_{1t}) + \gamma u(c_{2t}) + \gamma^2 u(c_{3t})$$

where $\gamma = 1/(1 + \delta)$ and δ is the subjective rate of time preference. We assume that u_t is twice-continuously differentiable, increasing and concave in each argument so that

$$u_{it} = \frac{\partial u}{\partial c_{it}} > 0 \quad \text{and} \quad \frac{\partial^2 u}{\partial c_{it}^2} < 0 \ (i = 1, \ 2, \ 3).$$

We further assume that

$$\lim_{c_{it} \to 0} u_{it} = \infty \quad \text{and} \quad \lim_{c_{it} \to \infty} u_{it} = 0.$$

A member of generation t also derives utility from the well-being of his parents and that of his descendants according to the Buiter-Carmichael (1984) specification of the utility function with two-sided altruism

$$V_t = (1 - \alpha\beta)u_t + \alpha u_{t-1} + \beta V_{t+1} \tag{4}$$

where α and β measure the concern of the current generation for the welfare of the previous and the next generation respectively.[3]

2.2   *Are transfers operative?*

The problem for the generation t household is to choose consumption in the three periods, transfers g_t and τ_t and loan repayment R_t so as to maximize (4) subject to the budget constraints (1) and (2′) and the following non-negativity constraints:

$$\tau_t \geq 0 \tag{5}$$

$$g_t \geq 0 \tag{6}$$

$$\tau_t - \frac{R_t}{1 + r} \geq 0. \tag{7}$$

Conditions (5) and (6) preclude the possibility that the current generation imposes negative transfers on the younger and older generations. Condition (7) states that, if $R_t \geq 0$, the present value of loan repayment cannot exceed the amount of the loan. If transfers are operative, i.e. if $\tau_t > 0$ and (7) is binding, then the age 2 household acts as a bank for the young household. Note that if $\tau_t = 0$ there are no *inter vivos* transfers from parents to children. Further, if $-R_t > 0$, bequests flow from the older to the younger generation. Thus, the structure of the model is flexible enough to accommodate *inter vivos* gifts and loans, as well as bequests. Recalling that by assumption period 1 consumption is constrained by current disposable income, the first-order conditions for the maximization problem are:

$$u_{2t} = \gamma(1 + r)u_{3t} \tag{8}$$

$$u_{3t} \geq \frac{a}{1 + r}\, u_{3t-1} \qquad \text{(with equality if } g_t > 0\text{)} \tag{9}$$

$$u_{1t+1} \geq \gamma(1 + r)u_{2t+1} \quad \text{(with equality if } \tau_t > 0\text{)} \tag{10}$$

$$u_{3t} \geq \frac{\beta}{\gamma}\, u_{2t+1} \qquad \text{(with equality if } \tau_t - \frac{R_t}{1 + r} > 0\text{)}. \tag{11}$$

The Euler condition (8) states that along the optimal consumption path the household is indifferent between one additional unit of consumption at age 2 and the present value of $1 + r$ additional units at age 3. Conditions (9) and (10) determine whether gifts and transfers are operative. If at the optimum $g_t > 0$ and $\tau_t > 0$, then (9) and (10) hold with equality. Condition (9) then implies that the value of g_t is determined by the requirement that, at the optimum, the consumer is indifferent between consuming one additional unit himself, or deriving utility from the consumption of one additional unit by the parents. If $\tau_t > 0$, it follows from (10) that the consumption of generation $t + 1$ at age 1 is the same as it would be in the absence of borrowing constraints.

Finally, condition (11) determines whether transfers τ_t are mainly motivated by altruism $(\tau_t - R_t/(1 + r) > 0)$, or rather take the form of a loan $(\tau_t - R_t/(1 + r) = 0)$. In the first case, (11) holds with equality and net transfers are such that a member of generation t is indifferent between consuming one additional unit when old, or enjoying the indirect utility provided by an additional unit of consumption by his children. In the second case, a parent with free access to credit markets acts as a bank for his children.[4]

Since the main purpose of this paper is to determine whether the probability of receiving a transfer can be linked to observable characteristics of the population and to test whether transfers are targeted towards liquidity-constrained households, we need to study the conditions under which transfers and gifts are operative. Conditions (8), (9) and (10) imply that $g_t > 0$ and $\tau_t > 0$ if the following inequalities hold:

$$z_1^* = u_{2t}(c_{2t}) - \alpha\gamma u_{3t-1}(c_{3t-1}) < 0 \tag{12}$$

$$z_2^* = u_{1t+1}(c_{1t+1}) - \gamma(1 + r)u_{2t+1}(c_{2t+1}) > 0. \tag{13}$$

The latent variable z_1^*, evaluated at $g_t = 0$, measures the net marginal gain in utility of making a gift to the older generation. Similarly, the latent variable z_2^* evaluated at $\tau_t = 0$, represents the net gain for the young generation of receiving a transfer.

Consider first a gift to the older generation. The transfer will take place if the loss in utility suffered by the age 2 household is less than the gain obtained from transfering one unit of consumption to his parents. An increase in the donor's income lowers the value of z_1^* and widens the gap between the loss and the gain of giving. The opposite holds for an increase in the recipient's income. Thus

$$\frac{\partial z_1^*}{\partial e_{2t}} < 0 \quad \text{and} \quad \frac{\partial z_1^*}{\partial e_{3t-1}} > 0.$$

Consider now the decision of making a transfer to the young. Such transfer will take place if the marginal utility of consumption in the first period, evaluated a $\tau_t = 0$, exceeds the value of an additional unit of consumption in the second period. Obviously, this will be always true for a liquidity-constrained consumer.[5] Thus, transfers will be always operative when young households are rationed in the credit market. It follows that the Euler condition $u_{1t+1} = \gamma(1 + r)u_{2t+1}$ holds for the young generation as well. This is simply the implication of the assumptions that middle-aged consumers are not liquidity-constrained, that there are no informational asymmetries between parents and children and that altruism is sufficiently strong to induce dishonest children to repay their obligations. If the latter assumption is violated, then the amount that parents would be willing to lend would not exceed the present value of planned bequests.[6]

An increase in the prospective recipient's current income reduces the probability of receiving a transfer, while an increase in his future income has the opposite effect, other things being equal. The reason is that an increase in current income relaxes the borrowing constraint, while higher future income raises desired consumption and the stringency of the constraint.[7]

An increase in donor's income has no effect on the transfer decision if $\tau_t - R_t/(1 + r) = 0$. However, if the transfer is motivated by altruism, an increase in e_{2t} raises z_2^*. To summarize, the partial derivatives are:

$$\frac{\partial z_2^*}{\partial e_{1t+1}} < 0, \quad \frac{\partial z_2^*}{\partial e_{2t+1}} > 0, \quad \frac{\partial z_2^*}{\partial e_{2t}} > 0.$$

If there are no intergenerational loans, transfers to the young are independent from future income but still negatively correlated with current income. Even in this case, being liquidity-constrained increases the probability of receiving a transfer.

3   Identifying transfer recipients and liquidity-constrained households

In order to test the main implications of the model we require data on transfer recipients, current resources and proxies for future resources. Since the probability of receiving a transfer also depends on whether desired consumption exceeds currently observed consumption, we also need a variable to identify liquidity-constrained households. The data set is taken from the 1987 Bank of Italy Survey of Household Income and Wealth (SHIW).[8] The interviews were conducted at the beginning of 1988 and the data refer to the year 1987. The survey contains fairly accurate data on consumption, income, wealth and several demographic characteristics for a total of 8,026 households. In the survey, families are defined as individuals living at the same address.

Transfer recipients are defined as households in wich at least one member received a monetary transfer from a relative or a friend outside the household during the year 1987. This definition implies that the household, rather than the individual, is the decision unit, i.e. we do not count transfers among members of the same family. The total number of transfer recipients in the data set is 213, or 2.7 percent of the sample. In principle, one would like to distinguish loans from gifts, i.e. transfers motivated by altruism from those motivated by exchange. Empirically, however, this distinction is almost impossible since it is purely subjective. For example, if the repayment is a service from the children to the parents, then recipients may well treat as a gift what is in fact a loan (see Bernheim, Schleifer and Summers, 1985 and Cox, 1987). Since our main objective is to test whether transfers are targeted towards individuals who do not have access to official credit markets, the distinction is also irrelevant. In fact, the model in Section 2 indicates that both gifts and loans should benefit liquidity-constrained households.

The number of transfer recipients might underestimate the true number of total *inter vivos* transfers because one important transfer is omitted from the survey, namely the implicit rental value of housing that accrues to secondary family units that are sharing living arrangements with primary family units. Similarly, the variable does not include other transfers made within multifamily households; these may be important if extended families are widespread.[9]

Even if it is taken for granted that the number of transfer recipients is underestimated, the proportion of recipients is fairly small in comparison to other countries.[10] For example, Cox (1987) and Cox and Jappelli (1990) find that in the United States – the only country in which the determinants of private transfers have been empirically studied – about 10 percent of households received transfers in any year. However, the figure for the United States includes also bequests. But in any given year the proportion of individuals receiving a bequest is small – in Italy around 0.5 percent in the survey.

In addition to those listed above, there might be several other reasons why we observe a small proportion of transfer recipients. First, transfers may not be operative for low-wealth households. Second, some authors argue that the bequest motive is weak, and limited at most to high-wealth households.[11] Third, parents may not be willing to transfer resources to the young, even if they have the means to do so "because families remain paternalistic long after their offspring reach official adulthood" (Hall, 1986, p. 52). Finally, in models in which transfers are motivated by exchange, and not by altruism, strategic considerations may render transfers not operative.

To study the connection between the probability of receiving a transfer and borrowing constraints, we also need an operational definition to identify liquidity-constrained households. One solution, adopted by Hayashi (1985) and Zeldes (1989), is to rely on *ad hoc* sample-splitting techniques, and to define a household to be liquidity-constrained if either its current savings – as in Hayashi – or its liquid assets – as in Zeldes – are below a predetermined threshold. As both authors point out, the major problem with this method is that one ends up including among the group of low-saving or low-wealth households many households that are not in fact liquidity-constrained, thus substantially overestimating the proportion of liquidity-constrained households in the population.

An alternative is to rely upon the direct information readily available in our data set. Let us define a consumer to be liquidity-constrained whenever current desired consumption exceeds current available resources. Desired consumption is not observable, though we can observe consumers who, while needing credit to finance expenditures on non-durable goods:

i) did apply for a loan in 1987 because they expected to be refused credit (1,194 households), or

ii) did actually apply for a loan in 1987, and were refused credit (55 households).[12]

We infer from this information that for 1,249 households, or 15.6 percent of the sample, desired consumption exceeds available resources. The proportion of liquidity-constrained is plausible, especially if one takes into account that we are missing all borrowing constraints arising in the mortgage market. Table 11.1 indicates that the total liabilities of the household sector in Italy are extremely low when compared with those of other developed economies. As shown by Guiso, Jappelli and Terlizzese (1994) and by Jappelli and Pagano (1989), these figures can be interpreted as evidence of widespread liquidity constraints in Italy, rather than as evidence of low propensity to borrow by Italian households.

Table 11.1 Ratios of household liabilities to financial assets and consumption for selected countries in 1986

Country	Liabilities	
	Financial Assets	Consumption
United States	24.8	98.0
France	38.0	79.0
Germany	8.6	19.0
United Kingdom	32.2	101.0
Sweden	63.1	116.0
Norway	73.3	93.0
Italy	6.1	12.2

Sources: OECD, *Financial Accounts*, 1987. The data for Italy are from Banca d'Italia, *Bollettino economico*, 6, 1986, p. 53. Consumption: OECD, *National Accounts*, vol. 1, 1987.

It is interesting to note that, according to our definition, the characteristics of liquidity-constrained households accord well with intuition. Among the young (less than 30 years old) the proportion of liquidity-constrained is much higher (20.8 percent) than among the elderly (11.6 percent in the group of over 65 years olds). Credit-constrained families have less disposable income than those with access to credit market (26.5 against 34.1 millions lire), and a considerably higher propensity to consume (83 percent against 73 percent).

Table 11.2 Sample means for selected variables *(a)*

Variables	Transfer recipients (1)	Non- recipients (2)	All consumers (3)
Proportion receiving transfers	1.000	0.000	0.027
Transfer amount	7,177	0	190
Income (net of transfers)	18,588	33,139	32,754
Consumption	20,288	24,356	24,249
Age	49	52	52
Education (years)	8	9	9
Males	0.718	0.855	0.851
Homeowners	0.390	0.599	0.593
Living in the North	0.451	0.624	0.620
Employed in the industrial sector	0.150	0.227	0.225
Employed in the service sector	0.178	0.219	0.218
Employed in the public sector	0.197	0.207	0.207
Liquidity-constrained households	0.498	0.146	0.158
Rejected applicants	0.042	0.006	0.007
Discouraged borrowers	0.455	0.140	0.149
Number of cases	213	7,813	8,026

(a) Current income, transfer amounts and consumption are in thousands of 1987 lire.

In Table 11.2 we report sample means of the variables that will be used in the estimation for the group of transfer recipients (column (1)) for those who did not receive transfers (column (2)) and for the whole sample (column (3)). It appears that transfer recipients are on average younger and have less income and wealth than households who did not receive transfers. It also appears that transfer recipients are more likely to be denied credit than the rest of the population. According to our definition, almost 50 percent of transfer recipients are liquidity-constrained. But among those who did not receive transfers, only 14.6 percent do not have access to credit markets. Note also that when transfers occur, their amount is substantial: for transfer recipients, they account for more than one third of consumption.

4   Estimation

As in Cox (1987) and Cox and Jappelli (1990), our approach is to infer behavior of the donors from the characteristics of the recipients. The theoretical model developed in Section 2 allows us to define a general reduced form for the latent variables z^*, relating the transfer decision of the donor to the current income of the recipient, demographic characteristics and proxies for future resources and borrowing constraints.

Assuming that the reduced form z^* is linear, indexing individuals by i ($i = 1, ..., n$), and adding a stochastic component ε_i, one can write

$$z_i^* = x_i'\beta + \varepsilon_i \tag{14}$$

where x_i is a (k x 1) column vector of attributes pertaining to the i-th household, β is a k-dimensional vector of unknown parameters, and the disturbance ε_i is assumed to be independently and identically distributed with zero mean and variance σ^2 ($i = 1, ..., n$). Let z_i be a dummy variable taking the value of 1 for a transfer recipient ($z_i > 0$), and of zero otherwise. Thus, the probability that a transfer takes place is given by

$$\text{Prob}(z_i = 1) = \text{Prob}(z_i^* > 0) = \text{Prob}(\varepsilon_i > -x_i'\beta) = 1 - F(x_i'\beta) \tag{15}$$

where $F(\cdot)$ is the cumulative distribution function for the disturbance ε_i. Further, assuming that $F(\cdot)$ is the logistic distribution function

$$\text{Prob}(z_i = 1) = \frac{\exp(x_i'\beta)}{1 + \exp(x_i'\beta)} \tag{16}$$

it is possible to estimate by maximum likelihood the vector of parameters β, up to a constant of proportionality.

The results of the logit estimation are displayed in column (1) of Table 11.3. As predicted by the model, current disposable income, net of transfers, has a negative and highly significant effect on the probability of receiving a transfer. At sample means a 10 percent increase in current income lowers the estimated probability by 1.5 percentage points.[13]

Table 11.3 Logit estimates on transfer receipts (a)

Variables	All households (1)		All households (2)		Independent family units only (3)	
	Coefficients	t-statistics	Coefficients	t-statistics	Coefficients	t-statistics
Income (net of transfers)	-0.382E-04	-5.32**	-0.380E-04	-5.27**	-0.118E-03	-9.20**
Age	-0.087	-3.07**	-0.088	-3.10**	-0.089	-2.78**
Age^2	0.602E-03	2.30*	0.613E-03	2.34*	0.613E-03	2.08*
Education	0.038	2.02*	0.038	1.99*	0.072	3.17**
Males	-0.445	-2.48*	-0.443	-2.46*	-0.089	-0.42
Homeowners	-0.246	-1.59	-0.239	-1.54	0.027	0.15
Living in the North	-0.149	-0.98	-0.144	-0.94	0.115	0.64
Employed in the industrial sector	-0.965	-3.72**	-0.983	-3.78**	-0.949	-3.00**
Employed in the service sector	-0.558	-2.21*	-0.579	-2.28*	-0.202	-0.68
Employed in the public sector	-0.555	-2.26**	-0.583	-2.36*	-0.383	-1.30
Liquidity-constrained households	1.418	9.13**			1.355	7.47**
Rejected applicants			2.100	5.26**		
Discouraged borrowers			1.376	8.71**		
Constant	0.226	0.29	0.253	0.32	0.651	0.71
Recipients	213		213		168	
Observations	8,026		8,026		5,994	
Likelihood at binomial	-983.16		-983.16		-766.15	
Final likelihood	-847.94		-846.46		-603.46	
Likelihood ratio test	270.44		273.40		325.38	

(a) Transfer receipts = 1 if transfer received, 0 otherwise. In column (3) the sample includes only independent family units. These are defined as families composed by a head and, if present, by a spouse and by children under the age of 18 who live at home and by non-working children – older than 18 – who live at home. – * Significant at the 5 percent level. – ** Significant at the 1 percent level.

Since future income is not observable, we proxy expected future resources with a set of demographic variables, such as age, sex, education, occupational and regional dummies. If earnings increase with age over the early part of the working life, being younger implies higher expected future income and higher desired consumption. Thus, one should find a negative relation between age and the probability of receiving a transfer. Indeed, we find that this probability decreases rapidly until the consumer is 40 years old, and more slowly thereafter.[14]

The coefficient of education is positive and significant. One possibility is that more education implies higher future income, other things being equal. However, education may be picking up other effects as well. For example, part of the effect may be due to tuition transfers targeted towards college students, i.e. towards students with above average education.

The sex, occupational and regional dummies indicate that transfers benefit disproportionately females, households in the South and in the rural areas. The interpretation of these coefficients is complex, since these variables may be picking up several effects. On the one hand, these groups of the population have less than average future resources, so they should, according to our model, receive more transfers. However, there are also other plausible explanations. For example, as we have suggested in the Introduction, where official markets are less developed – as in the rural and Southern regions – private transfers should be more widespread. Leigh (1982) suggests that women provide more services and interactions with their parents than men and therefore receive more transfers.

Finally, the coefficient of the liquidity-constraint variable is positive and very precisely estimated. At sample means, the probability of receiving a transfer is 1.7 percent higher for a consumer who is liquidity-constrained. This is remarkable, given that the unconditional binomial estimate is only 2.7 percent.[15] Since there may be errors of measurement in our proxy for liquidity constraints, we distinguish between discouraged borrowers and rejected applicants. The results, reported in column (2) of Table 11.3, confirm the finding of a strong correlation between liquidity constraints and transfer decisions. In addition, we find that those who have been explicitly denied a loan – who are unambiguously liquidity-constrained – are also those with the highest probability of receiving a transfer.

The results are also robust with respect to the proxy for liquidity constraints. We obtain the same pattern of results if we follow either Hayashi's (1985) or Zeldes' (1989) sample-splitting techniques to construct dummies for liquidity-constrained families.[16] The coefficients of the liquidity-constraint variable are 0.32 (with a t-value of 2.6) and 0.59 (with a t-value of 3.8), respectively. All three proxies are positive and significant.

But the direct measure for liquidity constraints displays the highest and most significant coefficient.

Our results may be criticized on the grounds that the dependent variable does not count as transfers those made within the family and, in particular, the implicit rental value of housing that accrues to secondary family units. If extended families are widespread, one should not be surprised to find few transfers outside the family as defined in the survey. Further, the coefficients of the logit equation could be potentially biased. For example, if secondary family units contain a disproportionate amount of women, the coefficient of males in columns (1) and (2) of Table 11.3 might be downward biased.[17] The correct strategy would be to treat each secondary family unit as a transfer recipient. Unfortunately, we lack information on most characteristics of these secondary family units, including whether they are liquidity-constrained.

In column (3) of Table 11.3 we report the results of estimating the logit equation in a subsample of independent family units only, defined as families composed by a head and, if present, by a spouse, by children under the age of 18 who live at home and by non-working children older than 18 who live at home. In the total sample there are 74.7 per cent independent family units. The proportion of transfer recipients is slightly higher than in the full sample. The effects of current income and of education are stronger than in the full sample estimates. But even in this case the effect of being liquidity-constrained increases the probability of receiving a transfer substantially.[18]

In order to test whether liquidity considerations affect also the amount of transfers, we have estimated equations for transfer amounts corrected for selectivity bias. The pattern of the result is the same as that reported in Table 11.3 for the transfer decision. The results indicate that being liquidity-constrained increases the average transfer by almost 2 million lire (roughly 8 percent of consumption), but the coefficient is not very precisely estimated.[19] For transfer recipients, the average transfer is more than 7 million lire, almost 40 percent of disposable income. Thus, the size of private transfers is large enough to enable at least some liquidity-constrained consumers to move closer to the unconstrained optimal consumption path.

5 Conclusions

Informal markets may provide the means for households to offset capital market imperfections and to smooth consumption over their life cycle. Using a cross-section of Italian households, we have investigated whether such system of family transfers exists, and to what extent it is able to overcome borrowing constraints. We have found substantial evidence that private transfers help remedy capital market deficiencies. Private transfers are in fact mainly targeted towards households which face binding credit constraints. This result is not sensitive to different proxies for liquidity constraints and to the importance of extended families. However, we have also found that many liquidity-constrained households received no transfer: out of 1,249 only 106 received transfers in 1987. Thus, a very substantial number of liquidity-constrained households remains after transfers have been made.

The data set that we have employed does not contain information regarding transfers that take place within multifamily units. As both theory and casual observation suggest, transfers between members of multifamily units should be even more closely linked to liquidity constraints than transfers that take place outside such units. Liquidity considerations might even be one of the main reasons why such families are widespread.

NOTES

* This paper was originally published in the *European Economic Review*, 35 (1991) and is here reprinted with permission. An earlier version was presented at the European Meeting of the Econometric Society, Munich, September 4-8, 1989. We thank Donald Cox, Bob Murphy, Daniele Terlizzese, Ignazio Visco and Guglielmo Weber for helpful comments. Errors are the authors' responsibility.

1 Alternatively, as in Stiglitz and Weiss (1981), we could assume that children are either high- or low-risk borrowers.

2 For example, suppose that the cost of default grows rapidly with age. Then credit rationing applies only to the younger generation.

3 As shown by Kimball (1987) and Abel (1987), there are restrictions on the values of the parameters α and β. First, altruism requires that both α and β be non-negative. Second, the "bounded altruism" condition is satisfied if $\beta < 1$ (Kimball, 1987). Third, consistency between parents and children decisions implies that $\beta\alpha \leq 1$ (Abel, 1987).

4 Note that if $R_t < (1 + r)\tau_t$, i.e. if bequests are operative, the distinction between a loan and a gift is arbitrary. This is precisely the reason why it is impossible to separate pure loans from pure gifts. As will be seen in Section 3, the distinction is irrelevant for the purpose of this paper.

5 If the discount rate γ would decrease between ages 1 and 2, then parents may find that a transfer is not in order, while their children would find that it is. However, we assume that the discount rate is independent from age and constant across generations. If γ is age-dependent, the optimal plan chosen at time t may not be optimal as of time $t + 1$. Thus, the optimal plan might be inconsistent. On the other hand, if consumers take into account the fact that tastes will be changing

over time, and if the discount factor is only a function of age, individuals will act as if they had a constant rate of time preference (Blanchard and Fischer, 1989, pp. 69-82).

6 A sufficient condition for private loans to be self-enforcing is that the utility of the child is greater if the child repays his obligations with the parent. Let V_n and V_d be the value of the child's utility if he honors his debt and if he defaults, respectively. Consider the case in which planned bequests, b_t, are below the loan repayment $(1+r)\tau_t$, and suppose that if the child defaults, parents set bequests equal to zero. Then the dishonest child will not default if:

$$V_n - V_d = \alpha\gamma^2[u(e_{3t} + ... + (1 + r)\tau - b_t) - u(e_{3t} + ... + 0)]$$
$$+ \gamma[u(e_{2t+1} + ... - (1 + r)\tau + b_t) - u(e_{2t+1} + ... + 0)] > 0.$$

The first term of the expression is positive, while the second is negative. We assume that the value of α is sufficiently large for this condition to be satisfied.

7 It is clear that even if all generations face borrowing constraints, provided that earnings are sufficiently hump-shaped, transfers from the middle-aged towards the younger generation would still be operative.

8 See the Methodological Appendix to this volume for a detailed description of the survey.

9 We try to deal with these issues at the end of Section 4.

10 The proportion of transfer recipients is similar to that produced by other surveys of Italian households. For example, the 1984 and 1986 surveys carried out by the Bank of Italy report that the proportion of households receiving transfers was 2.5 percent and 3 percent respectively, while the survey conducted by the Italian statistical institute (Istat) reports that 3.8 percent of the sample received a transfer in 1985. Interestingly, the latter survey, indicates that transfers between parents and children account for more than 70 percent of total transfers. The remaining 30 percent is accounted for by transfers between siblings and other relatives.

11 For example, Modigliani (1988) reviews the evidence for the U.S. and concludes that the share of bequeathed wealth accounts for less than one third of U.S. aggregate wealth. He also reports that the number of households that save to provide an estate for the family is substantially higher among the high-wealth households than in the total population.

12 The liquidity-constraint variable could overestimate the number of liquidity-constrained households because some families try to – or would like to – violate their intertemporal budget constraint, and because some consumers thought that they might be turned down for credit, but would not have wanted credit anyway. However, one should take into account the fact that the questions in the survey refer only to the market for consumer credit. Many households might instead be constrained in the mortgage market. Thus, we regard the information contained in the survey only as a proxy, and check the robustness of our results using also more standard proxies for liquidity constraints.

13 The coefficients reported in Table 11.3 show the effect of the explanatory variables on the odds, rather than on the probability itself. Denoting

with b the estimate of β, we then evaluate the partial derivatives, $x_{ik} = b_k \exp(x_i'b)/[1 + \exp(x_i'b)]^2$, at sample means.

14 An alternative interpretation is that the negative age effect is related to the increasing probability of being without parents when the consumer grows older. If this were the case, one should observe that the probability of receiving a transfer declines at a speed no greater than the increase in the probability of death of the parents. Assuming an average gap between generations of 25 years, the results indicate that the probability of receiving a transfer declines by 2 percent between ages 20 and 30. On the other hand, the 1985 survival table indicates that the probability of death increases by only 0.75 percent between ages 45 and 60 (from 0.36 to 1.11 percent). Thus, at least part of the negative relation between age and the probability of receiving a transfer cannot be explained by this effect.

15 We introduce a dummy for homeownership to proxy for the effects of borrowing constraints in the mortgage market. Houses may be used as collateral, and homeowners are less likely to apply for a mortgage to buy a house. The sign of the variable is negative as expected, but not significantly different from zero.

16 Hayashi (1985) includes in the group of liquidity-constrained each household with a level of consumption greater than 0.85 of disposable income plus 0.2 of financial assets. Zeldes (1989) defines as liquidity-constrained all households with liquid assets less than 0.167 of disposable income.

17 A transfer reported by a secondary family unit is conditional on having already received another transfer – in the form of implicit rent – by a primary family unit. In this case one would estimate the probability of receiving an additional transfer. If transfers are motivated by exchange and not by altruism, one should expect the coefficient of current income to be upward biased (Cox, 1987, p. 528).

18 Since the decision to be a multifamily unit is endogenous, the equation was reestimated controlling for selectivity bias. However, the selection-bias term was not significant and the results were very similar to those reported in column (3) of Table 11.3. Independent family units are more prevalent among males, non-homeowners and households in the South. This may help explain why the coefficients of these variables are not significantly different from zero in the sample of column (3).

19 The equation for transfer amounts, corrected for selectivity bias, is the following:

Transfer amount = $-1{,}475 - 0.154$ Income $- 98.8$ Age $- 1{,}530$ Male
                       (0.2)   (3.1)   (1.9)   (0.8)
                 $+436.3$ Education $- 524.8$ Homeownership
                    (2.6)   (0.4)
                 $+297.5$ North $+ 1{,}959$ Liquidity-constrained
                    (0.2)   (0.8)
                 $+6{,}237$ Selectivity term.
                    (1.3)

The mean of transfer amount for the sample of 213 recipients is 7,178 thousand lire. The R^2 of the regression is 0.12.

REFERENCES

Abel, A.B. (1987). 'Operative Gifts and Bequest Motives', NBER Working Paper 2331.

Altig, D. and S.J. Davis (1989). 'Government Debt, Redistributive Fiscal Policy, and the Interaction between Borrowing Constraints and Intergenerational Altruism', *Journal of Monetary Economics* 24: 3-29.

Arnott, R. and J.E. Stiglitz (1991). 'Moral Hazard and Non-Market Institutions: Disfunctional Crowding-Out or Peer Monitoring?', *American Economic Review* 81: pp. 179-90.

Barro, R.J. (1974). 'Are Government Bonds Net Wealth?', *Journal of Political Economy* 82: 1095-118.

Bernheim, D.B., A. Shleifer and L. H. Summers (1985). 'The Strategic Bequest Motive', *Journal of Political Economy* 93: 1045-76.

Blanchard, O.J. and S. Fischer (1989). *Lectures on Macroeconomics*, Cambridge, MA: MIT Press.

Buiter, W.H. and J. Carmichael (1984). 'Government Debt: Comment', *American Economic Review* 74: 762-65.

Cox, D. (1987). 'Motives for Private Income Transfers', *Journal of Political Economy* 95: 508-46.

Cox, D. and T. Jappelli (1990). 'Credit Rationing and Private Transfers: Evidence from Survey Data', *Review of Economics and Statistics* 72: 445-54.

Guiso, L., T. Jappelli and D. Terlizzese (1994). 'Why Is Italy's Saving Rate so High?', *this volume*.

Hall, R.E. (1986). 'Comment to: 'Liquidity Constraints, Fiscal Policy, and Consumption,' by G. R. Hubbard and K. L. Judd', *Brookings Papers on Economic Activity* 1: 51-59.

Hayashi, F. (1985). 'The Effect of Liquidity Constraints on Consumption: A Cross-Section Study', *Quarterly Journal of Economics* 100: 183-206.

Hubbard, G.R. and K.L. Judd (1986). 'Liquidity Constraints, Fiscal Policy, and Consumption', *Brookings Papers on Economic Activity* 1: 1-50.

Jaffee, D.M. and T. Russell (1976). 'Imperfect Information, Uncertainty and Credit Rationing', *Quarterly Journal of Economics* 90: 651-66.

Jappelli, T. and M. Pagano (1989). 'Consumption and Capital Market Imperfections: An International Comparison', *American Economic Review* 79: 1088-105.

Kimball, M.S. (1987). 'Making Sense of Two-sided Altruism', *Journal of Monetary Economics* 20: 301-26.

Kotlikoff, L.J. and A. Spivak (1981). 'The Family as an Incomplete Annuities Market', *Journal of Political Economy* 89: 372-91.

Leigh, G.K. (1982). 'Kinship Interaction over the Family Life Span', *Journal of Marriage and Family* 44: 197-208.

Modigliani, F. (1988). 'The Role of Intergenerational Transfers and Life Cycle Saving in the Accumulation of Wealth', *Journal of Economic Perspectives* 2: 15-40.

Stiglitz, J.E. and A. Weiss (1981). 'Credit Rationing in Markets with Imperfect Information', *American Economic Review* **71**: 393-411.

Zeldes, S.P. (1989). 'Consumption and Liquidity Constraints: An Empirical Investigation', *Journal of Political Economy* **97**: 305-46.

12 Bequests and saving for retirement. What impels the accumulation of wealth?*

FABRIZIO BARCA, LUIGI CANNARI
and LUIGI GUISO

1 Introduction

This paper is an attempt to answer an age-old but important question: namely, what is the relative importance of bequests and saving for retirement in the process of wealth accumulation? To this purpose we will provide evidence on the extent of intergenerational transfers using cross-section information on the origins of the real estate holdings of Italian households.

Before the life-cycle theory of Modigliani and Brumberg (1954) came to dominate the theoretical field of saving, there was probably little doubt that leaving a bequest was the main, or perhaps the only, motivation for saving. Indeed, at the end of the last century (and for many decades thereafter) the assessment of the relative importance of the origins of accumulated wealth was not a central question for economists. They were concerned, rather, with estimating the wealth of nations.

In fact, the belief that bequest was *the* motive for saving enabled the French statistician Alfred de Foville to put forward in 1887 a simple but ingenious method for estimating the wealth of a nation.[1] The idea was to use information on bequests received by the population in a given year to infer the value of the total stock of wealth. If bequests received are simply passed over to the next generation, and if the generational gap (i.e., the number of years between two successive transfers of wealth) and society's "demological laws" are not altered by rapid changes (Pantaleoni, 1890), then the wealth of a nation is simply equal to the generation gap times the flow of bequests observed in a given year.[2]

This method is now known as the method of flows (see Section 3), but given that it is now acknowledged that wealth is also decumulated before death,[3] the method is consistently used only to estimate that part of the stock of wealth due to intergenerational transfers.

There are several reasons for inquiring into the importance of transfers between generations as a source of accumulation. Besides the obvious intellectual curiosity of understanding people's behavior, the presence of significant bequests might have important consequences for policy, depending on the reasons people bequeath part or all of their wealth.

It is well known that the "Ricardian neutrality proposition" rests on the assumption that links exist between successive generations. These are made operative by a network of intergenerational transfers motivated by altruism. Moreover, the impact on the stock of wealth of variables such as life expectancy, retirement age, the composition of the population by age, the structure of the social security system and average household size may depend on whether saving is impelled by bequests (Modigliani, 1988). Furthermore, if one views inheritance as a way to transmit to future generations not only the *bien de famille* but also the ownership of productive capital (and hence the control over it), then bequests, as well as a determinant of the distribution of wealth, become a crucial factor in the efficient allocation of capital.

In Section 2 we summarize the available methods for evaluating the importance of bequests and contrast our approach with others. We outline the essential formal structure used in computation in Section 3 and present the results of the calculations made with our method in Section 4. In Section 5, to verify the robustness of the results, we provide an alternative estimation based on a variant of the method of flows (see next section). As a by-product we obtain a time series of the flows of bequests of land and buildings from 1954 to 1982. In Section 6 we offer additional empirical evidence on the role of bequests as a determinant of saving, based on examining self-reported motives for saving.

2   Evaluating the importance of intergenerational transfers

In spite of numerous shortcomings the share of a country's wealth that derives from bequests or gifts is widely accepted as a measure of the importance of intergenerational transfers in the process of accumulation.[4] Kotlikoff and Summers (1981), extending and improving on the methodology devised by White (1978) and Darby (1979), offer the startling finding that as much as 80 percent of the wealth held by households in the United States may derive from bequests, only 20 percent being then explained by life-cycle saving. They conclude, accordingly, that models of saving based on the life cycle as the primary source of accumulation should give way to approaches that shed light on the determinants of intergenerational transfers.

To estimate the share of inherited wealth, Kotlikoff and Summers adopt two alternative methods. The first, which we shall call the *method of flows*, uses the mortality rates and the distribution of wealth by age in a given year to estimate the flow of bequests. This is then converted into a stock by assuming that both the age difference between testator and legatee and the ratio of the value of bequests to that of capitalized earned income remain constant through time.

The second method is more complex and involves attributing total national earnings and consumption to the individuals belonging to the various age-groups by means of the profiles of consumption and earnings by age in a given year. The stock of wealth accumulated by each individual during his lifetime is obtained by cumulating and capitalizing his savings (defined as the difference between earnings and consumption) from working age onwards. This stock is defined as life-cycle wealth. The individual data are summed up to obtain aggregate life-cycle wealth. Inherited wealth is then obtained as the difference between total and life-cycle wealth. We shall call this procedure the *attribution method.*

Both methods have undesirable aspects that affect the quality of the estimate they produce. The first method rests on the rather strong assumption of the economy being in steady state. The estimated share of inherited wealth, moreover, is sensitive to the hypothesis regarding the age gap between the testator and the legatee. The second resorts to numerous assumptions whose effect on the final result cannot be readily interpreted. The choice of method is not inconsequential; for example, Kotlikoff and Summers calculate the share of inherited wealth at 46 percent using the method of flows and 81 percent with the attribution method.

In this paper we shall estimate the share of inherited wealth in Italy by means of an alternative method which avoids some of the problematic assumptions embedded in Kotlikoff and Summers' calculations and which does not require the economy to be in steady state. As will be discussed at length in Section 4 we use direct information on the source of households' wealth, drawn from the 1987 Bank of Italy Survey of Italian Household Income and Wealth (SHIW).[5]

3 The formal structure

Consider the equation of accumulation of wealth of a consumer or a household (if the latter is the economic unit of reference):

$$W_t = (1 + r)W_{t-1} + Y_t - C_t + E_t \tag{1}$$

where t is working age, W_t is the end-of-period stock of wealth, Y_t is after-tax earned income, C_t is expenditure on consumption. In every period the consumer may receive a bequest, E_t. Given his wealth from the preceding period (which yields a rate of return equal to r) and given the value of earned income and of the bequests received, the equation defines the stock of wealth holdings at the end of the period. His saving for the period is $S_t = Y_t - C_t$.

Assuming that the individual's stock of wealth is zero at the time he reaches working age ($t=1$), the current value of wealth W_t can be expressed as:

$$W_t = \sum_{i=1}^{t} (1 + r)^{t-i} S_i + \sum_{i=1}^{t} (1 + r)^{t-i} E_i = W_t^L + W_t^E. \qquad (2)$$

The first term of the expression is the sum of the individual's capitalized life savings to time t. This is the portion of wealth attributable to the life cycle under Kotlikoff and Summers' definition, which we designate as W^L. The second component, W^E, represents inherited wealth. A measure of the importance of intergenerational transfers in the process of accumulation is given by the ratio:

$$\alpha_E = \frac{W_t^E}{W_t}. \qquad (3)$$

This measure of the importance of bequests warrants some discussion. In the first place, bequests will be observed even in the absence of an express desire to make them when length of life is uncertain; these unintentional bequests, which may not be negligible, are obviously compatible with the life-cycle theory, whose basic implications are unaffected by the introduction of uncertainty regarding length of life.[6] However, a high value of α_E may signal the presence of significant intentional bequests.

In the second place, inherited wealth may be defined in different ways. In the equation above, W^E includes both bequests and the interest accrued thereon. This definition is consistent with the pure life-cycle model, where, in the absence of bequests, wealth consists of the capitalized value of the sum of earned income less the capitalized value of the sum of spending on consumption. An alternative course is to attribute the interest on bequests to current income and to define saving as $\tilde{S}_t = rW_{t-1} + Y_t - C_t$. In this case the breakdown of wealth is:

$$W_t = \sum_{i=1}^{t} \tilde{S}_i + \sum_{i=1}^{t} E_i = \tilde{W}_t^L + \tilde{W}_t^E. \qquad (4)$$

Modigliani (1988), in his critique of Kotlikoff and Summers, gives two reasons for preferring the second definition: because $\tilde{S}$ conforms with the usual practice of considering savings as the difference between disposable income (including all interest income regardless of the origin of the wealth on which it accrues) and consumption; and because "...one can measure directly what bequests have been received, but there is no way of telling whether some years later the wealth of the recipient will be larger by the capitalized value of the bequests, or whether instead the recipient will have consumed some or all of the return or even some of the principal" (p. 31).

Conformity with customary definitions is not in itself a good reason to prefer one procedure to another, except when it facilitates statistical comparison. Modigliani's other point is more substantial, as it brings to light the fact that the first procedure can result in a value of α_E that is greater than one. But this result is only apparently contradictory. It is obtained if the individual's lifetime consumption exceeds lifetime earnings and is thus financed by intergenerational transfers. In general which method is more appropriate depends on the effects on the level of consumption of interests earned on bequest.[7]

Thus, while the measure proposed by Kotlikoff and Summers provides a better representation of the share of inherited wealth if interest on bequest is fully saved, Modigliani's method is the correct one if interest on bequest is fully consumed. Lacking a way to solve this issue, we shall report the results obtained by applying both definitions of savings. The truth, as it is often the case, should lie in between the two.

4 Empirical findings

The SHIW provides data on the value of real estate holdings of households and the way they were acquired. Each individual property is identified as having been purchased, built to order by the household, inherited or received as a gift. In addition, respondents supply data on the year they assumed ownership, making possible a precise calculation of the capitalization of the return on bequests.[8]

Of a total sample comprising 8,027 households, 1,913 households (24 percent) either inherited real estate (21 percent) or received it as a gift (3 percent).[9] These households represent 38 percent of all real-estate-owning households. The fact that two out of five households acquired ownership of real estate through intergenerational transfers is by itself evidence that bequests play an important role in the accumulation of wealth.

Before presenting the results on the share of real estate wealth acquired through bequest, several points should be taken into account. First, the survey does not contain information on the origin of other forms of households' wealth, particularly durable goods and financial assets (including rights over fixed capital other than real estate), nor does it offer any evidence of the amount of taxation that people inheriting had to bear due to bequest itself. As a result, we can only estimate the gross real estate component of inherited wealth and then calculate its share of overall wealth.

The second point concerns two possible sources of underestimation of intergenerational transfer of real estate wealth in the survey. Real estate can be bequeathed by transferring the ownership of a company to which the estate belongs: in this case, the inheritance is likely not to be reported in the interview. Furthermore, inheritance being concentrated in high-income households, there might be significant underreporting.

A second source of underestimation can, instead, be taken care of. If an inherited property has been sold by the receiver before the time of the interview, it will be reported in the survey by the buyer as a property acquired through purchase. To correct for that, let q_k be the probability of the respondent indicating at time t that he inherited the property. Let Π be the probability of inheriting a property and p be the probability of an inherited property being sold in any given year. We have $q_k = \Pi(1 - p)^{t-k}$, where k is the year the property was acquired. Therefore, q_k/Π will indicate the probability of the inherited property not having been sold between the time it was inherited and the time of the interview.

Taking account of the above and using the symbols already introduced, the value of wealth inherited in the form of real estate can be estimated as:

$$W_t^E = \sum_{k=1}^{t} [(1 + r)/(1 - p)]^{t-k} E_k. \tag{5}$$

In the calculations it is assumed that the probability of an inherited property being sold is equal to the probability of a property being sold. Based on the data of the 1984, 1986 and 1987 surveys, this probability is estimated at 0.95 percent on an annual basis.[10]

The rate of return used for capitalization draws on survey data on the gross return on real estate and is equal to an average of 3.1 percent for leased properties[11] and 3.9 percent for owner-used properties. To obtain the value of the net return, it was assumed that buildings have an average life of 50 years and depreciate at a constant rate of 2 percent a year.

Table 12.1 shows the results of the calculations with and without the adjustment for the probability of sale of an inherited property and with and without the capitalization of the return on bequests. Bequests and gifts as a share of the total value of properties are shown respectively in the first two columns. Assuming gifts to be similar in all respects to bequests, total intergenerational transfers is reported in the third column.

Table 12.1 Wealth in the form of real estate inherited or received as a gift

	Bequests (a)	Gifts (a)	Total intergenerational transfers in the form of real estate	
			(a)	(b)
Not correcting for the probability of sale	26.2	3.5	29.7	19.3
Correcting for the probability of sale	31.4	3.9	35.3	22.9
Correcting for the probability of sale and capitalizing	44.0	4.9	48.9	31.8

(a) As a share of real estate wealth.
(b) As a share of total net worth.

Without the capitalization of interest, the share of intergenerational transfers is 35 percent, a considerable figure though not necessarily incompatible with the life-cycle model. If the return on bequests is capitalized, the share rises to 49 percent, nearly one and a half times that obtained without capitalization.[12]

The estimated value we obtain is high. It is nevertheless much lower than that estimated by Kotlikoff and Summers for the United States with reference to total wealth by means of the attribution method; it is more similar to their estimate based on the flow of bequests. These figures are consistent with the estimates of Rossi and Vendramin (1990), who apply to Italy the method of flows (once account is taken of the fact that they exclude gifts).

While we cannot supply an estimate of the share of total inherited wealth, we can provide a lower limit for it. Since wealth in the form of real estate represents roughly 65 percent of total households' wealth, the share of the latter attributable to intergenerational transfers is at least 32 percent when interest is capitalized and 23 percent when it is not (see the fourth column of Table 12.1).

These minimum levels are a good approximation of inherited wealth as a proportion of total wealth if we assume that individuals totally decumulate their financial wealth before dying, i.e. that no intergenerational transfers of financial assets are made. A glance at the cross-sectional age profiles of wealth shows that average rates of decumulation of real wealth and financial wealth are roughly similar. Between age-group 51-60, where maximum accumulation is reached, and age-group 76-80, total decumulation is approximately 60 percent *for both categories of wealth* (Table 12.2).

Table 12.2 Average real and financial wealth of households by age of head of household

Age of head of household	Real wealth *(a)*	Financial wealth *(a)*
≦ 40	66.4	47.3
41 – 50	119.4	63.4
51 – 60	135.0	64.8
61 – 65	101.6	45.7
66 – 70	82.3	43.4
71 – 75	83.5	35.8
76 – 80	53.8	21.1
> 80	42.7	13.9
Total	96.5	50.9

Source: 1987 Bank of Italy Survey of Italian Households Income and Wealth.
(a) Millions of 1987 lire.

If we assume that the two sources of underestimation of our share of real estate – bequeathing by transfering ownership of companies which own real estate and underreporting of wealthy households – compensate for the fact that we have not taken into account inheritance taxation, we could conclude that inherited wealth might not unreasonably account for some 50 percent of total wealth if interest on bequests is capitalized or 35 percent if Modigliani's methodology is followed.[13]

5   An alternative estimate

As an alternative to the method adopted above, the survey data can be used to estimate the *annual flow* of bequests of real estate for the population of households. Assuming that the economy is in steady state, the annual flow can be capitalized and transformed into a *stock* which can be compared with total observed wealth in the form of real estate. The method is similar to Kotlikoff and Summers' method of flows.

As noted in the Introduction, a problem with this procedure is that the economy must be assumed to be in a steady state. It is nonetheless useful to carry out the calculation as a control on the previous results, while a historical series of the flows of bequests of real estate can be obtained as a by-product. Unlike the previous case, the stock obtained will be compared to a stock of households' wealth in the form of real estate that is derived from a different source. The comparison might lead to an underestimation of the share of inherited wealth. In fact, previous work has shown that the Bank of Italy survey tends to underestimate households residential buildings:[14] flows of bequests of total real estate are then likely to be underestimated too.

Two key data are used to estimate the value of the flows of bequests (at 1987 prices): the year k when the bequest was received, and the age t of the head of household at the time of the interview. If the entire population living in year k were also alive at the end of 1987 (the survey year), the flow of bequests for year k could be estimated by scaling up the survey figure to the population. In fact, part of the population in year k did not survive to the end of 1987, so that individuals who received a bequest in year k and died before the end of 1987 were not included in the survey sample. As a result, the flow of bequests for year k obtained from the survey underestimates the real flow. This underestimation can be corrected, however, by dividing the flow of bequests in year k resulting from the survey by the probability of an individual aged $t-(1987-k)$ in year k having survived to the end of 1987. The correction was made by using the mortality tables for each year k starting in 1950. Earlier years were not considered because the variance of the estimate tends to increase as k diminishes.

Table 12.3 shows a 9-term centred moving average of the annual flow of bequests. A moving average was adopted because responses on the year of bequest tend to be concentrated at the end of decades, the latter having probably acted as a focal point.[15]

The data show that the flow of bequests grew rapidly from the fifties until 1972, then declined slightly and subsequently stabilized at around 34 (1987) trillion lire. An interpretation of the behavior of the series is beyond the scope of this paper.

In estimating a historical series of inherited wealth in the form of real estate, we use as a reference variable only the flow of bequests in each year, assuming the economy to be in steady state. For a growth rate of *per capita* output equal to n, the stock of inherited wealth, under the hypothesis of capitalization of interest, will be:[16]

$$W_E = \frac{e^{(r-n)g} - 1}{r - n} E \qquad (6)$$

where g is the average age gap between the testator and the legatee. We estimated the intergenerational age gap for 1987 at around 30 years. The lengthening of the average life span over the past 60 years has probably somewhat widened the gap. For the exercise we have to conduct, which capitalizes flows of bequests to recipients belonging to around 65 cohorts (from age 20 to age 85), it is more reasonable to assume a narrower gap of, say, 25 years.

Table 12.3 Annual flow of bequests

Year	Flow *(a)*	Year	Flow *(a)*	Year	Flow *(a)*
1954	18,325	1964	31,497	1974	34,300
1955	16,336	1965	38,043	1975	29,968
1956	23,634	1966	34,908	1976	35,700
1957	21,308	1967	36,027	1977	34,728
1958	23,001	1968	38,484	1978	33,731
1959	23,731	1769	39,457	1979	34,570
1960	24,271	1970	36,444	1980	31,560
1961	28,421	1971	40,884	1981	32,019
1962	28,414	1972	41,201	1982	34,034
1963	26,352	1973	35,358		

(a) Billions of 1987 lire.

In accordance with the hypotheses underlying the previous calculations, we assume a net rate of return of 1.6 percent. For productivity, it is reasonable to assume an average annual growth rate between 2.5 and 3 percent: in the computation we set $n = 0.028$.[17] With these values for the parameters g, r and n, the factor of capitalization is equal to 21.6. The series of the stock of bequests for the years from 1976 to 1982 is given in Table 12.4. The data are expressed in current prices to make them comparable with the series of the total stock of wealth in the form of real estate. The share of inherited wealth is shown in the fourth column. The estimate so obtained is lower than that previously obtained by direct calculation: the difference could be partly explained by the mentioned underestimation of real estate wealth in the survey.

The additional information concerns the stability of the share at around 32 percent from 1978 onwards. The fifth column shows the value of the share of inherited wealth in the form of real estate in the case of a golden-rule economy, where $r=n$; the factor of capitalization in this case is equal to g, so that the value of the stock is $W^E = gE$. The last column gives the estimate of the share in the absence of capitalization, again assuming average annual growth of productivity of 2.8 percent. The "blow-up" factor is in this case $(1-e^{-ng})/n$. The estimate of the share is similar to the one previously obtained. In the light of these figures, the results previously arrived at with the direct method appear to be relatively robust.

Table 12.4 Inherited and total wealth in the form of real estate *(a)*

Year	Flow of inherited wealth	Stock of inherited wealth *(b)*	Stock of real estate wealth	Intergenerational transfers as a share of real estate wealth		
				(c)	*(d)*	*(e)*
1976	7.8	168	394	0.43	0.50	0.35
1977	8.6	186	444	0.42	0.49	0.35
1978	9.6	207	531	0.39	0.45	0.32
1979	12.0	260	677	0.39	0.45	0.32
1980	14.5	314	892	0.36	0.42	0.30
1981	17.5	379	1029	0.37	0.43	0.31
1982	23.4	506	1304	0.39	0.45	0.33

(a) Trillions of current lire. The stock of real estate wealth is the sum of the stock of residential buildings estimated in Banca d'Italia (1986, p. 53, Table 5) and an authors' estimate of the stock of land and non-residential buildings.

(b) Obtained capitalizing the flow of bequests in the first column using the following parameter values: $g=25$; $r=0.016$; $n=0.028$.

(c) Computed capitalizing the interest on the flow of bequests, i.e. dividing the stock of inherited wealth reported in the second column by the stock of real estate wealth of the third column.

(d) Computed under the assumption that $r=n$ and $g=25$.

(e) Computed assuming non-capitalization of the interest on bequests and assuming $n=0.028$ and $g=25$.

6 Individuals' reported reasons for saving

This section supplements the results with available empirical evidence on the reasons individuals themselves give for saving. The way in which households classify and justify their own actions does not constitute a test of the significance of those actions (or their purposes) in the individuals' objective functions; nonetheless, if leaving bequests is an important reason for accumulating resources, this should be confirmed by the information supplied by individuals on the specific motives of their behavior. The practice of assessing alternative theories in the light of interviews on the subjective reasons for saving actually dates back to the early sixties, when the question of the importance of the bequest motive *vis-à-vis* the life cycle in determining the accumulation of wealth was already being raised (see Modigliani, 1988).

The evidence available to us comes from the Censis survey of households' savings and investments (1986), conducted on a nation-wide sample of 3,000 households, and the BNL report on saving (Banca Nazionale del Lavoro, 1988), based on a survey conducted by Doxa on a sample of 1,013 households.

The results of these surveys are set out in Table 12.5. The Censis survey contains a detailed breakdown of the reasons for saving and cannot be compared directly with the BNL-Doxa survey. The bequest motive (identified with the response "to provide for one's children") is designated as the primary reason by 23 percent of the respondents, "saving for old age" by 23 percent and "contingencies" (including illness) by 22 percent. These figures would appear to lend equal weight to the three main theories of saving, which can be labeled as "precautionary saving", "consumption smoothing" and "bequest-motivated saving". However, it is not easy to attribute the remaining share of responses, which is considerable.

The BNL-Doxa survey distinguishes among four prevalent "motivations" for saving: for future use, to supplement one's pension, for health care and for bequests. 25 percent of the respondents say they save in order to supplement their pension. This is the reason that most closely resembles life-cycle saving. A small share overall (6 percent) saves in order to be assured of health care, i.e. as a provision against contingencies, the proportion increasing with age. Around 12 percent of the respondents indicate they save mainly in order to leave bequests to their children, half as many as those who save mainly in order to supplement their pension.

These last figures appear to suggest that the bequest motive is less important than the others, which are closer to the life-cycle model. Nevertheless, such a conclusion might be mistaken, for more than half (57 percent) of the respondents indicate they save for future *use*, a choice that can be interpreted in various ways. In all likelihood the frequency of this response stems from its being a mere restatement of the *definition* of saving, which consists in forgoing current consumption of resources in favor of future *use*. "Use" does not necessarily mean consumption but could also signify "leaving an estate to one's children".

Table 12.5 Primary reasons for saving according to the Censis and BNL-Doxa surveys

			Reason			Censis survey	
	For old age	For contin-gencies	To provide for one's children	To buy a house or durable goods	To increase future income	Other	Total
Share of responses (%)	23.2	22.3	23.4	19.0	2.5	9.6	100

		Reason		BNL-Doxa survey	
	Future use	Pension supplement	Health care	Bequests to children	Total
Share of responses (%)	56.6	25.4	5.7	12.3	100

Sources: Censis (1986) and Banca Nazionale del Lavoro (1988).

This and the other ambiguities of the surveys suggest that they cannot be a substitute for studies of the behavior of individuals based on theory and real data.

7 Conclusions

Two out of five Italian households acquired ownership of their real estate through transfers from previous generations. The share of intergenerational transfers in the value of real estate ranges from 35 to nearly 50 percent depending on whether interest on bequests is excluded from or imputed to the stock of inherited wealth.

These figures can be interpreted as showing that bequests play a significant role in the accumulation of wealth. A deeper understanding of the inheritance process and of the policy implications of such widespread intergenerational transfers, however, requires closer study of the motives for leaving bequests. This is left for future research, and the magnitude of these figures surely indicates that research on the bequest motive is well worthwhile.

NOTES

* We wish to thank Elsa Fornero and Nicola Rossi for helpful comments. We are to be retained responsible for all remaining errors.

1 This was pointed out to us by Ignazio Visco.

2 The method, originally invented by Alfred de Foville (1887), was further discussed and implemented by several Italian economists, including Maffeo Pantaleoni (1890), Luigi Bodio (1891), Francesco Saverio Nitti (1905) and Francesco Coletti (1907). They thought that "blowing-up" the flow of bequests for a given year (estimated from information on probate duties), using as the blow-up factor an estimate of the average age gap between testator and legatee, was a way to estimate the wealth of the nation. Of course, this procedure is correct only if no decumulation of wealth takes place over the life cycle. Notice also that the de Foville formula applies to a stationary economy or to one growing on the golden rule path.

3 Wealth decumulation by the elderly is controversial. See, among others, Hayashi, Ando and Ferris (1988), Bernheim (1986), Mirer (1979), Hurd (1989) and Ando, Guiso and Terlizzese (1994).

4 See Modigliani (1988) for a discussion.

5 For details about the SHIW see the Methodological Appendix to this volume.

6 An indicator (probably biased downwards) of the importance of intentional bequests is the ratio of the annual average number of wills and deeds of gift to the annual average number of deaths of individuals aged 24 and more. Deaths of individuals younger than 24 are excluded from the denominator, which is a measure of the potential number of intergenerational transfers, since the probability of death of persons younger than 24 who are in a position to write wills is virtually nil. For the decade 1971-80 the average ratio is 30 percent. The number of wills and deeds of gift would be an improper measure of voluntary bequests, if those actions were taken only with the intention of determining the distribution among siblings of wealth *involuntarily* left at death. It is, however, reasonable that whenever there is concern for the division of an estate there is also concern for its extent.

7 Attributing interest on bequests to income involves the drawback of the resulting measure of life-cycle wealth not being independent of the value of these bequests. As Modigliani notes, the measure proposed by Kotlikoff and Summers also is not independent of the value of bequests if the latter influence consumption *choices*. If all interests on bequests are spent, the measure of life-cycle wealth proposed by Modigliani will be independent of bequests. By contrast, if all interests on bequests are saved, Kotlikoff and Summers' measure will be independent of the flows of bequests. This will always be true if in steady state the "golden rule" obtains so that $r=n$, where n is the growth rate of the economy.

8 Some survey respondents did not indicate the year they received the bequest. In this case (159 occurrences out of 2,354 observations) the year was imputed on the basis of the average year in which individuals of the same age-cohort received bequests.

9 In a survey conducted by Doxa in 1989, out of a total sample of about 1,000 households 25.4 percent reported to have been the beneficiary of an inheritance.

10 This value should underestimate p, since the probability of an inherited property being sold is almost certainly higher than the probability of a property-in-general being sold. In fact, sales of inherited properties accounted for about 67 percent of total property sales in 1987, the only year for which the survey allows us to draw this distinction.

11 For the period before a fair-rent law was introduced, the rate of return on leased properties should be the same as that on owner-occupied properties. By adopting a gross rate of return of 3.1 percent we are therefore underestimating the capitalized value of bequests.

12 Taking account of the fact that 60 percent of properties are used by their owners, the average net rate of return on properties implicit in the capitalization is around 1.6 percent. The average implicit capitalization period is thus about 20 years. Computed as a weighted average on total inherited wealth, using as weights the shares of bequests, the average period of capitalization is 18 years. Note that the average period of capitalization is different from the average intergenerational age gap that needs to be known if the method of flows is adopted. Using the survey sample, we estimate that gap at 30 years.

13 Without the contentious capitalization of interest, the share estimated for Italy is higher than that computed for the United States by Modigliani (1988), who places the share at between 17 and 20 percent. Our estimate of 35 percent is still higher but somewhat closer to that for the U.S. obtained by Hurd and Mundaca (1989) who, taking gifts into account, estimate a share in the range of 20-30 percent. The share of inherited wealth in Italy is instead equal to that for France and Canada reported by Kessler and Masson (1989).

14 According to Cannari and D'Alessio (1990), the survey underestimates the number of residential buildings by about 35 percent. The underestimation does not affect the first method, where the survey is the only source for the data.

15 This problem should not create any serious distortion in the previous calculation of the capitalization of the return on bequests if, as it may be reasonably assumed, the years in which bequests were actually received are symmmetrically distributed around the years reported.

16 This is the correct formula if all the bequests take place at death. It should be modified if intergenerational transfers occur before the date of death. On this point, see Modigliani (1988) and Kotlikoff (1988).

17 Per capita GDP grew at an average annual rate of 0.8 percent between 1931 and 1951, 4.9 percent in the period 1952-1970 and 2.0 percent in 1971-1985. The average annual growth rate for the entire period is 2.4 percent.

REFERENCES

Ando, A., L. Guiso and D. Terlizzese (1994). 'Dissaving by the Elderly, Transfer Motives and Liquidity Constraints', *this volume*.

364   Fabrizio Barca, Luigi Cannari and Luigi Guiso

Banca d'Italia (1986). *Bollettino economico* 6.

Banca Nazionale del Lavoro (1988). 'Rapporto Centro Einaudi sul risparmio e sui risparmiatori in Italia: Indagine Doxa 1988', *Quaderni di ricerca* 21.

Bernheim, B.D. (1986). 'Dissaving after Retirement: Testing the Pure Life Cycle Hypothesis', in Z. Bodie, J.B. Shoven and D. Wise (eds.), *Issues in Pension Economics*, Chicago: University of Chicago Press.

Bodio, L. (1891). *Di alcuni indici misuratori del movimento economico in Italia,* Editore G. Bartero: Roma.

Cannari, L. and G. D'Alessio (1990). 'Housing Assets in the Bank of Italy's Survey of Household Income and Wealth', in C. Dagum and M. Zenga (eds.), *Income and Wealth Distribution, Inequality and Poverty*, Berlin: Springer.

Censis (1986). *Risparmi e investimenti della famiglia Spa*, Milano: Angeli.

Coletti, F. (1907). 'La determinazione della durata della generazione e il calcolo della ricchezza privata di un Paese', *La riforma sociale* 17: 181-202.

Darby, M. (1979). 'Effects of Social Security on Income and the Capital Stock', Washington, DC: American Enterprise Institute.

de Foville, A. (1887). *La France économique. Statistique raisonnée et comparative,* Paris: Armand Colin.

Hayashi, F., A. Ando and R. Ferris (1988). 'Life Cycle and Bequest Savings', *Journal of the Japanese and International Economies* 2: 450-91.

Hurd, M.D. (1989). 'Mortality Risk and Bequests', *Econometrica* 57: 779-813.

Hurd, M.D. and B.G. Mundaca (1989). 'The Importance of Gifts and Inheritances among the Affluent', in R.G. Lipsey and H.S. Tice (eds.), *The Measurement of Saving, Investment and Wealth*, Chicago: University of Chicago Press.

Kessler, D. and A. Masson (1989). 'Bequest and Wealth Accumulation: Are Some Pieces of the Puzzle Missing?, *Journal of Economic Perspectives* 3: 141-52.

Kotlikoff, L.J. (1988). 'Intergenerational Transfers and Savings', *Journal of Economic Perspectives* 2: 41-58.

Kotlikoff, L.J. and L.H. Summers (1981). 'The Role of Intergenerational Transfers in Aggregate Capital Accumulation', *Journal of Political Economy* 89: 707-32.

Mirer, T.W. (1979). 'The Age-Wealth Relation among the Aged', *American Economic Review* 69: 435-43.

Modigliani, F. (1988). 'The Role of Intergenerational Transfers and Life Cycle Saving in the Accumulation of Wealth', *Journal of Economic Perspectives* 2: 15-40.

Modigliani F. and R. Brumberg (1954). 'Utility Analysis and the Consumption Function: An Interpretation of Cross-Section Data', in K. K. Kurihara (ed.), *Post Keynesian Economics*, New Brunswick, N.J.: Rutgers University Press.

Nitti, F.S. (1905). *La ricchezza dell'Italia. Quanto è ricca l'Italia. Come è distribuita la ricchezza in Italia*, Roux e Viarengo: Torino; English translation: *The Wealth of Italy. Its Amount and Distribution,* F. Centenari & Co.: Rome, 1907.

Pantaleoni, M. (1890). 'Dell'ammontare probabile della ricchezza privata in Italia. Dal 1872 al 1889', *Giornale degli economisti* (nuova serie) 2: 139-71.

Rossi, N. and A. Vendramin (1990). 'Il tasso di risparmio aggregato in Italia e il ruolo dei lasciti ereditari', in E. Fornero and O. Castellino (eds.), *Formazione e impiego della ricchezza delle famiglie*, Torino: Fondazione Giorgio Rota.

White, B.B. (1978). 'Empirical Tests of the Life Cycle Hypothesis', *American Economic Review* **68**: 547-60.

APPENDIXES

Methodological Appendix:
The Bank of Italy's Survey of
Household Income and Wealth*

ANDREA BRANDOLINI and LUIGI CANNARI

1 Introduction

The Bank of Italy's first Survey of Household Income and Wealth (SHIW) was conducted in 1965. Twenty-three further surveys have been conducted since then, yearly until 1987 (except for 1985) and every two years thereafter. The interviews for the twenty-fourth survey were completed in the Summer of 1992.

The aim of the SHIW is to gather information concerning the economic behavior of Italian families at the microeconomic level. Data on family income, saving, expenditure for consumer durables and real wealth have been collected since 1966, while the acquisition of details regarding total consumption expenditure started in 1980, essentially to improve internal consistency controls and to facilitate comparison with the Istat expenditure survey.

The methodology used in collecting the data and the definitions of the survey variables underwent several modifications over the years, hampering the possibility of using the survey evidence to perform intertemporal comparisons. The main features and modifications of the SHIW will be described in Section 2, while in Section 3 the results of the studies on the quality of the survey will be briefly presented.

2 A description of the survey design

2.1 The survey unit

The basic survey unit is the "household", which is defined as a group of individuals linked by ties of blood, marriage or affection, sharing the same dwelling and pooling all or part of their incomes. Persons living in nursing homes for the aged or ill, prisons, or military installations are not included.

On the basis of this definition, individuals who live together solely for economic reasons are not considered members of the same household; only one unit is recorded where two or more nuclear families, as registered at the registry offices, are linked by family ties and live together. This explains why the survey-based estimate of average family size tends to exceed the estimate based on records held at registry offices. The same pattern emerged from the survey on family structure and behavior carried out by Istat in 1983, according to which the average number of members in each household rose from 3.0 to 3.2 when the definition of a *de facto* household was used rather than the registry office definition. The relevant effect was on the number of single-member units which fell from 16.0 to 13.0 percent of the total, and it was most striking for the elderly population (cf. Istat, 1985a, Appendix A).

2.2   The sampling procedure

The sampling procedure remained essentially unchanged until the survey for 1983, after which major modifications were introduced (see Table MA.1). Sampling is carried out in two stages: the first consists in the selection of the municipalities and the second in selecting the families.

Municipalities were divided into 50 strata until 1980 and 85 strata (5 of which were empty) between 1981 and 1984, according to geographical and demographic characteristics (derived from the list of TV licences); they were then selected on the basis of criteria of convenience in the collection of data. This system had the undesirable effect that some "poor" areas of the country were probably underrepresented, owing to the absence of professional interviewers in those areas; moreover, the first-stage sample was not random, preventing researchers from computing actual sampling errors (see Fabbris *et al.*, 1986, p. 21). To obviate these problems, the sample design was entirely revised in 1986 and made consistent with that used by Istat in its survey of the labor force. Municipalities are now divided into 51 strata, defined by 17 regions and 3 classes of population size: over 40,000 inhabitants, 20,000-40,000 inhabitants, less than 20,000 inhabitants. All the municipalities in the first class are included; those in the second class are randomly selected with probability proportional to their demographic size; the same criterion is also applied to municipalities in the third class, after further stratification by altitude and by prevalent economic activity of the resident population.

Since access to registry office records is restricted, until 1983 the choice of families was based on the Electoral Register, from which a number of names equal to twice the desired sample size was drawn. This was likely to bias incomes upwards, because families with a higher number of adults, and hence a potentially higher income, were more likely to be selected. Since

1984 the collaboration of Istat and of the municipalities involved has made it possible to select families from the registry office records, thus eliminating the bias.

Table MA.1 Main changes in the design of the Survey of Household Income and Wealth, 1966-1989

Year (a)	Changes in the sample	Changes in the definition of income
1971 ↔ 1972	Oversampling of families living in Southern Italy	
1973 →		Imputed rents of owner-occupied housing included
1973 ↔ 1975	Oversampling of high-income families	Receipts from interest and dividends included
1981 →	Sample size raised to 4,000	
1982 →		Receipts from interest included
1984 →	Families drawn from registry office records instead of electoral lists	
1986 →	Revision of the sample design; random selection of first-stage units; sample size raised to 8,000	Interest on mortgages and dividends included
1987 ↔ 1987	Oversampling of high-income families	
1989 →	Introduction of a panel section	

Source: Brandolini (1993, Table 5).

(a) The symbol → denotes permanent changes, whereas the symbol ↔ means that the change or changes were applied only in the period indicated and were later dropped (although, in some cases, subsequently re-instated).

The sample size was initially set at 3,000 on the basis of considerations regarding the desired sampling error and confidence levels. It was raised to 4,000 in 1981 in order to increase the accuracy of estimates for regional subsamples (information at the regional level was, however, published for three surveys only, after being judged insufficiently reliable in 1984), and to 8,000 in 1986.

Frequent modifications have affected the proportionality between the sample size in each stratum and the corresponding population. Proportional samples were drawn from 1965 to 1970, from 1976 to 1980, and then again in 1986. In 1971 and 1972 families resident in Southern Italy were oversampled, whereas in 1973, 1974 and 1975 the attention focused on high-income families. Non-proportional sampling was reintroduced in 1981 to improve the quality of information at the regional level: one of three different sample sizes (200, 250 and 300) was assigned to each region depending on the desired sampling error. Within each region the number of planned interviews per stratum depended on the income variability within the stratum and was, therefore, not proportional to its population. In 1987 the families of senior white-collar employees and self-employed businessmen and professionals were oversampled to increase the frequency of high-income units. In order to allow for better comparisons over time, in 1989 about 15 percent of the sample (1,208 families) was obtained by reinterviewing families already interviewed in 1987. The criteria for selecting the families included in the panel are similar to those described above.

2.3   The realisation of the survey and the response rate

The actual conduct of the survey is contracted out to a private company, which provides professionally trained interviewers. Data are collected in personal interviews usually in the first months of a year and refer to family budgets in the previous calendar year, which in Italy coincides with the fiscal year (to avoid confusion we always refer to the year *for* which, and not the year *in* which a survey is conducted). Questions concerning the whole household are answered by the head of the family or by the person most knowledgeable on the family's finances; questions on individual incomes are answered by each member, unless he/she is absent. Each schedule is completed by the interviewers, who are given special training. Meetings are organised to discuss in detail the aims of the survey, the variables investigated and the structure of the questionnaire; after the first few interviews the entire data acquisition procedure is reexamined and possible systematic errors – due, for instance, to the misunderstanding of a question – are corrected so as to avoid their recurring in the remaining interviews.

For both responding and non-responding families interviewers are required to complete a section of the questionnaire on the family's characteristics such as the sex and age of the head of the family, the number of members and the quality and location of the home. The number of questions each family is asked to answer depends on its status and ranges between a minimum of 30 for a retired head of household without any property to a maximum of 300 for a wealthy family with numerous assets. Non-responding families are replaced with other units of similar characteristics.

Unlike Istat surveys, participation in this survey is voluntary. In order to overcome households' distrust, shortly before the interviews are scheduled every family is sent a letter explaining the aims of the survey and giving an assurance that all the information collected will be treated anonymously; families are provided on request with a copy of Bank of Italy's publications containing the reports of previous surveys. Interviewers carry special identification cards and letters of introduction. Finally, respondents are not asked to show pay-slips or other documents in answer to questions. Nonetheless, refusal to cooperate and "fear" account for the largest proportion of non-responses.

The response rate was slightly above 50 percent in the mid-seventies and oscillated around 60 percent until 1987, but dropped to only 37 percent in the survey for 1989. In this survey, the response rate was particularly low (23.3 percent) in the panel section, possibly because families had not been advised in advance. However, the figure of 41.2 percent for responses among non-panel families was about one third lower than that of earlier surveys. There are no obvious reasons to account for this sudden fall in the response rate except for the fact that, for the first time, interviewers were also paid for information provided for each non-responding unit. The decline could thus be explained either by the underreporting of non-responding units in previous surveys, or by an opposite tendency to inflate non-responses in 1989, or by a combination of the two. The first hypothesis is the most worrying, since it implies that the actual response rates might have been lower in the past than those officially recorded.

On the basis of the characteristics specified by the interviewers for all the families contacted, it seems likely that the response rate is inversely correlated with family income and wealth, leading to a probable underestimation of the mean and of the dispersion of incomes. In a recent analysis, Cannari and D'Alessio (1992) used the panel section of the latest survey to study the response rate and the reasons for non-responses in relation to family characteristics and income as reported in the 1987 survey. They found that the response rate falls from 26 percent for low-income families to 14 percent for the wealthiest families, fear being the main reason for non-response among the latter. As a result, the average income of responding families is about 5 percent lower than the average income computed across all families approached for the panel.

2.4 Processing of results

Questionnaires go through several checking procedures. Throughout the fieldwork, systematic reporting mistakes and missed answers are located manually; during this stage every wrong or incomplete questionnaire is returned to the interviewer for correction or completion. In the second stage, automatic controls are implemented to eliminate coding and computation errors as well as unreliable questionnaires. If important information is still missing (in particular, if the answers are insufficient to compute total family income) the questionnaire is discarded. In the third phase, each questionnaire showing inconsistent values of income, consumption and saving is analysed separately. If no explanation for the inconsistencies is found – possibly after further contacts with the interviewees – the questionnaire is discarded. Until 1987, the questionnaires relating to families who declared negative self-employment income were discarded. In general, more than 95 percent of questionnaires is utilised. The planned structure of the sample is reestablished through a process of post-stratification reweighting of family units, so that the published figures are corrected for differential response rates by sample stratum. The results for 1989 were corrected to make the socio-demographic structure of the panel section representative of the 1987 sample.

2.5 The information collected

The survey collects data on the social and demographic characteristics of household members. Sex, age and relationship to the head of the family are collected for all members; the education, professional status and economic sector are recorded for all income recipients. The design of the questionnaire has been considerably modified over the years; the changes have affected the number, quality and definition of the variables surveyed.

The basic definitions of income and its components were fairly stable until 1986 with the exception of income from property, the main difference being the inclusion or not of imputed rents, interest and dividends. The overall revision of the structure of the survey carried out in 1986 made the definitions closer to those used in compiling national accounts, by introducing the distinction between receipts in income account and transfers in capital account (e.g. inheritances, lottery wins, etc.), by recording receipts and disbursements of interest in the year they are due rather than in the year they are actually paid, and by distinguishing between income from private unincorporated enterprises and that from quasi-corporate enterprises. A further difference regards dividends and interest received: until 1986 interviewees were explicitly questioned on this item; since 1987, it has been calculated by multiplying a family's holdings of each financial asset by the relevant average market return (see Table MA.1). All income is recorded net of payments of taxes and social security contributions, and no information on taxation is collected.

The information on household expenditure for consumer goods has been gathered since 1980, with only minor modifications over the years, apart from the distinction between durables and non-durables, which is not available for 1986. Estimates of expenditure for durable goods are also available between 1966 and 1975. Data on holdings of financial assets have not been collected in a continuous way and have undergone frequent changes of definition. Estimates of households' real estate, on the other hand, are available for all surveys and are based on definitions kept largely unchanged over the years.

Raw data are generally collected on an individual basis and total figures are obtained by subsequent aggregation. Only interest and dividends, consumption and financial assets are surveyed at the household level. Separate records have generally been kept for each recipient of income. The exceptions are income from participation in unincorporated enterprises, which was assigned entirely to the main holder until 1987, and income earned by minors and/or below a certain threshold, which was attributed to the head of the family until 1976.

The results of the surveys have been published in the Bank of Italy's *Bollettino statistico* (until 1981 *Bollettino*) or in the series of *Supplementi al bollettino statistico*. The Statistics Unit of the Bank of Italy's Research Department is currently constructing a historical data set, starting in 1977, based on homogeneous criteria. Micro data are not available for the years before 1977.

3 The quality of the data

Several recent studies have assessed the quality of the survey data. Some of these have examined the selection bias generated by differential response rates and the underreporting of certain types of income. Another line of research has compared the survey data with information taken from other sources on the demographic structure of the country and the composition of the labor force, and with aggregate figures from the national accounts and flow of funds. The principal results and some data are presented in subsections 3.1-3.4.

3.1 Effects of selection bias and underreporting on income estimates

According to estimates by Cannari and D'Alessio (1992), when the negative correlation between response rates and income levels (see Section 2.3) is corrected the average family income for 1987 rises by about 5 percent. Using the 1989 survey, Cannari and Violi (1991) estimated on the basis of internal controls that the underreporting of self-employment income amounted to over 20 percent, which is lower than the 35 percent found by Pissarides and Weber (1989) for the United Kingdom. Cannari and D'Alessio (1990) corrected the underreporting of real estate by referring to declarations made by occupiers rather than owners (see, below, Section 3.3) and, on that basis, revised upwards the estimate of average family income for 1987 by about 4 percent, a figure that would probably rise in parallel with the level of family income.

3.2   Comparison between survey data and labor force statistics

In a comparison between survey figures and statistics derived from the Istat Labor Force Survey (LFS) for the years 1986, 1987 and 1989, Brandolini (1993, pp.17-8) found that the share in population of salaried employees was higher in the SHIW, while that of the self-employed was lower. The discrepancies in the other categories are relatively small. On balance, the employed appeared to be slightly overrepresented. This is also shown in panel I of Table MA.2.

More significantly, this table shows substantial differences between the SHIW and national accounts figures. The differences are evident mainly in the estimates of secondary jobs, which appear to be largely underestimated (as they are, incidentally, in the LFS). This discrepancy indicates the difficulties encountered by the SHIW in capturing the phenomenon of secondary jobs, even though, on closer scrutiny, the problem is less serious. On the one hand, all job positions are given equal treatment with no discriminating between full-time and part-time, or permanent and occasional jobs. By allowing for such differences and making the comparison on the basis of "standard equivalent labor units", the divergence between the SHIW and national accounts estimates is reduced by one half (see panel II). On the other hand, any adjustment of national accounts to take account of the hidden economy is by its very nature somewhat problematic and bound to produce estimates surrounded by considerable uncertainties. The estimates of secondary jobs, in particular, are recognised as constituting one of the "most sensitive points" (Istat, 1988b, p. 17).

3.3   Comparison between national accounts aggregates and survey estimates of household income and consumption

Aggregate estimates derived from national accounts are often used as an external yardstick to assess the quality of survey figures. In the United Kingdom, Kemsley, Redpath and Holmes (1980, p. 51) found that the widest discrepancies between the Family Expenditure Survey and the National Income Blue Book concerned self-employment income, investment income

Table MA.2 Comparison between SHIW, labor force survey and national accounts: employment, 1987 and 1989 (thousands of units)

	Survey of household income and wealth (a)		Labor force survey		National accounts (b)	
	1987	1989	1987	1989	1987	1989
			I. Job positions			
Employees:						
primary jobs	16,262	16,592	14,710	14,937	15,083	15,347
secondary jobs	153	66			1,034	1,117
Self-employed:						
primary jobs	5,266	5,164	6,126	6,067	6,139	6,075
secondary jobs	340	265			6,079	6,243
Total:						
primary jobs	21,528	21,756	20,836	21,004	21,222	21,422
secondary jobs	493	331	519(c)	407(c)	7,113	7,360
			II. Standard equivalent labor units			
Employees:						
primary jobs	16,262	16,592			14,566	14,773
secondary jobs	113	38			414	447
Self-employed:						
primary jobs	5,266	5,164			5,913	5,882
secondary jobs	158	123			1,436	1,465
Total:						
primary jobs	21,528	21,756			20,479	20,655
secondary jobs	271	161			1,850	1,912

Source: SHIW: Authors' calculations based on original data; Labor force survey: Istat (1988a, 1990), Tables 11 and 23; National accounts: Istat (1991), Tables 1.28-30, 1.34-36, 2.28-30, 2.34-36.

(a) Employment figures in standard equivalent labor units are computed by multiplying each secondary job by the ratio between hours worked in secondary and primary jobs recorded for 1989.

(b) Excluding non-resident foreign workers.

(c) Employed with one or more secondary jobs.

and private occupational pensions (–33, –67 and –51 percent, respectively). Atkinson and Micklewright (1983) basically confirmed this conclusion, but emphasised that part of the apparent discrepancy could be eliminated by putting figures on a comparable basis. Crystal and Shea (1990, p. 228) referred to evidence for the United States showing that unearned incomes are underreported by amounts that range typically between 20 and 50 percent. In Canada, underreporting of investment income and self-employment income was estimated at about 30 percent (Health and Welfare Canada, 1977, p. 51). In the Japanese National Survey of Family Income and Expenditure of 1984, according to Hayashi, Ando and Ferris (1988, p. 457), pre-tax earnings and pensions, and consumption were underreported by about 12-14 percent.

The evidence for Italy conforms to the experience of other countries (for earlier comparisons limited to total income see Lemmi, 1981, and Targetti Lenti, 1984, pp. 127-9). According to the figures shown in the first two columns of Table MA.3, the SHIW slightly overestimates wages and salaries, while underestimating self-employment income by one half; pensions fall short of the national accounts figures by almost one third. Among property incomes, net interest on financial assets emerges as a serious problem area, whereas rents are overestimated by about 7-9 percent (dividends are not examined on account of their marginal importance). On the whole, the shortfall for total disposable income appears to be around 25 percent, whereas for consumption it is about 30 percent. Part of the latter figure is explained by differences in definitions that have not been corrected: consumption from own production, which is not recorded in the SHIW; and expenditure for valuables, which is included among savings. These figures should be treated with caution in consideration of the large year-to-year variations typically associated with this sort of expenditure.

In the last two columns of Table MA.3, the estimates of wages and salaries and self-employment income are divided by the number of standard equivalent labor units, and transfers by the number of pensions. The resulting figures therefore represent labor income per standard equivalent labor unit and transfer income per pension, so that the shortfalls are now estimates of the underreporting only, as distinct from non-reporting. The outcome of the exercise is to turn the overestimation of earnings into an underestimation by about 10 percent, and to reduce the shortfall of self-employment income to 29 percent in 1987 and 44 percent in 1989; the average pension, on the other hand, appears to be estimated correctly.

Apart from the phenomena mentioned above of differential response rates, and of non-reporting and underreporting of income components that typically afflict surveys, other factors could perhaps contribute to some of the discrepancies that still remain (see Brandolini, 1993, Section 5.3, for further details). In the first place, the survey data are derived from a sample of families whose size has varied over the years between 3,000 and 8,000; the SHIW totals have to be grossed-up to the aggregates of national

Table MA.3 Comparison between SHIW and national accounts: income and consumption, 1987 and 1989 (percentage ratio of survey to national accounts figures)

	Unadjusted		Adjusted *(a)*	
	1987	1989	1987	1989
Types of income *(b)*:				
Wages and salaries	102.7	104.9	89.4	91.3
Self-employment income	48.6	44.0	70.7	56.2
Rents	109.1	106.9		
Interest	30.4	35.5		
Transfers	70.8	68.9	102.0	101.0
Total disposable income	74.7	74.8		
Consumption	71.9	69.6		

Source: Authors' calculations from the SHIW and national accounts.

(a) Wages and salaries and self-employment income are adjusted for the number of full-time equivalent workers; transfers, for the number of pensions.

(b) The *pre-tax* national accounts aggregates are defined as follows: *i) Wages and salaries:* compensation of employees less actual and net imputed social security contributions (contributions paid by the self-employed are deducted from the actual contributions); *ii) Self-employment income:* gross operating surplus of sole proprietorships with fewer than 20 employees, net of depreciation of physical assets, plus withdrawals from corporate and quasi-corporate enterprises (by construction net of the consumption of fixed capital) less contributions paid by the self-employed; *iii) Rents:* rents from land and royalties plus gross operating surplus of consumer households (which is essentially an estimate of imputed rents for owner-occupied houses); *iv) Interest:* interest on bank deposits, post-office deposits and government bonds, less interest on mortgages; *v) Transfers:* social security and assistance benefits net of benefits in kind. The *after-tax* aggregates are obtained by deducting *proportionally* from each item the current taxes on income and wealth net of some minor contributions (employees' contribution to Gescal, a housing scheme for employees, taxes on gambling games and lotteries, motor-vehicle taxes paid by households).

accounts. To this end, the SHIW average individual incomes and consumption were multiplied by the total number of resident individuals (excluding those living in institutions). The alternative procedure of grossing-up on a household basis would give different estimates and, in any case, the imprecision of survey-based estimates is amplified by the inadequacy of information on the size and distribution of the Italian population. Secondly, survey data do not account for institutional population, a fact that could be of some importance in explaining the underestimation of pensions. However, adjusting for non-household population is unlikely to raise total income by much more than 1 percent, since persons living in institutions constitute less than 1 percent of the total Italian resident population. For this reason, no adjustment was made to the figures in the table. Thirdly, the definitions used in compiling national accounts and those in the survey do not coincide, so that the figures from the two sources need to be rendered comparable. The main difficulty here is that direct taxes on income and wealth are not broken down by type of income, so that some arbitrary criterion of imputation has to be adopted. In this note, after-tax aggregate sources of income are derived from national accounts by assigning each type of income a proportional share of direct taxes. The national accounts figures come from the income account of households, and are aggregated into five types of income, as described in the notes to Table MA.3. Last but not least, the national accounts figures themselves are far from free of measurement errors, particularly on account of the obvious difficulties that arise in attempting to estimate the hidden economy.

3.4   Comparisons for household wealth estimates

Estimates of wealth are typically reputed to be less reliable than income figures and to vary dramatically in accuracy according to type of assets and liabilities. Statistics Canada (1979, p. 58) calculated that the estimates based on the Survey of Consumer Finances for 1977 understated the corresponding aggregates of the National Balance Sheet by about 33 percent for bank deposits and 39 percent for government bonds. Oja (1986) extended the comparison to 1983-84 data and found a much higher underestimate for bank deposits (61 percent), but a similar value for government bonds (41 percent); she computed the shortfall for total financial assets at about 50 percent, and that for company shares at over 86 percent. Figures of the same order of magnitude were estimated for Japan by Hayashi et al. (1988): –59, –35 and –69 percent are the discrepancies for bank accounts, bonds and stocks, respectively. Better results were achieved by the Surveys of Consumer Finances conducted in the United States (SCF). In a comparison between the 1983 survey and the Flow of Funds, Avery, Elliehausen and Kennickell

(1988) found underestimates of only 4 and 12 percent for corporate stocks and (federal, state and local) government bonds, respectively, though the figure rose to 44 percent for accounts at depository institutions. This result was largely attributable to the oversampling of high-income households: when these were excluded the shortfall for total financial assets rose from 15 to almost 35 percent. This was confirmed in subsequent studies by Curtin, Juster and Morgan (1989) and Juster and Kuester (1991), who extended the comparison to other U.S. household surveys.

The oversampling of high-income households, nonetheless, poses a series of problems. First, the response rate in supplementary high-income samples tends to be substantially lower than in the nationally representative probability samples: in the 1983 SCF, for instance, the former was about 10 percent compared with 71 percent in the latter. This casts doubt on the representativeness of the special high-income group. Second, the construction of weights for merging the two subsamples is made more difficult by the poor accuracy of the estimate of the upper-tail of the distribution in the nationally representative sample as well as by the different definitions of reporting units and variables used in the respective sampling frames. Finally, the high concentration of wealth leads to wide variability in the estimates and to the "outlier problem": frequently, it is difficult to determine whether a very high value of wealth is a reporting or a coding error, or the occurrence of a low-probability event. An instructive example is offered by the 1983 SCF. One individual, having one of the highest sample weights, reported a business worth that accounted for about a tenth of total household net worth in the United States. There were no evident reasons for dropping this observation as being wrong, until the reinterview for the 1986 follow-up survey showed that the amount had been incorrectly reported by the interviewer.

The oversampling of families of senior white-collar employees, businessmen and professionals carried out in the 1987 SHIW, with the aim of increasing the number of high-income households in the sample, raised similar problems with regard to the representativeness of the supplementary sample, as the average income of this group of households turned out to be significantly higher in the supplementary sample. The results of the oversampling were not, however, as satisfactory as for the SCF, possibly because the two sub-samples were merged using weights computed on the basis of the nationally representative sample only. Indeed, Cannari *et al.* (1990), when comparing the SHIW estimates of financial assets and the Flow of Funds figures, found discrepancies ranging from over 90 percent for private bonds, company shares and investment shares to about 50 percent for bank deposits (see Table MA.4).

Table MA.4 Comparison between SHIW and financial accounts: financial assets, 1987 (billions of lire)

	Survey of Household Income and Wealth		Financial accounts
	Unadjusted	Adjusted *(a)*	
Bank deposits	184,894	318,545	360,381
Post-office deposits	19,769	24,175	73,364
Government bonds	81,523	253,070	351,594
Private bonds, company shares, investment and trust fund shares	19,256	67,563	208,978
Total	305,442	663,353	994,317

Source: Cannari, D'Alessio, Raimondi and Rinaldi (1990), Tables 1 and 4.

(a) Figures derived by matching the SHIW with the survey conducted in 1987 by Banca Nazionale del Lavoro among its customers.

In the same paper, a method for adjusting financial assets for non- and underreporting was developed. Data were first corrected to impute financial assets to households reporting only the holding and not the amount. They were then adjusted for non-reporting and underreporting by comparing the SHIW figures with the estimates derived from a survey carried out in 1987 by Banca Nazionale del Lavoro (BNL) on a sample of its customers. This sample was not representative of the Italian population, but provided more reliable information on household financial assets, owing to the greater trust that customers are likely to place in their own bank. The integration (based on statistical matching procedures) of the SHIW subsample of families holding bank deposits with the BNL sample shows that adjusting for non-reporting would raise total financial assets by 16.3 percent, and adjusting for underreporting would add a further, more substantial 67.2 percent. The effect of these adjustments on total financial assets is to reduce the shortfall with respect to the flow of funds figures from 69.3 to 33.3 percent (see Table MA.4). As shown in Table MA.5, the age, education and job status of the household's head are significant determinants of underreporting. The elderly and self-employed seem to be especially unable or unwilling to divulge their financial situation, while the better educated are more likely to provide reliable information.

Table MA.5 Adjustment of household financial assets for underreporting and non-reporting, by family's head characteristic, 1987
(percentage ratio of adjusted to unadjusted figures)

Family head characteristics	Adjusted for non-reporting	Adjusted for underreporting and non-reporting
Age:		
30 and under	119.4	150.1
31 to 40	108.0	151.2
41 to 50	123.4	158.3
51 to 65	111.1	205.3
66 and over	122.7	306.1
Education:		
4 years and under	135.7	289.4
5 to 7	132.4	210.2
8 to 12	113.7	185.9
13 to 16	106.0	175.1
17 and over	97.4	184.1
Job status:		
Manual workers	131.8	143.8
Clerical workers	108.7	145.5
Managers, administrators	100.4	148.3
Employers, professionals	100.4	216.4
Other self-employed	112.3	218.7
Non-employed	123.4	273.9
All	116.3	194.4

Source: Cannari, D'Alessio, Raimondi and Rinaldi (1990), Table 2.

With regard to real estate, official statistics on the stock of houses are available in Italy only for Census years. Table MA.6 presents rough estimates obtained by a simple extrapolation of Census data for 1981 and 1991. On the basis of these figures, the SHIW detects about 65 percent of household dwellings: many of those undetected are rented properties, whereas owner-occupied dwellings tend to be overreported (note, however, that the Census-based estimates of owner-occupied dwellings should be revised upwards – and, accordingly, those of rented dwellings downwards – to account for the increased proportion of families living in their own homes). On the other hand, as noted by Cannari and D'Alessio (1990), declarations by occupiers would lead to better estimates of the stock of rented houses and reduce under reporting to below 20 percent.

Table MA.6 Comparison for household dwellings, 1987 and 1989
(thousands of units)

	Census-based estimates (a)		Survey of Household Income and Wealth estimates			
			as declared by the owner (b)		as declared by the occupier (c)	
	1987	1989	1987	1989	1987	1989
Occupied dwellings:						
Owner-occupied	10,875	11,113	11,817	11,873	11,817	11,873
Rented	6,083	6,216	971	658	5,970	5,411
Total	16,958	17,329	12,788	12,531	17,787	17,284
Unoccupied dwellings:						
Holiday houses	2,081	2,165	1,058	1,315		
Others	2,548	2,651	284	317		
Total	4,629	4,816	1,342	1,632		
Total dwellings	21,587	22,145	14,130	14,163		

Source: Authors' calculations from the Census of population and dwellings of 1981 and 1991, and the SHIW.

(a) Figures obtained by applying to 1981 figures (from Istat, 1985b) the average annual rates of growth over the period 1981-1991, computed separately for occupied and unoccupied dwellings (from Istat, 1992).

(b) Rented dwellings include houses leased to companies.

(c) Rented dwellings are houses rented by other households.

3.5   Concluding remarks

There are significant differences between survey data and estimates derived from independent sources, though the quality of the survey has greatly improved in recent years. Disaggregating the differences by type of income in order to identify the more problematic areas indicates that the survey is essentially similar to those of other countries. The quality of data differs across variables: estimates for wealth are less satisfactory than for income and consumption, on account of both the difficulty in interviewing the top wealth-holders and the greater reticence of families. On the whole, the survey seems to be sufficiently reliable for cross-section analyses, though less suitable for intertemporal comparisons on account of the problems created by the revisions of sample design and variable definitions.

NOTE

* This note draws heavily on material previously elaborated by the authors, in particular Brandolini (1993) and Cannari and D'Alessio (1990, 1992). For further methodological details see the note published in Banca d'Italia, *Bollettino statistico*, 1983, no. 3-4, the relevant chapters of Banca d'Italia (1986) and Banca d'Italia (1989, 1991).

REFERENCES

Atkinson, A.B. and J. Micklewright (1983). 'On the Reliability of Income Data in the Family Expenditure Survey 1970-1977', *Journal of the Royal Statistical Society*, Series A, 146, Part 1: 33-53.

Avery, R.B., G.E. Elliehausen and A.B. Kennickell (1988). 'Measuring Wealth with Survey Data: An Evaluation of the 1983 Survey of Consumer Finances', *Review of Income and Wealth* 34: 339-69.

Banca d'Italia (1986). 'Le indagini campionarie sui bilanci delle famiglie italiane', Special issue of *Contributi all' analisi economica*, Roma.

Banca d'Italia (1989). 'I bilanci delle famiglie italiane nell'anno 1987', *Supplemento al bollettino statistico* 42, 5.

Banca d'Italia (1991). 'I bilanci delle famiglie italiane nell'anno 1989', *Supplementi al bollettino statistico* 1 (nuova serie), 26.

Brandolini, A. (1993). 'A Description and an Assessment of the Sample Surveys on the Personal Distribution of Incomes in Italy', Discussion Paper 3, University of Cambridge, Department of Applied Economics, Microsimulation Unit.

Cannari, L. and G. D'Alessio (1990). 'Housing Assets in the Bank of Italy's Survey of Household Income and Wealth', in C. Dagum and M. Zenga (eds.), *Income and Wealth Distribution, Inequality and Poverty*, Berlin: Springer.

Cannari, L. and G. D'Alessio (1992). 'Mancate interviste e distorsione degli stimatori', Temi di discussione 172, Banca d'Italia.

Cannari, L., G. D'Alessio, G. Raimondi and A.I. Rinaldi (1990). 'Le attività finanziarie delle famiglie italiane', Temi di discussione 135, Banca d'Italia.

Cannari, L. and R. Violi (1991). 'Reporting Behaviour in the Bank of Italy's Survey of the Household Income and Wealth', paper presented at the Conference on Personal Income Distribution, Inequality and Poverty, Siena, October.

Crystal, S. and D. Shea (1990). 'The Economic Well-Being of the Elderly', *Review of Income and Wealth* 36: 227-47.

Curtin, R.T., F.T. Juster and J.N. Morgan (1989). 'Survey Estimates of Wealth: An Assessment of Quality', in R.E. Lipsey and H. S. Tice (eds.), *The Measurement of Saving, Investment and Wealth*, Chicago: University of Chicago Press.

Fabbris, L., G. Leti, E. Zaghini and A. Zuliani (1986). 'Aspetti metodologici delle indagini campionarie sui bilanci delle famiglie italiane', in Banca d'Italia (1986).

Hayashi, F., A. Ando and R. Ferris (1988). 'Life Cycle and Bequest Savings', *Journal of the Japanese and International Economies* **2**: 450-91.

Health and Welfare Canada (1977). 'The Distribution of Income in Canada: Concepts, Measures and Issues', Department of National Wealth and Welfare, *Research Report*, 4.

Istat (1985a). *Indagine sulle strutture ed i comportamenti familiari*, Roma.

Istat (1985b). *12º Censimento generale della popolazione, 1981*, Vol. II: *Dati sulle caratteristiche strutturali della popolazione e delle abitazioni*, Roma.

Istat (1988a). 'Rilevazione delle forze di lavoro – Media 1987', *Collana d'informazione* **13**.

Istat (1988b). 'Conti economici nazionali. Occupazione e redditi da lavoro dipendente – Anni 1980-1987', *Collana d'informazione*, 23.

Istat (1990). 'Rilevazione delle forze di lavoro – Media 1989', *Collana d'informazione* **20**.

Istat (1991). 'Occupazione e redditi da lavoro dipendente – Anni 1980-1990', *Collana d'informazione* **42**.

Istat (1992). *13º Censimento generale della popolazione e delle abitazioni, 20 ottobre 1991. Primi risultati*, Roma.

Juster, F.T. and Kuester, K.A. (1991). 'Differences in the Measurement of Wealth, Wealth Inequality and Wealth Composition Obtained from Alternative U.S. Wealth Surveys', *Review of Income and Wealth* **37**: 33-62.

Kemsley, W.F.F., R.U. Redpath and M. Holmes (1980). *Family Expenditure Survey Handbook*, London: HMSO.

Lemmi, A. (1981). 'Un tentativo di confronto aggregato fra le stime del reddito familiare della Banca d'Italia e i valori della contabilità nazionale, nel periodo 1970-1978', *Note economiche* **2**: 125-35.

Oja, G. (1986). 'The Wealth of Canadians: A Comparison of Survey of Consumer Finances with National Balance Sheet Estimates', Statistics Canada, Staff Reports, December.

Pissarides, C.A. and G. Weber (1989). 'An Expenditure-Based Estimate of Britain's Black Economy', *Journal of Public Economics* **39**: 17-32.

Statistics Canada (1979). *Evaluation of Data on Family Assets and Debts, 1977*, Ottawa.

Targetti Lenti, R. (1984). *Struttura produttiva e distribuzione personale del reddito: una verifica del caso italiano*, Milano: Giuffrè.

Statistical Appendix

The Italian National Accounts were substantially revised in 1985 and official estimates released since then only cover the years since 1970 for most of the variables of interest in a study on saving. As part of the project that has led to this volume, a major reconstruction of the data has been undertaken. Analytical income accounts from 1970 onwards and aggregate time series since 1951 have been constructed by Giuseppe Marotta and Patrizia Pagliano and by Patrizia Pagliano and Nicola Rossi in the two essays published in "Income and Saving in Italy: A Reconstruction", Temi di discussione 169, Banca d'Italia, June 1992.

These data have been used in the time series estimates presented in Chapter 2 of this book and, after being updated to match the new release of official statistics by Istat, to produce the income and consumption flows, general government accounts, wealth measures and saving rates presented in the tables which follow. Social security wealth has been estimated by Luca Beltrametti; for the methodology followed see Appendix B to the working paper version of Chapter 2 (N. Rossi and I. Visco, "Private Saving and Government Deficit in Italy (1951-1990)", Temi di discussione 178, Banca d'Italia, October 1992).

Table SA.1 Measures of income
(billions of lire at current prices)

	Gross domestic product	National disposable income				Household disposable income			Gross domestic product deflator 1985=1
		Gross	Net (a)	Net adjusted (b)	Net adjusted (c)	Gross	Net (a)	Net adjusted (b)	
1951	12,069	12,143	10,186	11,038	11,226	8,988	8,519	n. a.	.065
1952	13,082	13,148	11,069	12,282	12,440	9,812	9,279	9,427	.067
1953	14,440	14,549	12,386	13,048	13,176	10,845	10,259	10,271	.070
1954	15,397	15,478	13,234	14,647	14,862	11,490	10,879	10,732	.071
1955	17,015	17,099	14,737	15,943	16,165	12,734	12,108	12,181	.074
1956	18,509	18,626	16,065	17,393	17,670	13,887	13,239	13,228	.077
1957	19,950	20,134	17,481	18,846	19,075	15,064	14,385	14,474	.078
1958	21,429	21,653	19,005	20,141	20,457	16,301	15,612	15,556	.080
1959	22,742	22,965	20,291	21,818	22,088	17,216	16,519	16,780	.080
1960	24,673	24,906	22,080	24,776	25,071	18,629	17,899	17,939	.081
1961	27,573	27,848	24,851	28,009	28,257	20,730	19,966	20,008	.084
1962	31,001	31,292	28,082	32,073	32,124	23,635	22,796	22,445	.090
1963	35,598	35,883	32,308	35,161	35,380	27,063	26,130	24,980	.097
1964	38,936	39,220	35,345	38,039	38,361	29,224	28,162	27,320	.104
1965	41,834	42,210	38,194	41,546	42,065	32,122	31,028	30,398	.108
1966	45,450	45,905	41,669	45,891	46,578	34,780	33,654	33,378	.110
1967	50,062	50,491	45,991	49,668	50,394	37,749	36,563	36,516	.115
1968	54,114	54,556	49,802	54,826	55,718	40,755	39,507	39,341	.115
1969	59,686	60,241	55,018			45,182	43,787	43,660	.120

Year									
1970	67,178	67,645	61,470	61,180	61,979	51,111	49,452	47,844	.129
1971	72,994	73,529	66,753	64,921	65,790	56,612	54,845	52,847	.137
1972	79,810	80,458	72,998	72,834	73,804	62,755	60,865	58,663	.146
1973	96,738	97,175	87,777	87,760	88,221	75,923	73,524	67,856	.165
1974	122,190	122,165	109,257	109,263	108,596	94,802	91,648	78,222	.198
1975	138,632	138,492	122,419	122,357	120,508	112,079	108,265	90,560	.231
1976	174,869	174,734	154,605	154,482	157,256	138,098	133,398	121,609	.274
1977	214,398	214,493	189,672	189,842	189,995	169,530	163,865	140,051	.324
1978	253,536	253,321	223,919	223,779	227,276	201,255	194,591	177,439	.370
1979	309,834	311,519	276,124	275,383	279,096	242,128	234,150	209,015	.428
1980	387,669	389,493	344,949	344,185	344,737	297,001	286,936	241,373	.513
1981	464,030	462,618	406,158	406,626	414,952	368,369	355,612	309,475	.610
1982	545,124	542,949	475,205	475,696	493,810	432,304	416,915	378,702	.715
1983	633,436	631,095	553,129	554,297	575,465	503,155	485,454	448,052	.823
1984	725,760	723,138	634,682	636,002	658,823	567,174	547,171	511,817	.919
1985	810,580	806,468	706,280	707,057	733,678	629,954	607,544	578,855	1.000
1986	899,903	890,331	782,365	782,625	811,537	679,924	655,730	639,031	1.079
1987	983,803	975,190	858,341	859,803	897,176	746,194	719,859	719,057	1.143
1988	1,091,837	1,081,766	953,514	954,354	993,647	819,595	790,998	779,850	1.219
1989	1,193,462	1,178,034	1,037,467	1,038,192	1,084,401	904,326	873,044	857,151	1.295
1990	1,312,066	1,292,079	1,137,827	1,141,416	1,194,822	1,009,318	975,060	954,780	1.394
1991	1,426,580	1,396,981	1,229,445	1,231,402	1,281,732	1,101,609	1,064,494	1,021,256	1.497
1992	1,507,190	1,473,314	1,288,165	1,289,406	1,354,123	1,178,851	1,137,922	1,114,777	1.567

(*a*) Net of depreciation. – (*b*) Adjusted for inflation. – (*c*) Adjusted for inflation and for the services on the stock of durables.

Table SA.2 Measures of consumption
(billions of lire at current prices)

	Final domestic consumption expenditure				Economic consumption (a)	Deflator: 1985=1		
	Non-durable goods and services	Durable goods	Services on the stock of durables	Total consumption expenditure		Non-durable goods	Durable goods	Total
1951	7,498	340	319	7,838	7,817	.074	.108	.075
1952	8,335	387	423	8,722	8,758	.077	.111	.078
1953	9,070	435	402	9,505	9,471	.079	.106	.080
1954	9,422	470	390	9,892	9,812	.081	.110	.082
1955	10,147	493	496	10,640	10,644	.084	.109	.084
1956	11,104	566	548	11,670	11,652	.087	.111	.088
1957	11,827	631	643	12,458	12,469	.089	.112	.090
1958	12,588	687	619	13,275	13,207	.091	.113	.092
1959	13,154	759	745	13,913	13,899	.091	.114	.092
1960	14,114	884	740	14,998	14,854	.092	.113	.093
1961	15,321	1,055	809	16,377	16,131	.093	.111	.094
1962	17,289	1,350	850	18,639	18,139	.098	.114	.099
1963	20,048	1,812	781	21,860	20,829	.105	.116	.106
1964	22,180	1,873	1,063	24,053	23,243	.111	.123	.112
1965	23,876	1,841	1,245	25,717	25,122	.115	.123	.116
1966	26,190	1,955	1,576	28,145	27,766	.118	.122	.118
1967	28,756	2,201	1,866	30,957	30,622	.121	.121	.121
1968	30,745	2,366	2,019	33,111	32,765	.123	.122	.123
1969	33,745	2,618	2,324	36,364	36,069	.126	.124	.126

Year							
1970	37,551	2,812	2,411	40,363	39,962	.133	.126	.132
1971	40,880	3,211	2,733	44,091	43,613	.140	.132	.139
1972	45,026	3,585	3,142	48,611	48,168	.149	.139	.148
1973	54,565	4,610	3,246	59,175	57,811	.170	.160	.169
1974	68,647	5,814	2,909	74,461	71,557	.205	.203	.205
1975	80,511	6,564	2,717	87,075	83,228	.237	.250	.238
1976	98,775	9,024	8,747	107,799	107,522	.278	.304	.280
1977	119,718	12,177	7,816	131,895	127,534	.327	.360	.330
1978	139,176	15,160	12,740	154,336	151,917	.370	.411	.374
1979	168,690	20,981	15,314	189,671	184,003	.423	.476	.429
1980	213,945	27,413	15,837	241,358	229,782	.510	.575	.516
1981	257,177	31,961	27,450	289,137	284,626	.603	.662	.609
1982	305,961	36,540	41,652	342,501	347,613	.708	.761	.713
1983	354,981	41,157	49,546	396,138	404,527	.814	.869	.819
1984	405,417	47,014	54,790	452,431	460,207	.915	.943	.917
1985	453,173	54,633	61,732	507,806	514,905	1.000	1.000	1.000
1986	498,108	61,441	67,984	559,549	566,093	1.065	1.040	1.063
1987	544,427	69,593	81,010	614,020	625,437	1.124	1.083	1.119
1988	595,641	80,541	88,177	676,182	683,818	1.192	1.122	1.183
1989	652,596	91,949	102,324	744,545	754,921	1.272	1.171	1.258
1990	712,509	97,950	116,197	810,459	828,706	1.352	1.237	1.337
1991	780,711	105,277	118,961	885,988	899,672	1.449	1.286	1.428
1992	838,637	112,376	139,266	951,013	977,903	1.531	1.340	1.506

(a) Sum of non-durable goods and services on the stock of durables.

Table SA.3 Consolidated general government account: receipts
(billions of lire at current prices)

				Receipts			
	Gross operating surplus	Interest	Direct taxes	Indirect taxes	Social security contributions	Other	Total
1951	37	16	423	1,116	647	105	2,344
1952	41	19	518	1,257	807	121	2,763
1953	45	24	602	1,449	968	153	3,241
1954	48	26	669	1,645	1,163	170	3,721
1955	57	35	727	1,807	1,287	204	4,117
1956	63	40	839	2,072	1,505	237	4,757
1957	71	41	939	2,205	1,606	282	5,143
1958	74	49	1,040	2,288	1,794	290	5,536
1959	83	50	1,129	2,460	2,059	311	6,092
1960	90	62	1,238	2,787	2,302	353	6,832
1961	98	60	1,296	3,067	2,531	380	7,433
1962	115	76	1,622	3,412	2,991	386	8,604
1963	131	104	1,797	3,781	3,755	436	10,003
1964	152	115	2,161	4,177	4,340	395	11,341
1965	170	125	2,403	4,471	4,405	449	12,023
1966	182	172	2,595	4,796	4,711	570	13,026
1967	196	250	2,754	5,558	5,405	648	14,811
1968	204	209	3,208	5,892	6,174	623	16,310
1969	217	283	3,487	6,345	6,471	736	17,539

1970	282	608	3,439	6,973	7,613	730	19,645
1971	314	761	3,896	7,384	8,621	1,064	22,040
1972	350	777	4,709	7,566	9,483	1,220	24,105
1973	407	1,072	5,394	8,726	11,469	1,332	28,400
1974	498	1,689	6,614	10,778	14,434	1,467	35,480
1975	569	2,055	8,280	10,937	17,769	1,606	41,216
1976	698	3,354	11,831	14,788	22,285	1,763	54,719
1977	774	3,216	16,107	19,179	26,626	2,065	67,967
1978	923	4,251	21,963	22,021	31,357	2,953	83,468
1979	1,111	4,549	26,109	24,934	39,570	3,548	99,821
1980	1,263	4,799	37,291	33,522	49,493	4,712	131,080
1981	1,614	5,953	50,916	38,297	59,493	5,821	162,094
1982	1,998	6,439	64,534	46,649	74,608	5,902	200,130
1983	2,437	6,519	78,402	57,987	88,838	9,452	243,635
1984	2,849	8,149	91,416	67,283	98,522	10,126	278,345
1985	3,308	9,668	105,466	72,661	110,230	13,938	315,271
1986	3,919	12,394	115,683	81,743	125,498	18,649	357,886
1987	4,519	12,331	130,611	93,240	135,761	16,263	392,725
1988	5,551	11,848	145,720	109,076	149,381	17,271	438,847
1989	6,544	12,384	170,697	123,867	167,472	19,392	500,356
1990	7,398	14,372	189,101	139,465	189,309	21,777	561,422
1991	8,036	14,997	207,002	159,191	210,004	26,811	626,041
1992	9,797	15,276	220,934	166,544	226,358	28,225	667,134

Table SA.4 Consolidated general government account: disbursements
(billions of lire at current prices)

				Disbursements				
	Final consumption expenditure	Subsidies	Transfers	Transfers to other government subsectors	Other	Interest	Total	Net saving
1951	1,398	112	704	60	29	129	2,432	−88
1952	1,587	110	928	58	29	155	2,867	−103
1953	1,665	149	1,073	80	38	164	3,168	73
1954	1,851	142	1,238	70	37	219	3,558	163
1955	2,008	176	1,390	69	40	242	3,925	192
1956	2,176	230	1,598	72	45	274	4,394	363
1957	2,334	242	1,694	66	46	269	4,652	491
1958	2,568	227	1,976	77	48	251	5,147	389
1959	2,743	277	2,199	84	51	330	5,683	409
1960	2,974	397	2,366	107	49	355	6,247	585
1961	3,288	266	2,579	112	55	369	6,669	764
1962	3,806	392	3,040	131	67	397	7,833	771
1963	4,637	373	3,674	149	81	414	9,328	675
1964	5,239	498	4,114	80	106	429	10,466	875
1965	5,945	586	5,052	105	127	475	12,289	−267
1966	6,333	606	5,552	106	118	602	13,316	−290
1967	6,760	740	5,821	149	127	743	14,339	472
1968	7,368	962	6,610	196	107	816	16,059	250

1969	7,987	1,105	7,151	179	128	941	17,491	48
1970	8,709	1,103	8,049	157	342	1,093	19,453	192
1971	10,634	1,275	9,285	194	468	1,370	23,226	-1,186
1972	12,082	1,362	10,803	225	497	1,667	26,636	-2,531
1973	13,936	1,404	12,733	181	811	2,235	31,300	-2,900
1974	16,805	1,802	15,652	247	857	3,362	38,725	-3,245
1975	19,563	3,838	20,099	294	1,190	4,911	49,895	-8,679
1976	23,438	4,368	25,131	505	1,313	7,004	61,759	-7,040
1977	29,529	5,760	29,857	467	1,288	9,183	76,084	-8,117
1978	35,850	7,063	37,607	493	1,927	12,859	95,799	-12,331
1979	44,962	8,664	43,809	583	1,504	15,504	115,026	-15,205
1980	57,013	11,068	54,696	706	2,038	20,479	146,000	-14,920
1981	74,156	13,298	72,805	578	2,227	28,583	191,647	-29,553
1982	87,386	16,898	88,609	663	2,697	38,857	235,110	-34,980
1983	103,568	18,381	109,355	1,488	3,307	47,320	283,419	-39,784
1984	118,034	22,446	121,556	2,097	3,566	58,113	325,812	-47,467
1985	133,265	22,878	139,055	1,729	5,064	65,069	367,060	-51,789
1986	145,960	27,693	154,826	1,454	6,497	76,370	412,800	-54,914
1987	163,880	26,093	170,500	1,949	6,556	78,199	447,177	-54,452
1988	184,291	26,577	189,065	2,391	7,987	88,924	499,235	-60,388
1989	198,517	29,837	209,963	2,982	11,487	106,624	559,410	-59,054
1990	228,375	29,577	238,585	3,465	9,360	126,069	635,431	-74,009
1991	249,773	32,487	261,359	3,718	12,503	145,410	705,250	-79,209
1992	263,137	30,867	288,488	4,465	13,717	171,763	772,437	-105,303

Table SA.5 National, household, private and public sector wealth
(billions of lire, end-of-period stocks)

	Households					Other private sector			Public sector			National wealth
	Dwellings and land	Durable goods	Financial assets	Net worth	Social security wealth	Fixed capital & stocks	Financial assets	Net worth	Fixed capital	Financial assets	Net worth	
1951	54,860	2,123	8,628	65,611	5,778	21,214	−538	20,676	5,996	−4,090	1,906	88,193
1952	54,856	2,385	9,730	66,970	11,309	22,388	−1,179	21,209	6,332	−4,551	1,781	89,961
1953	54,898	2,478	10,797	68,173	13,708	23,076	−1,650	21,426	6,745	−5,029	1,716	91,315
1954	55,040	2,720	11,388	69,148	16,144	23,177	−1,643	21,534	7,265	−5,624	1,641	92,323
1955	55,240	2,955	13,185	71,381	17,451	24,372	−2,827	21,545	7,768	−6,247	1,521	94,446
1956	55,514	3,228	14,505	73,247	18,199	26,111	−3,854	22,257	8,426	−6,609	1,817	97,321
1957	55,726	3,490	16,085	75,301	20,732	27,855	−5,067	22,788	9,240	−6,997	2,243	100,332
1958	55,917	3,796	17,519	77,232	35,833	28,921	−6,021	22,900	9,583	−7,522	2,061	102,193
1959	56,317	4,131	19,084	79,531	38,100	30,179	−6,809	23,370	10,214	−8,355	1,859	104,760
1960	56,456	4,458	20,640	81,554	36,144	33,189	−6,946	26,243	11,057	−9,784	1,273	109,070
1961	56,528	4,963	23,539	85,030	41,975	37,113	−9,154	27,960	12,146	−10,692	1,454	114,443
1962	57,187	5,891	26,894	89,972	53,156	41,282	−11,641	29,641	13,739	−11,744	1,995	121,608
1963	58,359	7,184	28,449	93,991	64,271	48,844	−12,871	35,974	15,658	−12,568	3,090	133,055
1964	58,769	8,510	30,903	98,182	67,499	50,865	−14,543	36,321	18,073	−13,509	4,564	139,068
1965	69,879	9,448	34,514	113,841	92,321	51,507	−15,949	35,558	23,595	−15,499	8,096	157,495
1966	80,058	10,362	39,479	129,899	131,390	55,797	−17,769	38,028	25,258	−18,242	7,016	174,942
1967	85,165	11,447	44,879	141,490	117,253	60,316	−20,805	39,511	27,415	−20,624	6,791	187,792
1968	98,634	12,662	50,719	162,015	124,716	66,613	−23,624	42,989	24,990	−23,231	1,759	206,763
1969	120,402	14,036	58,135	192,573	139,304	73,460	−28,402	45,058	28,362	−25,593	2,769	240,400

Year												
1970	116,973	15,596	66,908	199,477	145,432	86,585	-37,127	49,458	32,982	-25,589	7,393	256,328
1971	124,576	17,787	78,563	220,926	148,239	97,771	-43,267	54,504	36,366	-30,952	5,414	280,844
1972	150,252	20,159	92,825	263,235	195,380	108,735	-49,538	59,197	39,320	-38,772	548	322,980
1973	223,804	24,974	108,046	356,824	223,077	137,515	-60,757	76,759	49,090	-45,173	3,917	437,500
1974	277,618	33,764	125,856	437,239	248,620	188,767	-71,484	117,283	63,996	-53,193	10,803	565,324
1975	351,047	43,064	152,710	546,821	312,037	229,958	-88,750	141,207	78,210	-62,758	15,452	703,480
1976	431,530	55,143	182,997	669,670	381,148	291,799	-109,051	182,748	98,154	-73,161	24,993	877,411
1977	486,638	69,738	214,212	770,588	595,206	358,108	-113,178	244,930	121,662	-99,679	21,983	1,037,500
1978	580,263	85,124	259,004	924,392	734,012	421,878	-124,060	297,818	145,780	-132,383	13,397	1,235,607
1979	739,257	107,734	310,990	1,157,981	897,398	510,163	-136,213	373,950	180,772	-167,643	13,129	1,545,060
1980	988,427	143,577	383,748	1,515,752	1,039,354	656,110	-180,626	475,484	233,150	-198,748	34,402	2,025,638
1981	1,156,128	179,003	459,290	1,794,421	1,470,088	816,211	-224,416	591,795	296,880	-243,397	53,483	2,439,699
1982	1,493,830	218,084	541,099	2,253,012	1,893,598	979,010	-245,317	733,693	351,724	-311,063	40,661	3,027,367
1983	1,593,048	261,588	655,980	2,510,615	2,274,879	1,110,836	-272,189	838,647	401,286	-403,516	-2,230	3,347,032
1984	1,730,735	298,189	789,311	2,818,235	2,713,220	1,256,540	-313,622	942,918	448,114	-496,865	-48,751	3,712,402
1985	1,894,628	335,628	986,697	3,216,953	2,972,307	1,415,871	-415,926	999,945	505,176	-591,544	-86,368	4,130,529
1986	1,870,332	372,150	1,215,414	3,457,896	3,236,974	1,522,736	-543,886	978,850	532,820	-689,062	-156,242	4,280,505
1987	2,150,306	413,871	1,368,169	3,932,346	3,640,668	1,654,917	-591,363	1,063,554	568,138	-799,511	-231,373	4,764,527
1988	2,315,819	462,339	1,545,459	4,323,617	4,126,499	1,808,917	-647,355	1,161,563	617,965	-916,240	-298,275	5,186,904
1989	2,476,293	520,181	1,712,442	4,708,915	4,685,233	1,980,650	-693,488	1,287,162	669,857	-1,045,784	-375,927	5,620,151
1990	2,708,689	585,462	1,892,447	5,186,599	5,134,683	2,165,787	-766,416	1,399,371	738,574	-1,178,369	-439,795	6,146,175
1991	3,056,187	647,002	2,113,979	5,817,168	5,540,631	2,354,545	-815,231	1,539,314	802,124	-1,334,577	-532,453	6,824,029
1992	3,588,968	712,558	2,344,820	6,646,346	n. a.	2,521,957	-912,888	1,609,069	850,156	-1,473,704	-623,548	7,631,867

Table SA.6 National, household, private and public sector saving rates
(in percent of national disposable income)

	National		Private sector		Public sector		Households	
	Gross	Net (a)	Gross	Net (a)	Gross	Net (a)	Gross	Net (a)
1951	24.0	9.4	24.7	10.5	-0.7	-1.1	9.5	6.7
1952	21.6	6.9	22.4	8.1	-0.8	-1.2	8.3	5.1
1953	23.4	10.0	22.9	9.8	0.5	0.3	9.4	6.3
1954	24.3	11.4	23.2	10.5	1.1	0.9	10.5	7.6
1955	26.3	14.5	25.1	13.5	1.1	0.9	12.5	10.2
1956	26.0	14.2	24.0	12.3	1.9	1.9	12.2	10.1
1957	27.1	16.1	24.7	13.6	2.4	2.4	13.5	11.7
1958	27.6	17.5	25.8	15.8	1.8	1.7	14.7	13.1
1959	28.3	18.8	26.5	17.2	1.8	1.6	15.2	13.8
1960	28.8	19.7	26.4	17.4	2.3	2.3	15.5	14.2
1961	30.4	22.0	27.6	19.2	2.7	2.7	16.6	15.5
1962	29.2	21.1	26.7	18.7	2.5	2.4	16.9	15.8
1963	27.0	18.9	25.1	17.2	1.9	1.7	15.3	14.1
1964	26.2	18.1	24.0	16.0	2.2	2.1	14.1	12.6
1965	26.1	18.4	26.8	19.5	-0.6	-1.1	16.3	15.2
1966	26.1	18.6	26.7	19.7	-0.6	-1.1	15.7	14.6
1967	26.3	19.1	25.4	18.4	0.9	0.6	14.4	13.3
1968	26.7	19.7	26.2	19.5	0.5	0.1	14.9	13.8
1969	27.1	20.2	27.0	20.5	0.1	-0.3	15.4	14.3
1970	28.0	20.8	27.7	20.8	0.3	..	16.4	15.4
1971	26.2	18.7	27.8	20.8	-1.6	-2.1	17.6	16.8

1972	25.4	17.8	28.5	21.6	-3.1	-3.8	18.4	17.7
1973	25.5	17.5	28.5	21.1	-3.0	-3.6	17.9	17.1
1974	26.0	17.2	28.6	20.5	-2.7	-3.3	17.3	16.5
1975	23.8	13.8	30.1	21.2	-6.3	-7.4	18.9	18.2
1976	25.7	16.0	29.7	20.9	-4.0	-4.8	18.2	17.5
1977	26.0	16.3	29.8	20.8	-3.8	-4.5	18.8	18.3
1978	26.3	16.6	31.2	22.4	-4.9	-5.8	19.9	19.5
1979	26.2	16.7	31.0	22.5	-4.9	-5.8	18.3	17.8
1980	24.6	14.9	28.4	19.5	-3.8	-4.6	15.5	14.6
1981	22.6	11.8	29.0	19.3	-6.4	-7.5	18.2	17.6
1982	22.1	11.0	28.6	18.6	-6.4	-7.6	17.8	17.1
1983	22.2	11.3	28.5	18.7	-6.3	-7.5	18.4	17.8
1984	22.4	11.6	28.9	19.3	-6.6	-7.7	17.1	16.4
1985	21.7	10.6	28.1	18.2	-6.4	-7.6	16.4	15.5
1986	21.6	10.8	27.8	18.1	-6.2	-7.3	14.4	13.3
1987	21.0	10.2	26.5	16.9	-5.6	-6.7	14.3	13.2
1988	20.9	10.3	26.5	17.0	-5.6	-6.7	13.7	12.6
1989	20.3	9.5	25.3	15.6	-5.0	-6.1	13.9	12.8
1990	19.9	9.0	25.6	15.9	-5.7	-6.9	15.7	14.8
1991	19.0	8.0	24.7	14.9	-5.7	-6.9	15.8	14.9
1992	17.8	5.9	24.9	14.6	-7.1	-8.7	15.6	14.7

(a) Net of depreciation.

Table SA.7 Saving rates adjusted for inflation and durables
(in percent of national disposable income)

	National		Private sector		Public sector		Households	
	Gross	Net	Gross	Net	Gross	Net	Gross	Net
1952	23.6	7.9	24.1	8.8	−0.5	−0.9	10.6	6.0
1953	25.2	10.7	23.8	9.4	1.3	1.3	11.2	6.6
1954	25.8	11.6	23.1	8.8	2.7	2.8	11.6	7.1
1955	28.0	15.2	26.2	13.4	1.8	1.8	14.2	10.6
1956	27.7	14.8	24.8	11.7	2.9	3.1	13.7	10.1
1957	29.0	16.9	25.9	13.6	3.1	3.3	15.3	12.0
1958	29.4	18.1	26.6	15.3	2.8	2.9	16.2	13.1
1959	30.1	19.6	28.1	17.6	2.0	1.9	17.8	15.0
1960	30.7	20.4	27.6	17.2	3.1	3.2	17.8	15.0
1961	33.0	23.6	29.6	20.1	3.4	3.5	19.0	16.5
1962	32.5	23.4	28.6	19.3	3.9	4.0	18.8	16.3
1963	30.9	21.6	26.3	16.8	4.6	4.8	16.7	13.8
1964	29.9	20.5	25.5	16.0	4.3	4.5	15.8	12.5
1965	29.4	20.3	28.2	19.4	1.2	0.9	18.0	15.0
1966	29.2	20.3	28.4	19.8	0.7	0.4	17.6	14.7
1967	29.4	20.8	27.4	19.0	2.0	1.8	16.8	13.7
1968	29.7	21.3	28.1	19.8	1.7	1.5	17.0	14.0
1969	30.1	21.8	28.8	20.7	1.3	1.1	17.4	14.4

1970	30.8	22.1	28.2	19.6	2.5	2.5	16.5	13.3
1971	27.7	18.2	26.7	17.4	1.0	0.8	17.9	14.7
1972	28.6	19.3	29.0	20.0	-0.4	-0.8	18.2	15.1
1973	29.2	19.5	27.9	18.3	1.3	1.2	15.9	12.2
1974	30.0	19.4	25.5	14.5	4.5	4.9	11.4	6.9
1975	28.0	15.6	26.6	14.3	1.4	1.3	11.9	7.0
1976	29.3	17.6	28.3	16.7	1.0	0.9	14.3	9.9
1977	30.6	18.7	26.9	14.6	3.7	4.1	12.8	8.0
1978	30.7	18.9	29.5	17.8	1.2	1.1	16.9	12.8
1979	31.2	19.6	28.8	17.0	2.4	2.6	15.1	10.6
1980	30.3	18.2	24.9	12.1	5.4	6.1	10.3	4.7
1981	27.9	14.8	25.2	11.8	2.7	2.9	12.6	7.2
1982	26.9	13.3	24.9	11.3	2.0	2.1	13.2	7.7
1983	26.8	13.3	24.9	11.3	1.9	1.9	14.5	9.1
1984	27.0	13.6	26.3	13.1	0.7	0.5	14.5	9.2
1985	26.5	13.0	26.6	13.3	:	-0.3	15.1	10.2
1986	26.5	13.2	27.7	14.9	-1.2	-1.7	15.0	9.9
1987	26.0	12.8	27.7	15.0	-1.6	-2.2	16.1	11.2
1988	26.3	13.2	27.5	15.0	-1.2	-1.8	15.3	10.2
1989	25.9	12.5	25.9	12.8	:	-0.4	15.1	9.8
1990	25.4	11.9	25.8	12.6	-0.4	-0.8	16.1	10.9
1991	24.6	10.7	24.1	10.5	0.5	0.2	15.3	9.9
1992	23.2	8.5	24.7	10.7	-1.4	-2.2	15.8	10.3

Index